AF304779

GLASSTRESS NEW YORK

NEW ART FROM THE VENICE BIENNALES

OPEN PROJECT BY ADRIANO BERENGO

SKIRA

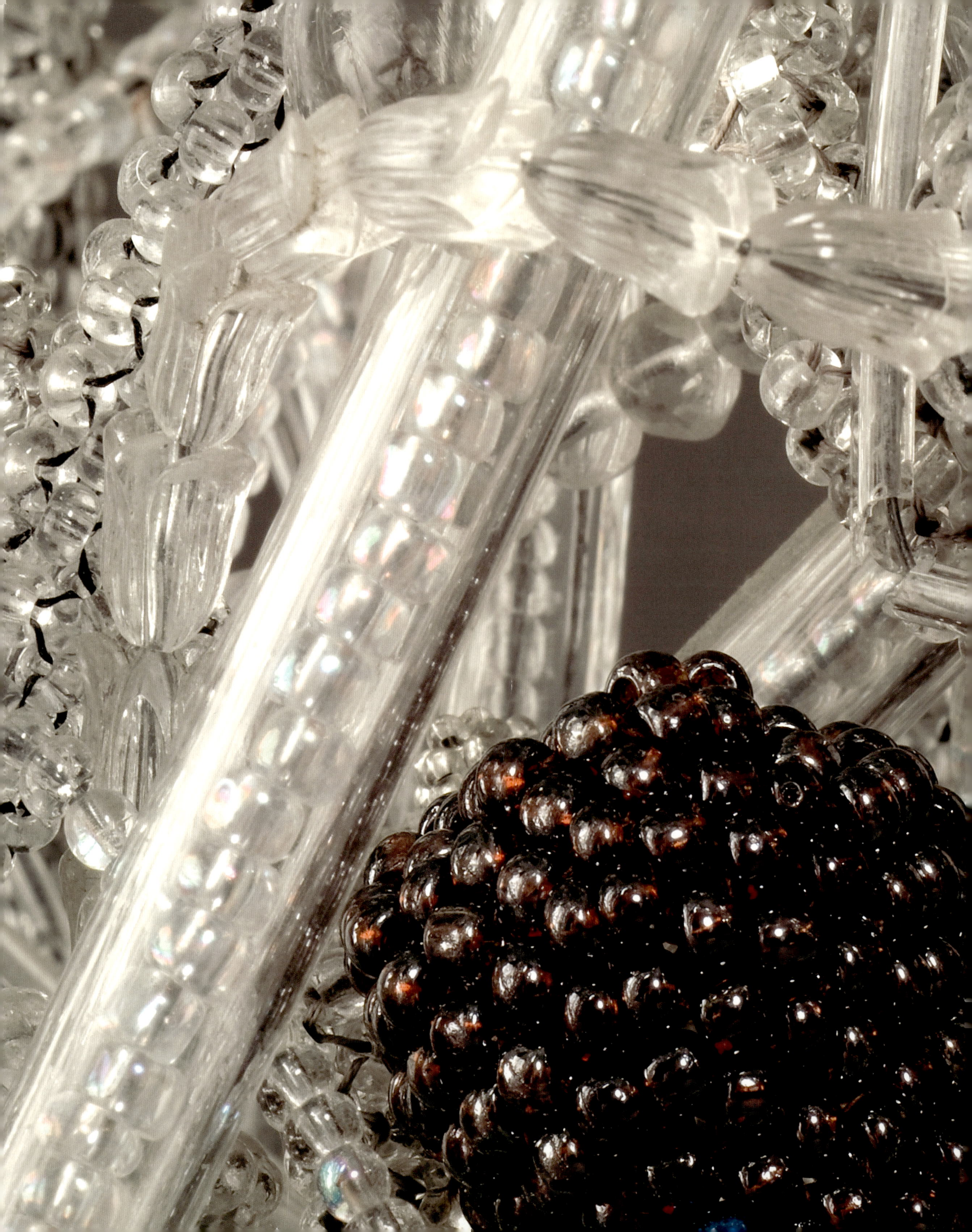

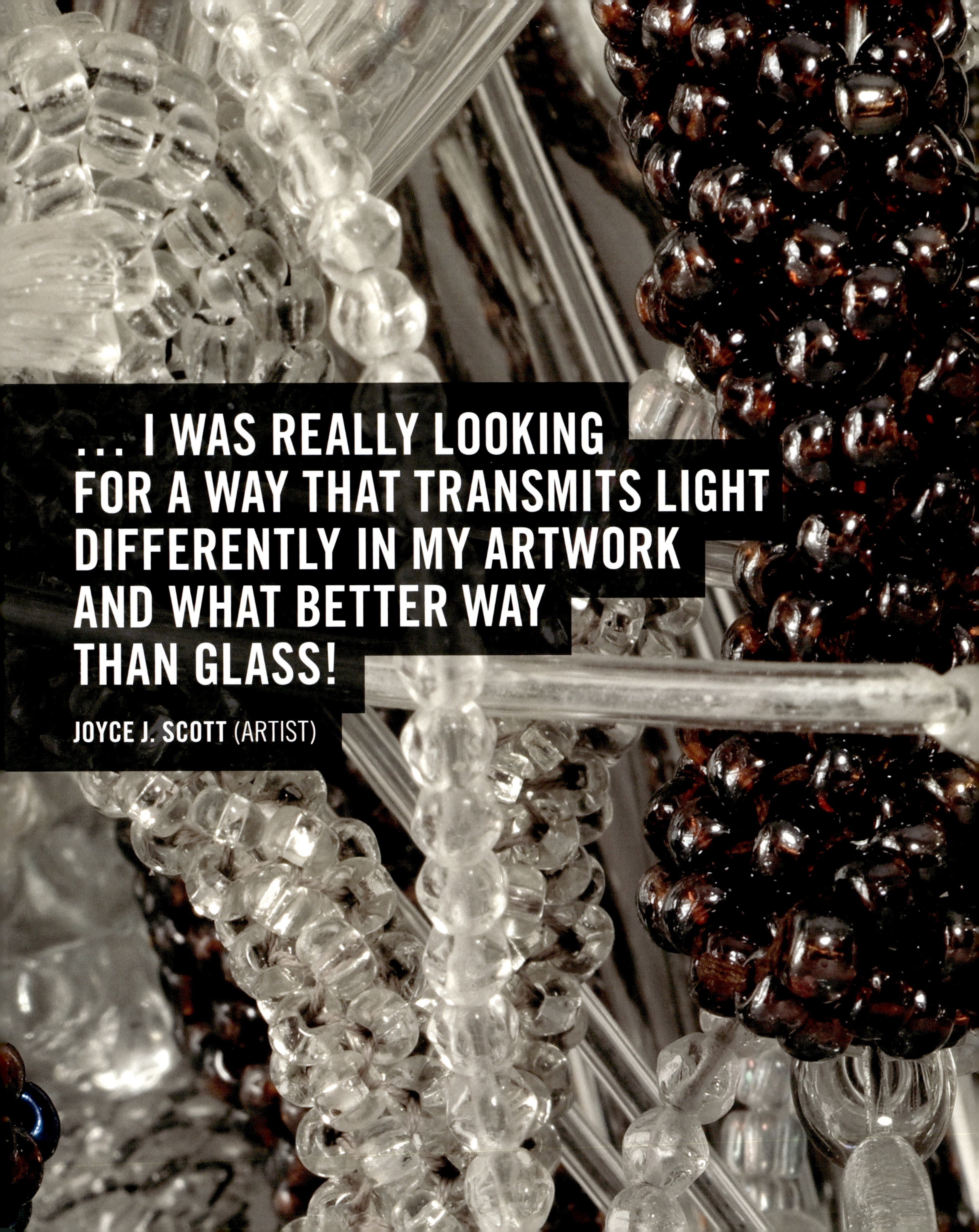
… I WAS REALLY LOOKING FOR A WAY THAT TRANSMITS LIGHT DIFFERENTLY IN MY ARTWORK AND WHAT BETTER WAY THAN GLASS!
JOYCE J. SCOTT (ARTIST)

GLASSTRESS NEW YORK
New Art from the Venice Biennales

New York, 14th February > 10th June 2012

The Museum of Arts and Design
2 Columbus Circle, New York
USA

Conceived by
Adriano Berengo

Organized by
The Museum of Arts and Design (MAD), New York
Venice Projects | Berengo Studio 1989, Venice

Curators
Adriano Berengo, Holly Hotchner, David McFadden

Supported and Cooperated by

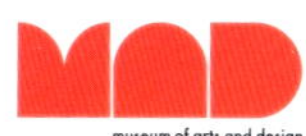

VENICEPROJECTS

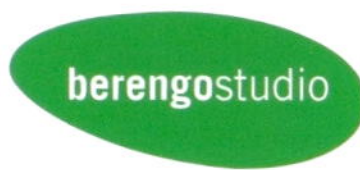

Sponsored by

Cordover Family Foundation
Shintaro Akatsu School of Design
Solidere
The Amb Way
The Inner Circle, leadership support group of MAD

SASD
SHINTARO AKATSU SCHOOL OF DESIGN

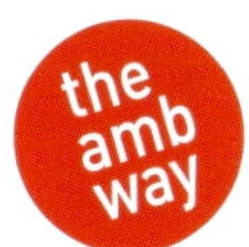

solidere

This catalogue was made possible through the generosity of Goya Contemporary Gallery, Suzi Cordish, and an anonymous donor.

GOYA CONTEMPORARY
GOYA-GIRL PRESS

**Exhibition Management –
The Museum of Arts and Design (MAD)**

General Coordination
Elizabeth Kirrane

Exhibition Staging
Dorothy Globus

Shipping Department
Ellen Holdorf
Brian MacElhose

*Communication
and Graphic Design*
Linda Florio, Florio Design

Info Press
Marisa Bartolucci

Sponsorship Department
Judith Kamien

**Exhibition Management –
Venice Projects
Berengo Studio 1989**

General Coordination
Marco Berengo
Laura Bresolin

Exhibition Staging
Koen Vanmechelen
Giovanni Scarpa
Stefano Dono

Shipping Department
Stefano Dono
Mauro Falcier
Gianni Gallo
Roberto Lazzari
Marino Zaffalon

Thanks to our collaborators
Danilo Zanella
Dawn Bennett
Metal Riv- Giuseppe Bonini
Romano De Angeli
Daniele Donà
Massimo Lunardon
Jane Rushton
Falegnameria Santini
Andrea e Paolo
Valle Romano
di Valle Alessio

Special thanks to
Shintaro Akatsu
Savino Cancellara
Max Casacci and Vaghe Stelle
Ronald and Barbara Cordover
Marcello and Valeria Forin
Paolo Grossi
VeneziaNews

**Contributing Galleries,
Collections, and Institutions**
Gallery Fons Wetters, Amsterdam
Pieke Bergmans – Design Virus, Amsterdam
Angelos Bvba Collection, Antwerp
Goya Contemporary, Baltimore
Private Collection, Baltimore
Galleria Toni Tàpies, Barcelona
Studio Plensa, Barcelona
Artbug Gallery, Bassano
Private Collection, Bassano
Galleria Fumagalli, Bergamo
lorch+seidel contemporary, Berlin
Max Hetzler Gallery, Berlin
Buchmann Galerie, Berlin/Lugano
Josef Albers Museum Quadrat Bottrop, Bottrop
Galleria Massimo Minini, Brescia
Galerie Rodolphe Janssen, Brussels
Xavier Hufkens Gallery, Brussels
Goodman Gallery, Johannesburg, Cape Town
Collection Cingoli
Galerie Gisela Capitain, Cologne
De Nul Collection
Joanne Katz Private Collection, Florida
Keith Johnson
Marlborough Gallery, London
Spring Projects, London
Stephen Friedman Gallery, London
Zaha Hadid Architects, London
Urs Meile Gallery, Beijing, Lucerne
Moss Private Collection, Miami
Collection Orsi, Segrate, Milan
E. Righi Collection, Milan
Fondazione Marconi, Milan
Galleria Raffaella Cortese, Milan

Studio Urquiola, Milan
Kosuke Mori
Triumph Gallery, Moscow
Robert and Dianne Moss
Claire Oliver Gallery, New York
David Zwirner, New York
Estate of Robert Rauschenberg, New York
Lehmann Maupin Gallery, New York
Private Collection, New York
R 20th Century Gallery, New York
Tracy Williams ltd., New York
Galerie Lelong, New York-Paris
Orrefors Kosta Boda AB, Orrefors
The Pace Gallery
Saazs, Paris
Thaddaeus Ropac Gallery, Paris, Salzburg
Private Collection, Piacenza
Collection Lise and Thierry Prevot
Latvian National Museum of Art, Riga
Joseph Kosuth Studio, Rome
Galleria Continua, San Gimignano, Beijing, Le Moulin
Susan and Fred Sanders
Kukje Gallery, Seoul
Shanghart Gallery, Shanghai
Zhang Huan Studio, Shanghai
Galerie Karsten Greve AG, St. Moritz
Angelika Knapper Gallery, Stockholm
Istituto Italiano di Cultura, Stockholm
Millesgården Museum, Stockholm
SCAI, The Bathhouse, Tokyo
Tokujin Yoshioka inc., Tokyo
Yumiko Chiba Associates, Tokyo
Tucci Russo Studio per l'Arte Contemporanea, Torre Pellice, Turin
Galleria Michela Rizzo, Venice
Istituto Veneto di Scienze, Lettere ed Arti, Venice
Peggy Guggenheim Collection, Venice
Museum of Glass, Tacoma, Washington

Special thanks to all the artists for the enthusiasm they brought to this project

CONTENTS

GLASSTRESS NEW YORK

GLASSTRESS ANTHOLOGY

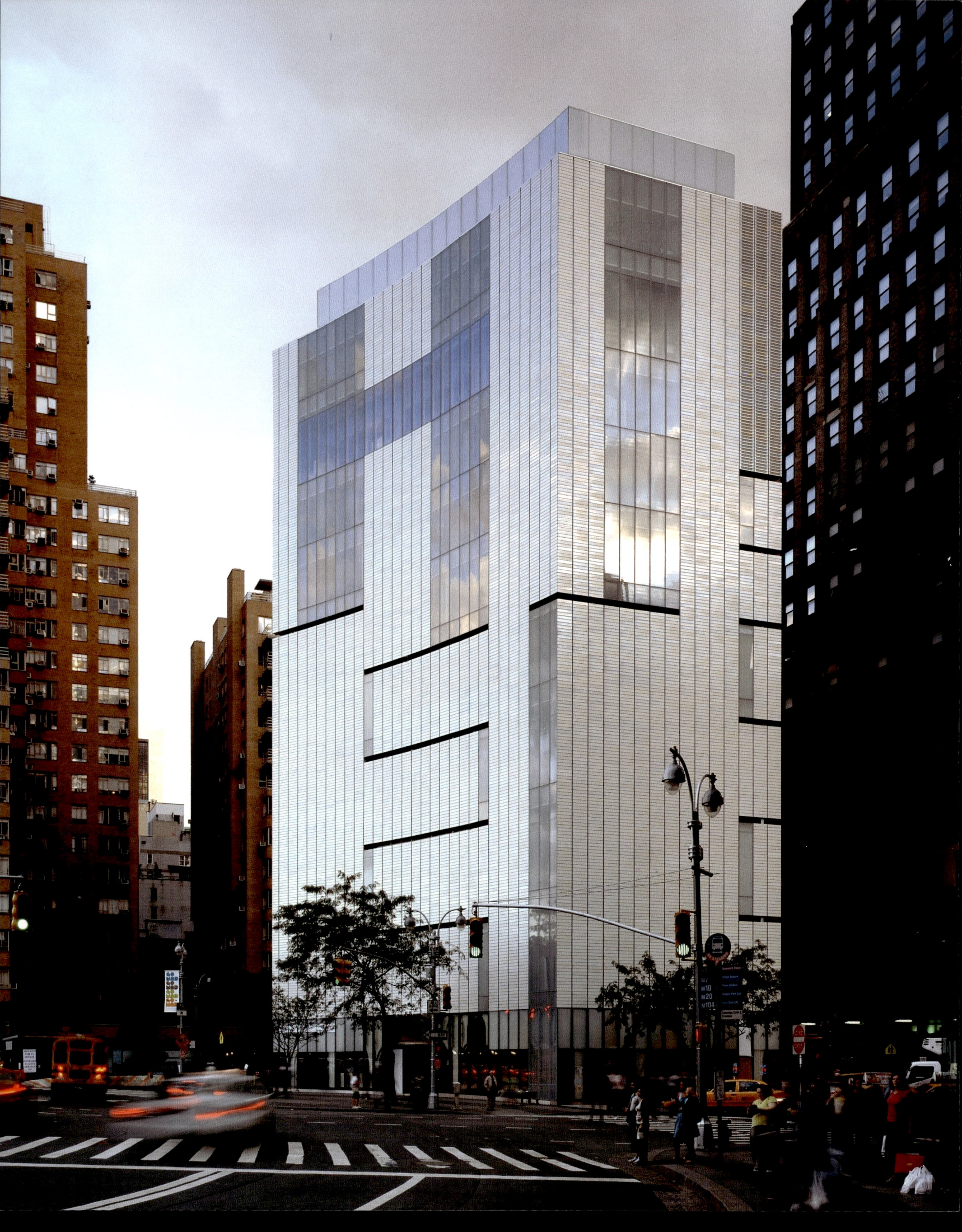

GLASSTRESS NEW YORK

NEW ART FROM THE VENICE BIENNALES

The Museum of Arts and Design (MAD, then known as the Museum of
Contemporary Crafts) opened in 1956. Two years later the museum organized
Louis Comfort Tiffany, a groundbreaking retrospective of America's most
renowned and influential glass designer around the year 1900. Since that
time, the museum has been a pioneer in the United States, organizing
exhibitions that have explored glass in its many forms. The exhibitions have
focused both on individual studio practitioners and thematic overviews of
glass as a global medium. This year America salutes the fiftieth anniversary
of the founding of the American studio glass movement, a renaissance
of artistic innovation in this medium launched in 1962 through the efforts
of two pioneers: Harvey Littleton and Dominick Labino. The legacy of
creativity and expertise in glass making that they founded has inspired
and challenged hundreds, if not thousands, of young creators to embrace
this most amazing of materials.
In this historic year The Museum of Arts and Design is proud to present
Glasstress New York, an extraordinary international gathering of glass sculpture
created in Murano at the studio of entrepreneur and mentor Adriano Berengo.

FOREWORD

HOLLY HOTCHNER

Berengo, the founder of Venice Projects, has engaged artists, architects,
and designers from such diverse countries as the United States, China, Italy,
Germany, The Netherlands, and Spain. The resulting works were originally
commissioned for and presented at the Venice Biennales of 2009 and 2011.
The pieces are dramatic and often provocative, ranging from independent
sculptures to installations incorporating sounds and light to prototypes for
production. The spirit of innovation and experimentation pervades the works
in this exhibition; many of the artists and designers were given their first
opportunity to work with this challenging medium, and in collaboration with
the brilliantly capable master glass artisans assembled by Adriano Berengo.
Since the beginnings of glassmaking in ancient Mesopotamia and its meteoric
rise to international prominence in the Roman Empire, the magical medium
of glass—a solid that takes on the appearance of a liquid—has attracted
innovative artists and designers to continue to push the medium into new
realms. The history of the decorative arts in the West over the past two
millennia is a testament to the limitless potential of the medium in both the
realms of functional design and independent works of art. Ubiquitous
in Roman-era glassmaking are vials, bowls, and containers to hold liquids
or other materials, while one need only remember the stunning brilliance
of the stained glass windows at St. Chapelle in Paris to realize that this
material can achieve the heights of aesthetic needs.

Throughout the history of glass as an art and design medium, the majority
of the skilled practitioners capable of working this demanding (and often
dangerous) superheated material have remained anonymous. By the
nineteenth century, industrial methods of glass production and a complex
system of distribution of glass rendered this formerly prized material
available to a massive audience of middle-class consumers. At the same time,
this democratization of the material rendered it commonplace.
It was not until the end of the nineteenth century when artists embraced
the material as a valid and valuable medium for creating unique works of
art; such luminaries as Louis Comfort Tiffany in the United States and Emile
Gallé in France renovated the artistic reputation of glass, and from that point
forward, the intimate relationships between glass and glassmaking as an art
medium, a skilled craft, and as a design medium were forged. The twenty-first-
century manifestation of this holistic phenomenon is seen in the works created
by the diverse artists and designers who have participated in *Glasstress*.
From its earliest incarnation and to some degree the result of the properties
of glass to simulate organic forms, whether plants, flowers, or animals,
nature has remained a powerful inspiration. This remains true for many
of the artists represented in *Glasstress*. Such artists as Jan Fabre and Kiki
Smith make use of glass in their sculptural installations featuring brilliant
blue shitting pigeons and a colony of frogs, respectively. While the subject
matter of the works are recognizable and familiar, their translation in glass
moves them into a jewel-like hyperreality.
More abstract studies of nature are found in the work of Yutaka Sone, whose
radiant studies of snowflakes in transparent glass make the ephemeral into
a permanent form, while Britain's Luke Jerram uses glass to take the viewer
into the world of the microscopic by revealing the eerily beautiful world
of deadly viruses. Ursula von Rydingsvard captures the rough tactility of
wood in her *Glass Corrugated*, 2010, an ironical allusion to the destruction
of wood (the artist's primary material) by fire, a ritual burning without
which glass could not exist. The delicacy of bamboo is evoked in the Starn
Brothers' assemblage of fragile glass rods, a delicacy and fragility in glass
that contrasts with the limber flexibility of the organic material. Likewise,
Marya Kazoun's *Frosty Ground: The Beginning*, 2009, is suggestive of the
evanescent crystallization of moisture, the hoarfrost that coats grasses and
twigs for a fragile moment. A profound intimacy between art and nature is
recorded in *The Seed of Narcissus*, 2011, by Tomáš Libertíny; the artist has
used a mirrored glass ovoid as a foundation upon which bees have built a wax
mantel that encapsulates the alien glass form, effecting a fusion between the
inert and the living, between the permanent and the ephemeral.
The human form is also explored by several artists in *Glasstress*, notably
Jaume Plensa, in the poignant and meditative elongated head of *Cristina's
Frozen Dreams*, 2010, and in the expressive *Laura's Hands*, 2011, both made
from cast glass. The artist uses the ability of the material to capture and
transmit light to give each of the works an inner radiance that evokes the
spiritual presence of the sitter. The same light-capturing property of glass,
combined with the jewel-like colors that can be achieved in the medium, is
effectively exploited by German artist Thomas Schütte, in his red and green
male busts that stare blankly at each other across space with the same

air of alienation evoked by traffic lights in an empty middle-of-the-night
intersection. American artist Joyce Jane Scott, long known for her provocative
figural imagery created with glass beads, has extended her repertoire by
creating a memorable cast glass figural group for *Glasstress*.
The world of industrial design is represented in *Glasstress* by the lively
animated works of Spanish artists Jaime Hayon and Patricia Urquiola.
Hayon's *Testa Mecanica*, 2011, are spunky and engaging robot heads, more
innocently toy-like than confrontive. Urquiola has created a menagerie
of eccentric and perverse shapes that find their genetic core in a strange
mutation part functional vessel—vases, bowls, pitchers—and surf-and-turf
creatures ranging from jellyfish to barnyard fowl.
Time and its passing and the contradictory nature of memory is examined
from several points of view in *Glasstress*. Silvano Rubino's *Addizione sottrattiva*,
2009, is a dining room table notable for the absence of accoutrements—plates
and cutlery that would normally inhabit this domestic space are presented
as empty cutouts of space and, by implication, the interaction between two
diners. Michael Joo's lonely museum stanchions made entirely of glass
are a pointed and humorous commentary on security and regimentation of
institutions that create systems to control and monitor access to some desired
goal. The artist's title for the work *Expanded Access*, 2011, underscores
this dichotomy of freedom and control.
Time as a force of both physical and psychic presence is made tangible in
Javier Pérez's *Carroña*, 2011, a blood red chandelier made in the grandest of
Venetian ornamental styles that has crashed to the ground, leaving behind
only fragments of what was once perfect and beautiful, fragments being
picked over by black crows. Among the simplest of the works in *Glasstress*

and yet one of the most provocative is Vik Muniz's untitled hourglass
containing a full-sized clay brick rather than sand. In this work, time has
literally and figuratively stood still. The rough and tactile presence of
the brick is pitted against the fragile transparency of the glass. Time as
we experience it is held in limbo, a metaphor for the vague territory that
separates the physical world from the realms of the spirit.

MAD has defined its role in the global museum community as an institution
dedicated to the exploration of materials and process in the arts and design,
and to the creative transformation of materials that results in works
of significant visual, emotional, and intellectual content. MAD also rejects
the traditional hierarchies and boundaries that have separated art, craft,
and design over the centuries. The diversity of creators involved in this
exhibition, and the quality of the works that they have produced, are
testaments to this belief and this commitment.

We are deeply indebted to Adriano Berengo for his ceaseless energy, vision,
and generosity for making *Glasstress New York* a reality, and for making
it possible to premiere this exhibition at MAD. I also want to thank Susan
Scherman, a founder of Venice Projects, for her commitment to new talent
in glass. Many thanks also to Marco Berengo who has taken these projects
around the world and to Laura Bresolin who coordinated the US exhibition.
From MAD, thanks go to David McFadden who helped to curate the exhibition,
and to Elizabeth Kirrane, Nurit Einik, and Dorothy Globus who made the
exhibition at MAD come to life. And finally to Goya Contemporary Gallery, Suzi
Cordish, and an anonymous donor who made this new catalogue a reality.
We hope that with these new experimentations in glass the artists have
expanded their horizons and opened a new chapter in glass history.

I became interested in glass around 1985. An interest in modern and contemporary art had prompted me, right from the beginning, to study the way in which glass had been used in the context of modernism—that is, since the split from nineteenth-century aesthetic canons and the search for new forms of expression expanded to include materials which, until that time, had been considered foreign to the plastic arts. Despite this new direction and the degree to which glass working techniques had developed over the centuries, with the *objects* created reflecting a particular style and having incomparable formal qualities and elegance, glass continued, even in modernist times, to be considered a material more in keeping with design than with the art of sculpture.

Glass was thought to be inadequate for the creation of works of art, mainly because of the ways in which the material was worked, requiring the use of specialized labor. Indeed, if art has always welcomed such materials as wax, clay, marble, or wood, the same cannot be said for glass, which can only be shaped at extremely high temperatures. The artist who chooses to work with glass can design a form; define its color, weight, and transparency;

GLASS, MON AMOUR

ADRIANO BERENGO

and monitor the different stages of the process. Yet he is rarely able to manipulate this incandescent material himself. It could be argued that bronze sculptures also require the use of master craftsmen (though this has never made bronze a material foreign to the plastic arts). However, these sculptures come from forms that the artist's own hand has molded or assembled using other materials. On the other hand, it cannot be denied that, over the last half century, artists have increasingly entrusted to skilled artisans the production of their works, using ever more varied materials. If artists in the early decades of the twentieth century earned the right to appropriate everyday objects, from the 1960s onwards—namely, with pop art in the US and new realism in Europe—the new frontier became a definitive statement that a work's intrinsic value is found as much in its conceptual qualities as in its formal ones. This conception asserted, once and for all, that the author of a work is the one who conceives it and oversees its outcome, and not the one who carries out its actual production. This shift can be traced back to two fundamental starting points in the 1960s when it first became fashionable to entrust the construction of extremely large works to skilled workers from outside the artist's workshop and then later, when pop art began to borrow images from advertising and glossy magazines. The latter could be considered the basis for the vision of the world that, in the second half of the 1970s, came to be known as postmodernism. Thus, the fact that, in choosing to use glass, the artist could not fully control or change the shape of his work, after having second thoughts or new insights, ceased to be a problem.

As I said before, my interest in glass arose in the mid-1980s when postmodernism manifested its artistic identity through the repetition of images and forms borrowed from the past as well as through the bold use of all material. Recalling the cultural climate of those years, I now find my decision to create on Murano first, in 1989, Berengo Studio and later, in 2009, Venice Projects to have been a natural one. Berengo Studio was set up as an experimental workshop in which artists could create their own works with the help of skilled artisans, but also as a place where it was possible to meet critics and come into contact with the best glass craftsmen working on Murano. As for Venice Projects, it came about from the need for a space in which to exhibit and promote some of the works created in my workshops, with a particular focus on developments in contemporary art.

I sensed that art was becoming increasingly interdisciplinary and multisensory and that this would change radically our relationship to the works of art themselves. At the same time, I was sure that glass, thanks to its distinctive qualities, could attain the same status in art as any other medium. Nevertheless, I realized that the difficulty of working with glass and the high production costs related to the need for a skilled workforce (that sadly was disappearing) were major obstacles. I wanted to give artists the opportunity to create works that would have been difficult for other workshops to produce. Over time, this has given me the opportunity to work with such artists as Monica Bonvicini, Barbara Bloom, Tony Cragg, Jan Fabre, Kendell Geers, Michael Joo, Liu Jianhua, Oleg Kulik, Vik Muniz, Jaume Plensa, Thomas Schütte, Fred Wilson, and Zhang Huan, to name just a few.

For years, I had cherished the idea of setting up an international exhibition to be held every two years in Venice during the Biennale, but I was not able to make it a reality until 2009. I wanted to create an international event that showed the best works made of glass. This is how *Glasstress* came into being. The event's success was instantaneous and, in many ways, beyond my wildest expectations. After such important milestones as the exhibitions at the Latvian National Museum of Art in Riga and Stockholm's Millesgården Museum, *Glasstress* today has arrived at The Museum of Arts and Design in New York, with a selection made together with Holly Hotchner and David McFadden, and which offers an original and critical vision of the works.

Art cannot be separated from the processes of its creation and production; otherwise it would be something else, a philosophy: the technical and manual aspects are essential components of a work. Today, artists are increasingly turning to other professionals, including artisans whose work weds precision with imagination. However, let us not forget that it is the conceptual dimension—namely, *that which is implicit in its appearance and shape*—that confers its identity on a work in glass. In other words, it is this conceptual dimension that lets us recognize that a work in glass conveys something that no other material could express.

Focusing on only some of the works on display in the latest editions of
Glasstress at Palazzo Cavalli Franchetti in Venice, part of the 54th Venice
Biennale, and now chosen for a further limited selection for this exhibition
at The Museum of Arts and Design in New York, does not mean they are
more important than the others, but simply that they are best suited for
a reflection on the use that an artist can make of glass today.
Rather than an art material, glass has long been considered a material
for furnishings. With few exceptions, such as Duchamp's *The Large
Glass*, glass was used more in the twentieth century to create design
objects than veritable works of art. This way of understanding glass was
lacking in the early 1980s with the strengthening of the postmodern view,
which considered the experiences of the past with an eye to using them
instrumentally in new contexts. Moreover, this way of understanding
art continues to this day, as demonstrated by *Expanded Access*, made by
Michael Joo in 2011 for *Glasstress*.
Interested in the way men tend to limit their personal freedoms by
subordinating them to the needs of social organization, Michael Joo has

GLASSTRESS IN NEW YORK

DEMETRIO PAPARONI

repeatedly dealt with barriers created to make certain areas inaccessible
or to indicate obligatory routes. The most common among these are the
string or cloth barriers supported by columns of steel or wood that each
of us has seen in theaters or museums. Not being immoveable, these objects
mostly tend to inform us that there is a boundary beyond which one cannot
go. Therefore, they act exclusively on a psychological level.
In Adriano Berengo's kilns, in Murano, Michael Joo created examples of
these boundaries from blown glass polished to a mirrored finish, giving them
a sense of extreme fragility. While bumping into ordinary steel barricades
and rope does not involve special risks, hitting the glass barriers made by
Michael Joo means inevitably damaging them. Furthermore, the skill with
which these glass barriers are made deceives the spectator, who at first
glance is led to believe that they are made of steel. It is a sort of visual trap
that can lead one to get dangerously close to the work without perceiving
its fragility. Glass has allowed Michael Joo to give an ambiguous identity
to a physical object and thwart the function that its shape suggests.
Expanded Access takes advantage of both the theories and dynamics of early
twentieth-century Duchamp and those that characterized the conceptualism
of the 1970s. Using blown glass rather than a resistant material—such
as bronze, steel, marble, or resin—to reproduce the barriers is in itself a
choice sufficient to define the content and meaning of the work. The language

remains unchanged, which is that of sculpture, even though what does
change is the way it relates to the spirit of the time.

From Duchamp onwards, many sculptors speculated a good deal on the
possibility of altering the meaning of an object through the title of the work
or by creating unlikely associations, namely transferring the idea of beauty
from the visual plane to the mental one. Aware of the fact that beauty is
manifested by arousing astonishment and wonder, the artist embraced
the opportunity to engage the spectator on a conceptual level through
images capable of revealing an intuition. *Expanded Access* by Michael Joo
demonstrates that this aesthetic vision, which implies the encroachment
of art into areas once considered the prerogative of philosophy, is still
relevant today. While on the one hand these boundaries promise to protect,
the use of a brittle material such as blown glass means they can easily break,
injure, or harm. The work is thus a reflection on how what seems to be and
what actually is are not the same.

A similar idea of fragility is expressed by *Carroña*, an installation by Javier
Pérez also made for the 2011 edition of *Glasstress*. The work consists of
a classic Venetian red chandelier with leaves, flowers, and rings that the
artist broke into pieces by letting it drop to the floor from up high during a
sort of performance. On it are crowded ten stuffed crows that seem to feed
voraciously on its fragments. The ancient fables tell us that the plumage
of the crow, once white, became black as punishment for the sin of excessive
vanity. Through the symbolic use of color, this bird is thus linked to the
concept of guilt.

Blood vessels are frequently depicted in Javier Pérez's work, sometimes
under the guise of red horsehair, other times as branches or shrubs.
In *Carroña* the blood vessels are brought to mind by the joints of blown glass
that support the goblets. As much as the chandelier is like a found and
modified object, shattered on the floor, it evokes flesh and blood and on the
symbolic level becomes a dramatic representation of history crumbling into
a thousand pieces. Hence *Carroña* equates the existential crisis assailing and
tearing up contemporary individuals with the impossibility of the West to see
their history reconstructed and projected into the future. The crows gathering
the shards highlight that we are at a tipping point of no return; the contrast
between the black and the red, between the impenetrability of the black
and the transparency of the red, envelopes the entire scene in a pall of
bereavement.

In Catholic countries, on an individual level, death is experienced as calamity
and misfortune, while theologically and culturally it is associated instead
with the hope of the Resurrection, the promise of an afterlife. The funeral
rituals and the period of mourning have always been the necessary steps for
channeling the pain within a cathartic process tied to the idea that becoming
necessitates death because it goes from "what has been" to "what will be."
Over time the idea of becoming and that of progress became increasingly
intertwined, ending up being the same thing in most cases. Starting from
the French Enlightenment and German Idealism, in particular, and moving
through the Industrial Revolution of the second half of the nineteenth
century, the idea of progress found its natural outlet in the avant-garde
concept developed by the first modernist art movements. The twentieth

century thus experienced the death of the cultural experiences that had preceded it as a liberation from the numerous constraints that the past had placed on art, preventing them from designing a better future. From this perspective, the death of theories, phenomena, and trends now considered foreign to the spirit of the times was seen as a celebration and not as bereavement. In the postmodern era artists have considered it a limitation only to endeavor to look forward. Consequently, they have looked back, without nostalgia and with utilitarian behavior, to recover the fragments in random order, *improperly* assembling them and placing them in contexts related to the contemporary. Hence the use in today's art of old objects, forms, and materials, glass included.

Like *Carroña* by Javier Pérez, Antonio Riello's installation, *Ashes to Ashes*, 2009/2010, also presented at the 2011 edition of *Glasstress*, is a dramatic representation of history that is crumbling. The installation consists of about twenty containers of blown glass in the shape of wine glasses, hermetically closing within the swollen stem the ashes of a book the artist took from his library and burned. About 35 to 40 centimeters high each, and with a diameter of between 6 and 25, these reliquaries aligned on glass shelves have been *soffiati al lume* based on a design by the artist, in Massimo Lunardon's glassworks, in the province of Vicenza. The very thin glass binds these artifacts to the glassmaking tradition of Central and Northern Europe, which is very different from that of Venice. At a formal level these glasses are inspired by the Italian Medieval and Renaissance periods, but also by forms taken from international design.

Book burning is unanimously considered a barbaric profanation. Inevitably the mind returns to the book burning of 1933, in Berlin, at the hands of the Nazis, a ritual that was to consecrate the superiority of German culture over the rest of the world by erasing the memory of written words. Burning the books he has loved the most and placing them in an urn is one way for Antonio Riello to consign them to Eternity instead, turning them into tutelary deities. In *Ashes to Ashes* we find individual goblets engraved with the names of Kafka and Joyce, Russell and Bateson, but also with the titles of comics and science fiction stories. Conceived as a work in progress—many titles will be added by the artist—the installation refers to the many volumes that have crowded the shelves of the spatially infinite library of Jorge Louis Borges. Burning his favorite books is also a propitiatory and apotropaic gesture for

Antonio Riello: the ashes are not scattered to the wind, but lovingly collected and piously protected in special reliquaries. The books kept in these glass goblets thus represent the mark left by every book in the existence of people who, as artists, transcend their own individuality.

Other examples of interesting glass works included in this exhibition are *Hourglass*, 2010, and *Sheet of Bubble Wrap*, 2011, by Vik Muniz. The first is a large hourglass with a crumbly red brick inside it. Despite having the shape and materials of an hourglass, this object does not in fact have its function. *Sheet of Bubble Wrap* looks like a sheet of bubble wrap sinuously folded over itself. Vik Muniz has chosen glass to imitate this most appropriate material for packing fragile objects, such as those made of glass itself. In these as in other

works by the artist we recognize the object as a model, but what we see does not correspond to the real nature of the elements that constitute it. In both of these works, the aim is to demonstrate the misleading nature of the image in relation to its historical memory and to the experience of the spectator.
Apart from the many implications expressed by the works under consideration, what I wish to emphasize is the originality of the use of glass, which thanks to its properties becomes part of itself. In other words, these examples are intended to show that glass material is not alien to contemporary art and that actually, precisely because it has been kept at the margins of modernist experimentation, can now tap unexplored areas. This is demonstrated by the work of Kiki Smith, an artist who has devoted much attention to the expressive possibilities of this material. Glass, says Kiki Smith, "has excellent qualities and a special light that seems to come from the contemplation of a Christ of ice; like the skin, it gives the illusion of being fragile and impenetrable at the same time."[1]
As much as there has been an attempt in recent decades to distance itself from modernism, to go beyond it, the works cited above show that today's art is moving in the path traced by the historical avant-gardes who, particularly with Constantin Brancusi and Marcel Duchamp, redefined the concept of sculpture. Prior to Brancusi's modular masses with no pedestal, and before Duchamp's readymades, sculpture was understood as statuary made primarily of wood, marble, and bronze. These were the materials that lent themselves best to that way of understanding sculpture and the execution of bas-relief sculpture, i.e. the construction of narratives with figures emerging from a plane. Clay, ceramics, and glass, on the other hand, were the domain of the applied arts and considered artistic expressions closer to a craft, which however fine the quality did not, however, enjoy the same consideration as the plastic arts.
Thanks to art nouveau, between the late nineteenth and early twentieth century, at the same time as the political and economic rise of the bourgeoisie and the socio-cultural change triggered by the Industrial Revolution, glass took on a significant role in the creation of artistic objects. After all, glass has always been an ideal material for decorations because of its transparency, its letting light shine through lending brightness to the colors. Nevertheless, however hard the artist strove to embody a new style linked to the spirit of the times, art nouveau objects made of glass—or of glass combined with other materials—had a purpose of use and therefore remained linked to the context of the applied arts. Doors and windows, chandeliers, plates, vases and jewelry had not yet received the full dignity of plastic art works, as has happened in recent times.
In the second half of the nineteenth century, when the inquietudes that would lead to the birth of the avant-garde movements were already apparent, artists were rejecting the idea that a work of art could have a useful function. At the same time as the invention of photography, which had freed art from the documentary role, the new languages did not concede anything to the taste of the old bourgeoisie, which wanted to subvert the aesthetic values. The decline of portrait painting was not simply because a photograph could reproduce reality more faithfully and more quickly than a painting, it also responded to the need to make the work an object for its own sake.
With the end of commissions by the aristocracy and the Church, and with

the emergence of a new conception of the market that led artists to work for themselves and sell their works personally—the first private galleries would appear shortly thereafter—there was also the idea that besides being useless in practical terms, art no longer needed to aspire to beauty. Modern artists preferred to identify with the harshness of the tribal sculpture (beginning to find space in Parisian museums) and in the banality of industrial objects in common use (baked in large quantities by the new factories) rather than in the refined elegance of handmade glass objects from Murano, France, and Bohemia such as mirrors and chandeliers, which had been very popular with the French aristocracy and bourgeoisie of the eighteenth and nineteenth centuries. What had once been a strength of glass art—particularly the elegance of those items made by hand in Venice from the 1200s onwards—was considered a weakness by the avant-gardes.

It was starting from a view of the world that assigned negative attributes to beauty as it had been understood in earlier centuries that the dadaists came to theorize the *aesthetic of indifference*, a programmatic definition that summarized the need to focus attention on objects that were also chosen by virtue of their anonymity. Since the objects dearest to the old bourgeoisie were those related to furnishings and practical use, emphasizing a clear separation between the applied arts and the noble arts responded both to a formal and linguistic strategy and to the desire to affirm the spirit of the times. This was true despite there being no lack of important formal solutions in the applied arts like those developed by the Bauhaus (1919–1933), in the vanguard from a linguistic perspective while still aiming to create useful objects.

Nevertheless, because the Bauhaus claimed that form must follow function and not vice versa, it marked an important turning point in the way design and architecture were conceived and perceived. The presence of such artists as Paul Klee, Wassily Kandinsky, Oskar Schlemmer, László Moholy-Nagy, and Josef Albers as teachers in a school of architecture and design, the Bauhaus itself showed there was an intention to eliminate the distinction between fine arts and applied arts, overlapping them until they coincided. The Bauhaus manifested interest in glass as a material suitable for design, but also for art. There was so much interest, in fact, that it led to the establishment of a workshop for glass decorating, whose direction was entrusted first to Paul Klee (in 1919) and then to Josef Albers (in 1923). In the spirit of social revolution, which viewed art as a community asset and not the privilege of a few, artists dressed the part of creator in public, but in the privacy of their studios made a clear distinction between applied arts and plastic arts. No matter how many people may argue the opposite, the handmade objects created in the Bauhaus resemble art more than being works of art. In any case, the debate about what distinguishes design from art is an unresolved question and open to conflicting interpretations.

Unlike what happened with marble and wood, which could also be used as raw materials, and therefore be "found," during the years of the historical avant-gardes there were many who felt that glasswork and ceramics necessarily implied the production of elegant objects, more suitable for the

homes of the bourgeoisie than for places of art. As materials to be shaped,
glass and ceramics thus brought into play the manual intervention of the
artist, while starting with Duchamp and dada, as mentioned before, sculpture
was not conceived of as a mass shaped by its author, but an assembly of
objects that the artist could appropriate by changing its meaning. Duchamp's
inverted urinal presented with the title *Fountain* is perhaps the most explicit
example of this dynamic: the artist does not personally mold the shape
he needs, but chooses it in a process that presumes a relative interest in
the material with which to create the work. From this perspective, glass
became part of the modernist work as a found object (bottles, glasses, balls,
ampoules, display cases, crockery) and not as material to be shaped.
Between 1913 and 1915, Marcel Duchamp gave a glass ampoule the title of
Paris Air. The greatest emphasis on glass, however, is found in his work *The
Bride Stripped Bare by Her Bachelors, Even*, also known as *The Large Glass*.
Duchamp worked on this emblematic example of modernism from 1915 to
1923, leaving it unfinished. Consisting of two glass panels framed by wooden
and steel mounts, *The Large Glass* is seen as a spacious window with cryptic
forms inside created with oil paint, silver and lead foils, and wires. As is well
known, during transport the glass suffered several cracks, but the artist
decided to accept the intervention of chance as an integral part of the work.
Apart from the diverse and conflicting interpretations that have been given
to *The Large Glass*, the fact remains that one of the fundamental
characteristics of this work is that it allows the eyes to see through it, which
is why the viewer can grasp the physical space that it houses.
Before the historic avant-gardes changed the direction of Western art,
sculpture still had materials that helped to define an idea of style. Suffice
it to say that even an extraordinarily innovative formal sculptor like Auguste
Rodin is now considered to be tied more to the nineteenth-century conception
of sculpture than to that of the twentieth-century, not only because of the
choice of subjects represented, but especially because they were created in
marble and bronze.
The impact of the materials in connoting the art object is such that even
a revolutionary work like the bronze sculpture *Unique Forms of Continuity
in Space*, 1913, by Umberto Boccioni lends itself to be perceived more as an
expression of a renewed classicism than as a real break with tradition.
Entering into modernism not only meant renouncing the themes and
languages that had characterized the visual culture from the fourteenth to
the nineteenth century, from the Middle Ages to Romanticism, it also meant
giving up materials that had characterized classical statuary and sculpture.
Therefore, it was not a matter of substituting one material for another, but
rather of making the selected material a functional tool for the formal and
conceptual result that the artist tended. In light of all of this it can be argued
that, having expanded the catalogue of usable materials, artists favored the
identification of their work with the chosen materials.
In the 1960s, synthetic materials like plastics and resins appeared in avant-
garde art. A decade later, the choice of material played such a significant
role in the work of individual authors that it became a determining factor in
defining their aesthetic. For example, fire refers to the art of Yves Klein, shit
to that of Piero Manzoni, and felt and animal fat to the work of Joseph Beuys.

Similarly, the mirror makes us think of Michelangelo Pistoletto, wax and the bundles are associated with Mario Merz, iron with Jannis Kounellis, Richard Serra, and Carl Andre, stones and earth with Robert Smithson and Richard Long, granite with Giovanni Anselmo, felt with Robert Morris, pitch with Gilberto Zorio, and frost (obtained with the resistance of a refrigerator) with Pier Paolo Calzolari. Many other examples could be cited as well, including artists of the decades that followed. Even though the individual artist's choices may not be tied to one material or another—so each one's body of work of is actually far more complex—the examples above show that for many of them the material used is a sort of trademark. The innovation of this aesthetic vision also lies in the fact that artists can make use of any material or medium that helps achieve the pre-established goal, provided the use has a theoretical justification.

The 1960s and 1970s were the years of poor and discarded materials: iron, chalk, wax, straw, burlap, glass splinters. Although uncommon and of little value, within the work they obtained the same dignity as wood, marble, and bronze. There was nothing that could not become a part of the work, including ashes or organic materials *found* in nature (plants, fruits, vegetables, etc.). In this context, glass obviously became a part of the work as an industrial product and not as a mass to be molded since it requires an elaborate and expensive process and a specific skill to obtain it and shape it by hand.

The turning point that led to a different perception of glass as a material also suitable to sculpture took place in the 1990s, with the second generation of postmodernism: the generation that had seen the enthusiasm for materials of traditional sculpture metabolize in the previous decade. It was a turning point, however, anticipated by Luciano Fabro's *Foot* series. As the title indicates, these are sculptural representations of very large feet, each one of them different and made of stone, marble, glass, and bronze, which form the base for a column of fabric. The choice of materials recalls the Renaissance and Baroque tradition. Contrary to what happened in the past, however, this cycle of Fabro's works placed more emphasis on the base of the column (the foot) than on the column itself, which was assigned the principal role in the classical architectural tradition. By using Murano glass for one of these *feet*, Fabro showed the tendency of the neovanguards to look at the expressive forms of the past with a more forgiving eye than what their predecessors had done at the turn of the century. After all, we are at the doors of postmodernism, i.e. at a conception of art that by reversing the logic of the avant-gardes, rather than trying to invent new styles, languages, and forms, preferred to take possession of the styles, languages, and forms belonging to tradition to combine them so that their contrasts emerge.

This (then new) aesthetic vision involved painters, sculptors, performers, designers, and architects, but also poets, novelists, film and theater directors, musicians, set designers, and scriptwriters. There was also the tendency to give body to the sculptures shaped by the hands of its author, interested in following the entire process leading to the bronze casting. Artists started to feel attracted to the fire of the kilns again, thus looking at glass as a sculptural material. This is highlighted in this exhibition, which shows how glass offers artists, as well as designers, expressive possibilities that transcend the memory of elegant, useful objects created in the best glassworks decades and centuries ago.

One of the effects of the renewed interest in traditional expressive forms was a return to the idea that the freedom of art is linked to its uselessness. Is it perhaps not a restriction to subordinate form to a function? Once again we have the debate about the distinction between plastic arts and design. Every aesthetic vision that came from the historical avant-gardes was, after all, the result of overcoming a pre-existing vision, which by nature was to be overcome quickly in the space of a decade. From this perspective, drawing a boundary between the various arts does not mean classifying them, but defining the identity of the creative work (also) through its ability to stand out. As repetitive as it might sound, it is by accepting the differences that the qualities free themselves from discrimination and take on dignity, which is not the same as claiming a return to order. The path of art is an evolutionary one, in the sense that everything the artist does takes into account what was done by those who came before him. As many have pointed out, it is this knowledge that makes us realize that current art, compared with what preceded it, is not better or worse, just different. And it is this awareness that allows us to identify in the alternation of themes and contrasting visions the return of paths that cyclically present themselves in a new look.

The marriage between art and design has expanded the area of expressive possibilities for the former as well as the latter. Understanding that the plastic artist is free to manufacture an object intended for use, and the designer to create an object as a single exemplar with no practical function, we feel the need for new criteria to evaluate both art and design. It is a need revealed by the inability of art in recent decades to move beyond modernism—of which postmodernism is the tail—with the same determination and radicalism with which modernism ferried the new man in the century of psychoanalysis, ideological revolutions, and discoveries in science and technology once considered utopian. In anticipation of an art that expresses the new turning point, there is nothing left to do but once again question the rules of the game made outmoded by also being taken up in the classrooms of provincial academies.

1) *Il ritorno di Kiki*, interview with Manuela Valentini, *Artribune*, September 27, 2011.

BARBARA BLOOM
EL ULTIMO GRITO
JAN FABRE
JAIME HAYON
LUKE JERRAM
MICHAEL JOO
MARYA KAZOUN
MARTA KLONOWSKA
TOMÁŠ LIBERTÍNY
BETH LIPMAN
VIK MUNIZ
TONY OURSLER
JAVIER PÉREZ
JAUME PLENSA
SILVANO RUBINO
URSULA VON RYDINGSVARD
JUDITH SCHAECHTER
THOMAS SCHÜTTE
JOYCE JANE SCOTT
KIKI SMITH
YUTAKA SONE
MIKE + DOUG STARN
PATRICIA URQUIOLA
KOEN VANMECHELEN

GLASSTRESS NEW YORK

NEW ART FROM THE VENICE BIENNALES

OPEN PROJECT BY ADRIANO BERENGO

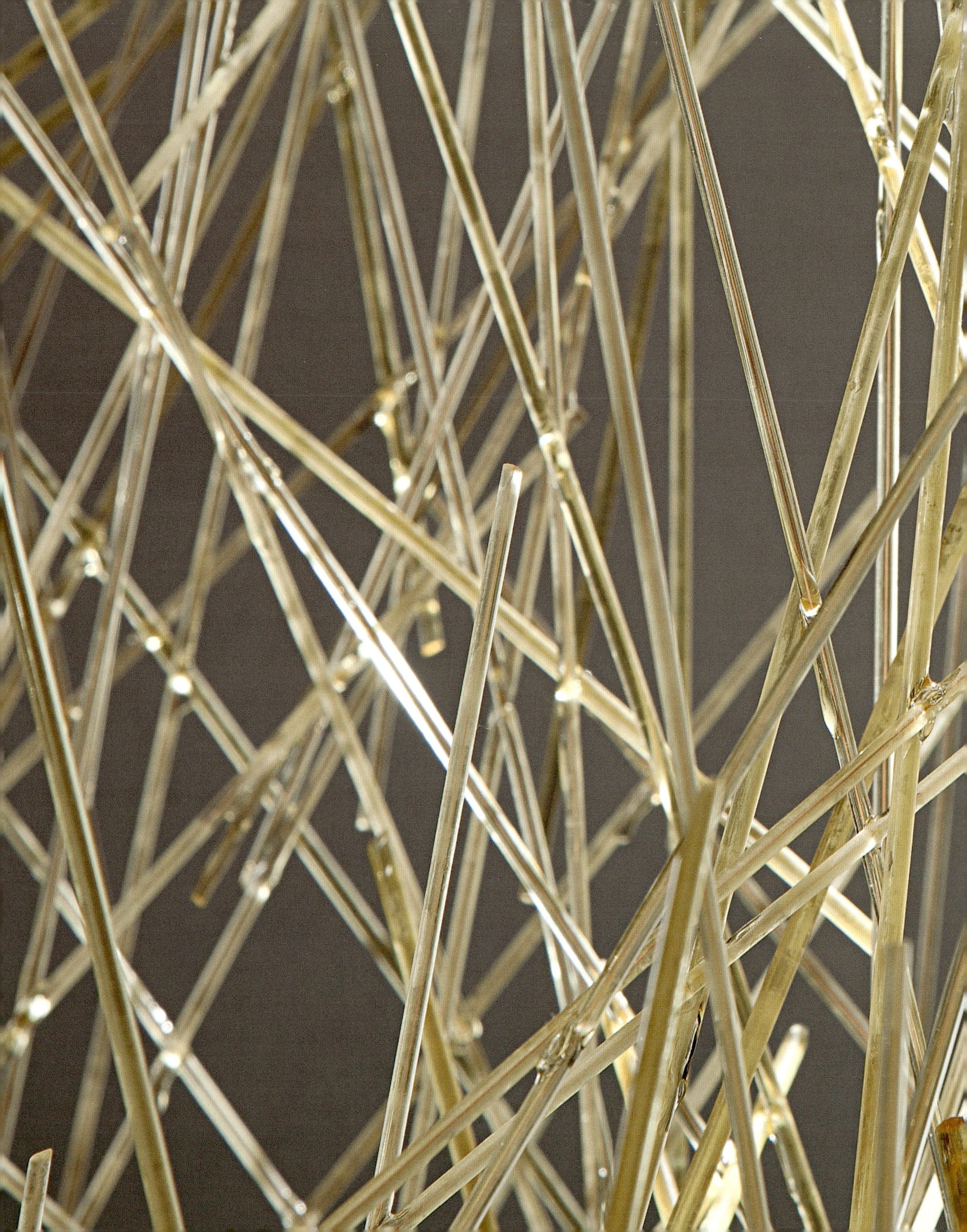

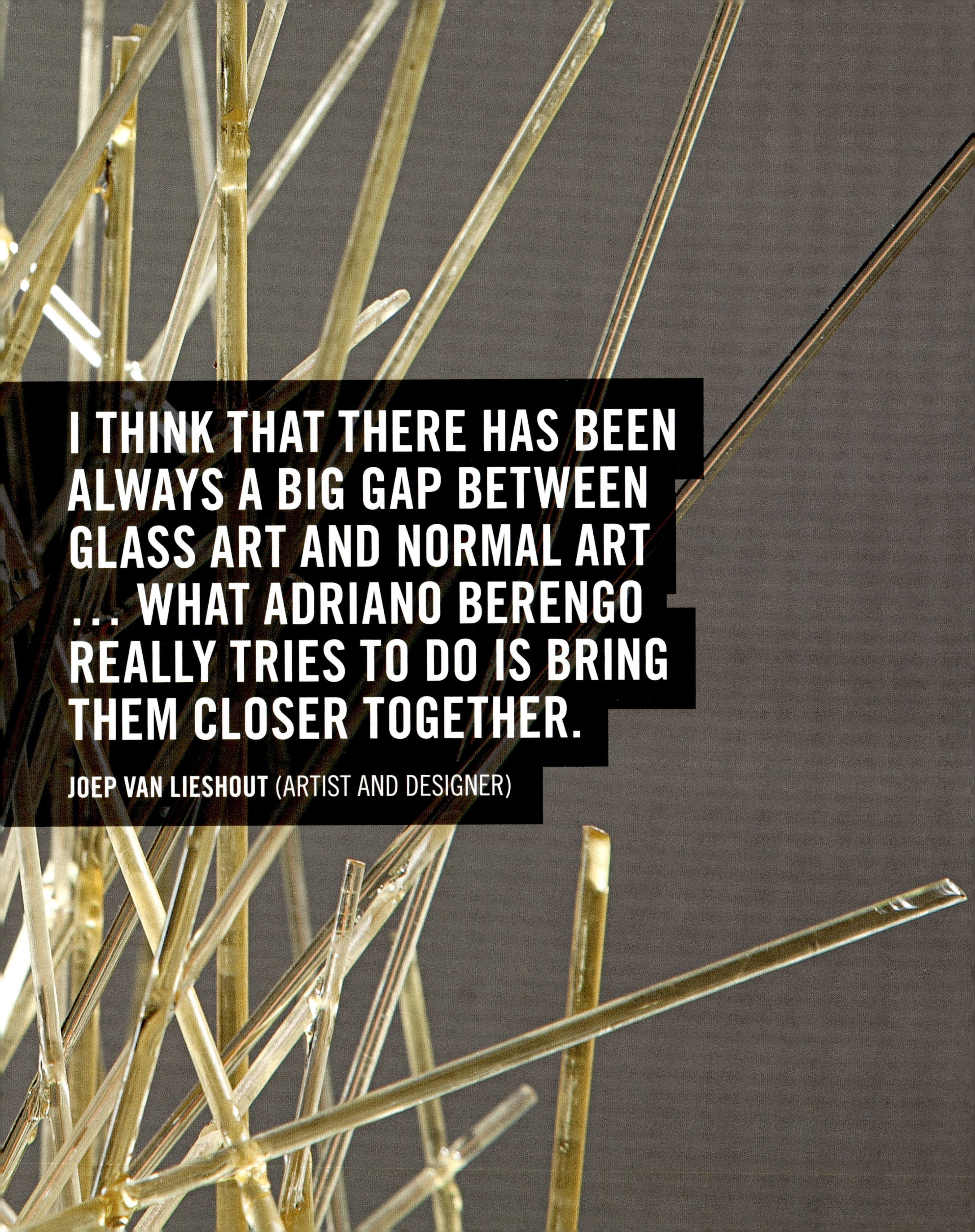
I THINK THAT THERE HAS BEEN ALWAYS A BIG GAP BETWEEN GLASS ART AND NORMAL ART … WHAT ADRIANO BERENGO REALLY TRIES TO DO IS BRING THEM CLOSER TOGETHER.
JOEP VAN LIESHOUT (ARTIST AND DESIGNER)

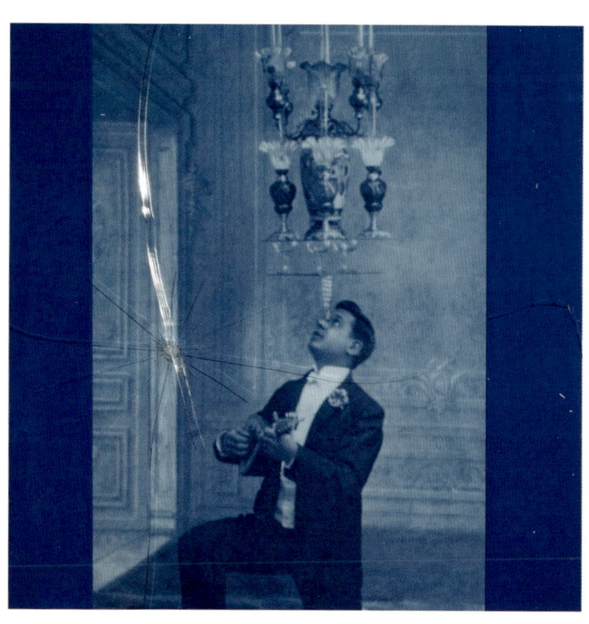

BARBARA BLOOM

Barbara Bloom was born in Los Angeles in 1951. She lives and works in New York. She is an installation artist, a designer, and a photographer. Once she completed her studies at the California Institute of the Arts, she lived for many years in Amsterdam and Berlin. Known for her meticulously crafted works, precisely detailed and flawlessly executed, Bloom focused her research on the relationships between objects and images and the meanings implicit in their placement and combination. In her artwork, beauty is a premise for investigating illusion, fragility, and transience to expose the subliminal ideologies of modern visual culture. Her witty and elegant installations combine objects that she has collected in her vast archives with manufactured ones, and challenges conventional perceptions with wry commentaries on the shifting notions of value and the practice of collecting, the desire for possession. Moreover, she examines the concept of the artist as an eccentric, narcissistic collector and curator of her own history, producing works of great visual glamour together with installations which include different media: video, sound, and photography. Her work has been exhibited in museums such as MoMA in New York, the Museum of Contemporary Art, Los Angeles, the MAK, Vienna, the Serpentine Gallery in London, and several other international prominent venues such as the Venice Biennale where, in 1988, she received the Due Mille Award. In 1989, she received The Louis Comfort Tiffany Foundation Award, and was the recipient of awards from the Guggenheim Foundation, the Wexner Center for the Arts, and the Getty Research Institute.

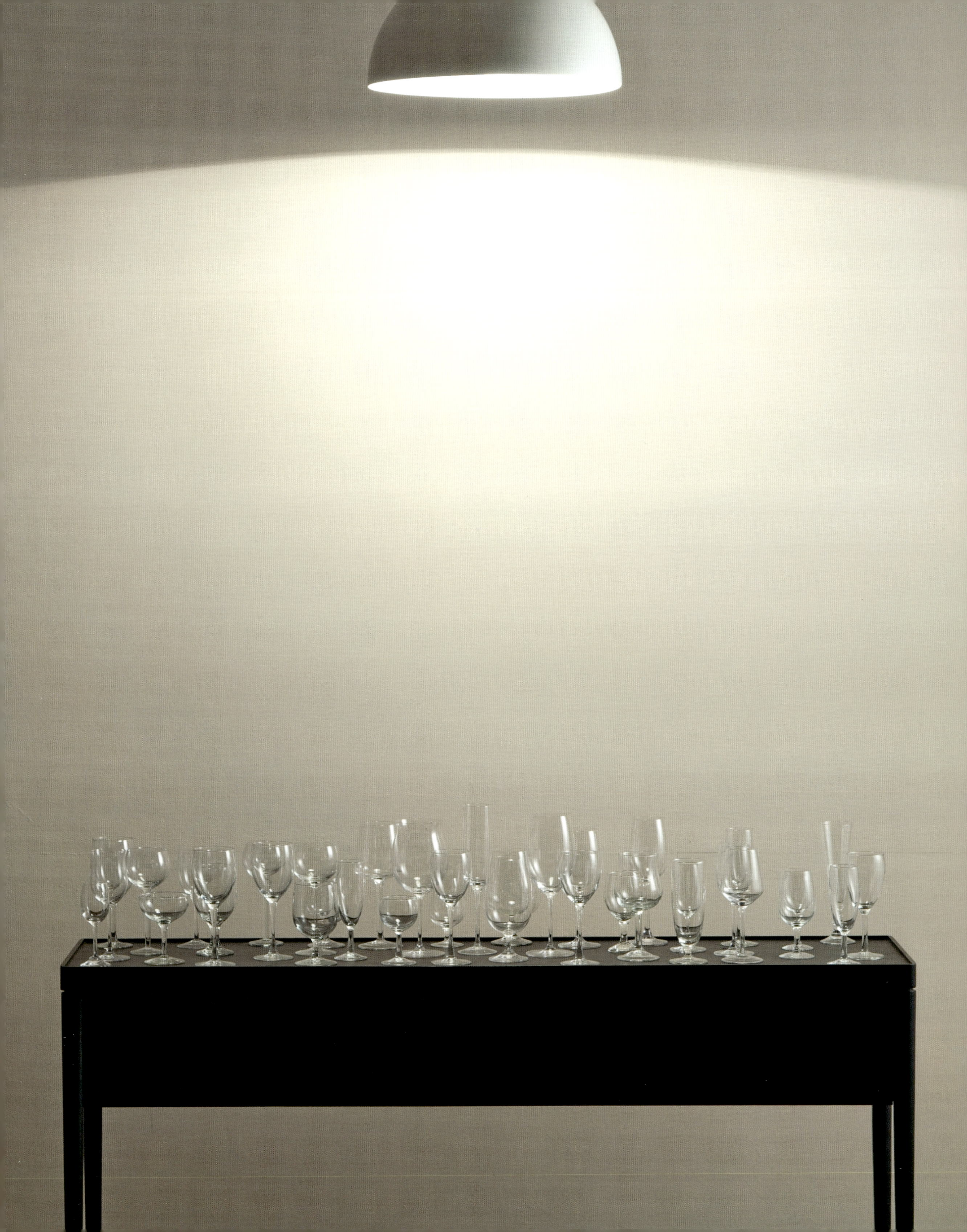

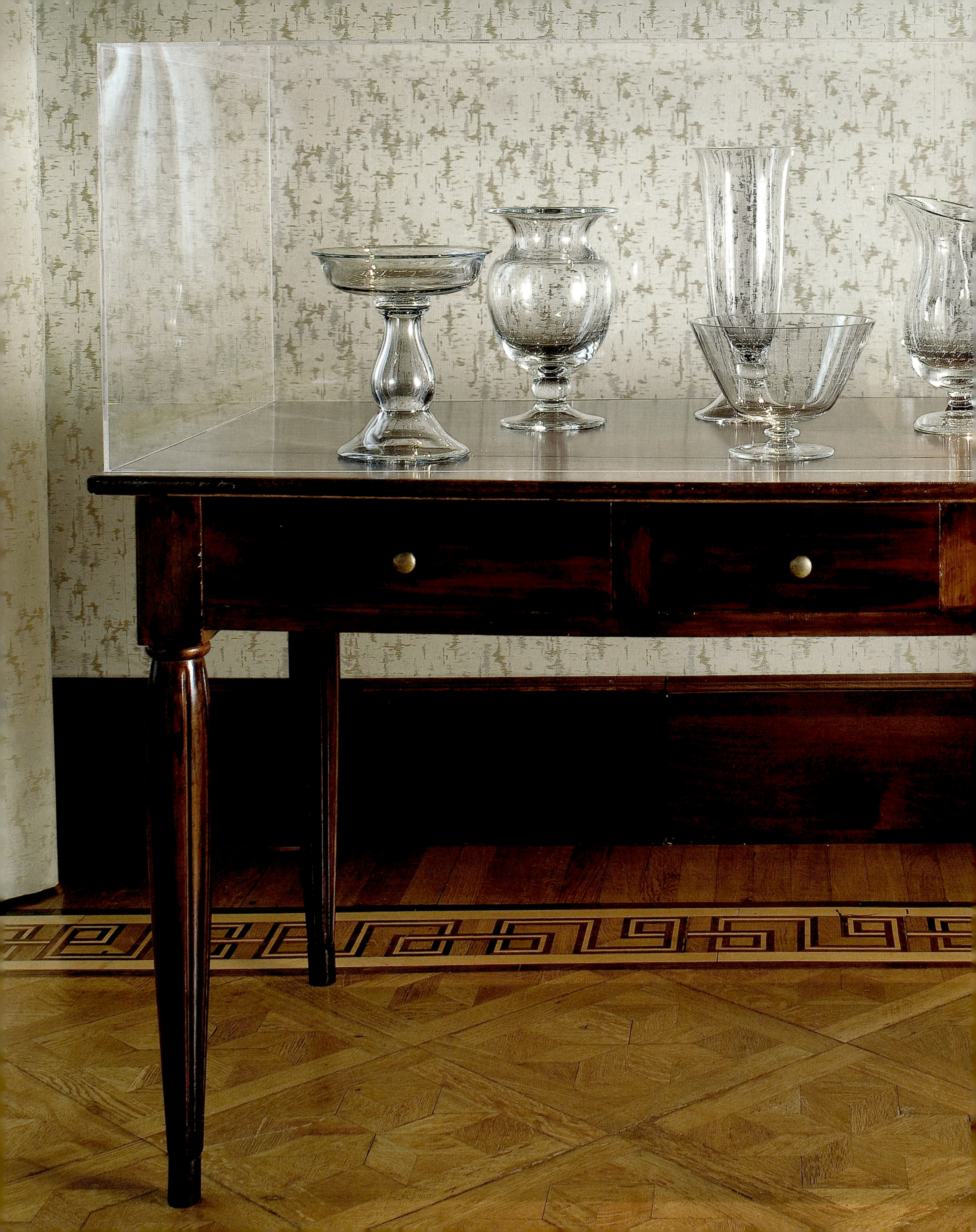

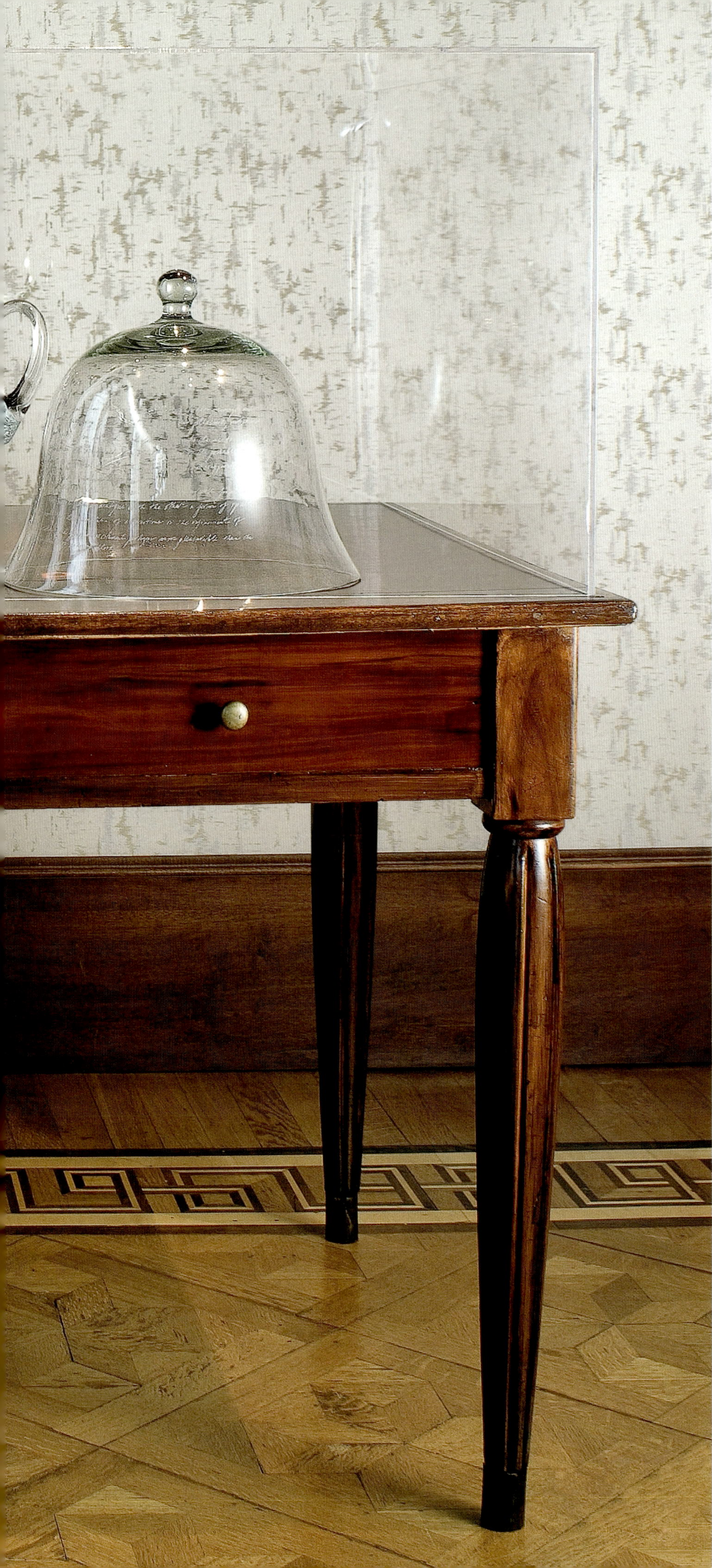

FLAUBERT LETTERS II
1987–2008
ED. 2/3 THREE VERSIONS, EACH UNIQUE
VARIABLE DIMENSIONS
COURTESY PRIVATE COLLECTION, PIACENZA

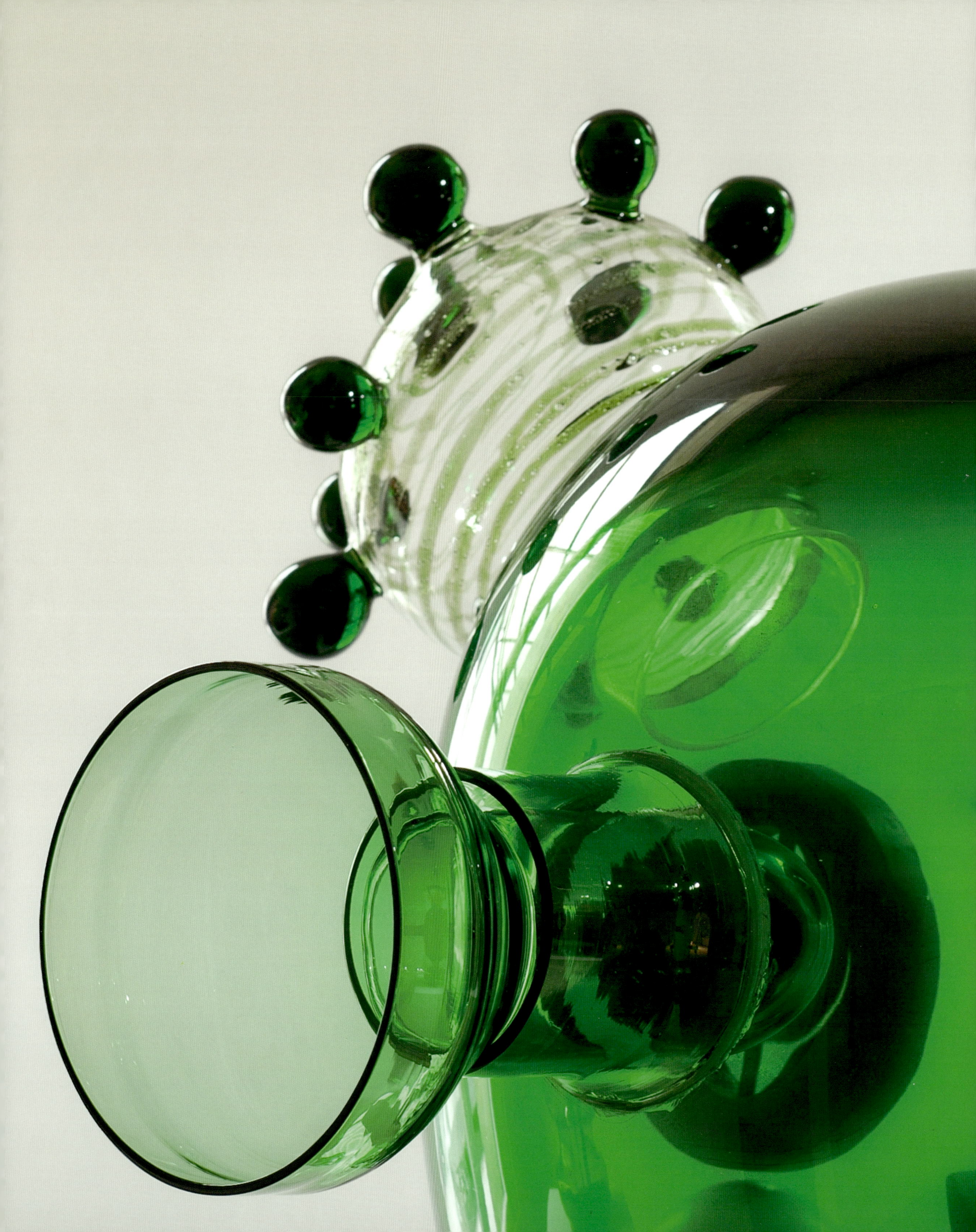

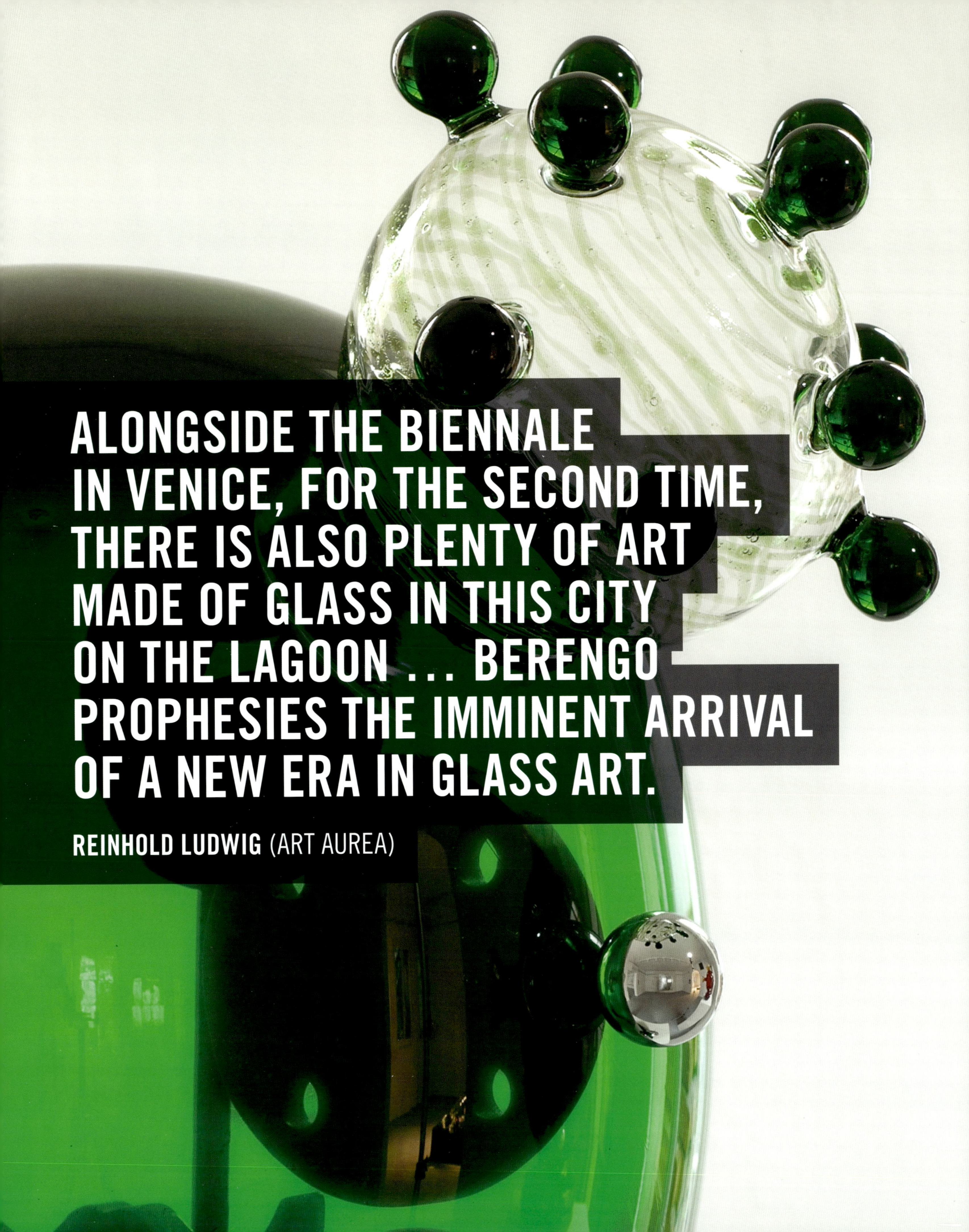
ALONGSIDE THE BIENNALE IN VENICE, FOR THE SECOND TIME, THERE IS ALSO PLENTY OF ART MADE OF GLASS IN THIS CITY ON THE LAGOON … BERENGO PROPHESIES THE IMMINENT ARRIVAL OF A NEW ERA IN GLASS ART.
REINHOLD LUDWIG (ART AUREA)

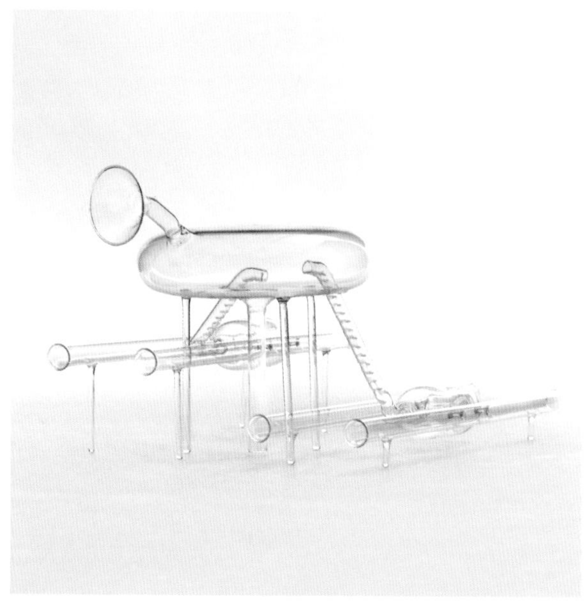

EL ULTIMO GRITO

El Ultimo Grito is the creative partnership between Rosario Hurtado and Roberto Feo. Hurtado was born in Madrid (1966) and Feo was born in London (1964); both work and live in London. El Ultimo Grito was founded in London in 1997. The name "El Ultimo Grito" translates from Spanish to English as "the last shout" reflecting the witty names they give to their products, summing up the heart, intelligence, and humor of the idea. The focus of their work is on one's relationships with objects and culture, which they continuously research, exploring those relationships across disciplines in a wide variety of projects which range from interior design to graphics.

El Ultimo Grito describe their work as a creative studio that places its focus on design and where the idea takes center stage. They receive inspiration from ordinary daily tasks and various materials after experimenting with their tactile or engineering properties. Their most recent work, including *Imaginary Architectures*, 2011, questions cultural and social preconceptions and asks how contemporary culture incorporates, reuses, and reinterprets the systems and structures it has inherited from the past.

While the designers have steered away from preconceived definitions and prescribed design paths in their work, this strategy did not prevent them from teaching at some of the most prestigious design colleges, including Kingston University, Royal College of Art, and Goldsmiths University in London.

Nor did it prevent them from working for renowned companies and institutions like Selfridges, Budweiser, Hugo Boss, the Victoria and Albert Museum, and Southwark Council.

In 2008 El Ultimo Grito curated *nowhere/now/here Exploring New Lines of Investigation in Design* at the LABoral in Gijón, Spain. The exhibition explored "experimental design" and seeked to challenge the conception we have of design. The exhibition presented over sixty works, which were shown in a colorful space designed by Patricia Urquiola studio with graphics created by Fernando Gutierrez.

The work of El Ultimo Grito has been collected by leading museums and galleries including the Victoria and Albert Museum, Crafts Council and British Council in London; MoMA in New York; Stedelijk Museum in Amsterdam; and Kulturehusset in Stockholm. They have also participated in numerous solo and group exhibitions including *Curious Minds, New Approaches in Design* (2011–2012) at the Israel Museum, Jerusalem; *Escape into the Upper Air* (2011) at Spring Projects, London; *Sitting and Looking* (2010) at Innovative Craft, Edinburgh; and *El Ultimo Grito New Work* (2008) at Appel Gallery, Berlin.

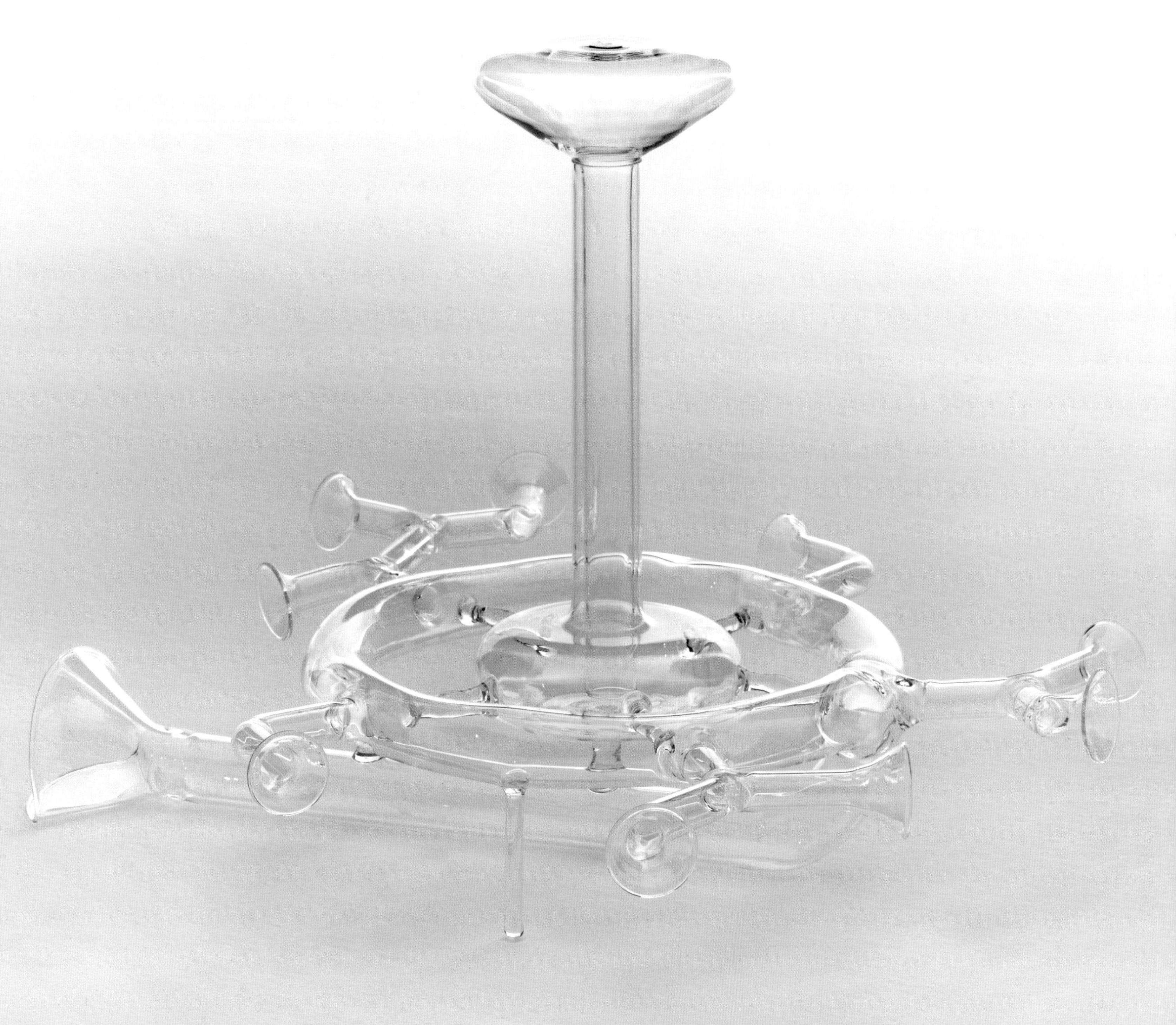

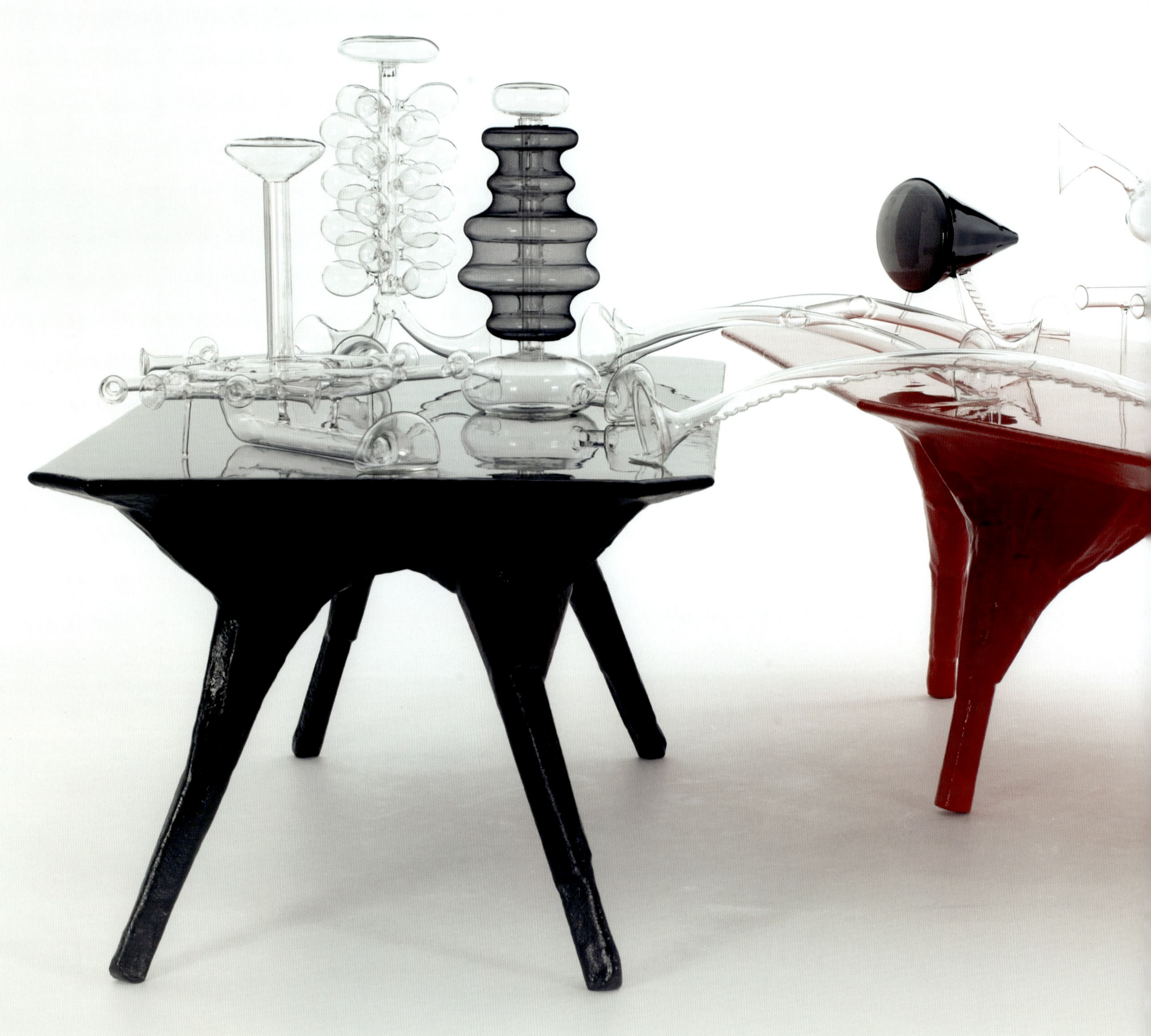

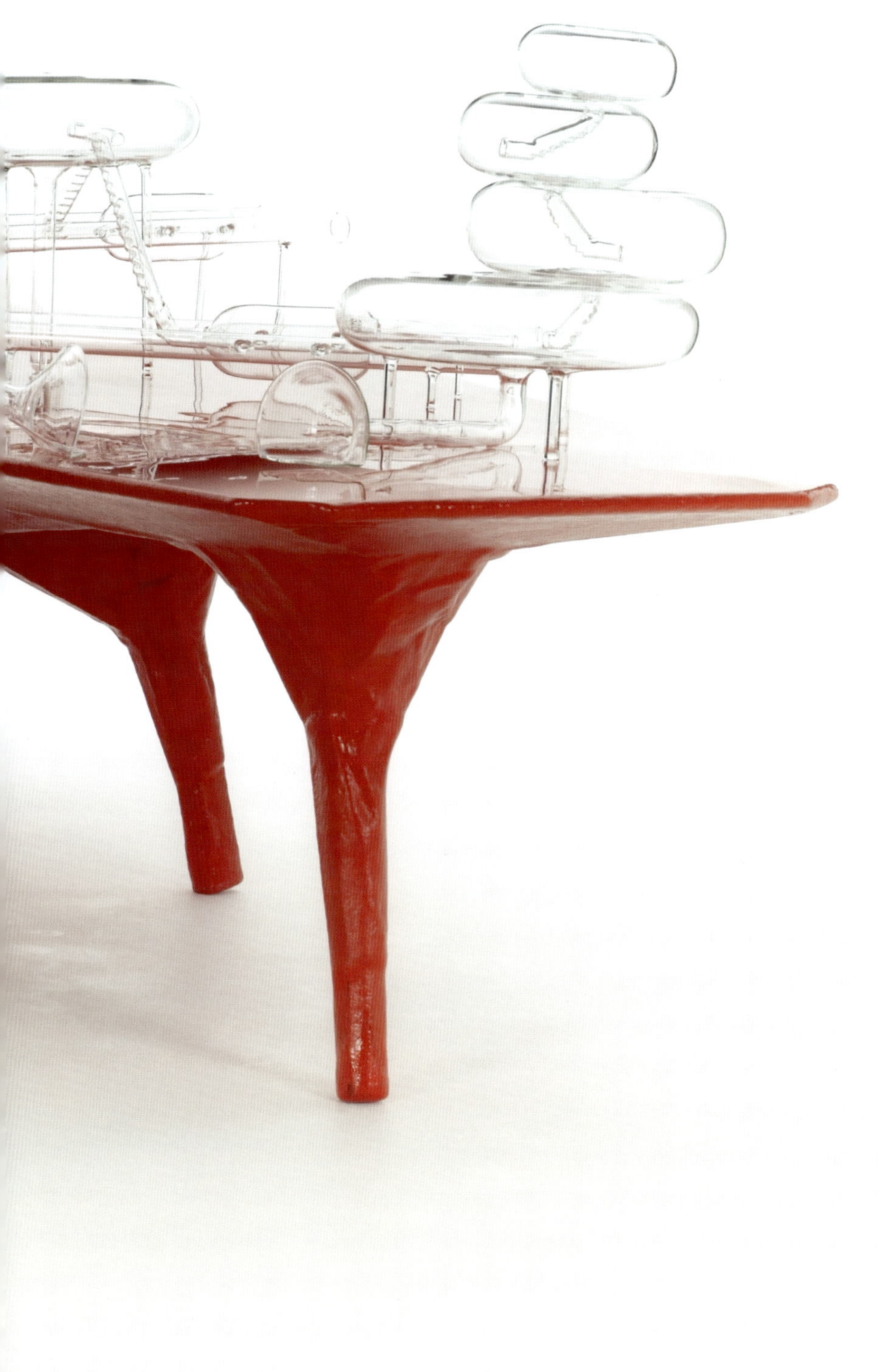

IMAGINARY ARCHITECTURES
2011
VARIABLE DIMENSIONS
COURTESY SPRING PROJECTS, LONDON

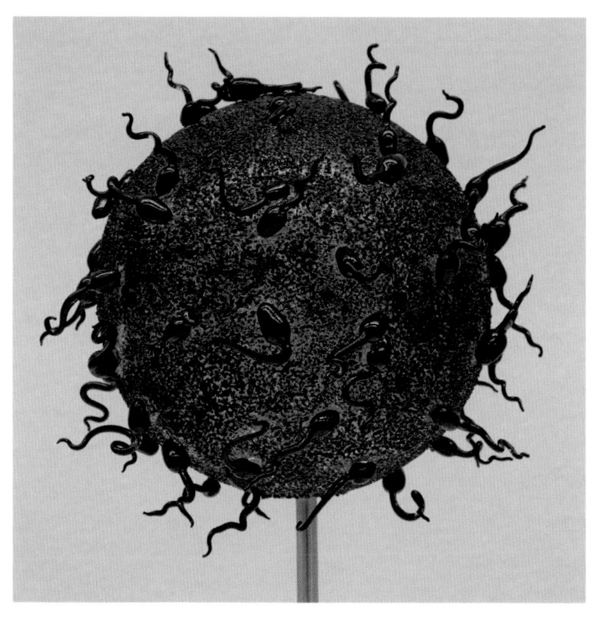

JAN FABRE

Jan Fabre was born in 1958 in Antwerp, where he lives and works. Fabre is known as a versatile figure: a visual artist, a choreographer, a filmmaker, and a writer, he has gained equal fame in each field of action. His work has an all-absorbing and interdisciplinary character. In Fabre's research the study of the human body and its transformations prevails, and he deals with the concept of metamorphosis, through the extreme exploration of human corporeity. A kinsman of the famous entomologist Jean-Henry Fabre, he is attracted to the study of nature and has a real passion for the sciences, entomology in particular. The use of insects is a distinctive feature of his work. He has also created a particular "bic blue" that he uses to coat different kinds of surfaces. Man, nature, and their mutual relations are his favorite themes. The many venues where his works have been displayed include the Venice Biennale in 1984, 1990, and 2003, Documenta in 1987 and 1992, Kassel, Bienal de São Paolo in 1991, Lyon Biennale in 2000, Valencia Biennale in 2001, Istanbul Biennale in 1992 and 2001. Amongst the leading exhibitions there are *Anthropology of a Planet* at Palazzo Benzon, Venice, in 2007, *Jan Fabre au Louvre. L'Ange de la metamorphose*, in 2008, *From the Cellar to the Attic. From the Feet to the Brain* at Kunsthaus Bregenz, in 2009 *From the Feet to the Brain* at Arsenale Novissimo, Venice, *Art kept me out of jail. Performance installations by Jan Fabre 2001–2004–2008* at M HKA, in 2010. In 2011, the Kröller-Müller Museum, Otterlo, hosted the solo exhibition *Hortus / Corpus*.

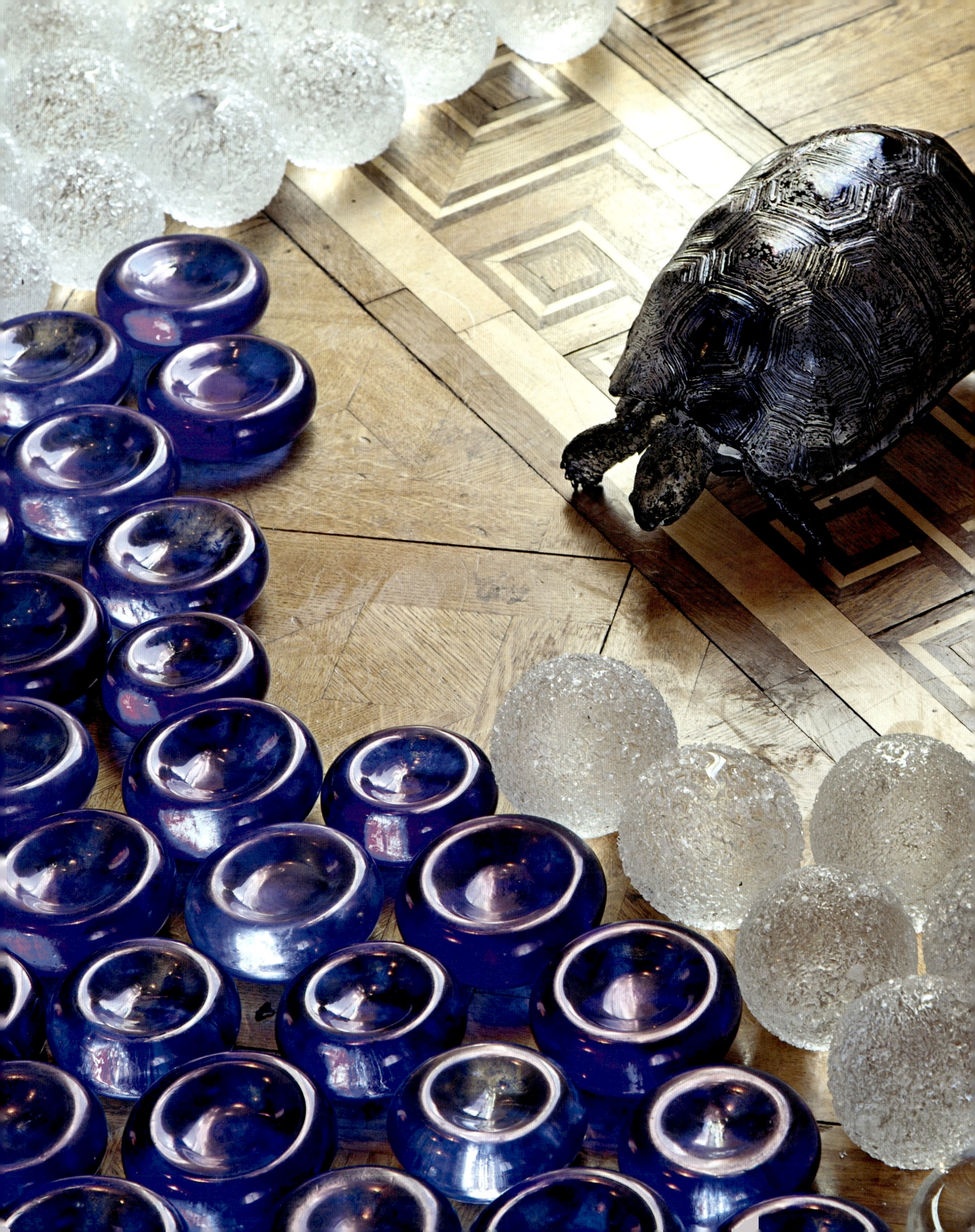

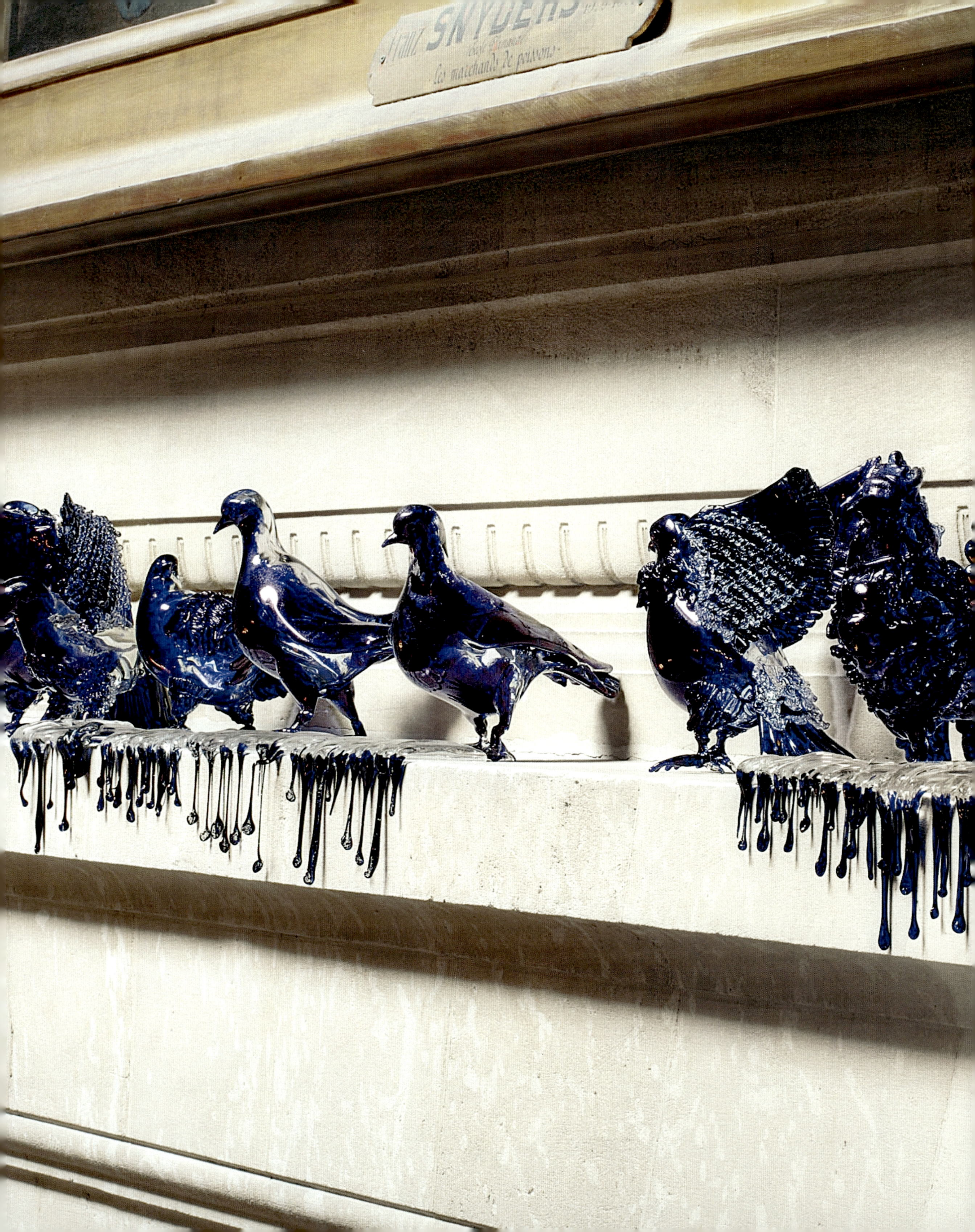

Franz SNYDERS
les marchands de poissons

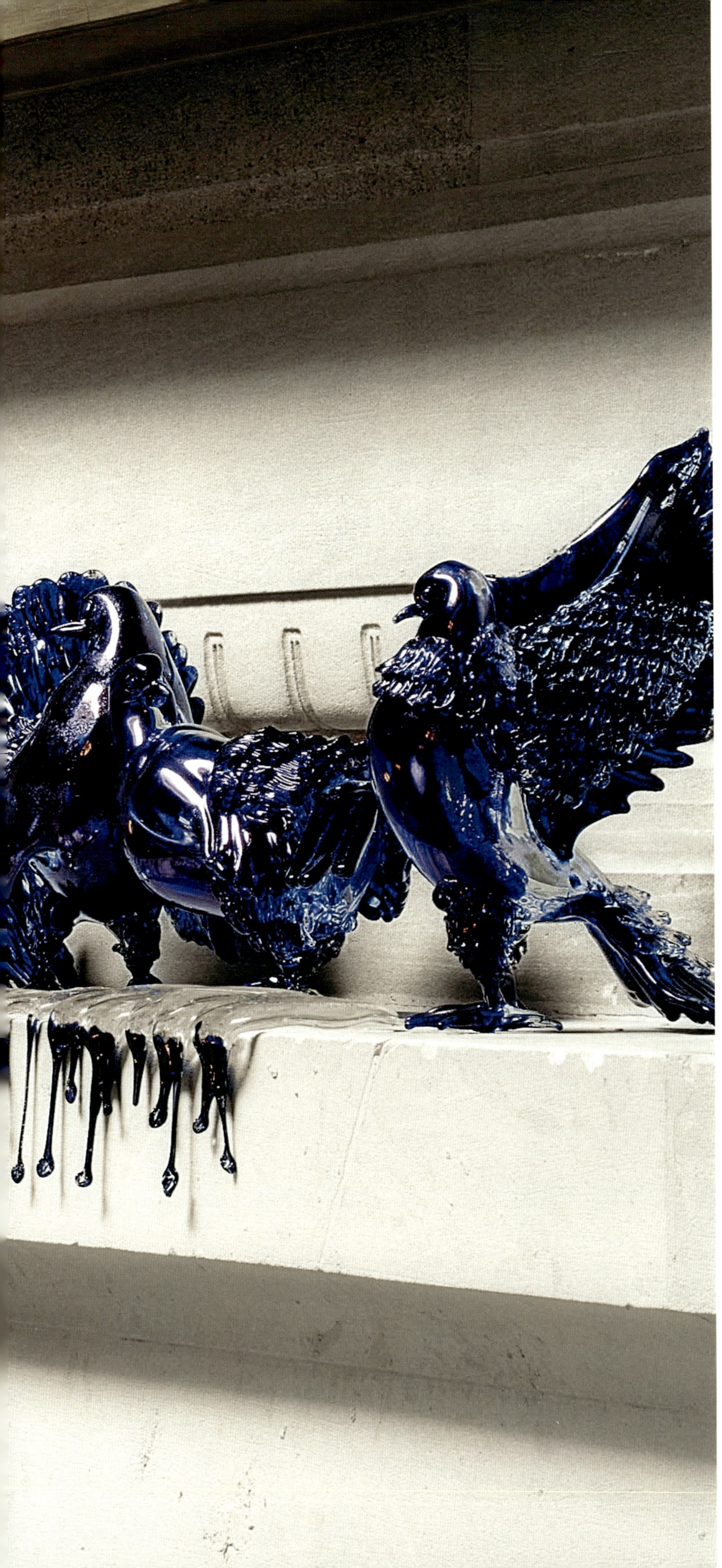

SHITTING DOVES OF PEACE AND FLYING RATS
2008
25 x 260 x 25 CM / VARIABLE DIMENSIONS
COURTESY BERENGO PRIVATE COLLECTION, VENICE

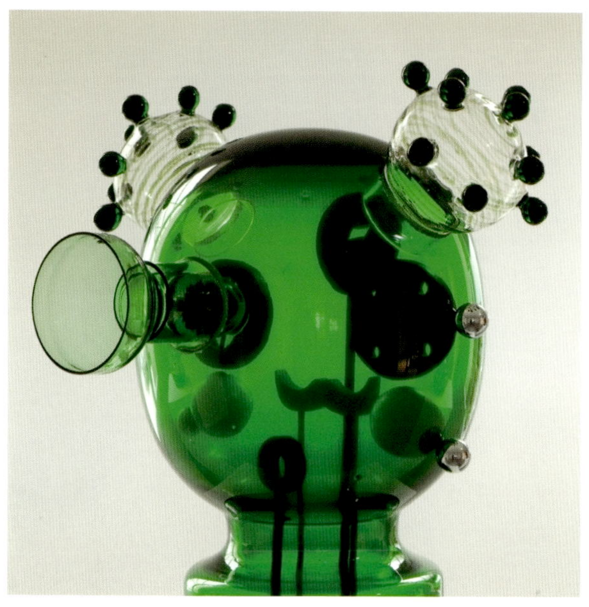

JAIME HAYON

Spanish artist and designer, born in Madrid in 1974.
As a teenager, he plunged into the worlds of skateboarding and graffiti,
passions that, in the years ahead, would lay the groundwork for his art
and which are still predominant today in the detailed and bizarre work that
sets him apart. He studied Industrial Design in Madrid and Paris. In 1997,
he joined Fabrica, the design and communication academy founded by
Benetton, where he worked closely with the legendary photographer Oliviero
Toscani. In a very short time, he moved from being a student to head of the
Design Department.
Eight years later he branched out on his own, making his debut with
Mediterranean Digital Baroque, at the David Gill Gallery in London,
an exhibition that revealed his altogether unique vision, blending irony
and surrealism primarily through the use of ceramics. It was followed, first,
by *Mon Cirque*, seen in Frankfurt, Barcelona, Paris, and Kuala Lumpur;
by a solo show at the Aram Gallery in London; and appearances at the Salone
del Mobile in Milan, the Museum of Design in London, the Vivid Gallery in
Rotterdam, the Gronginger Museum as well as Art Basel.
Hayon's profound knowledge of artisanal potential and quality combined
with his creativity have allowed him to go beyond the barriers and limitations
imposed by the various materials, resulting in the many collections he has
created for such clients as Established and Sons, Moooi, Metalarte, Swarovski,
Berhardt Design, Piper Heidsieck, Gaia and Gino, Fritz Hansen, Se London,
BD Barcelona, Camper, and Bosa Ceramiche Ceccotti. In addition, he has
produced noteworthy collections for Bisazza, the "Crystal Candy Set" collection
for Baccarat, and "Fantasy" for the Spanish porcelain manufacturer Lladró.
These collections have placed Jaime in the vanguard of the production of pieces
that blur the line between design, art, and decoration by creating sophisticated
artisanal objects whose complexity is a perfect reflection of the world of
contemporary design.
He has won numerous awards including "Best Installation" (*Icon Magazine*),
"Breakthrough Creator" (*Wallpaper Magazine*), and, in 2006, the Elle Deco
International Award. Jaime was the guest of honor at the 2008 Interieur
Biennial in Belgium, becoming the youngest person ever to receive this honor.
Jaime is currently working on designing the interiors of leading hotels,
restaurants, and shops around the world.

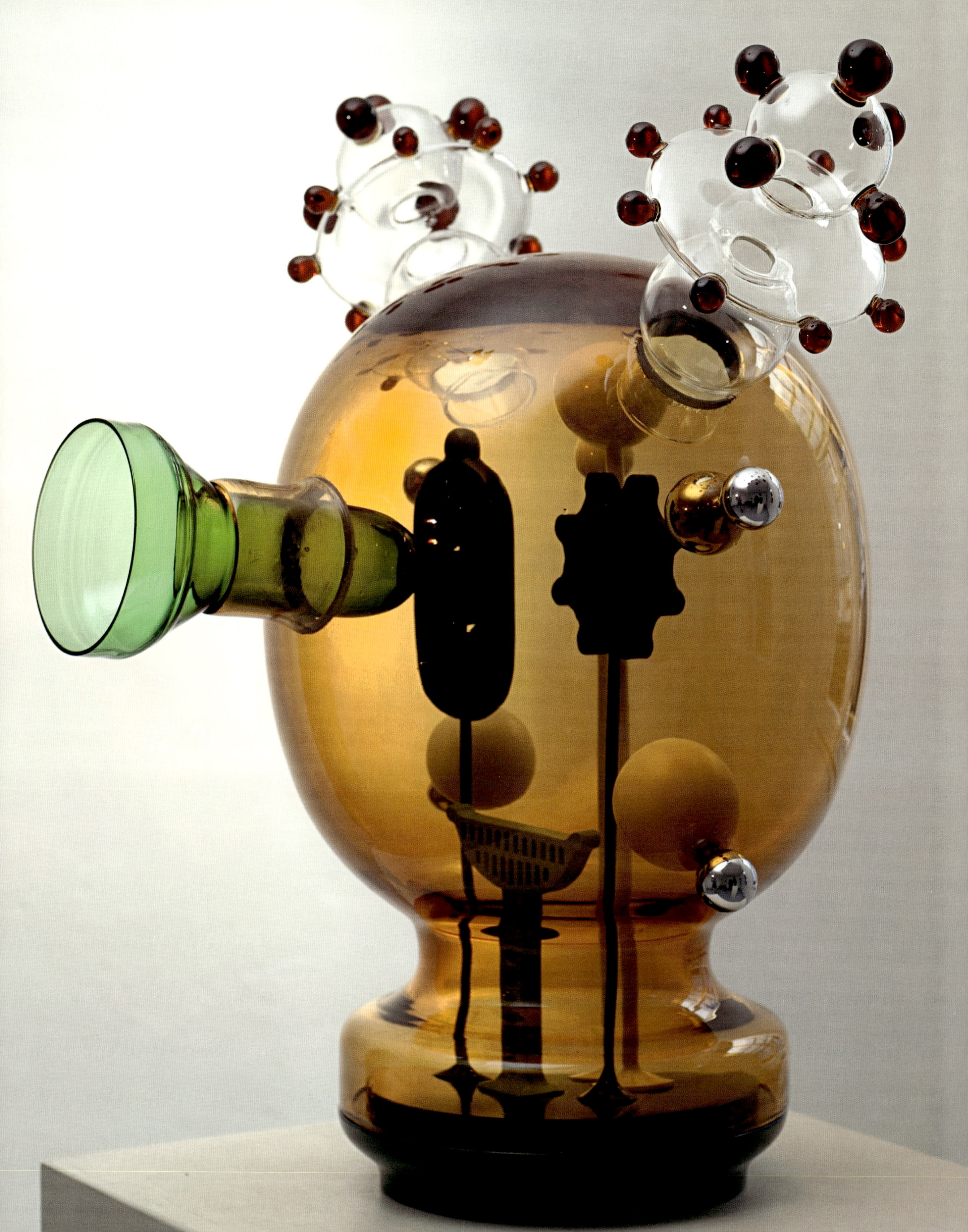

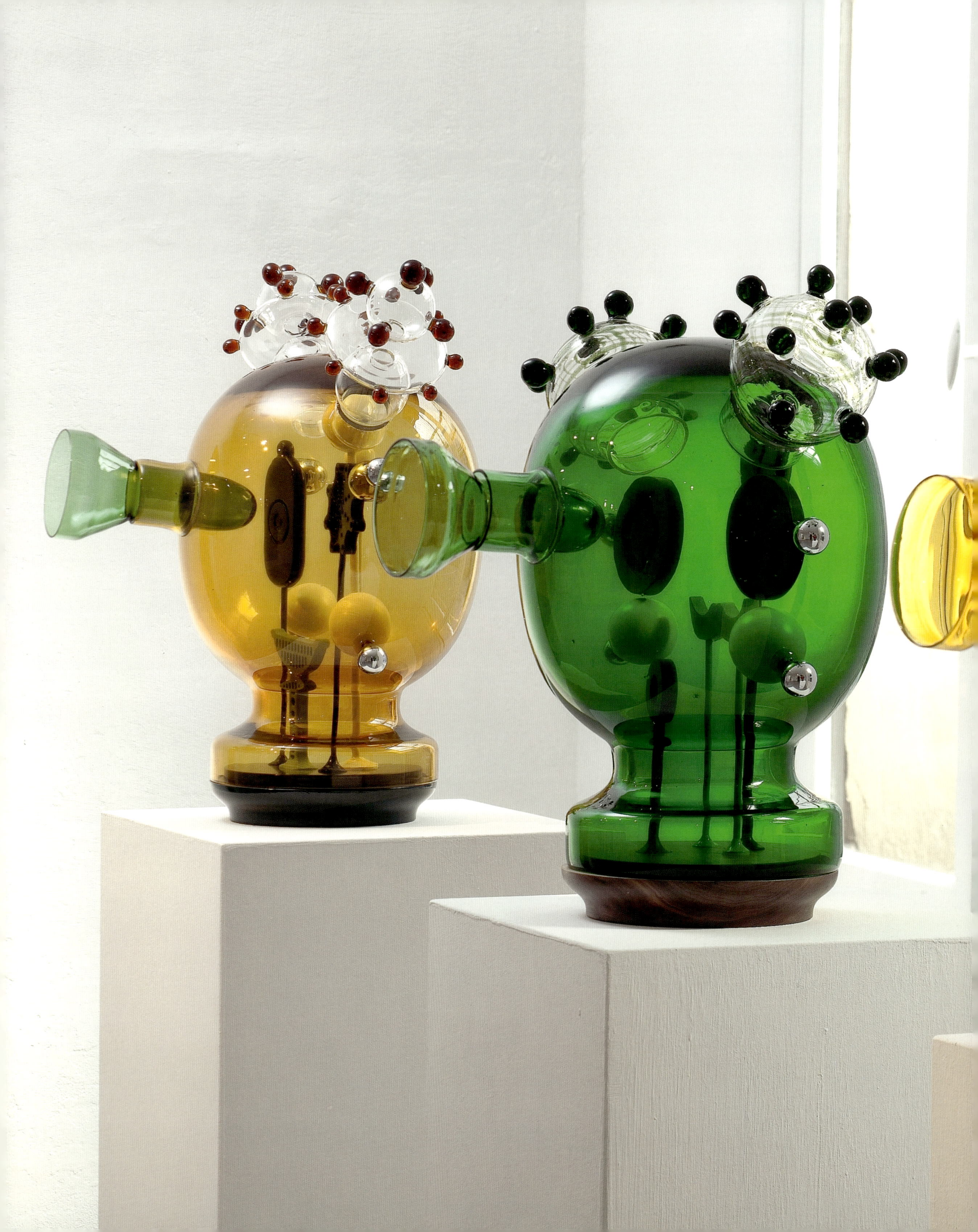

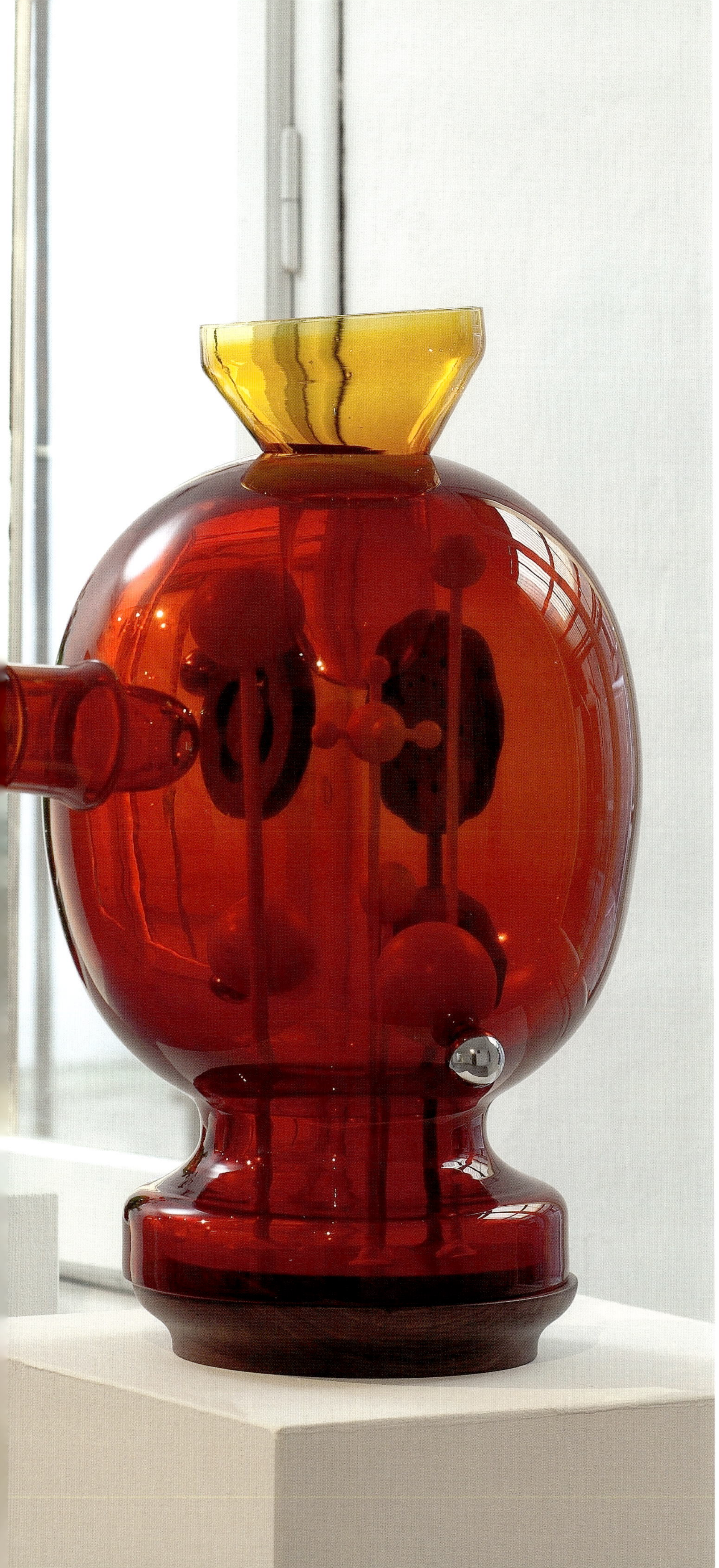

TESTA MECANICA
2011
55 x 52 x 43 CM (GREEN) / 53 x 35 x 43 CM (RED) /
55 x 52 x 43 CM (YELLOW)
COURTESY THE ARTIST
AND BERENGO PRIVATE COLLECTION, VENICE

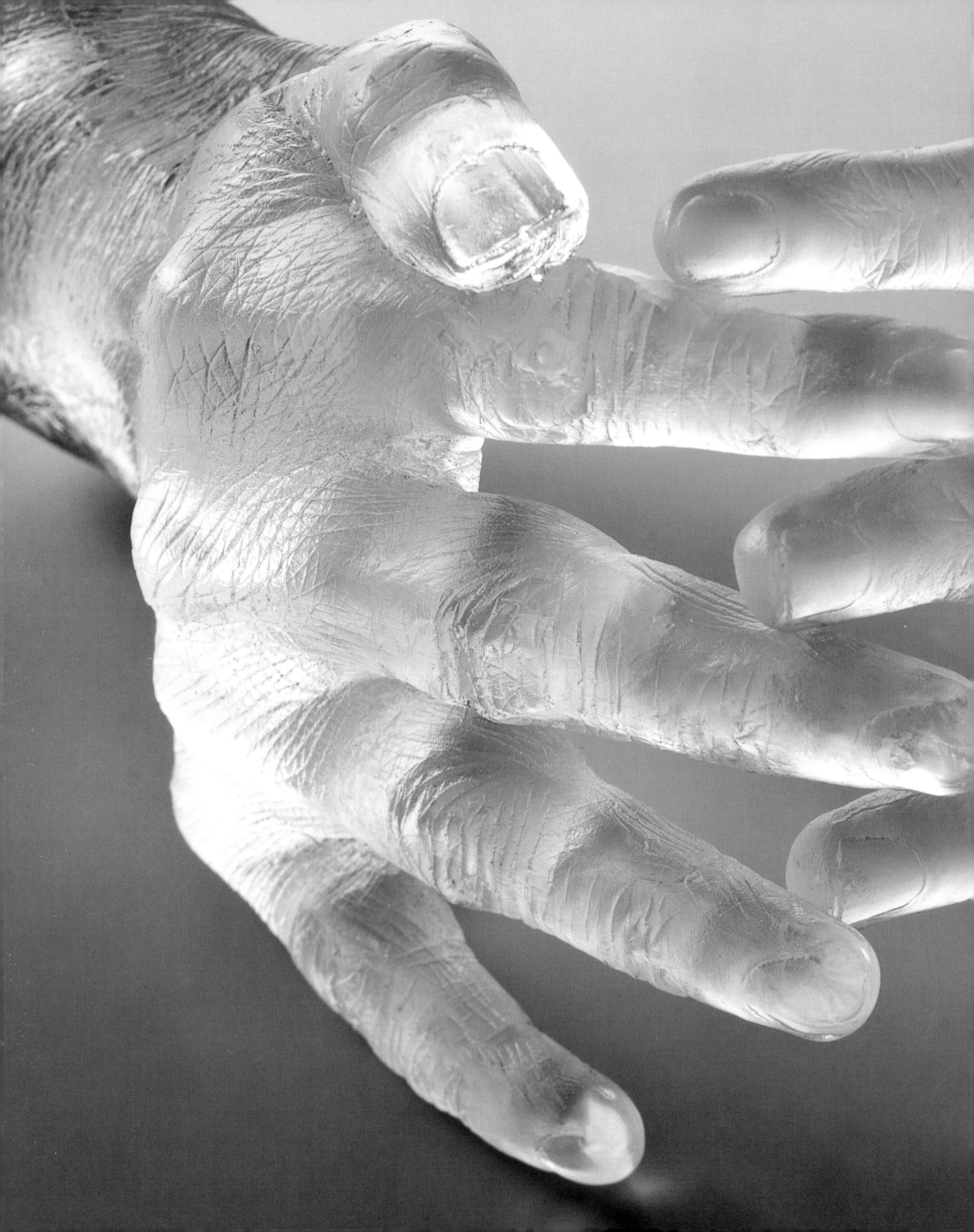

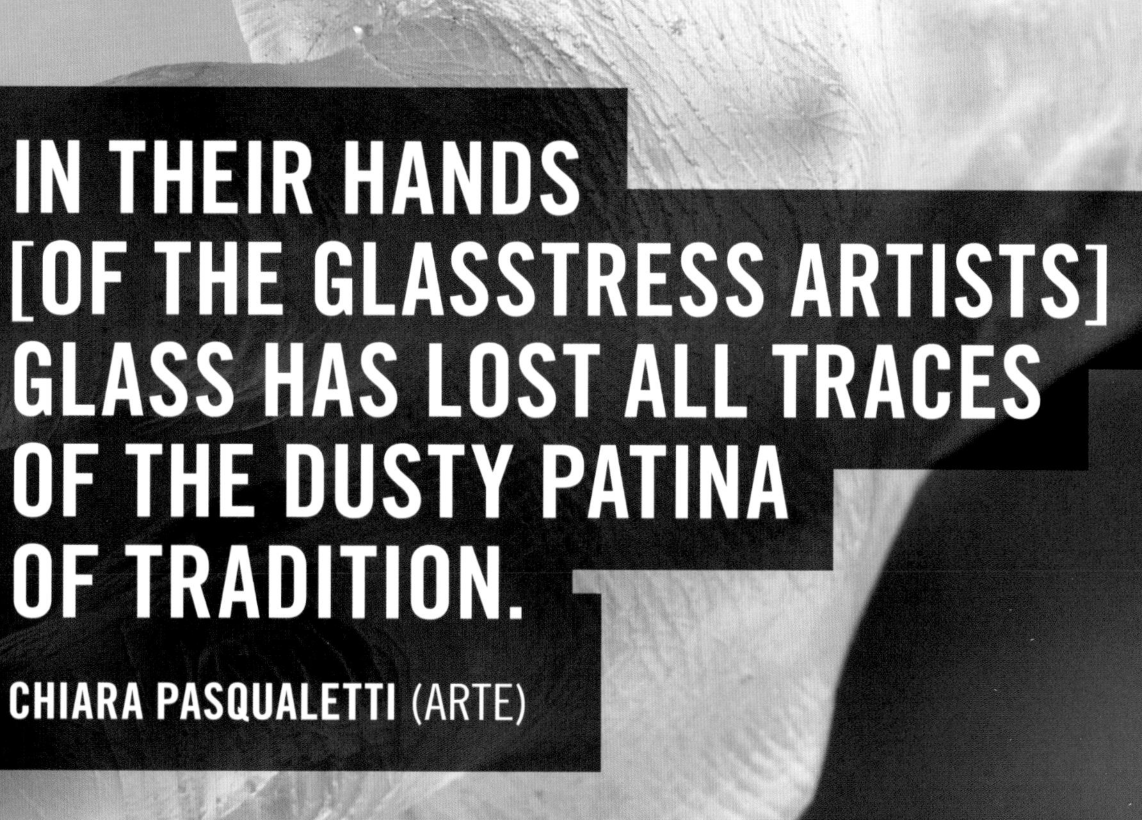

IN THEIR HANDS
[OF THE GLASSTRESS ARTISTS]
GLASS HAS LOST ALL TRACES
OF THE DUSTY PATINA
OF TRADITION.

CHIARA PASQUALETTI (ARTE)

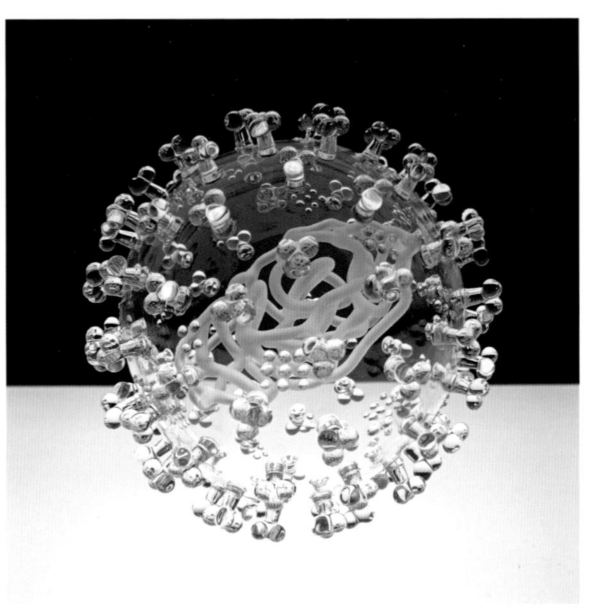

LUKE JERRAM

Luke Jerram, an English artist and researcher, was born in Stroud in 1974 and currently lives and works in Bristol. He graduated with honors in Fine Arts at the University of Wales Institute in Cardiff in 1997. Thanks to his craftsmanship and his interest in experimentation, Jerram was able to establish himself immediately first on the English stage and then worldwide. He is appreciated for the peculiarity of his glass creations, the subject of which are viruses and bacteria, designs that Jerram has called "Glass Microbiology." Versatile and creative, his artistic expressions encompass various techniques ranging from sculpture to installations up to live arts projects.

The artist's interest in microbiology has led him to investigate human perception and its limits, the contrast between the beauty of art works themselves and what they represent for people. The artist pays great attention to sensations and perceptions as he himself suffers from a visual deficit that prevents him from recognizing colors. Although he has worked as a researcher at the University of Southampton and his team consists of scientists, Jerram insists that he is not a scientist; in fact, he finds the fields of applied science too specialized and limiting in comparison to the world of art.

He is very popular in the United States, and his works have been exhibited in such major American museums as MoMA and the Museum of American Glass. Through a series of science-like activities, he has received several honors, including the 2007 Medical Imaging Institute Award, the 2010 Rakow Award, and a fellowship at The Museum of Glass in Washington in 2011.

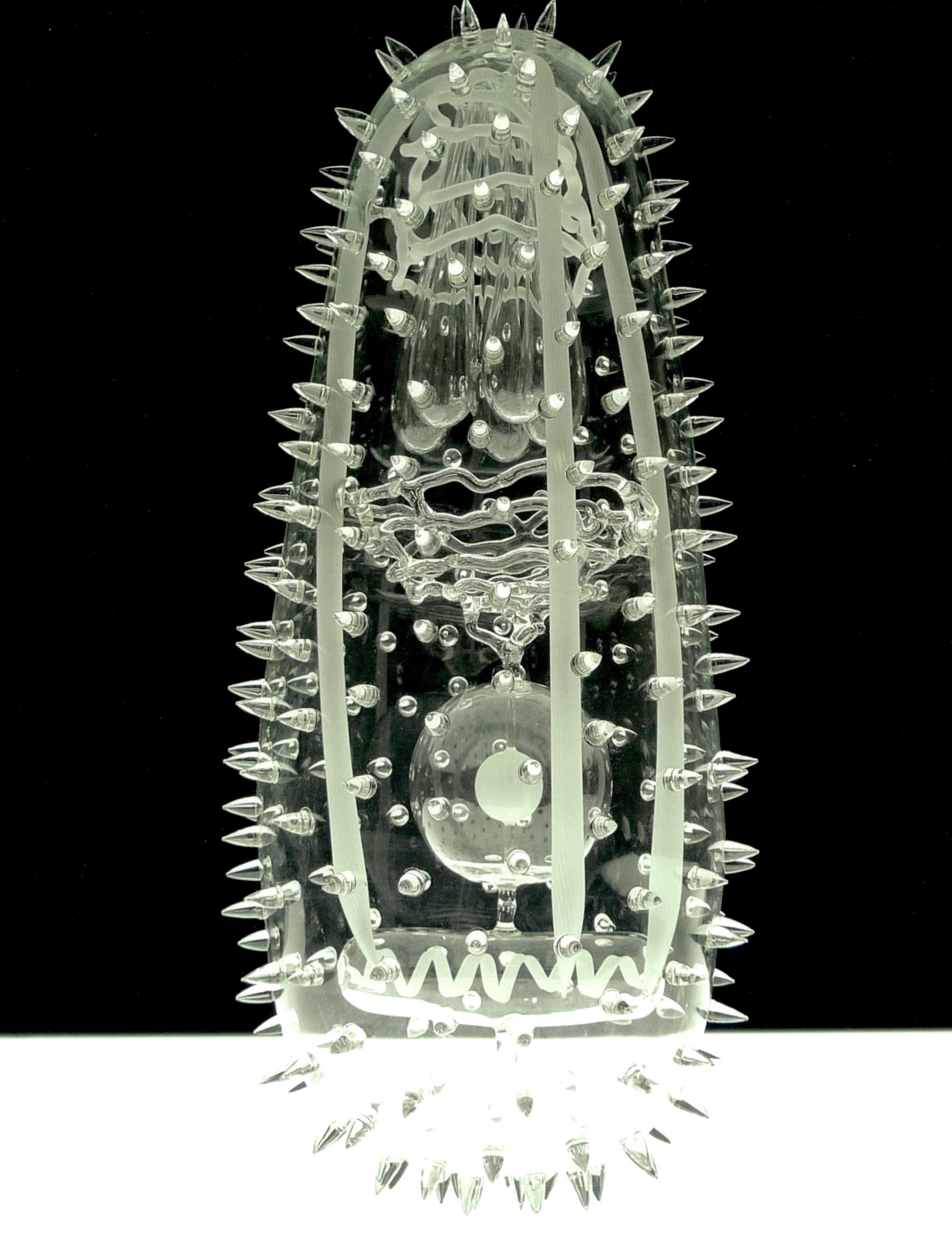

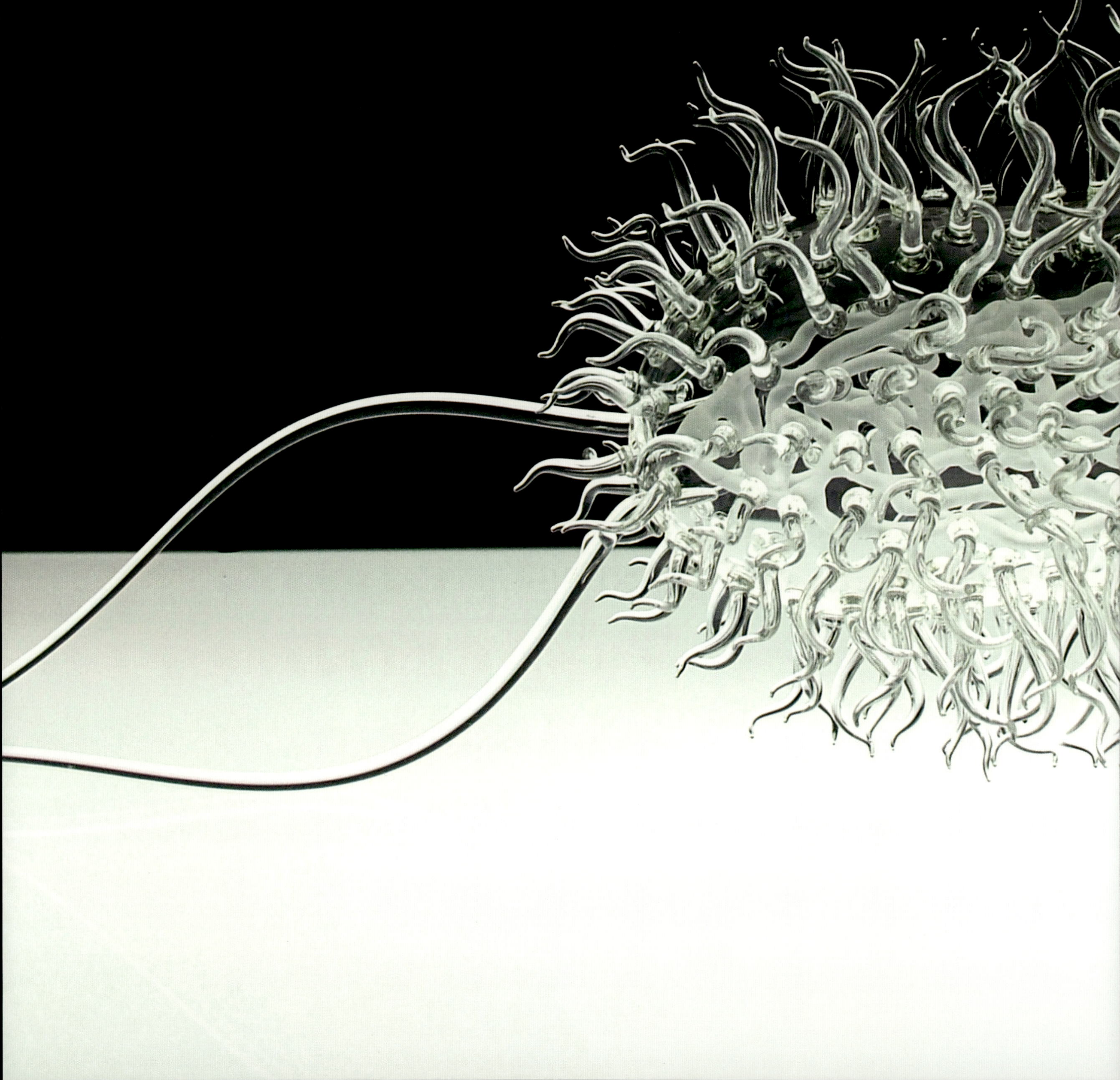

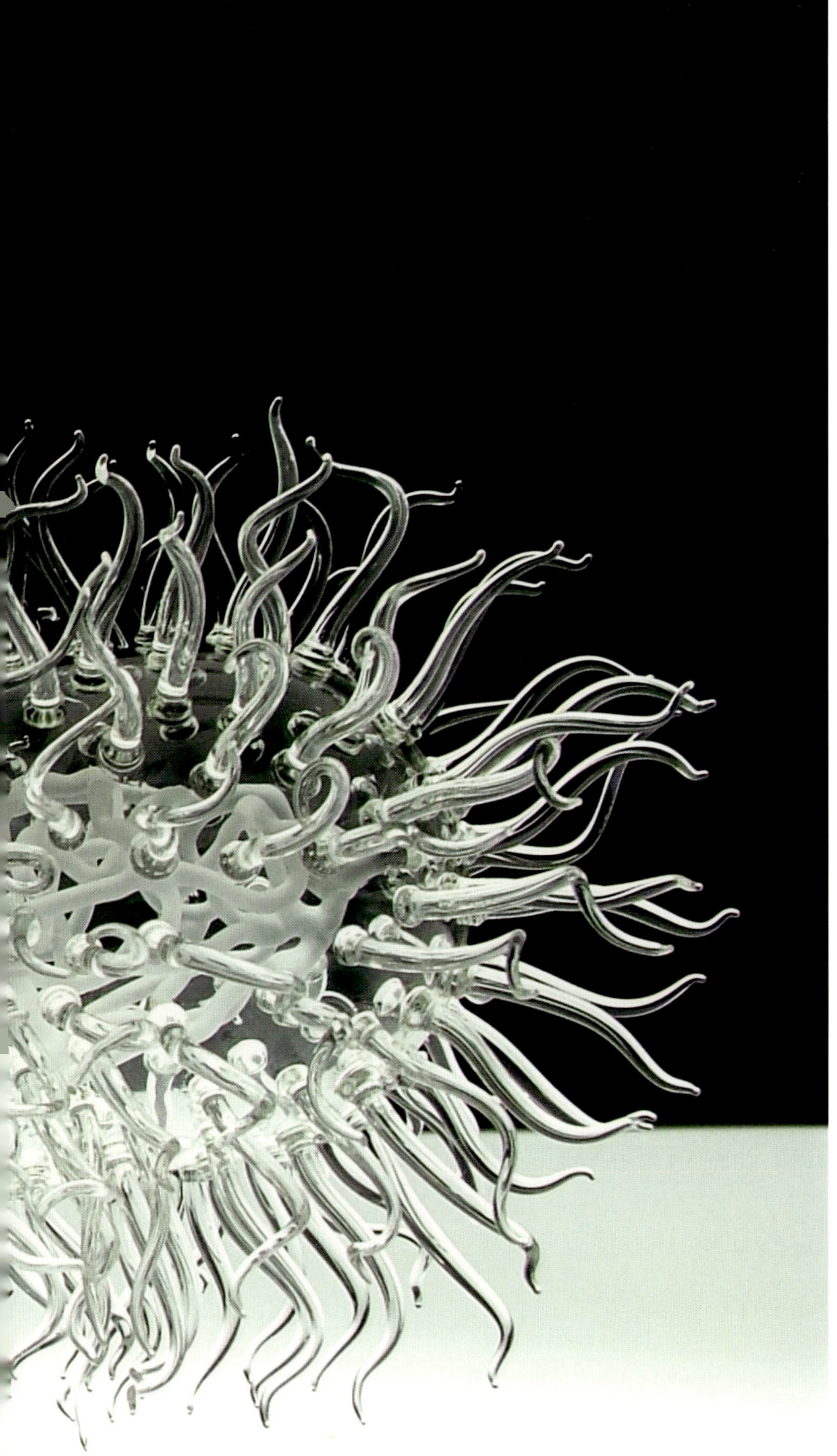

E. COLI
2010
24 x 128 x 30 CM
COURTESY DE NUL COLLECTION, BELGIUM

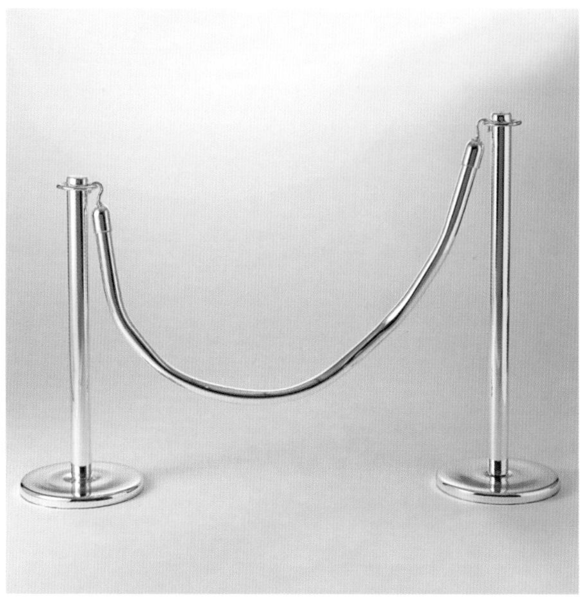

MICHAEL JOO

Michael Joo was born in Ithaca (New York) in 1966 to Korean parents.
He graduated in Biology from Washington University in 1989 and then received
his Master's in Fine Arts in 1991 from the Yale School of Art. He now lives
and works in New York.
Ever since the beginning of his artistic exploration, in his works he has always
tried to link the mechanisms through which visible and living entities, such as
the human body, plants, and animals, are connected to invisible entities,
i.e. the energy they need to affirm their existence.
He later focused his work on the exploration of his own identity and on the
intersection of binary concepts such as nature-science, East-West, religion-
ethics, inner-outer: the simultaneous presence of contrasting elements reveals
his aspiration to re-compose an essential order of the universe.
His work is an invitation to reflect on the concept of hybrid, through a process
that begins by deconstructing the object and ends with a dis-uniform union of
deconstructed objects, as in *Family (tradition)* … presented at the 49th Venice
Biennale, showing four bronze figures, representing a family, connected one
to the other via an element of style beginning at the father's knees, through
the mother's back, then the head of the older daughter, to end at the penis
of the younger son, closing a generational circle of cultural transformation.
He recently tried to reconcile in his work Buddhist spirituality and the analytic
approach of Western civilization. In 2006 he participated in the 6th Gwangji
Biennale, winning the Grand Prize with *Bodhi Obfuscatus* (*Space Baby*),
according to the critics "a clear example of West reconciling with the East."
In addition to representing Korea again at the 2001 Venice Biennale,
he exhibited at the Whitney Biennial in 2000, and in many other museums
and galleries in Europe and the United States, such as the Stedelijk Museum
in Amsterdam, the Walker Art Center in Minneapolis, and the Serpentine
Gallery in London. His works are included in the permanent collection of the
Guggenheim Museum and the MoMA in New York, the UCLA Hammer Museum
in Los Angeles, the Moderna Museet in Stockholm, and the FNAC in Paris.

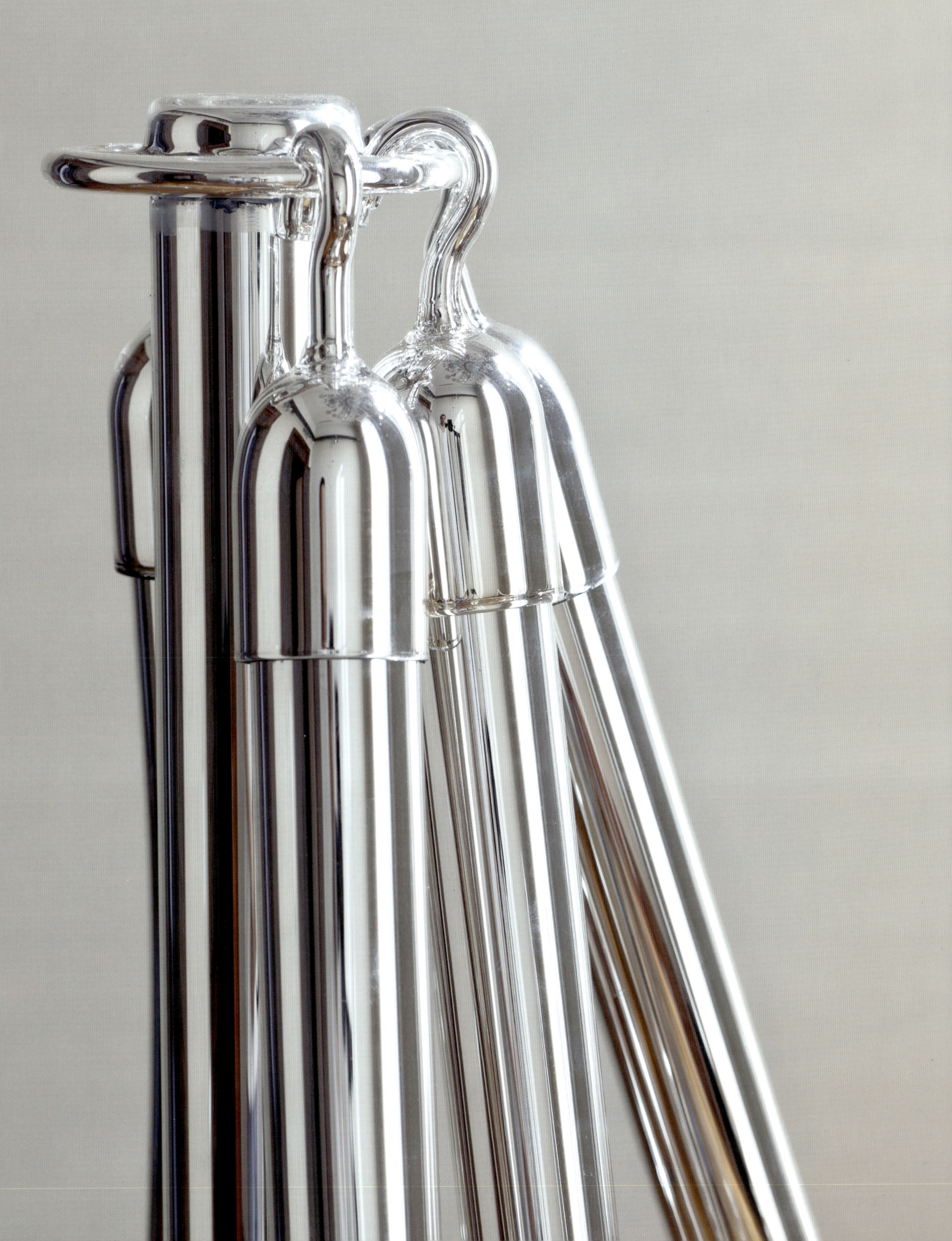

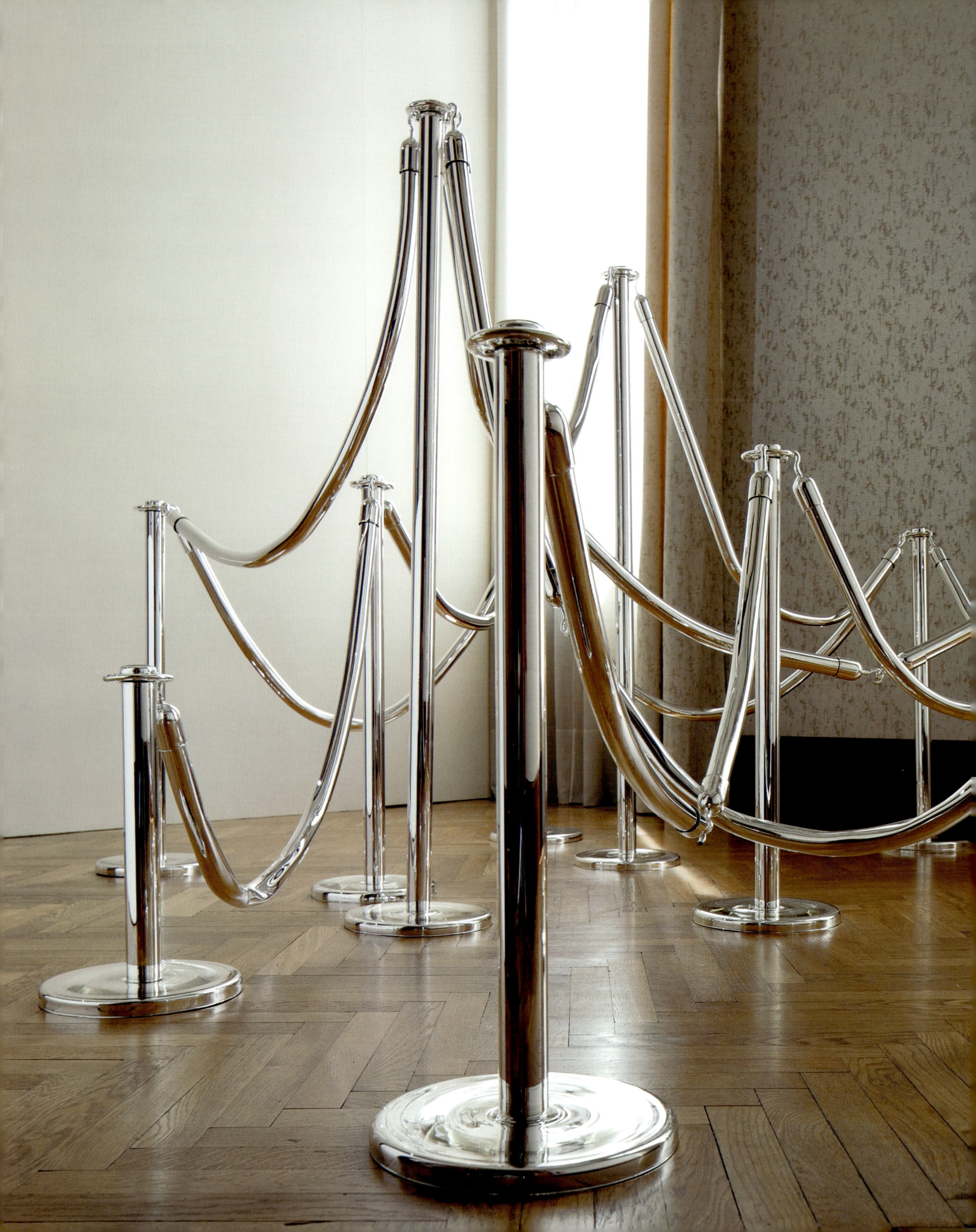

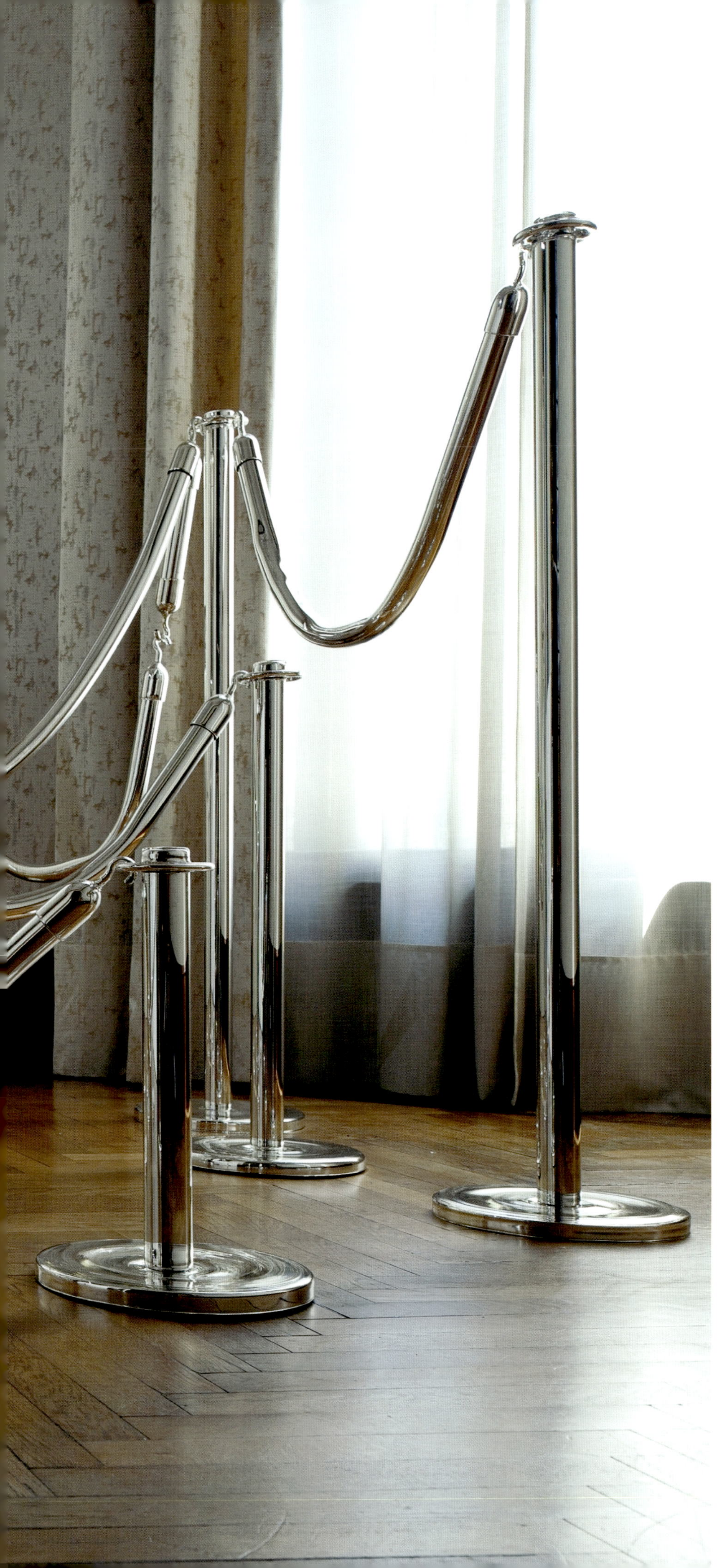

EXPANDED ACCESS
2011
155 x 290 x 290 CM / 85 x 67 x 8 CM
COURTESY THE ARTIST
AND BERENGO PRIVATE COLLECTION, VENICE

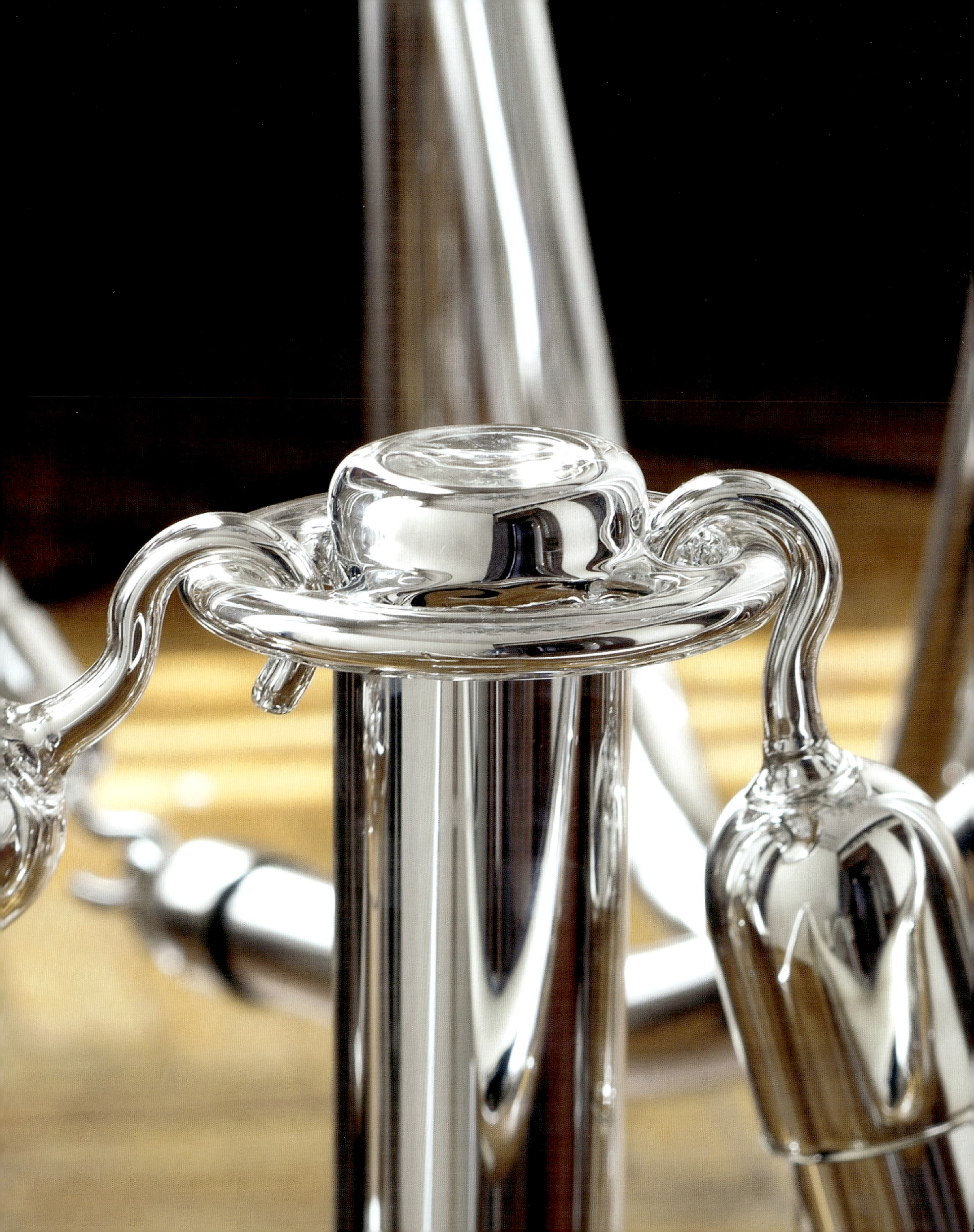

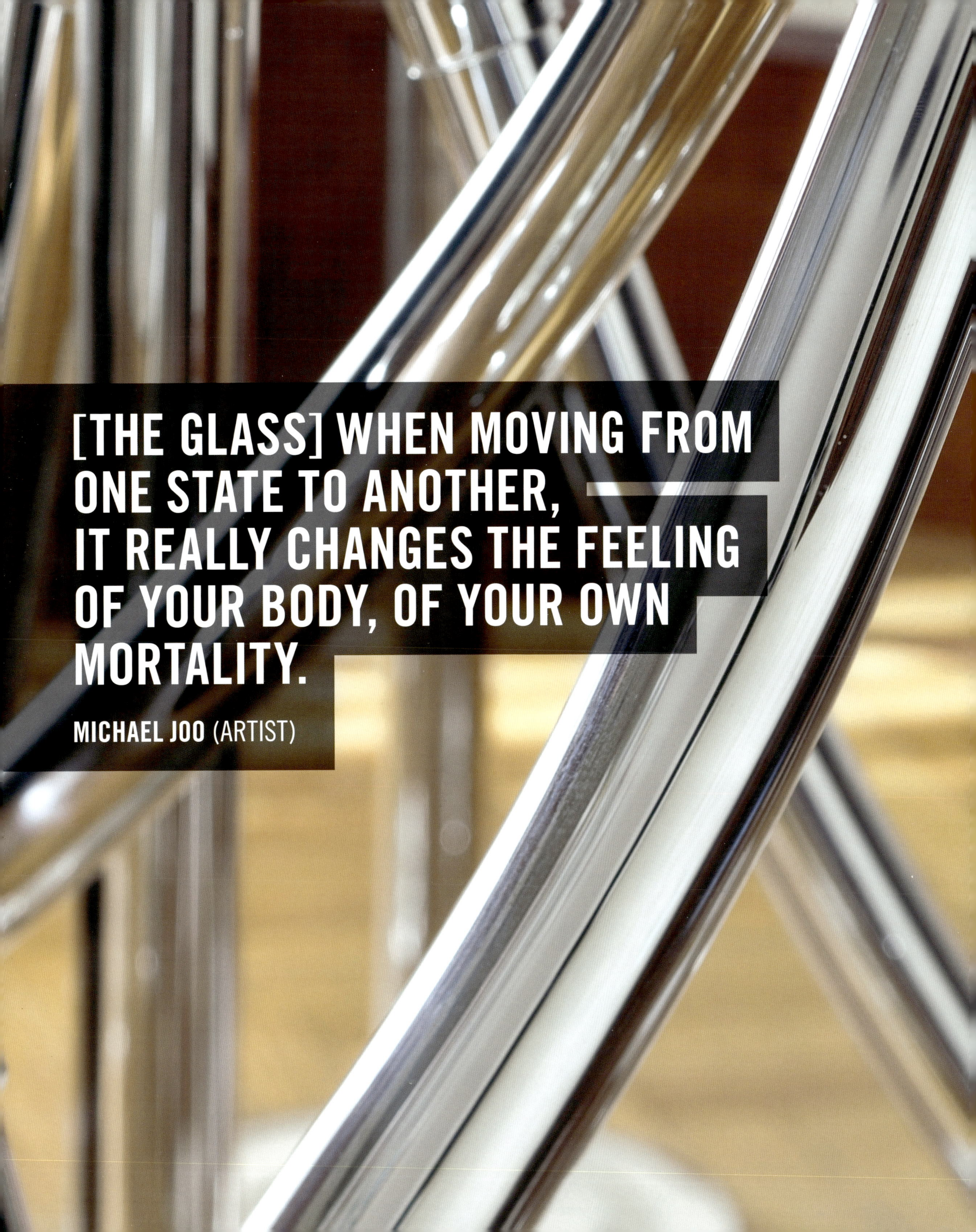

[THE GLASS] WHEN MOVING FROM ONE STATE TO ANOTHER, IT REALLY CHANGES THE FEELING OF YOUR BODY, OF YOUR OWN MORTALITY.
MICHAEL JOO (ARTIST)

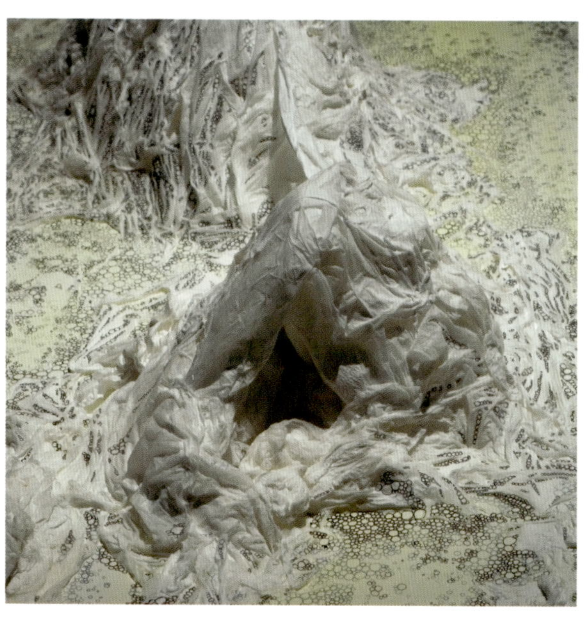

MARYA KAZOUN

Marya Kazoun was born in Beirut in 1976. She lives and works in New York and Venice. Marya Kazoun grew up in Beirut during the war years. In 1984 her family fled the war the first time by moving to Switzerland. Later she lived in Montreal with her family where she became a Canadian citizen. She later returned to Beirut and completed degrees in Interior Architecture and Fine Arts at Lebanese American University. In 2001 she moved to New York and completed an MFA in Fine Arts at the School of Visual Arts. Her works are mainly installations and performances; she uses 3D low reliefs, painting, drawing, and photography as support for her installation pieces. Her art is a personal perception of reality. She creates worlds that are parallel to the one we live in. She explores the micro vs the macro, the extremely beautiful vs the extremely repulsive. She gives a voice to herself at five years old. Her art is an attempt to domesticate the dark. She uses very common materials like tissue and fabric to transform them and give them another life. Her approach to art is strongly feminine, emphasized by her dexterity with materials and mastery of ancestral techniques like sewing and weaving. She took part in the 51st Venice Biennale in 2005 with a solo show, *Personal Living Space.*

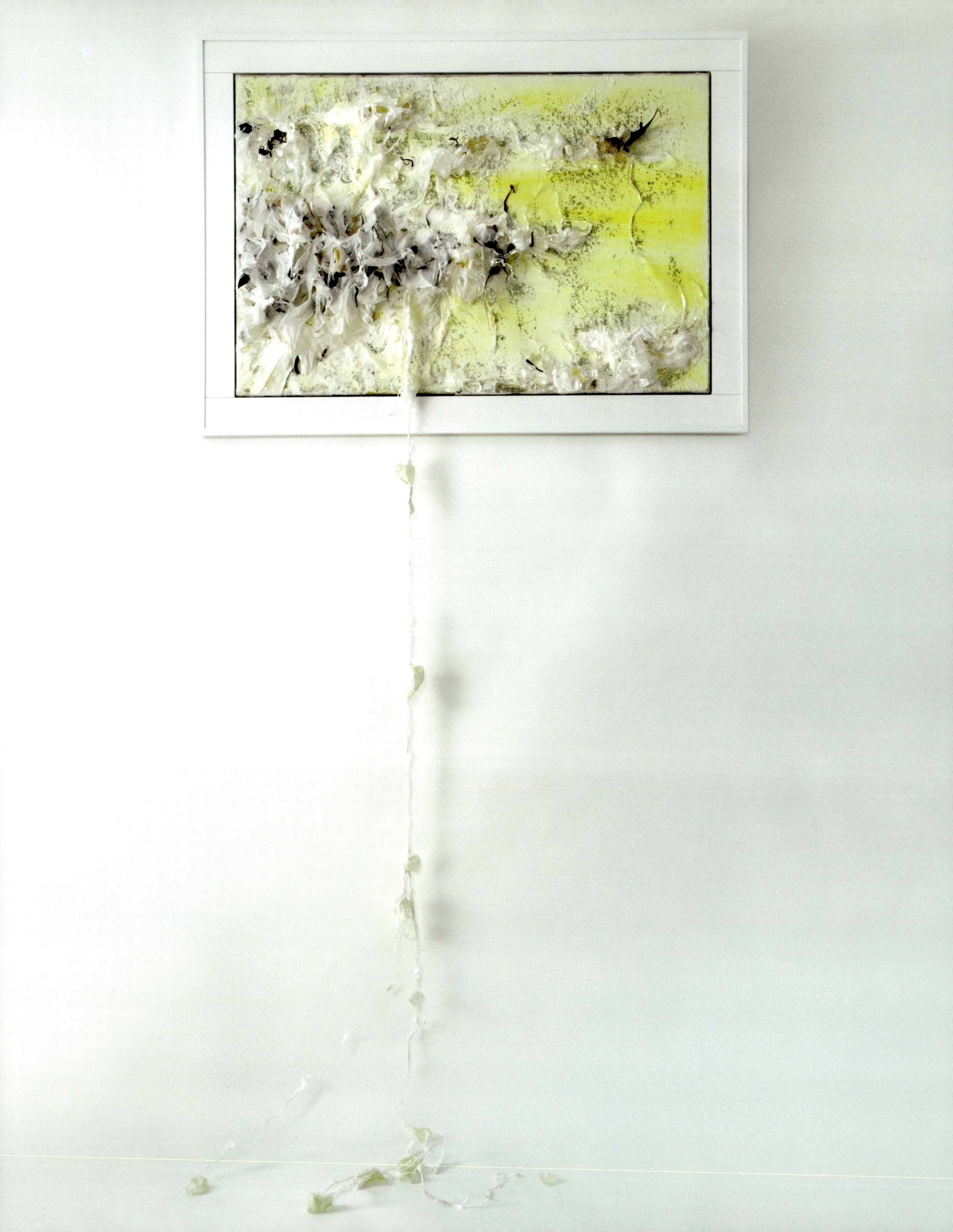

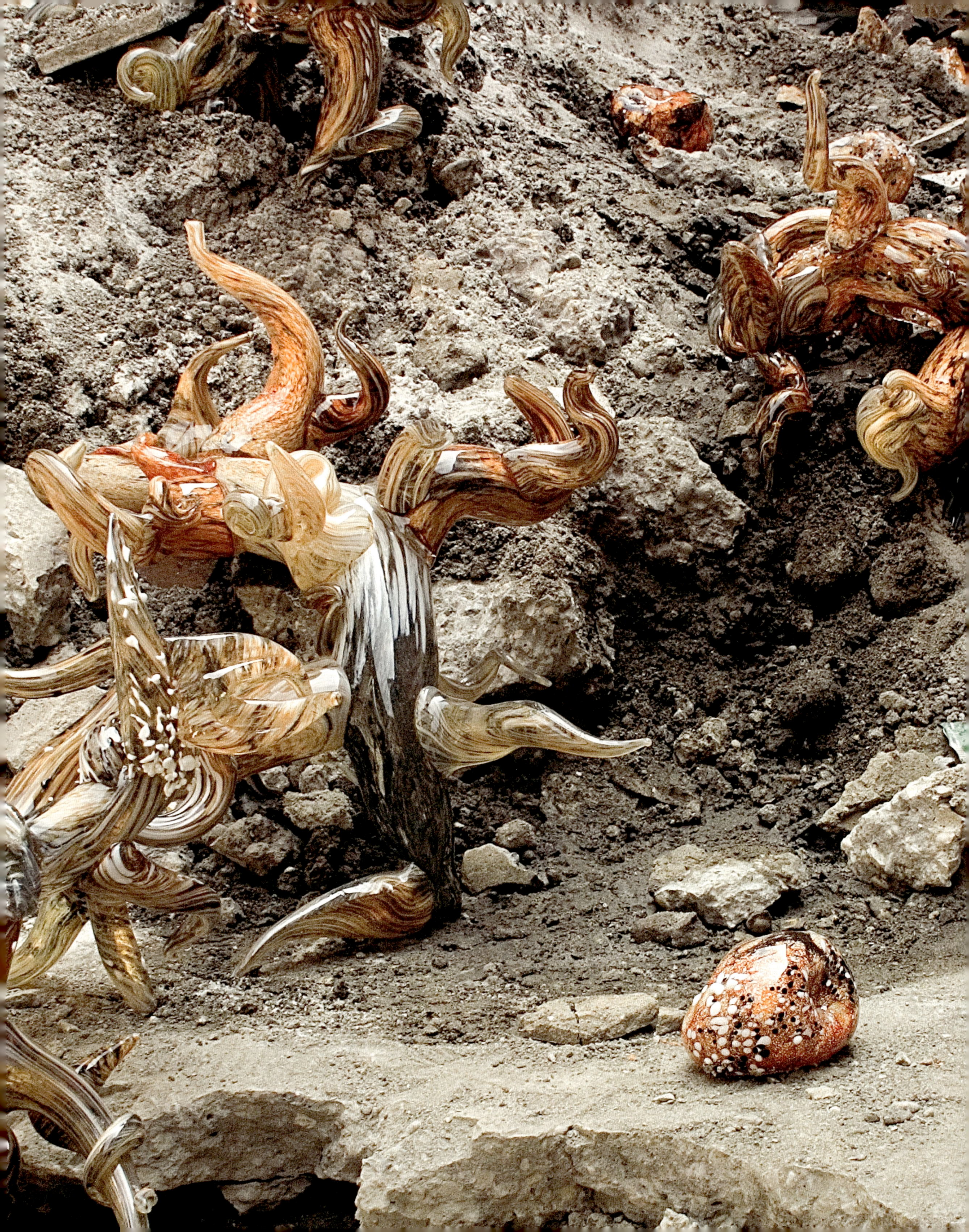

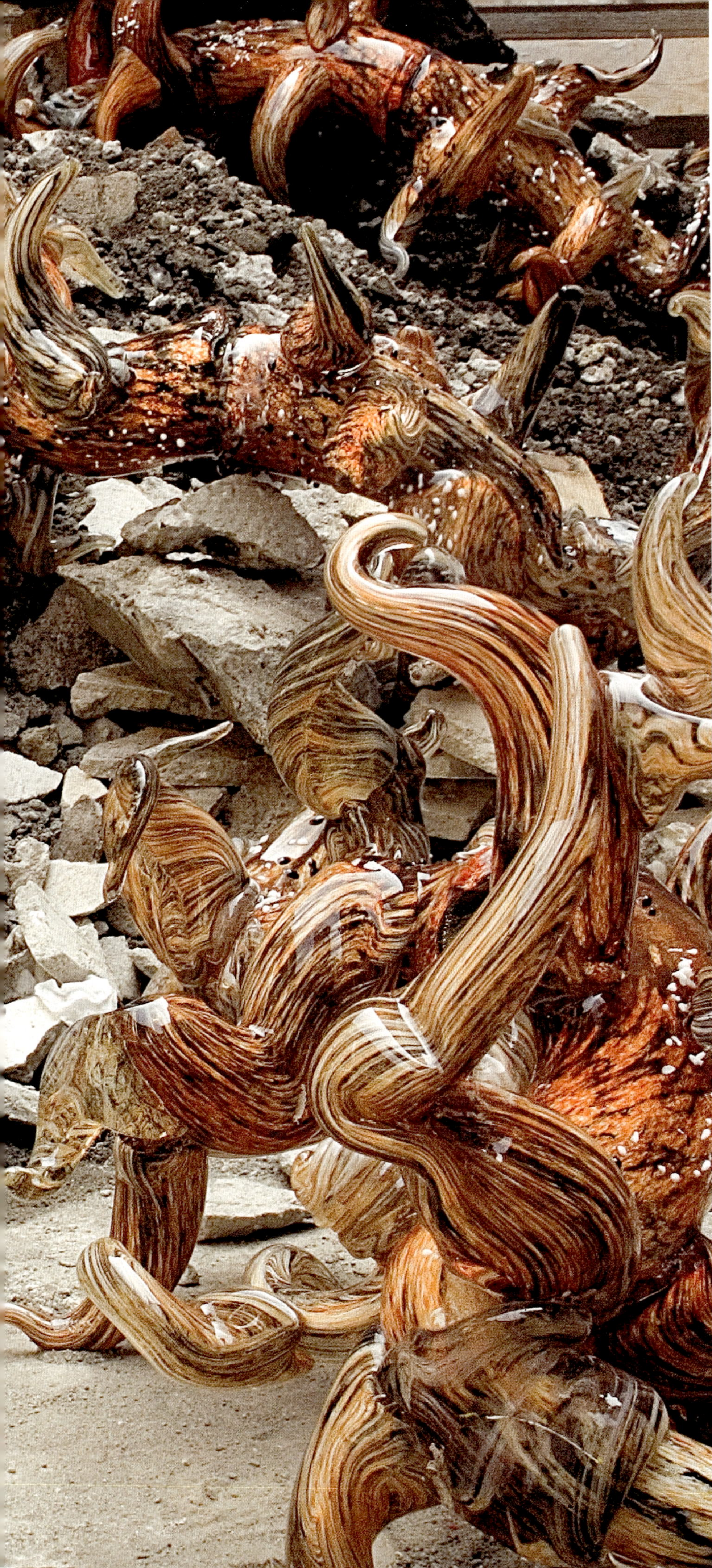

PETRIFIED SKINS
2007 / DETAIL
VARIABLE DIMENSIONS
COURTESY THE ARTIST

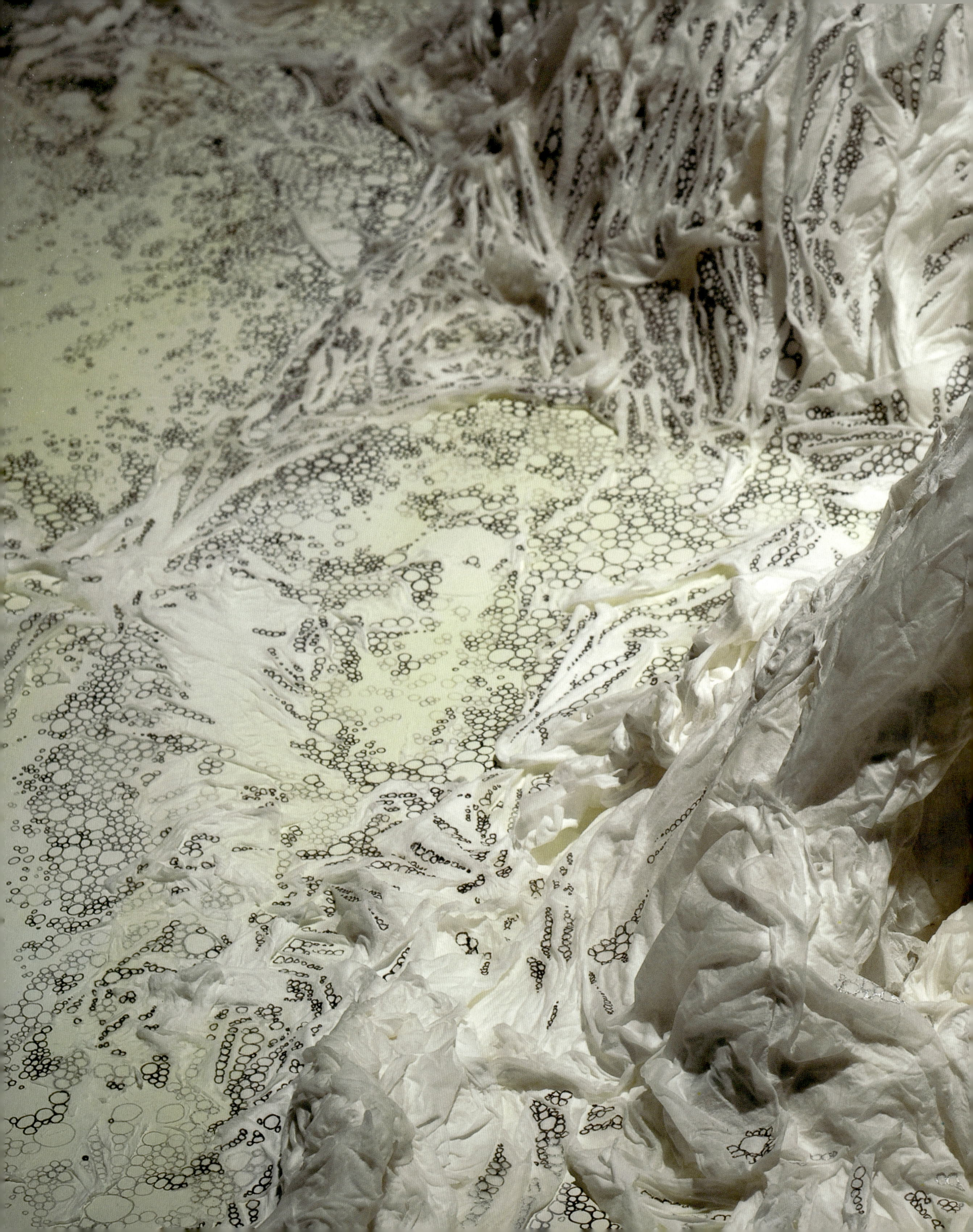

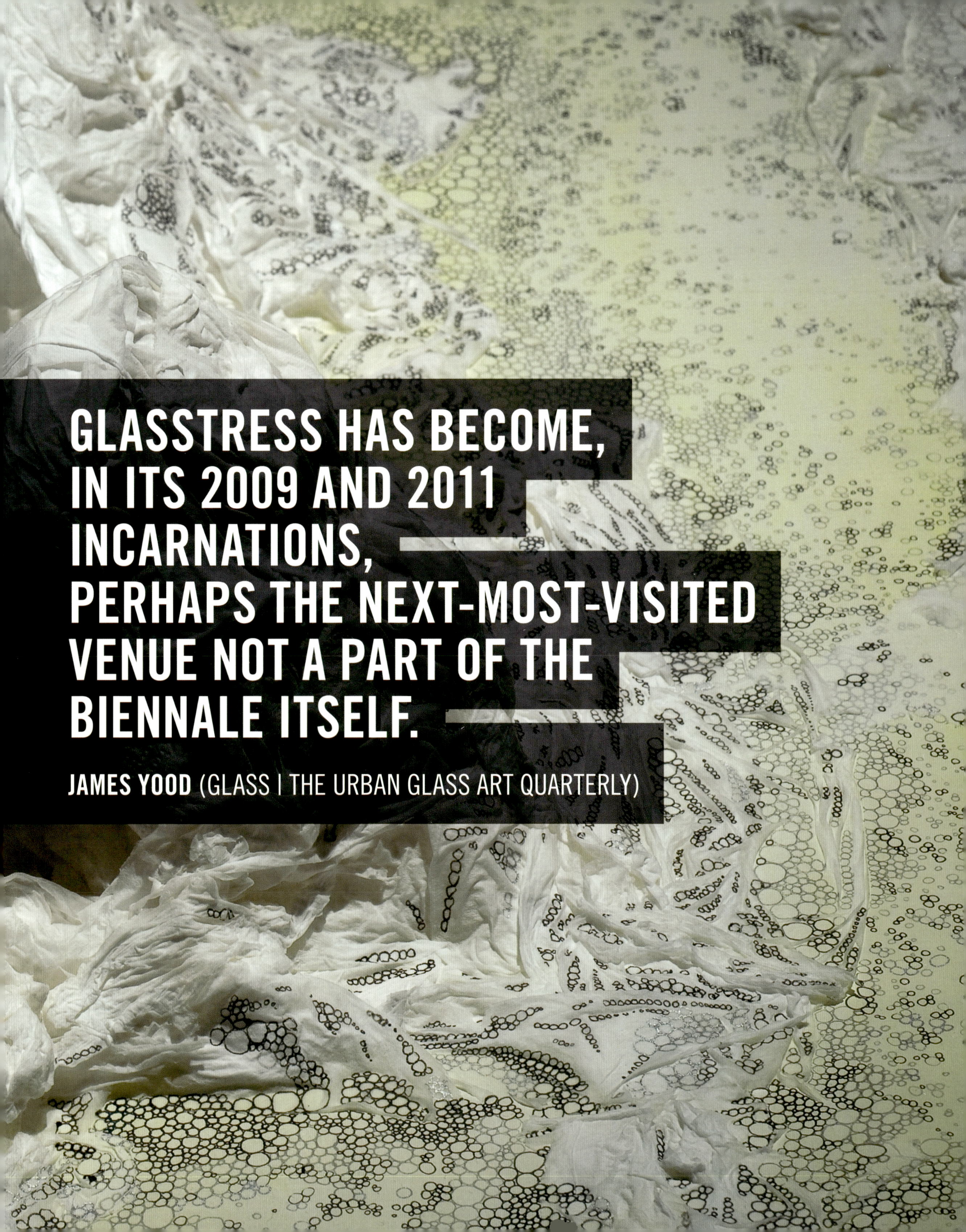

GLASSTRESS HAS BECOME,
IN ITS 2009 AND 2011
INCARNATIONS,
PERHAPS THE NEXT-MOST-VISITED
VENUE NOT A PART OF THE
BIENNALE ITSELF.

JAMES YOOD (GLASS | THE URBAN GLASS ART QUARTERLY)

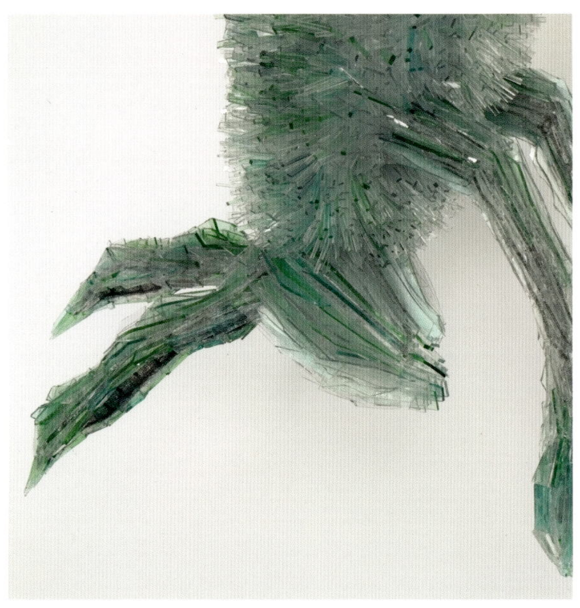

MARTA KLONOWSKA

Marta Klonowska was born in Warsaw in 1964. She currently lives and works in Düsseldorf.

Already during her studies at the Academy of Fine Arts in Wroclaw, Poland, and later at that of Düsseldorf, glass had become her preferred artistic medium. Today she is known for her numerous canine sculptures that depict the four-legged companions of important historical figures, capturing their natural poses in colored glass. For the subjects of her works, the artist finds inspiration in the paintings of the great masters, in which pets—mostly dogs—are side by side with the subjects, acting almost like prestigious objects that are exhibited as synonyms for wealth and power. Thanks to her work, the artist succeeds in telling the secondary stories of these ancillary characters. Marta Klonowska calls attention to the interplay of historical and artistic references reproducing each painting (usually in the original size) in a single color that matches the color of the glass chosen for the sculpture. To construct these works, she starts with a metal skeleton that is then carefully covered with sharp shards of glass, as in *The Morning Walk*, 2006.

She has received such important awards as the 1999 Artist in Residence at the Cité International des Arts in Paris and the 2002 Artist in Residence at the Akerby Skulpturpark in Sweden. She was also a finalist in the 2006 Bombay Sapphire Prize in London.

Among her most recent exhibitions are *And Domestic Animals* at the Finnish Glass Museum in Riihimäki (2009) and *t.b.a.* (2011), and *Geschöpfe* (2011) at the lorch+seidel gallery in Berlin.

Since 2011, one of her works has been on display at the Corning Museum of Glass for the *Ben W. Heineman* exhibition at the Sr. Family Gallery of Contemporary Glass in New York.

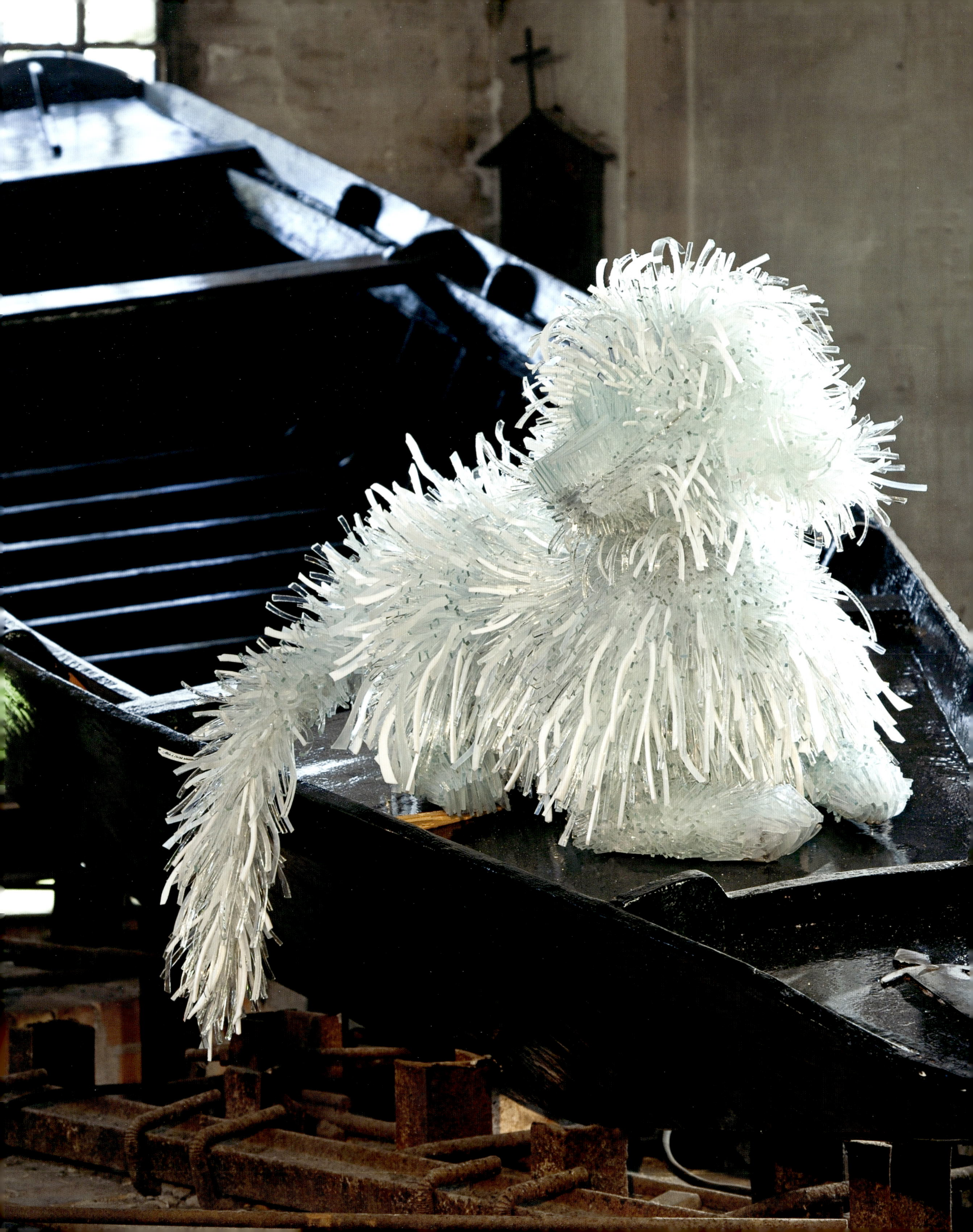

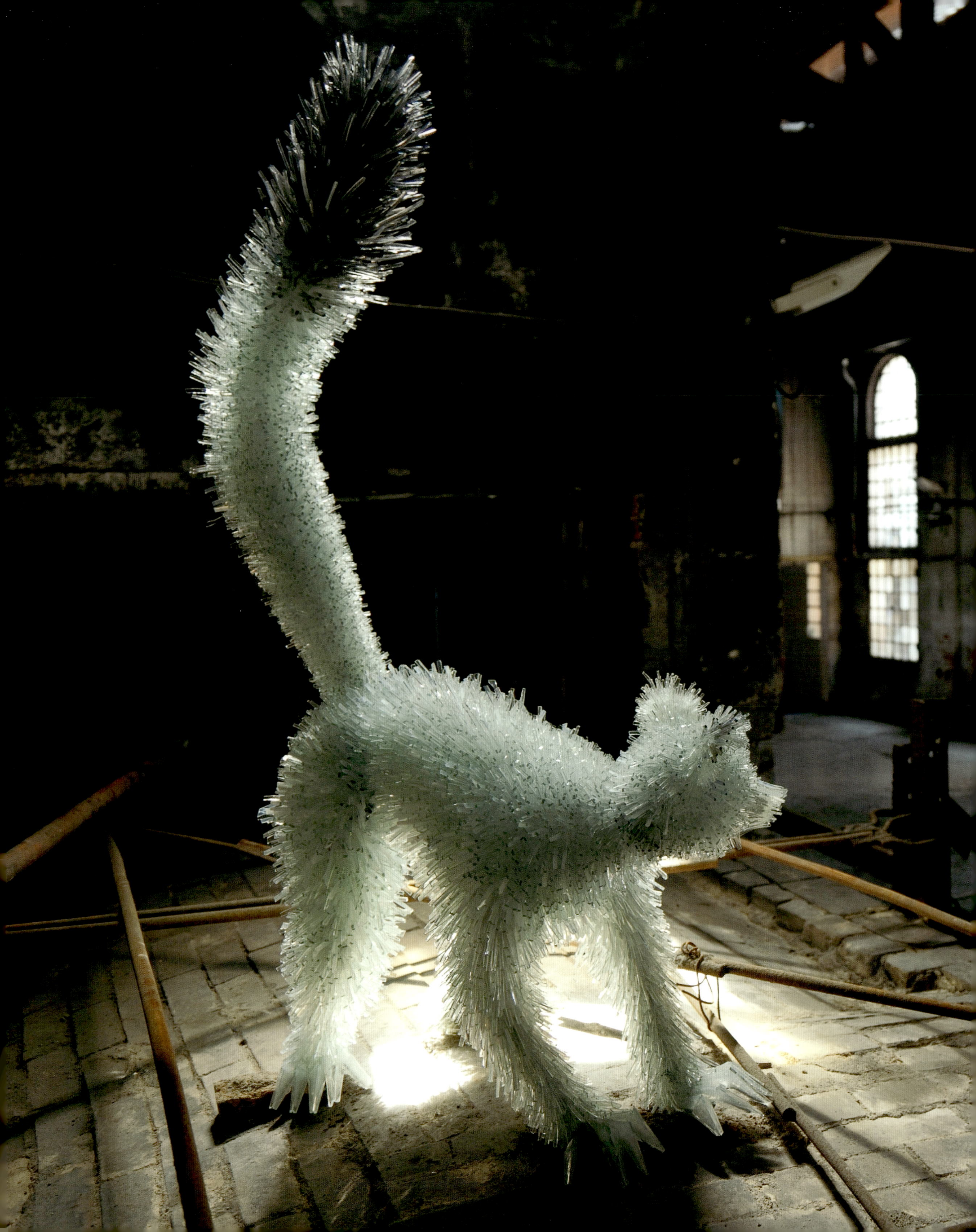

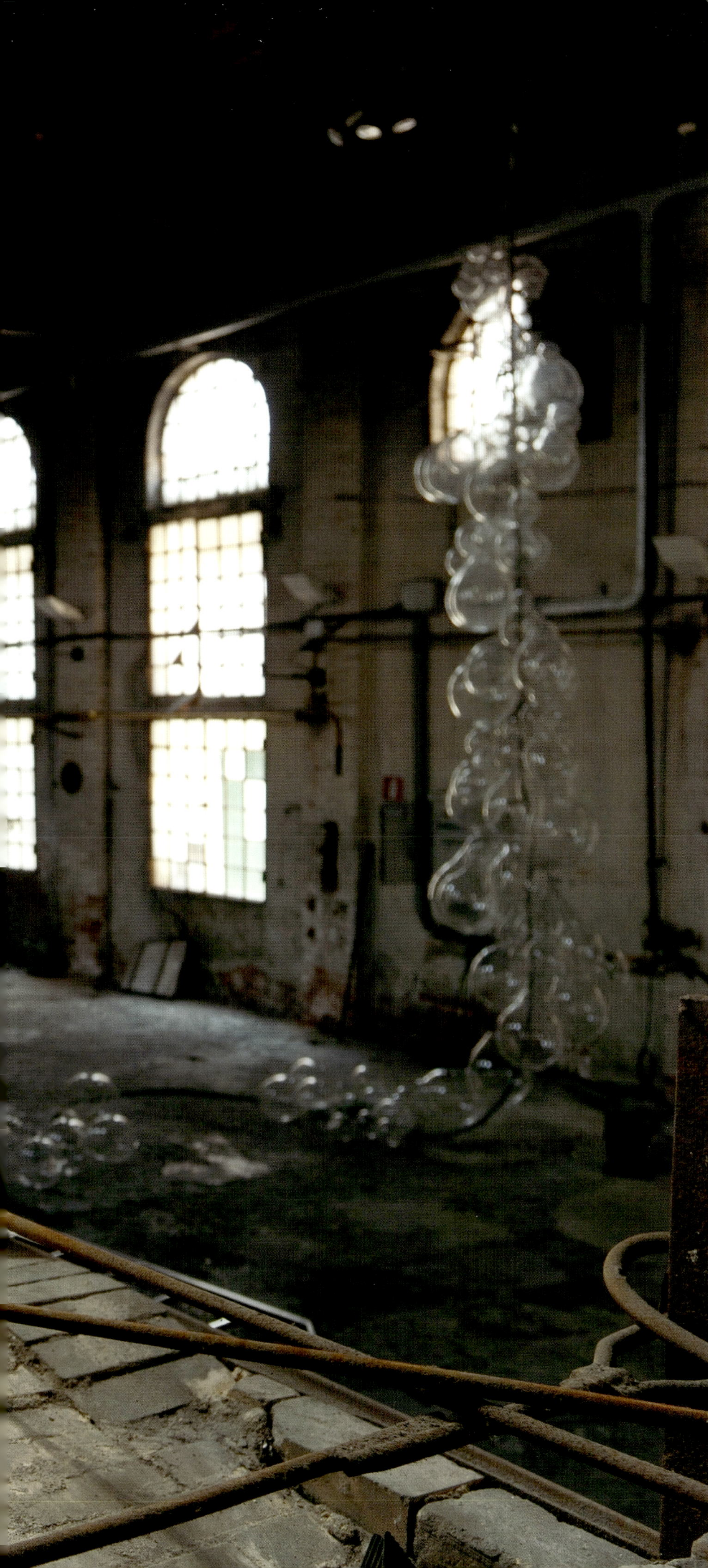

BESTIARIUM: MAKI
2011
124 x 80 x 37 CM
COURTESY SUSAN AND FRED SANDERS

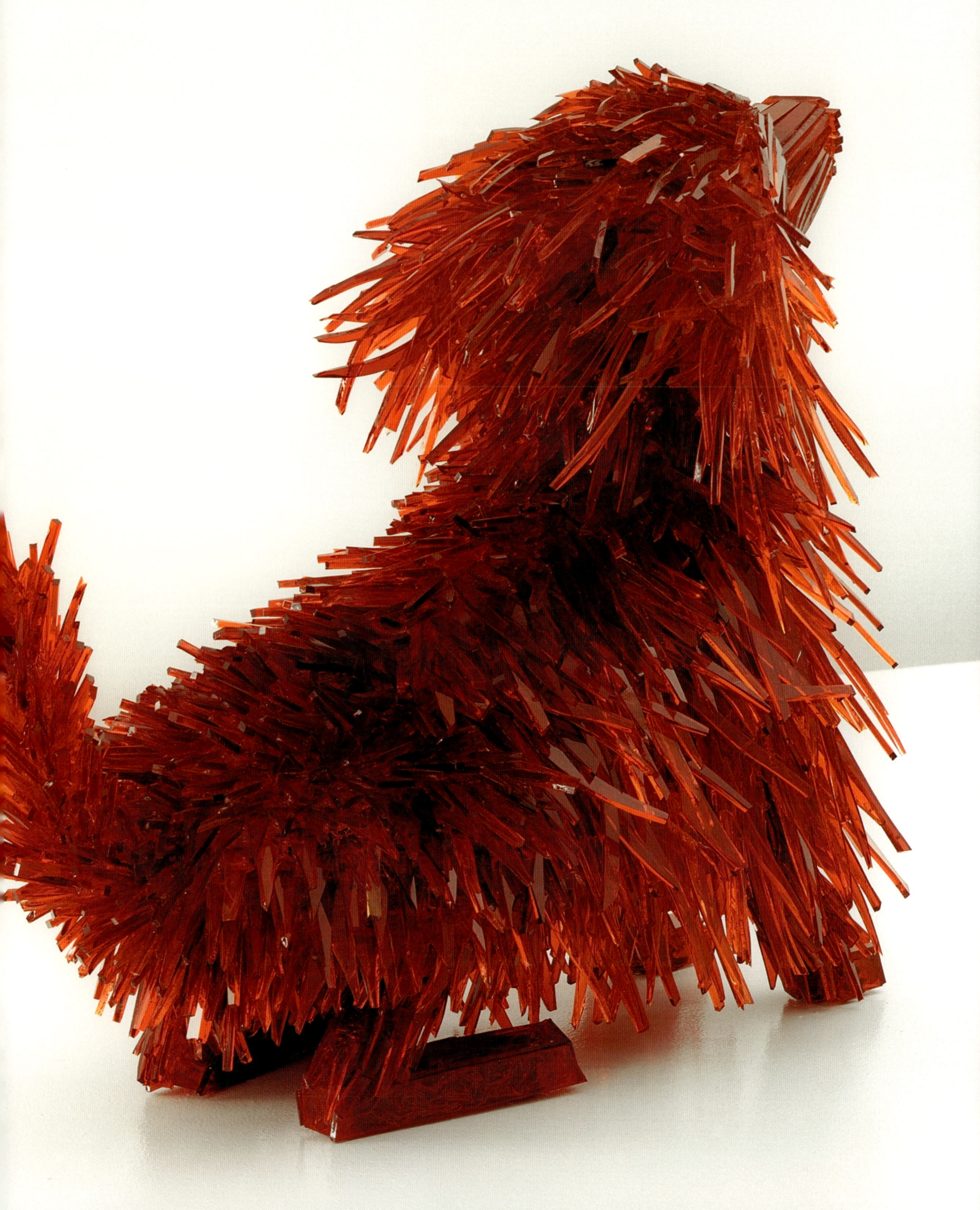

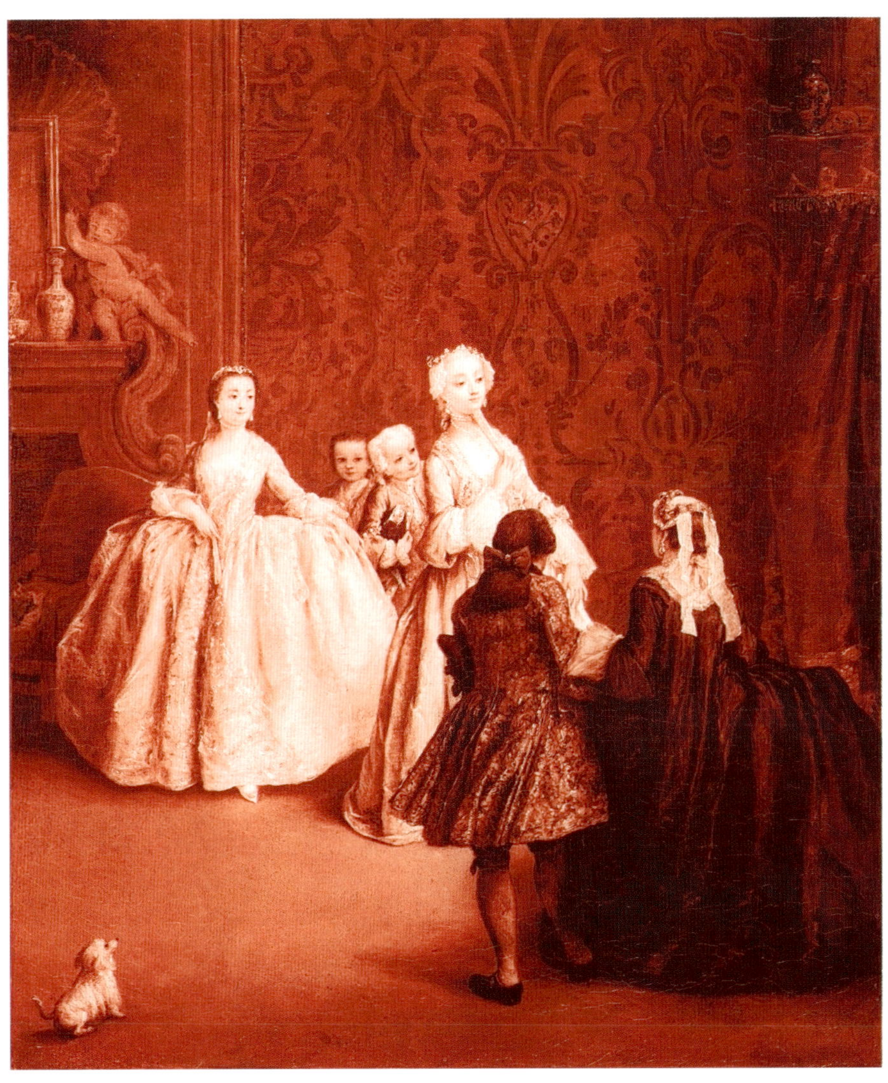

LA PRESENTAZIONE
AFTER PIETRO LONGHI, 1741
2005
25 x 40 x 25 CM (DOG) /
66 x 55 CM (INKJET PRINT ON PAPER)
COURTESY THE ARTIST
AND LORCH+SEIDEL CONTEMPORARY, BERLIN

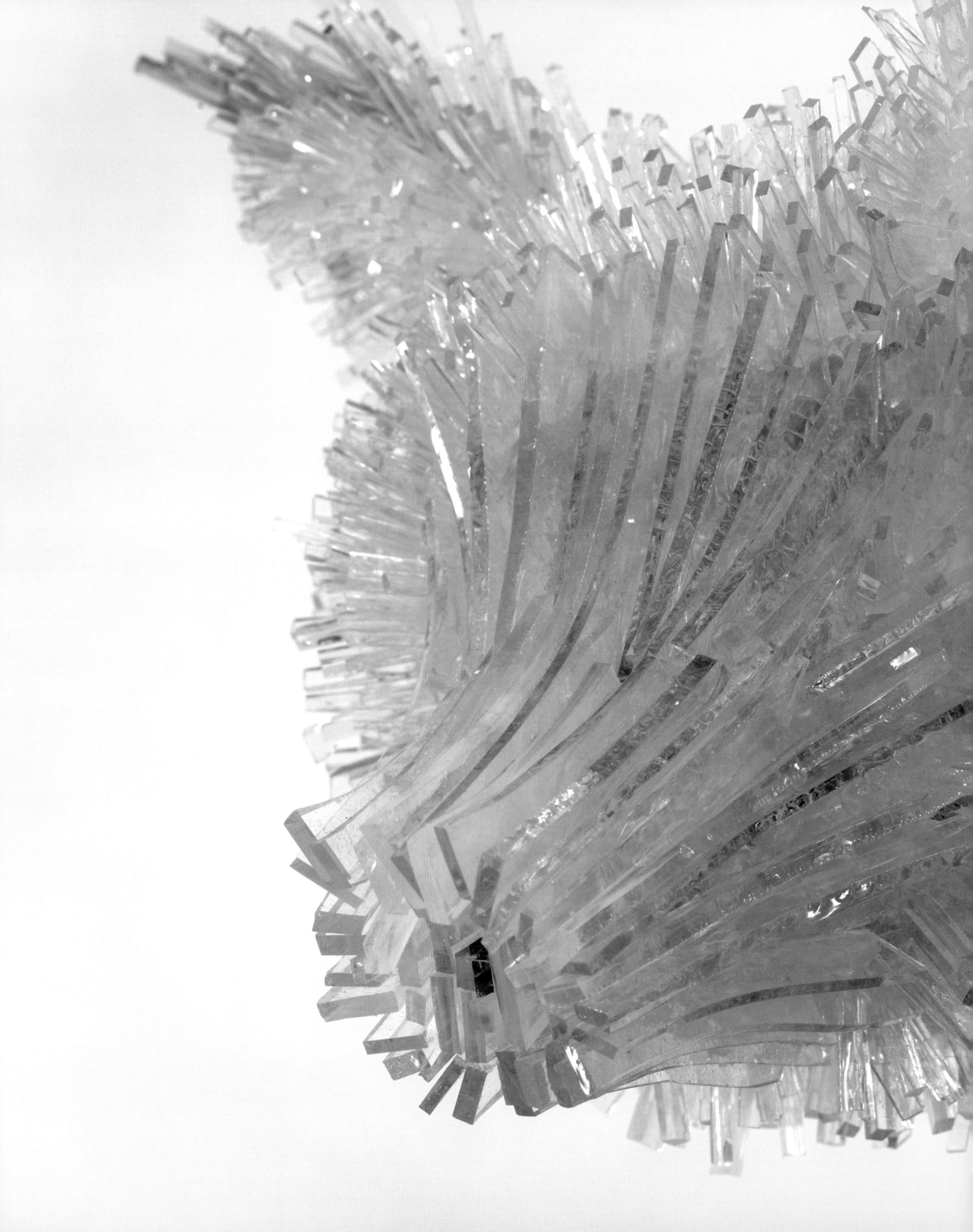

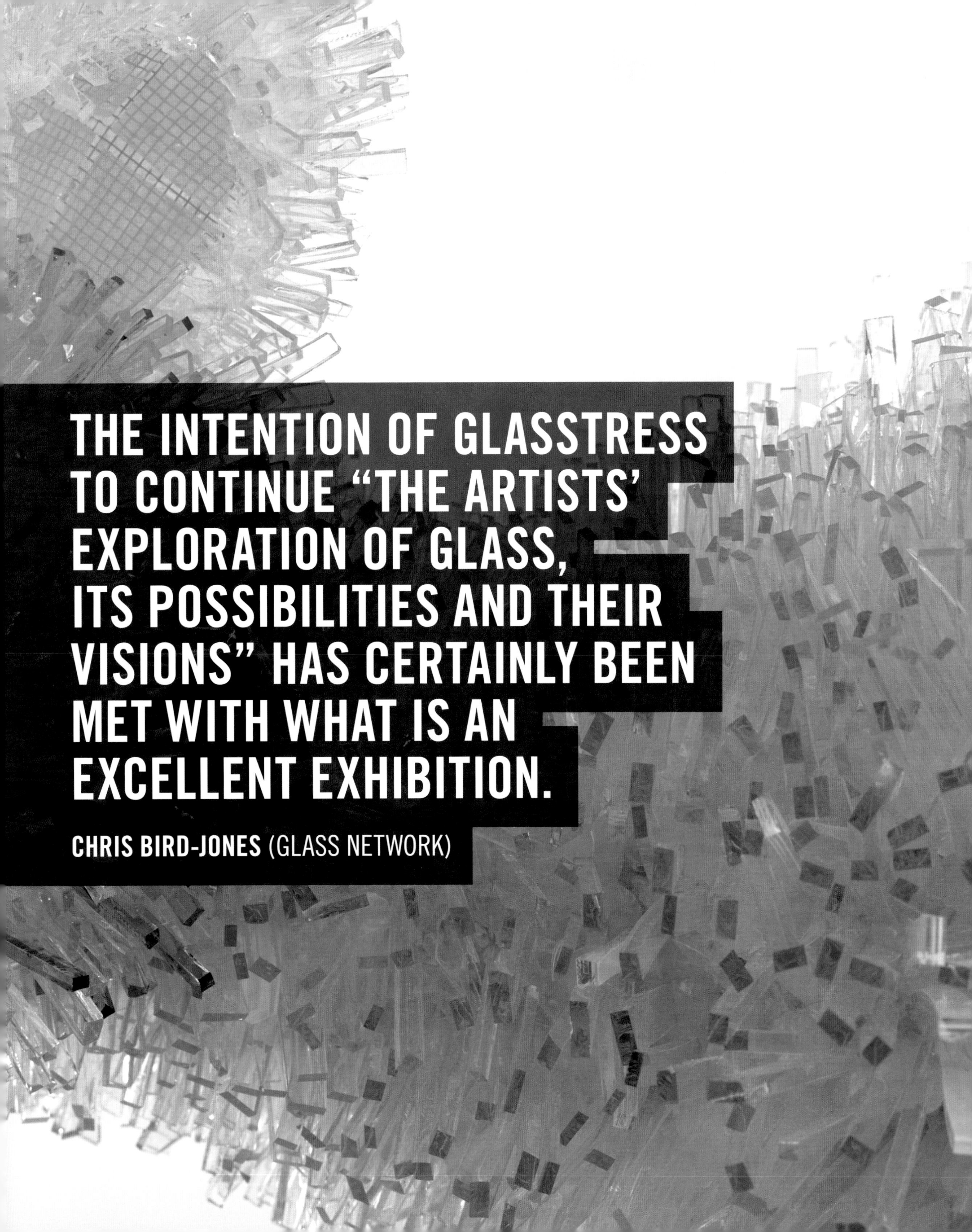

THE INTENTION OF GLASSTRESS TO CONTINUE "THE ARTISTS' EXPLORATION OF GLASS, ITS POSSIBILITIES AND THEIR VISIONS" HAS CERTAINLY BEEN MET WITH WHAT IS AN EXCELLENT EXHIBITION.

CHRIS BIRD-JONES (GLASS NETWORK)

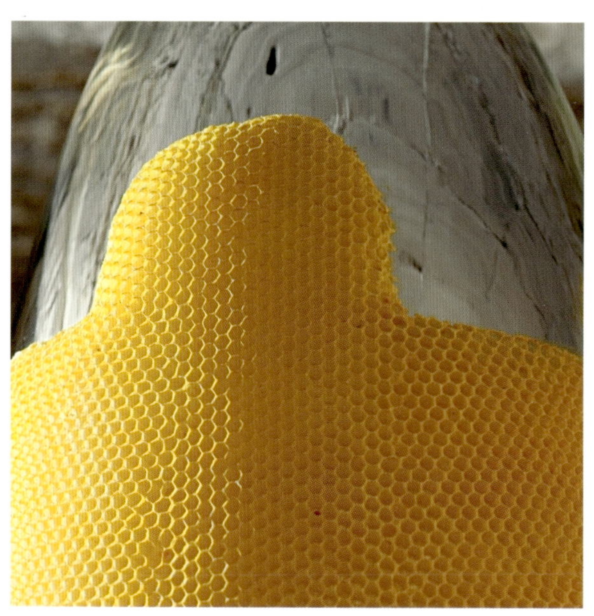

TOMÁŠ LIBERTÍNY

The artist and designer Tomáš Libertíny was born in 1979 in Slovakia where, in 1999, he began his university studies by attending the School of Industrial Design. In 2001, when he won a scholarship from the George Soros Open Society Institute, he decided to study at the University of Washington in Seattle. Soon after, he decided to continue his education at the Academy of Fine Arts and Design in Bratislava. He became interested in design, conceptual art, and the technique of construction and disassembly. In 2006, he finished university obtaining an MFA from the Eindhoven Design Academy, achieving a fully mature style. The artist, in fact, definitively abandoned the idea of using a pictorial method of painting for his works and began to explore the use of new construction materials to express his ideas. In 2007, he exhibited *Honeycomb Vase* at the Salone del Mobile in Milan, introducing the concept of "slow prototyping" and the theme of the contrast between nature and culture. Feeling the need to provide a conceptual basis to his art, he began writing a series of critical essays that drew inspiration from such sources as Freud and Lipovetsky that gathered his thoughts on the creation of a work of art. In 2007 he opened a studio in Rotterdam where he has devoted himself to studying new artistic techniques and new design strategies. His works are in the permanent collections of several world-class museums including MoMA in New York, the Museum Boijmans Van Beuningen in Rotterdam, and the Cincinnati Art Museum. In 2009 he was named Designer of the Future at Design Miami/Basel and was a winner of the Dutch Design Award.

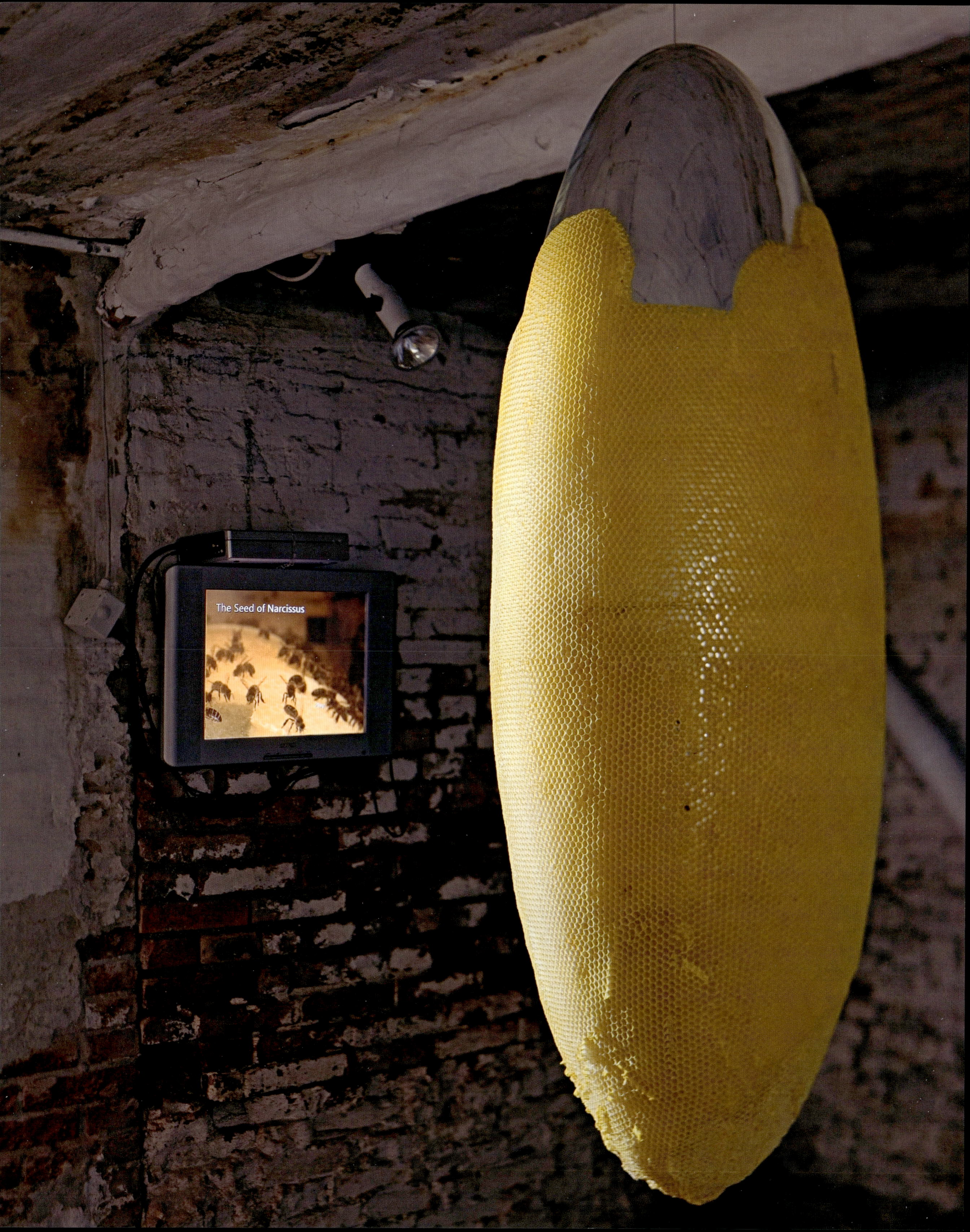
The Seed of Narcissus

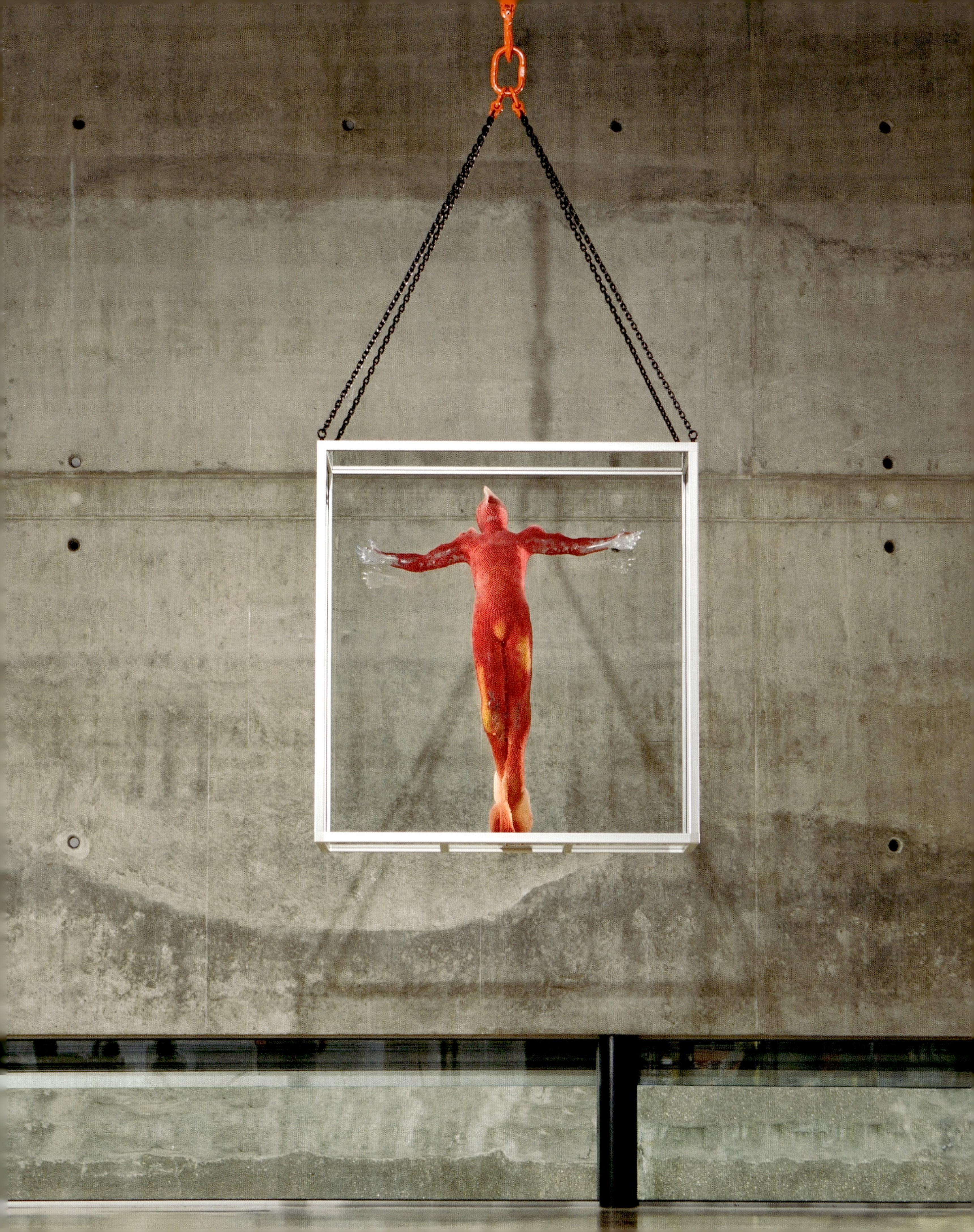

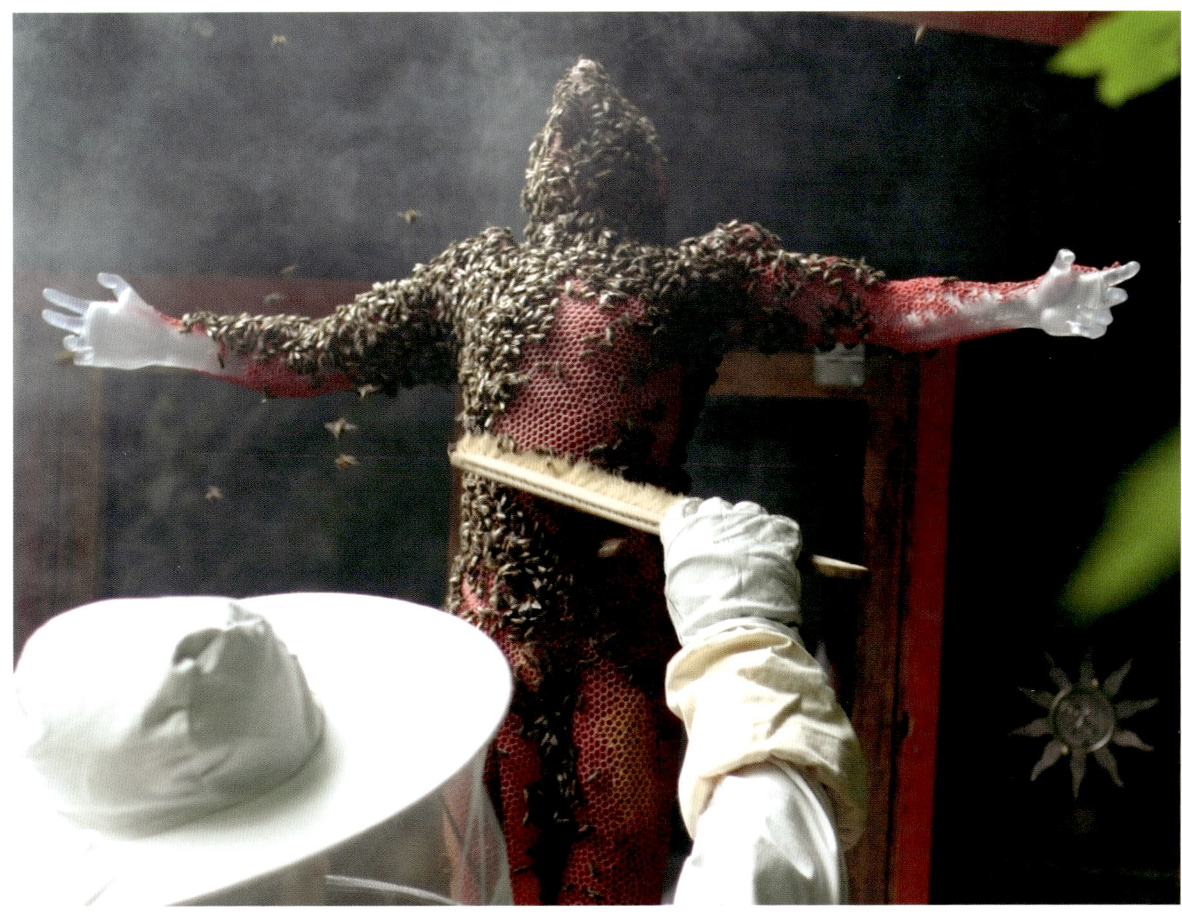

THE UNBEARABLE LIGHTNESS
2010
120 x 120 x 45 CM
COURTESY CARPENTERS WORKSHOP GALLERY,
LONDON, PARIS

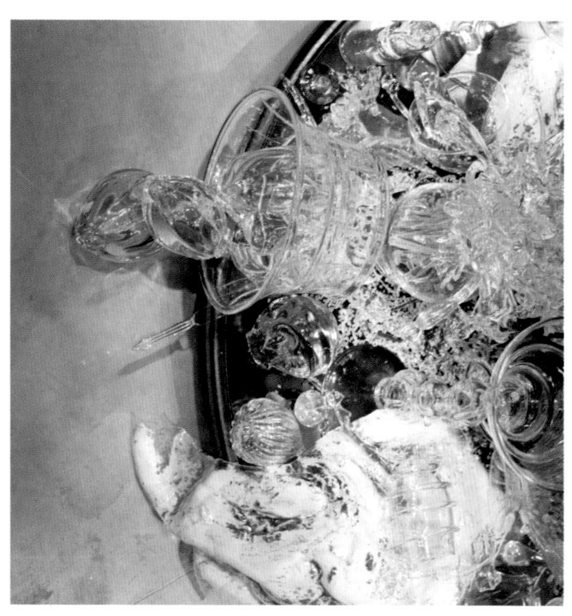

BETH LIPMAN

Beth Lipman was born in Philadelphia, in 1971. The artist now lives and works in Sheboygan Falls, Wisconsin.

Optimizing glass's clarity, fragility, and absence of color, Beth Lipman's opulent sculptures and photographs of meticulous, glass-based compositions are a contemporary response to and homage of still life paintings from the seventeent–twentieth centuries. Contemporizing the tradition of depicting real life objects dates back to the first century, Lipman speaks to the ephemerae nature of life and our universal truths, interpreting on a political, moral, and theological level current economic or socio-cultural events. One can draw a direct parallel between the tradition of still life painting and art made from traditional craft processes, for instance glass, and Lipman explores the possibilities in her studio practice. She studied at the Tyler School of Art, Temple University (Philadelphia), the Massachusetts College of Art (Boston), and the Pilchuck Glass School (Seattle). Lipman's work has been exhibited internationally including exhibitions at the Institute of Contemporary Art/ MECA, Maine, RISD Museum, Rhode Island, Milwaukee Art Museum, Wisconsin, Gustavsbergs Konsthall, Sweden, and the Smithsonian American Art Museum, Washington, DC. She is the recipient of numerous awards including a Louis Comfort Tiffany Foundation Grant, a USA Artists Grant, Wisconsin Arts Board Fellowship, and a Ruth Chenven Foundation Grant. Lipman's work is in the permanent collections of the Brooklyn Museum of Art, the Smithsonian American Art Museum, and the Corning Museum of Glass, in New York, among other prestigious international institutions.

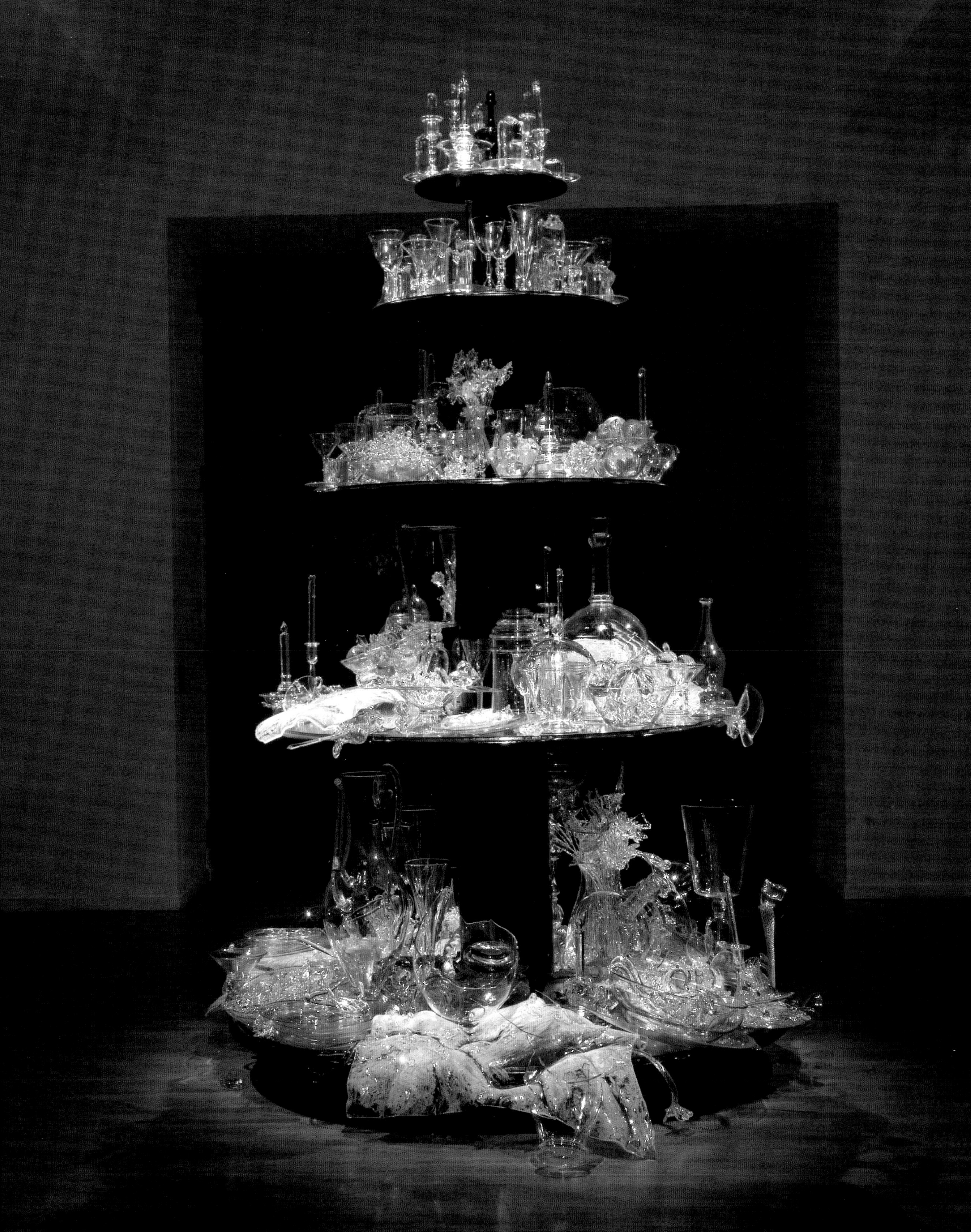

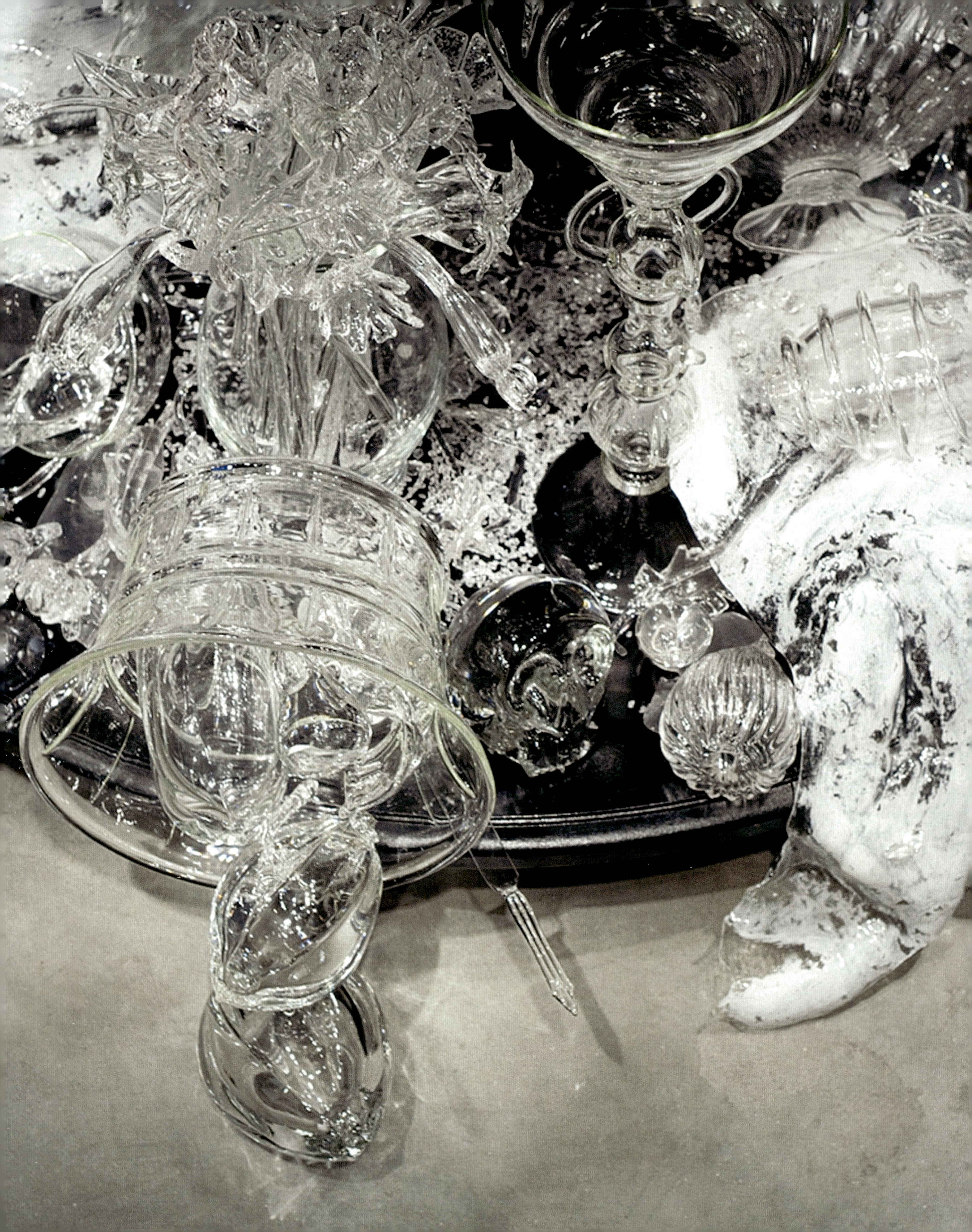

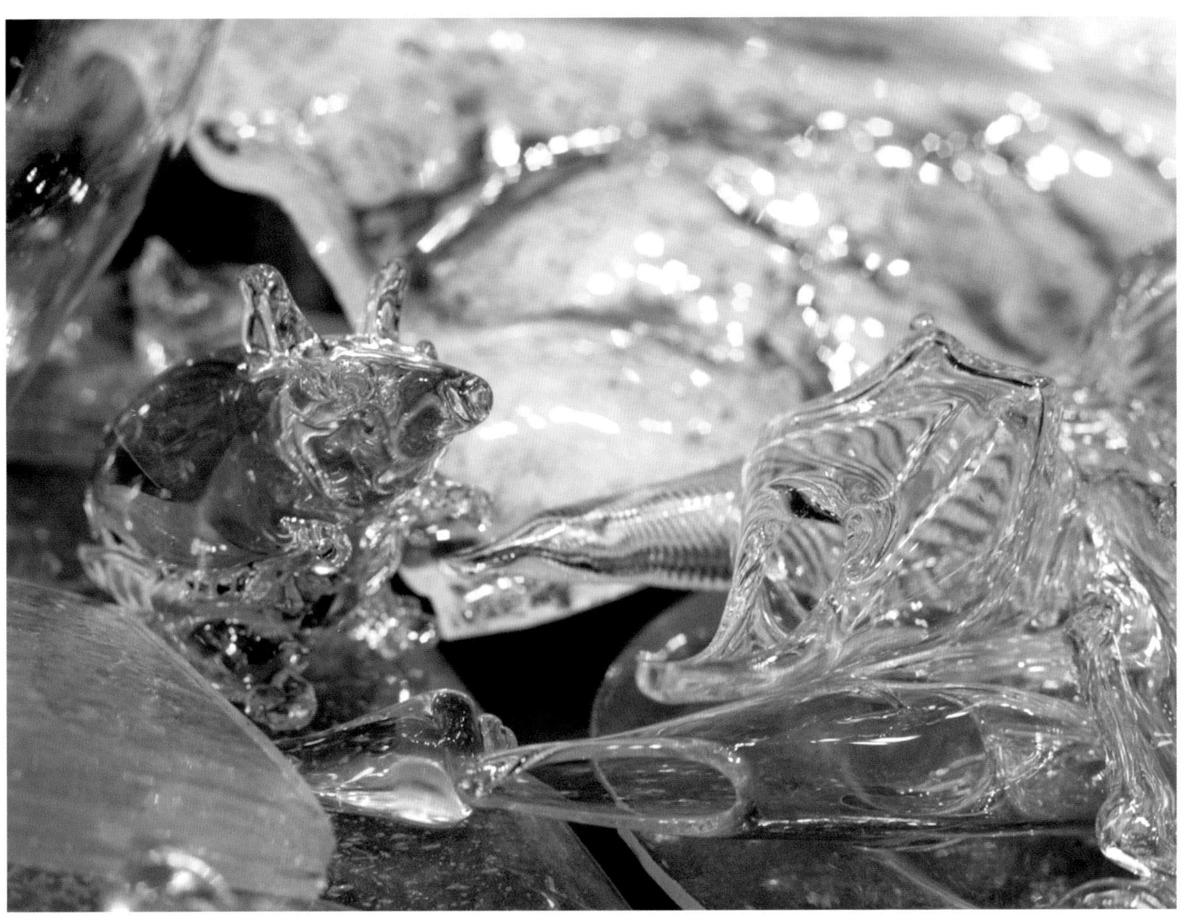

BRIDE
2010 / *DETAIL*
305 x 228 x 228 CM
COURTESY CLAIRE OLIVER GALLERY, NEW YORK

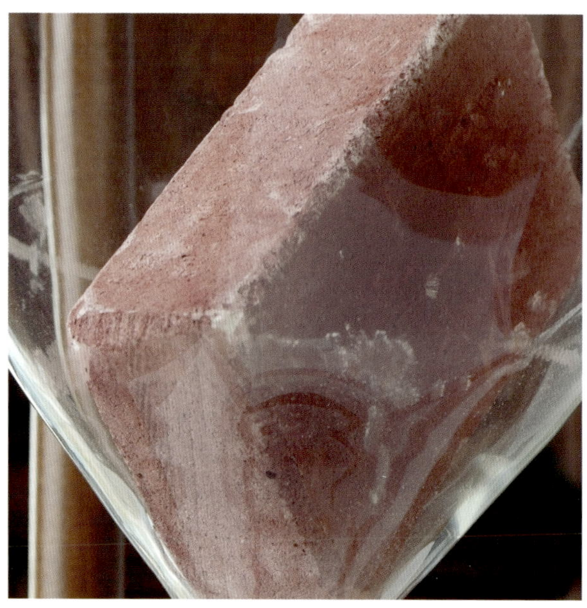

VIK MUNIZ

Vik Muniz was born in São Paulo, Brazil, in 1961. He lives in New York.
Initially, a draftsman and sculptor, photography took center stage in his
art beginning in the 1980s, after also working in the world of advertising.
Muniz's interest is directed especially at photographic reproduction of his
own 3D works.

In his works, however, the photograph is just the last link in a series
of interlocking steps that connect technical reproducibility, manual skills,
and collective memory. His artistic exploration mixes expressive codes
and languages, thanks also to his use of unconventional elements.
Chocolate, peanut butter, honey, sand, dust, tomato sauce, dirt, wire, and
cotton wadding are the elements he has used to create the visual compositions
later recaptured through an optical device. The end result is, therefore,
a photograph of the work and not the work itself, which, in fact, has been
destroyed.

In his series *Pictures of Dust*, 2000, Muniz uses dust, collected over a number
of months in the Whitney Museum, to create works that reproduce the
museum's collection of minimalist and post-minimalist sculptures.

The materials he uses frequently offer an opportunity for reflection and
social criticism, as in the *Sugar Children* series, 1996, which condemns the
exploitation of children who work harvesting sugar by reproducing their faces
and their poses as they work, precisely by using various types and colors
of sugar itself.

His cinematographic work *Wasteland*, 2010, also continues in this direction
with the artist's portrait of *catadores*, the rubbish collectors who live and work
in Jardim Gramacho, the landfill on the outskirts of Rio de Janeiro.

Vik Muniz has exhibited his work in numerous American and European
museums, including the Metropolitan Museum of Art in New York and the
Centre National de la Photographie in Paris (1998), the Venice Biennale,
the Museu de Arte Moderna in Rio de Janeiro, and the Whitney Museum
of American Art (2001), as well as the Menil Collection in Houston (2002).

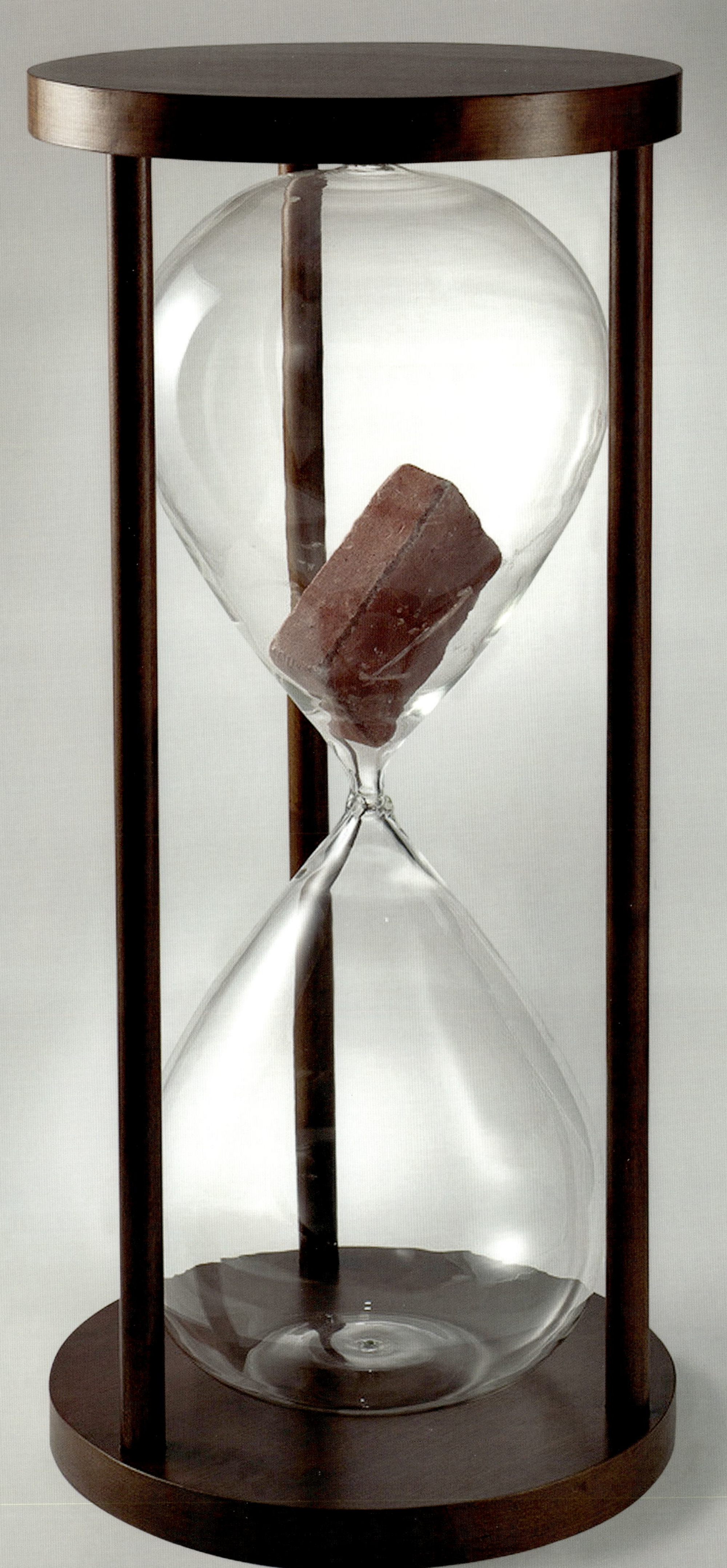

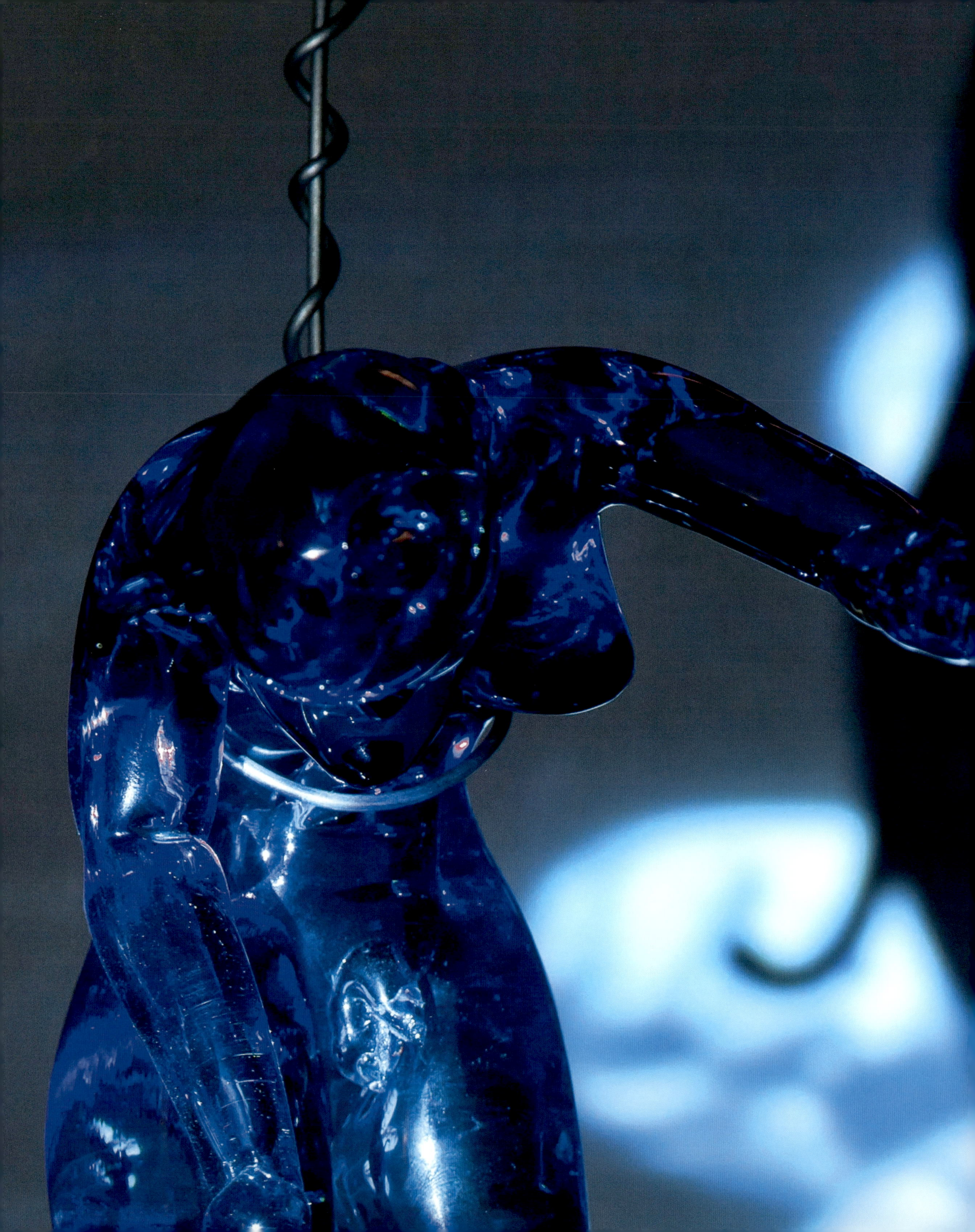

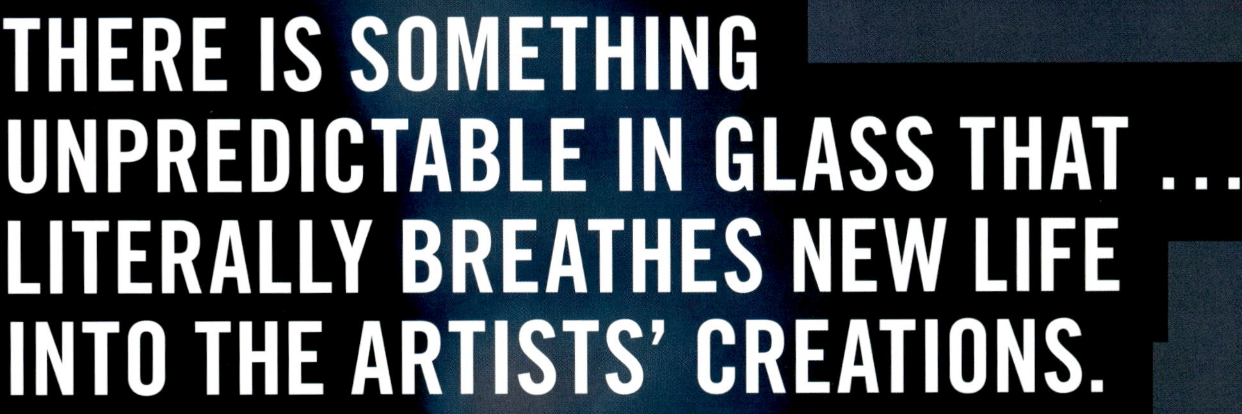

THERE IS SOMETHING UNPREDICTABLE IN GLASS THAT … LITERALLY BREATHES NEW LIFE INTO THE ARTISTS' CREATIONS.

CHIEKO HASEGAWA (NICHIDO GALLERY)

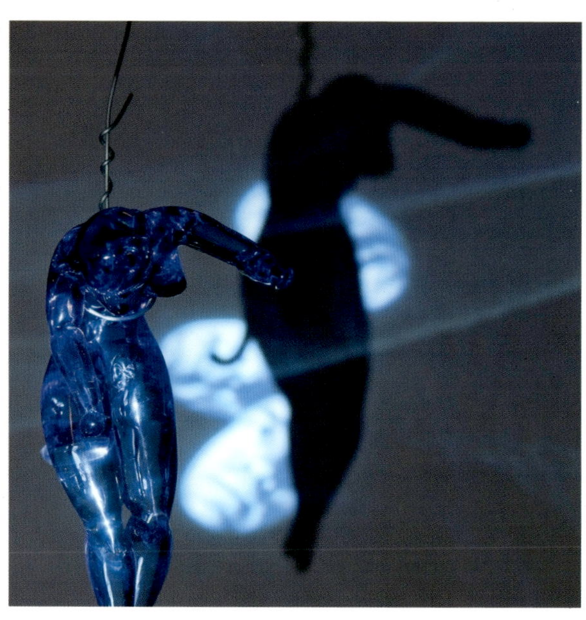

TONY OURSLER

Tony Oursler, a prominent figure in the recent history of video art, was born in 1957 in New York City, where he still lives and works.

In the 1980s he began to create short videos and later designed installations in which he used sound and video. Since the 1990s the use of dummies, puppets and dolls, trees and clouds of steam have become a constant in his work. Oursler is interested in the relationship between the individual and the language of mass media, which he feels is responsible for the profound changes in the modes of expression and communication in our times.

The multimedia works that have made him famous are videos shown in 3D, often on spherical surfaces that accentuate the subject's expressiveness: deformed faces recite monologues from intimist and somewhat delirious repercussions, shown on irregular masses as they talk, observe, yell (the *Talking Heads* series, 1998). These were then replaced by showing eyes (the *Eyes* series, 1998), that display dilated pupils, blinks, and irises. Combining sculpture, multimedia, and recordings of the human voice, Oursler explores interacting with the public and the animation of philosophical and psychological concepts. With this new technique, he has become the first to take video beyond the limitations of a screen and by projecting an image on a uniform surface that lets the public interact with the sculpture itself. Because of this, he has been called the mastermind of video-sculpture.

His works are in the collections of major museums worldwide, including MoMA, the Whitney Museum, and the Metropolitan Museum in New York; the Musée d'Orsay and the Centre Georges Pompidou in Paris; the Tate Gallery in London; and the National Museum in Osaka. He has also participated in numerous solo and group exhibitions around the world, including *Disparities and Deformations: Our Grotesque* (2004); *Studio: Seven Months of My Aesthetic Education (Plus Some)* at the Metropolitan Museum of Art, New York (2010); and *Lock 2,4,6* at the Kunsthaus Bregenz (2010).

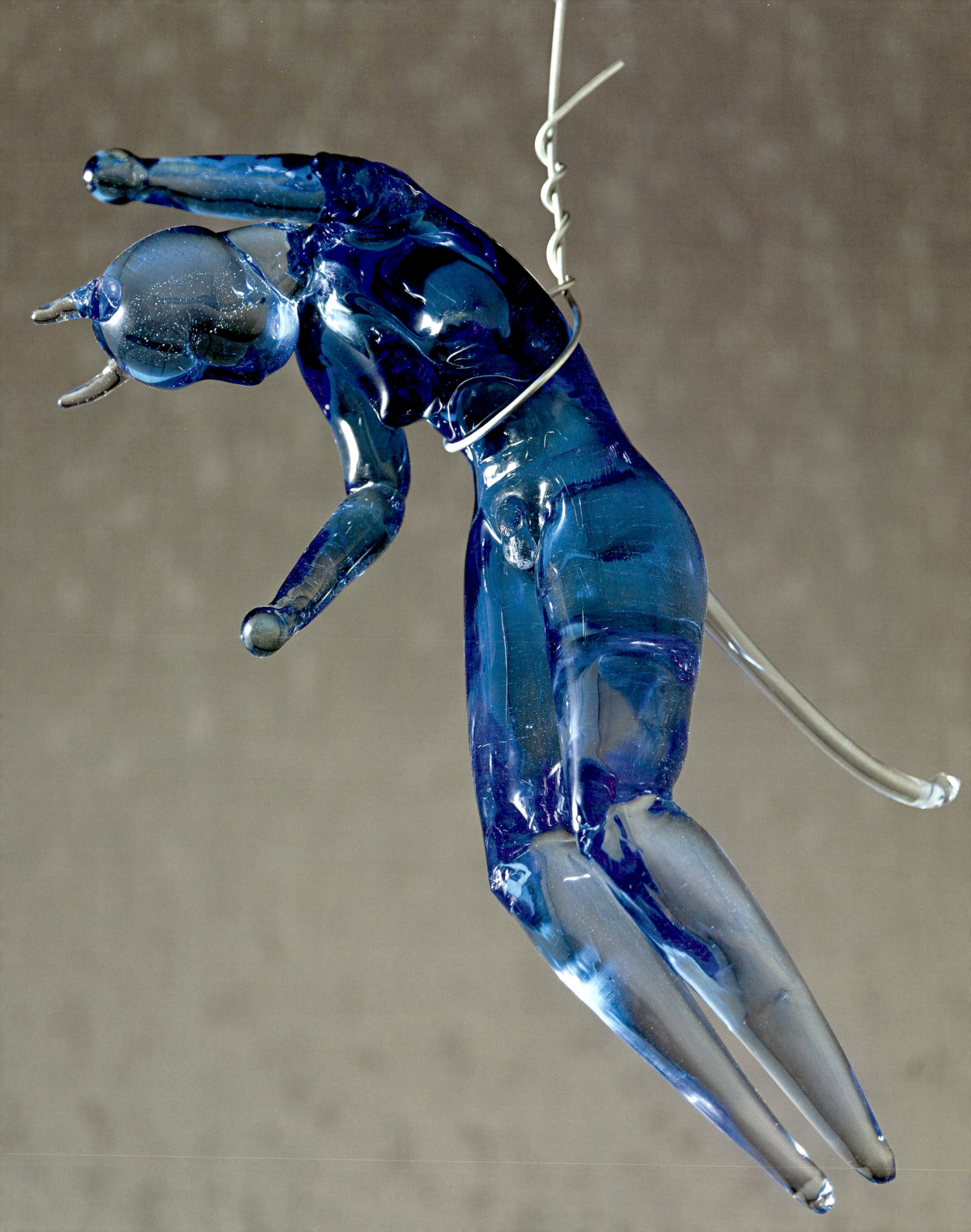

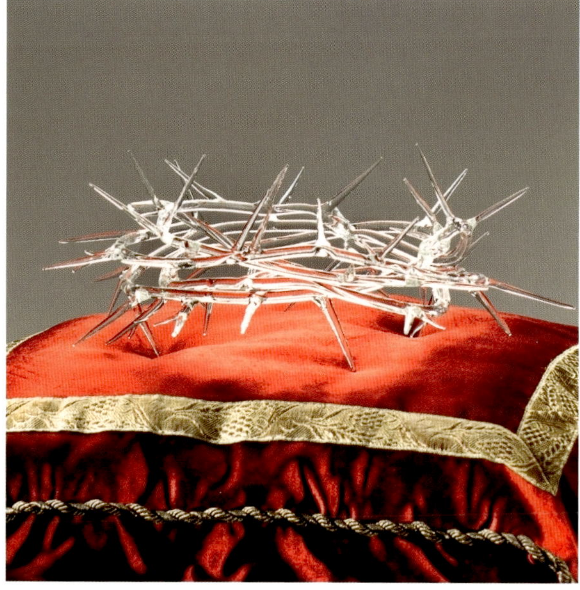

JAVIER PÉREZ

Javier Pérez was born in Bilbao in 1968. He lives and works in Barcelona. His work is permeated by a strong symbolism and accompanied by an intense use of metaphor. His works are characterized by a certain syncretism, both in the methods and the materials used. Drawing, sculpture, and video are used both independently and together to create installations in which interaction and exploration are essential.

The artist's favorite subjects for addressing the impermanence and cyclic nature of life are the body and time. The stages of life (birth-life-procreation-death) as well as social and cultural rites of passage indeed exert powerful influences on his work. Works such as *Mutaciones*, 2004, a mixed media installation exhibited at the Palacio de Cristal in Madrid, or *Tempus fugit*, 2002, emphasize the inexorable passage of time and the inevitable traces that it leaves on the body from a biological but, above all, an existential point of view. The idea of cyclicality, circularity, and the line between an individual and the environment, between inside and outside, the internal and external worlds is stated clearly in his graphic works. In the *Metamorphosis* series, 2004, as in the work *Capilares II*, 2002, this message is conveyed by the repetition of graphic signs that are almost always red and strongly connected to the idea that the venous capillaries ensure life by allowing the blood to circulate.

To create his art, Pérez uses strong, often antithetical, means of communication like horsehair and polyester, silkworm cocoons and ceramics, or cattle intestines and blown glass. Playing with the contrasts, the artist confronts humanity with its own condition, torn between body and spirit, purity and impurity, attraction and repulsion, beauty and horror.

In 2001 he was invited to represent Spain at the Venice Biennale. In 2008 the Guggenheim Museum in Bilbao exhibited Pérez's 1997 work, *Màscara de seducciòn,* and bought it for its own collection. He has had other exhibitions at the Museum of Modern and Contemporary Art in Strasbourg (1997), the Museo Nacional Centro Reina Sofía in Madrid (2004), and the Museo Vasco de Arte Contemporaneo in Vitoria (2006).

Some of the artist's works are in the collections of Marseille's CIRVA, the Fondation Guerlain, and Strasbourg's Museum of Modern and Contemporary Art as well as the Basque Parliament.

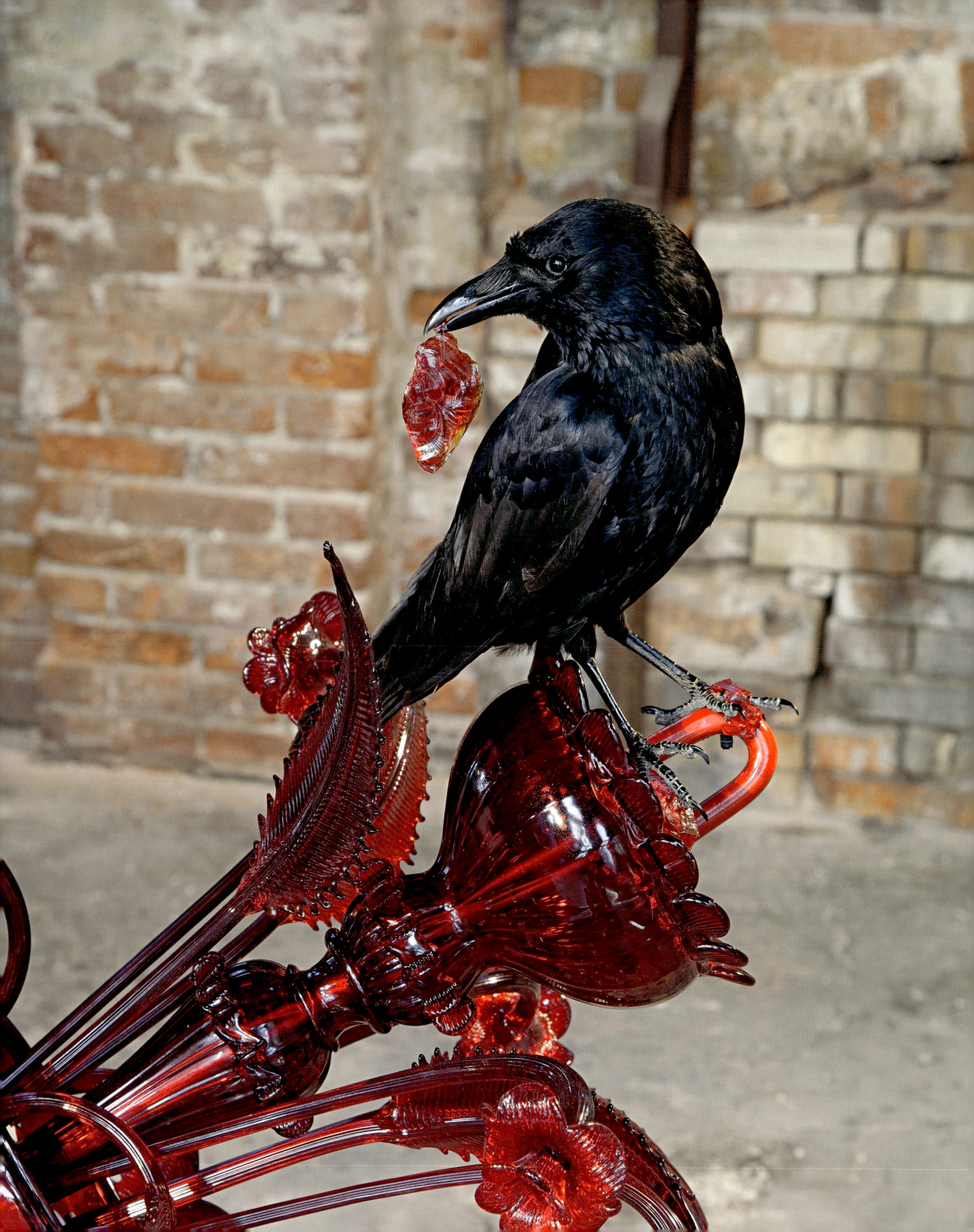

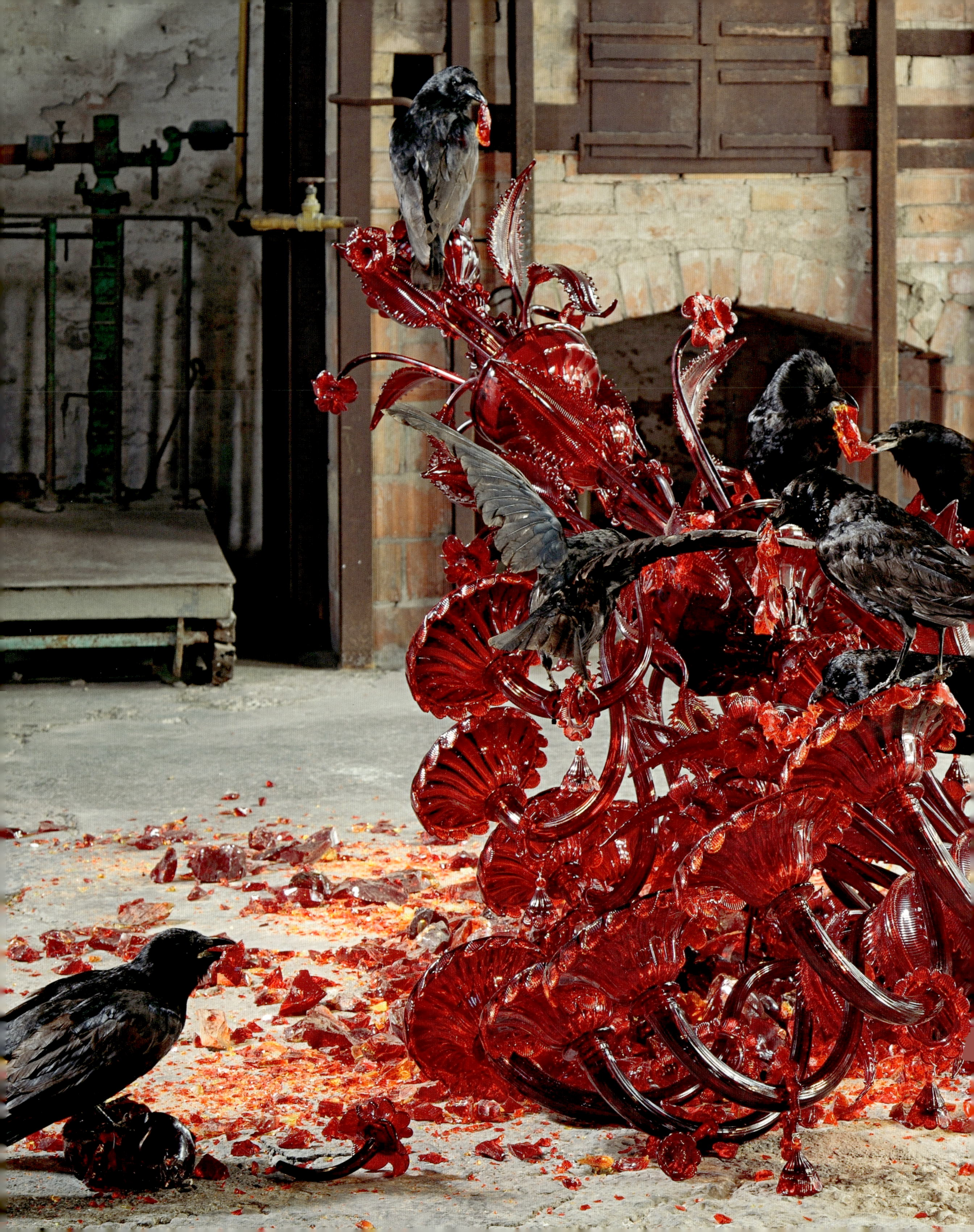

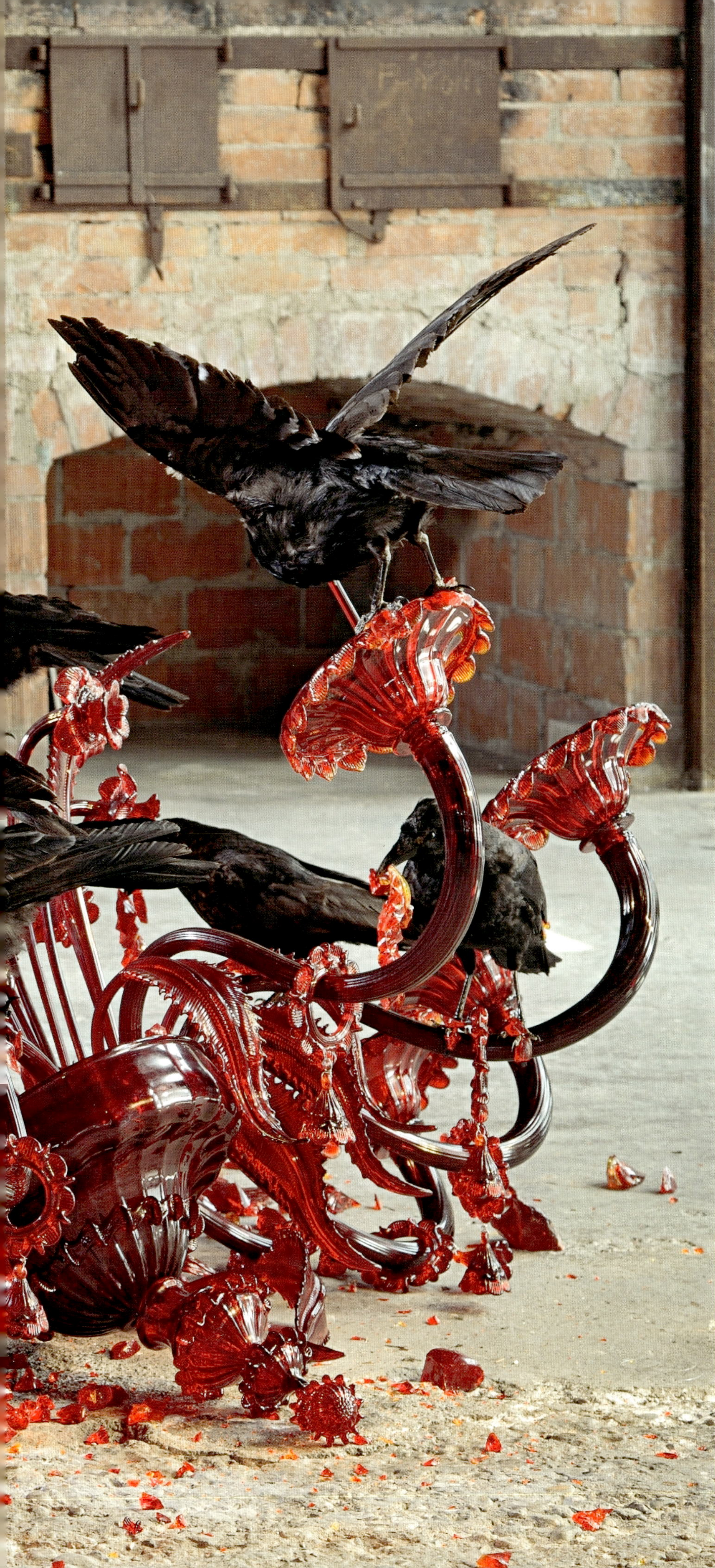

CARROÑA
2011
120 x 235 x 300 CM /
VARIABLE DIMENSIONS
COURTESY VENICE PROJECTS, VENICE

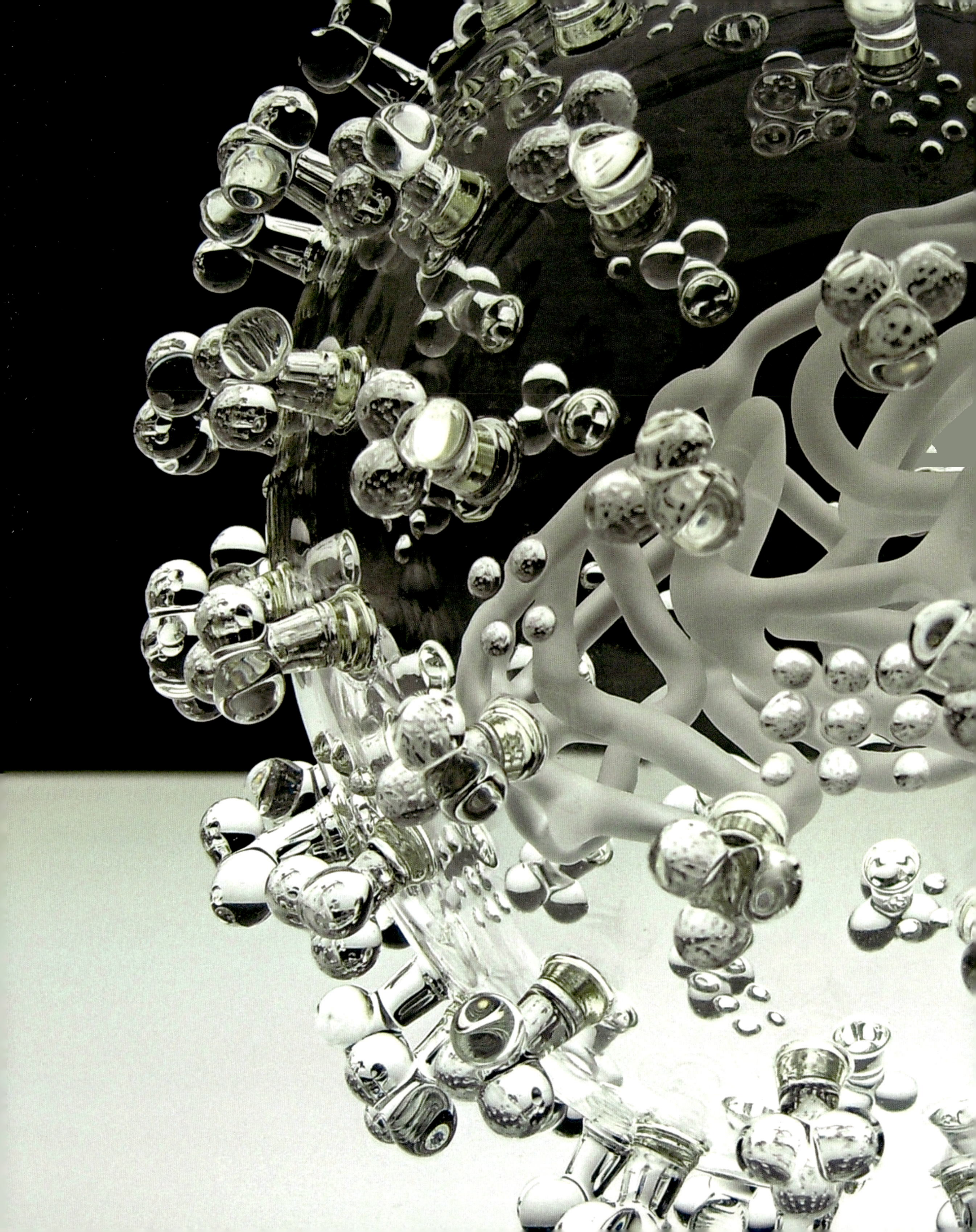

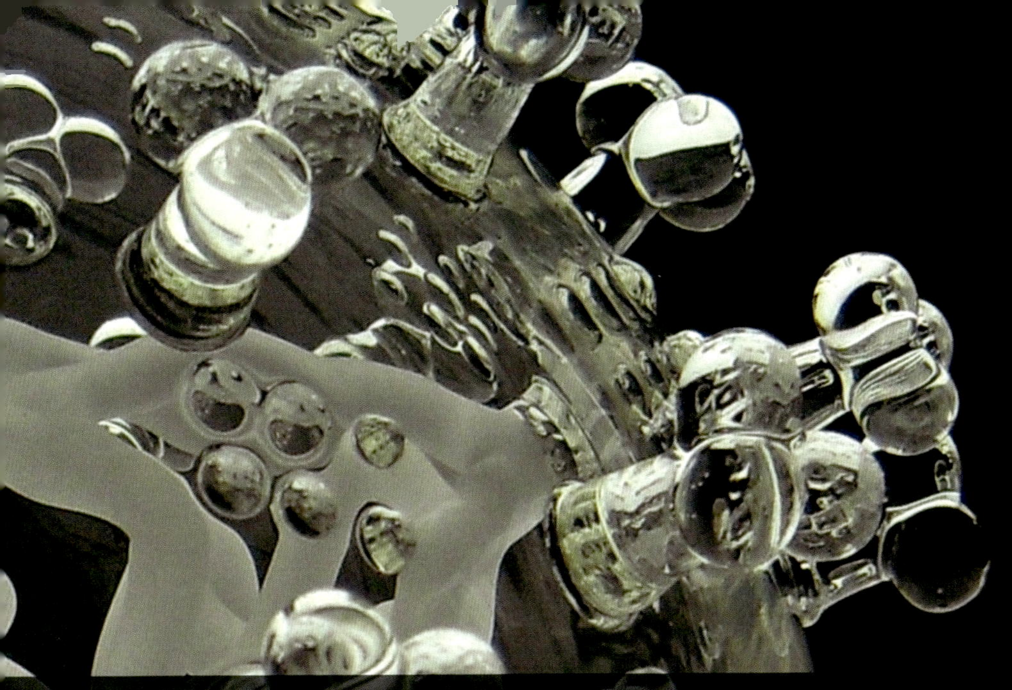

ITS FRAGILITY, TRANSPARENCY,
VERSATILITY, AND ABILITY TO CONTAIN
YET SIMULTANEOUSLY REVEAL
HAVE MADE GLASS ONE OF THE RICHEST
MEANS OF ARTISTIC EXPRESSION.

FAUSTO PETRELLA (PSYCHIATRIST)

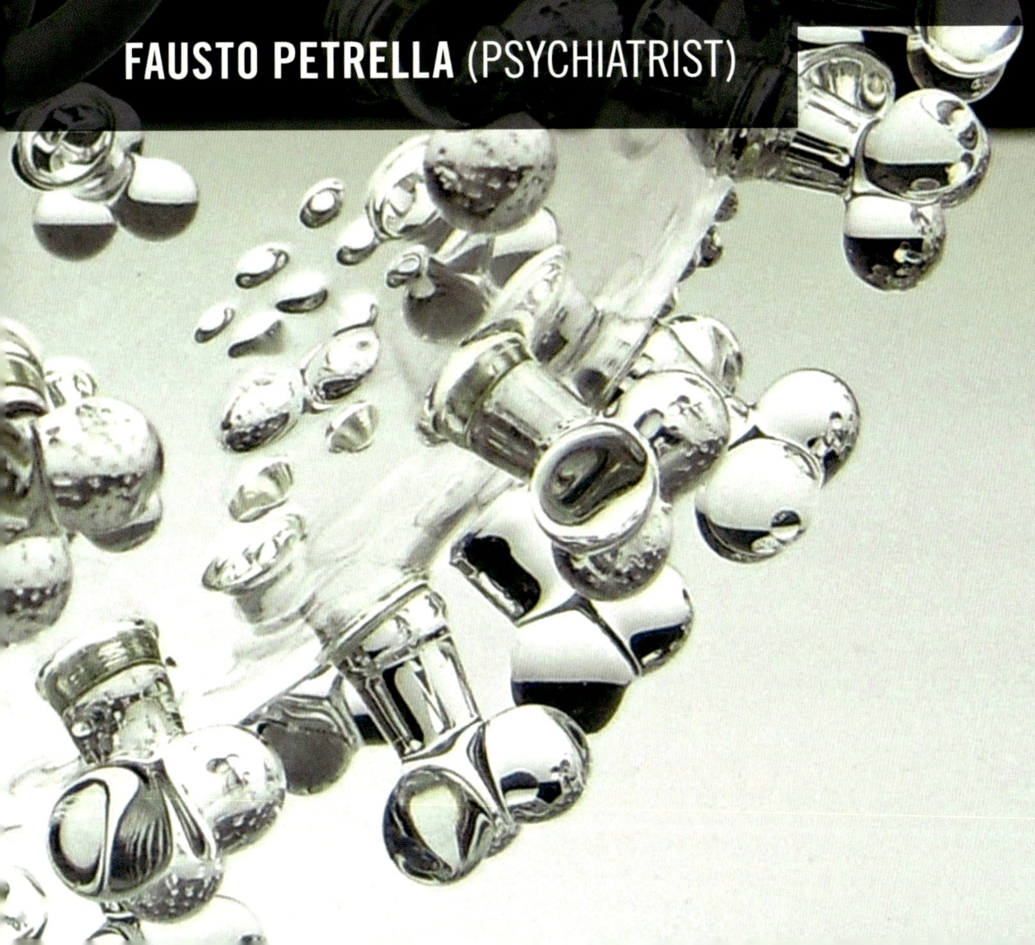

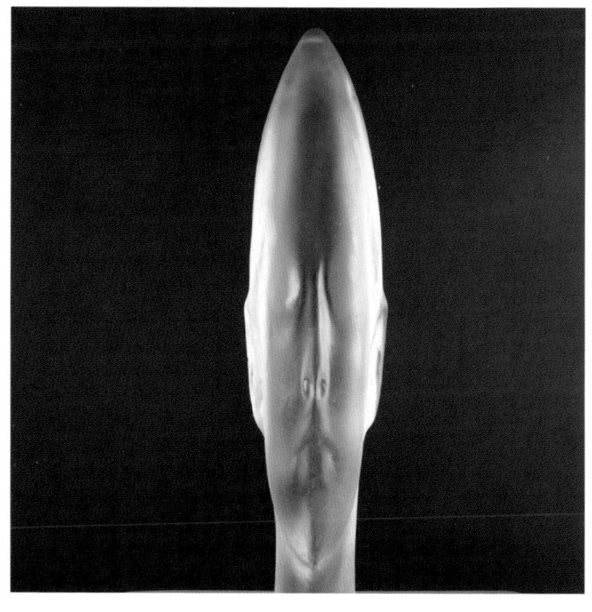

JAUME PLENSA

Born in 1955 in Barcelona, Jaume Plensa lives in both his hometown and
in Paris.

The artist's early works are characterized by anthropomorphic forms made
of heavy materials like iron and bronze. Over time, he has experimented
with new synthetic plastics as well as glass and alabaster, intrigued by the
luminous effects and the shapes they can take on.

Many of his sculptures depict a seated human figure that has been created
by an assembly of alphanumerical characters from various languages.
When combined, they become poems or parts of words that are particularly
meaningful to the artist.

Through the use of letters and symbols belonging to various peoples, the
artist seeks to celebrate diversity and to emphasize the importance of cultural
unity, as in his work *The Nomad*, 2007. Located on the Saint-Jaume bastion
in Antibes, the work encourages the endless passage between space and
sculpture but also the continuous exchange between different cultures. Using
conventional sculptural materials (such as glass, metal, bronze, aluminum)
together with other unusual ones (such as water, light, sound, and video),
Plensa always prompts a dialogue between the work itself and the space
surrounding it. In *Crown Fountain*, 2000–2005, at Millennium Park in Chicago,
the artist wanted to create a free, fun space for people: a fountain constructed
of glass, steel, black granite, but also LED screens where videos of 1,000
different faces were shown. Consisting of two, 16-meter high towers and
placed on a water surface of 70 x 14 meters, the fountain creates several water
features connected to the images gradually screened.

Parallel to the sculptures, the artist has created an equally important body
of works on paper.

Since 1995 he has collaborated with the theater group La Fura dels Baus,
designing theatrical costumes and some sets.

Since 1992 he has won several awards, both nationally and internationally.
In 2005 he received an honorary doctorate from the School of the Art Institute
of Chicago.

He has participated in numerous exhibits including ones at the Fundació Joan
Miró in Barcelona (1996); the Galerie Nationale du Jeu de Paume in Paris
(1997); the Museo Nacional Centro de Arte Reina Sofía in Madrid (2000); the
Fondation Européenne pour la Sculpture in Brussels (2002); and the Palazzo
delle Papesse in Siena (2004). He is also the only living artist who has had
an exhibition at the Nasher Sculpture Center in Dallas, United States.

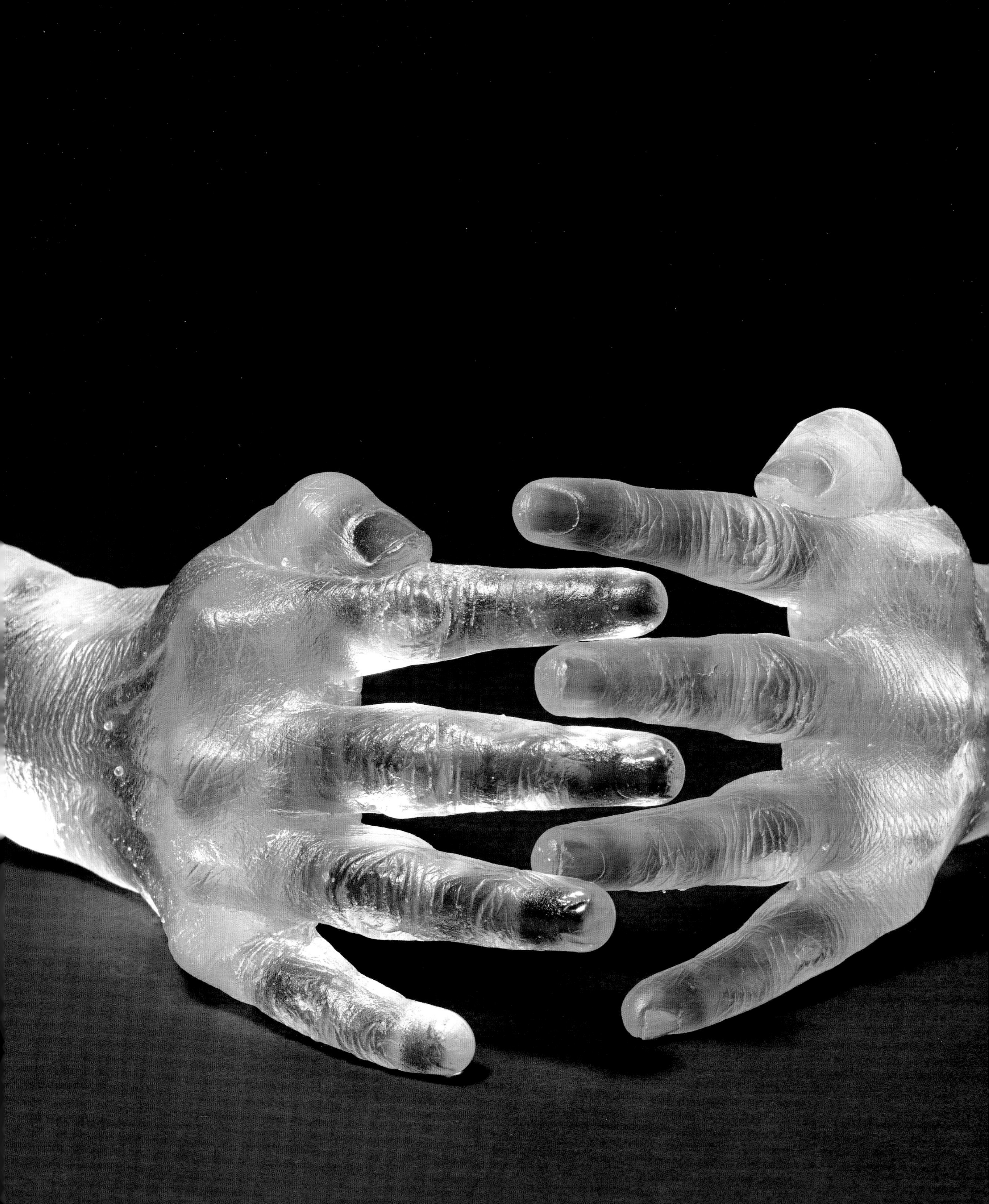

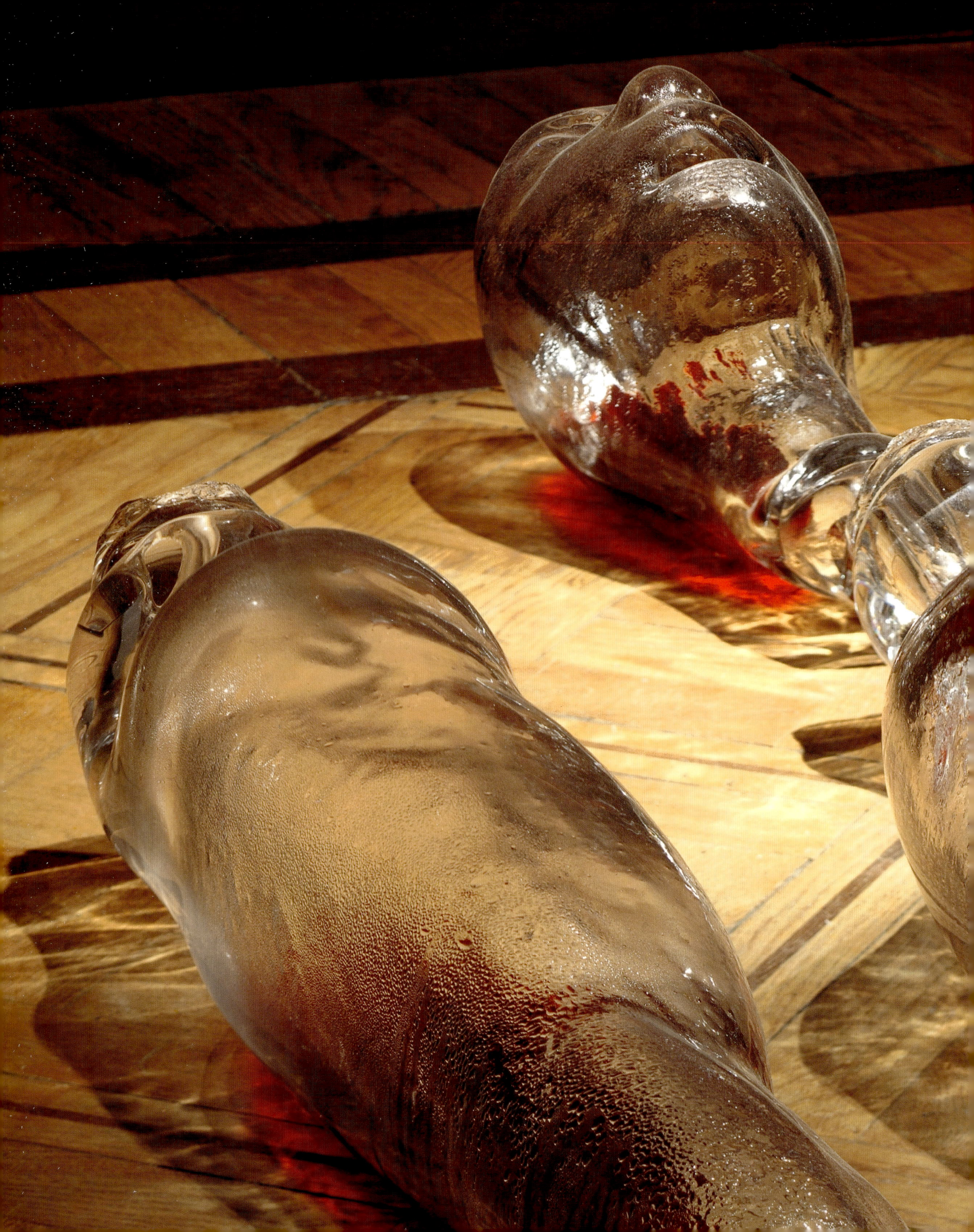

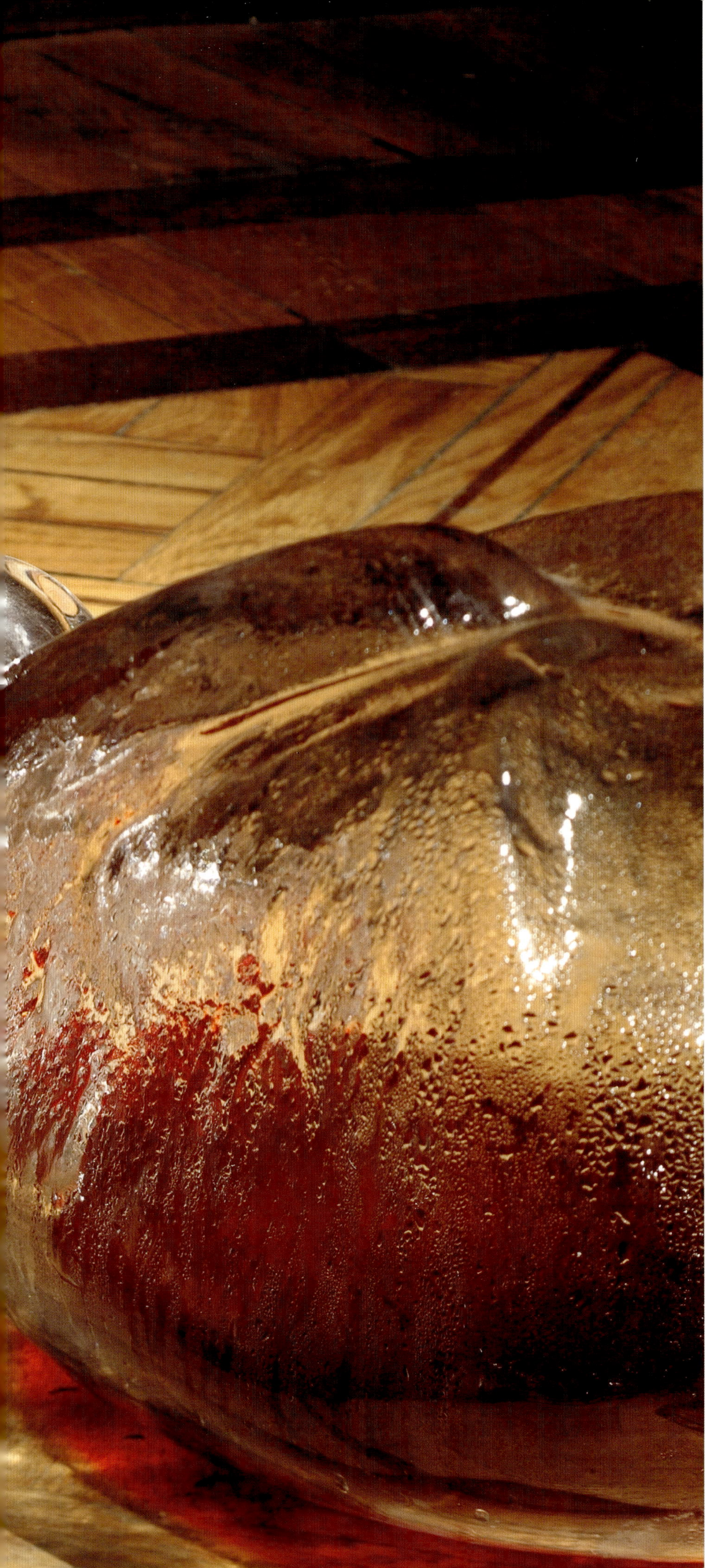

GLASSMAN II
2004 / DETAIL
30 x 250 x 90 CM
COURTESY THE ARTIST
AND GALERIE LELONG, PARIS

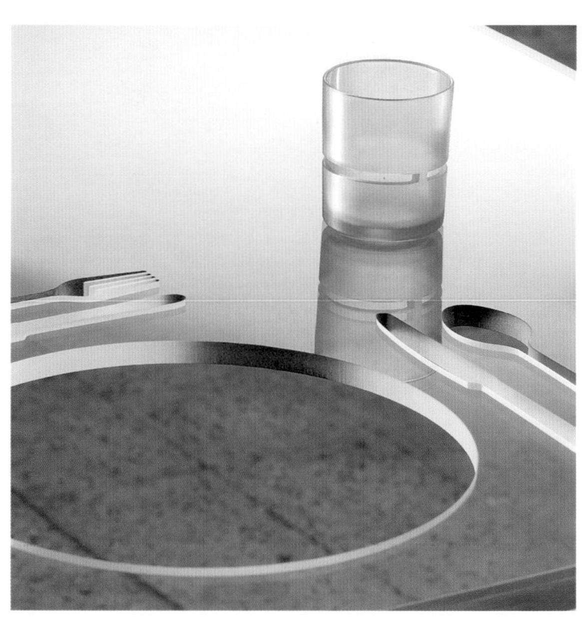

SILVANO RUBINO

Silvano Rubino was born in 1952 in Venice, where he lives and works.
He studied Painting and Fresco at the Istituto d'Arte and at the Accademia
di Belle Arti in Venice. Since 1984 he has also created set and costume design
for theater and dance performances, achieving great scenic effect.
His artistic activity includes large-format photography, video, and installations,
always aiming at relating the artwork to the individual space, environment,
and observer. His artistic research in glass consists in giving new shapes and
dimensions to commonly used items. His glass works enhance the ambiguity
of the material, which is glass but could be something else, and concentrates
on forms. He actually gives his works a self-sufficient and autonomous life,
exploiting the deceptive effects of the material. He has taught Drawing and
Planning at the Abate Zanetti School of Glass in Murano. His works were
presented in *Glass in the World Today* at the Istituto Veneto di Scienze, Lettere
ed Arti in Venice in 2004, *In Perfect Scale* at the Galleria Michela Rizzo in
2006, and at Palazzetto Tito, Fondazione Bevilacqua La Masa, Venice, with
the exhibition *In equilibrio tra due punti sospesi*.

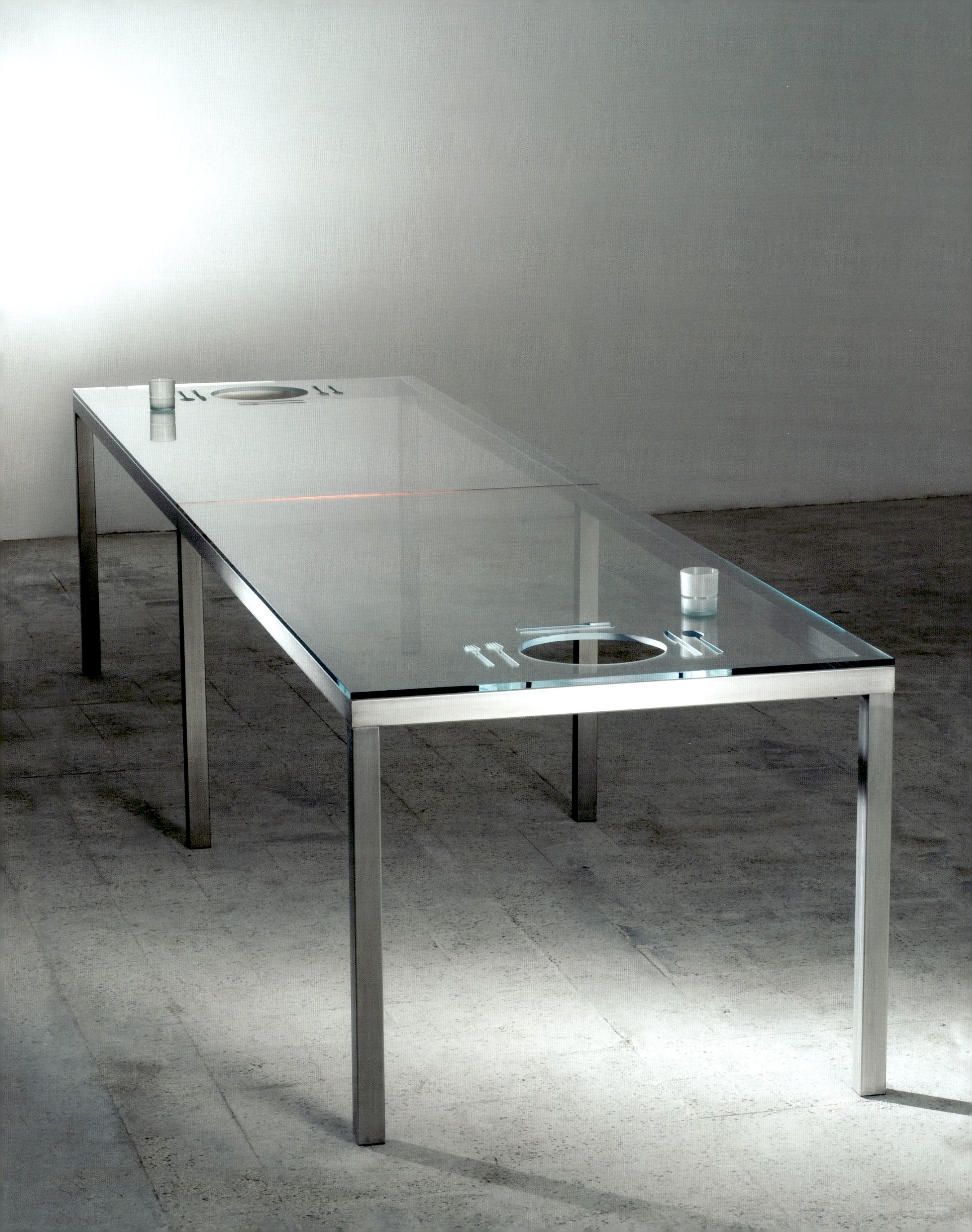

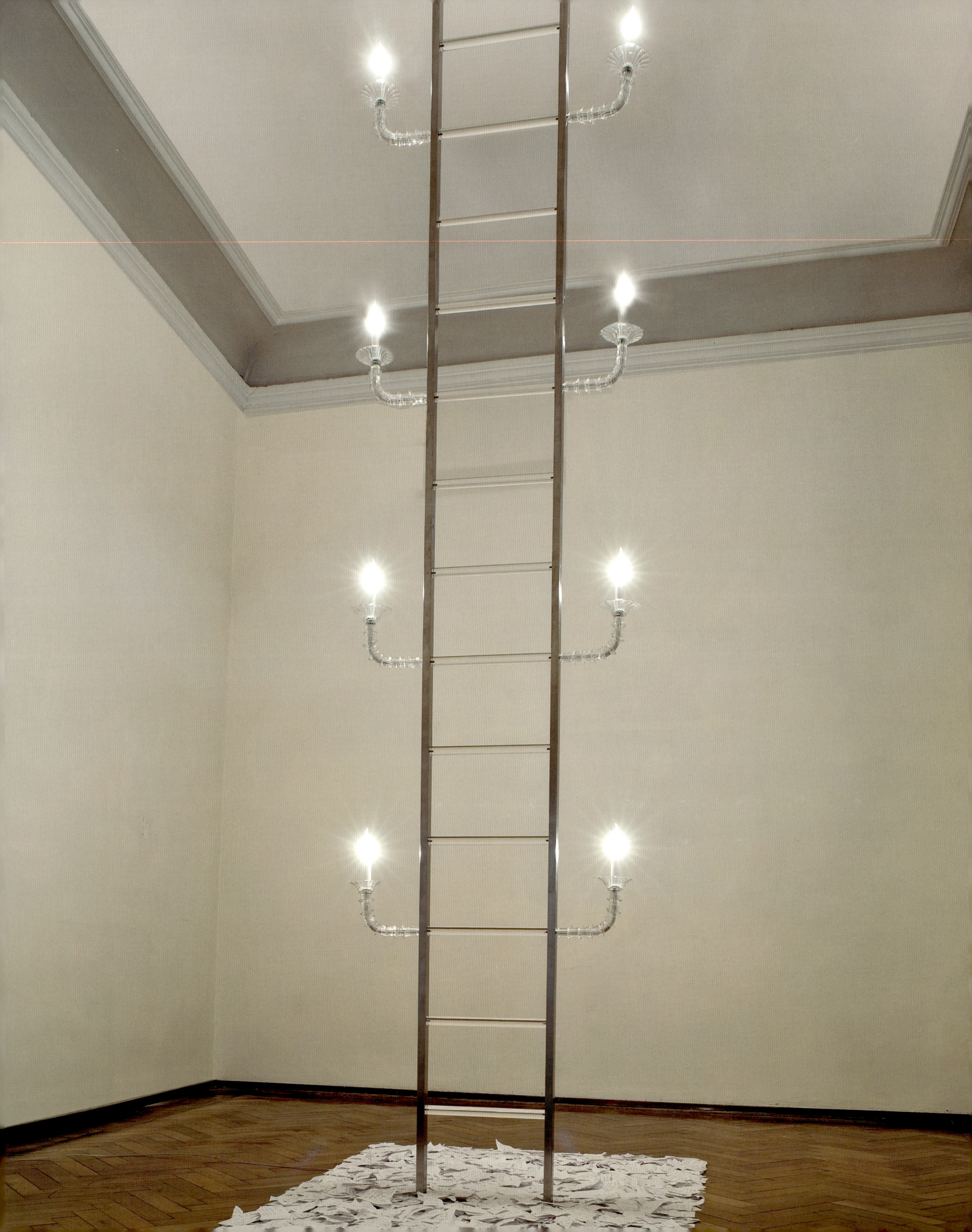

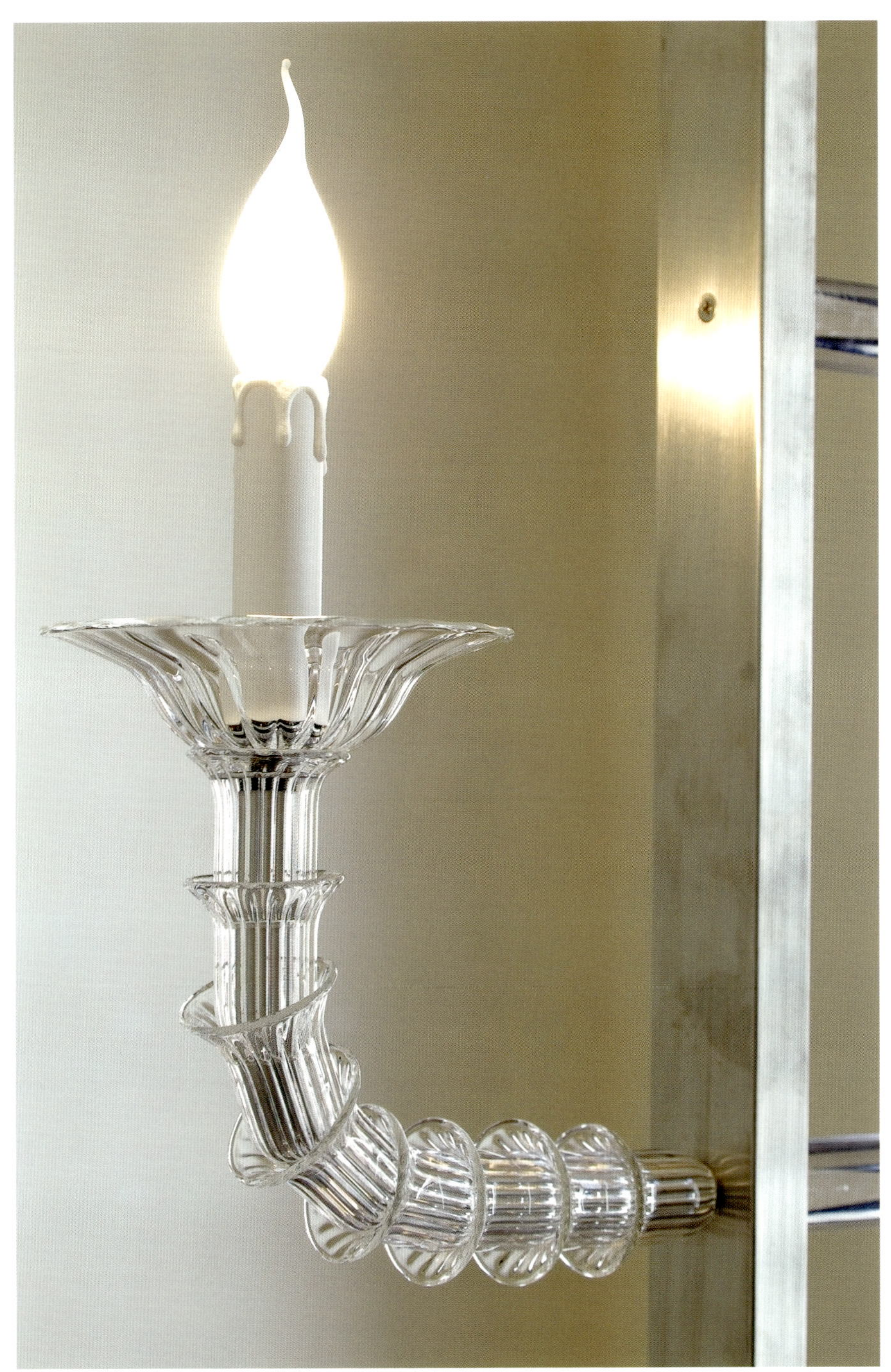

SCALA ILLUMINANTE
2010
420 x 150 x 250 CM /
VARIABLE DIMENSIONS
COURTESY THE ARTIST

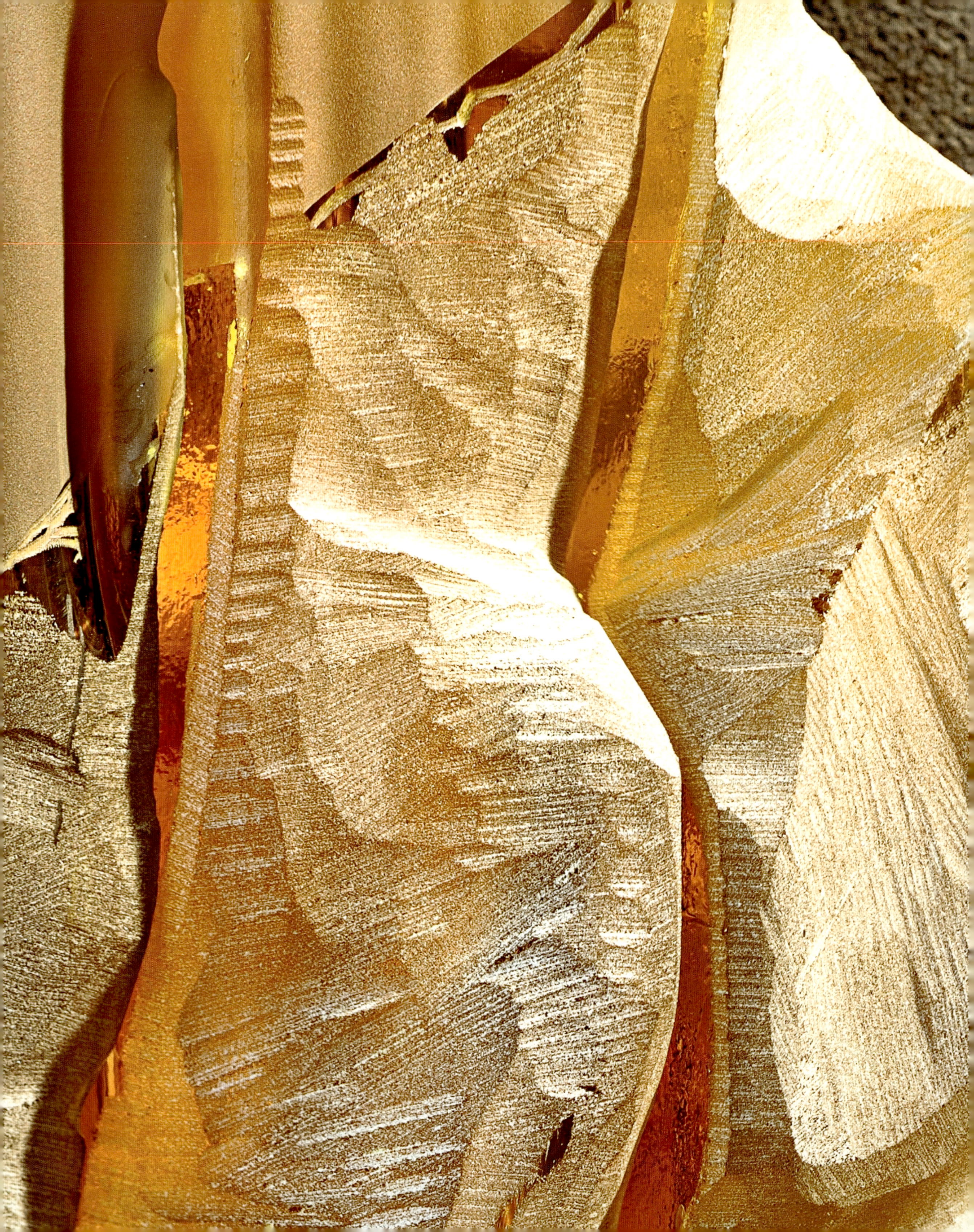

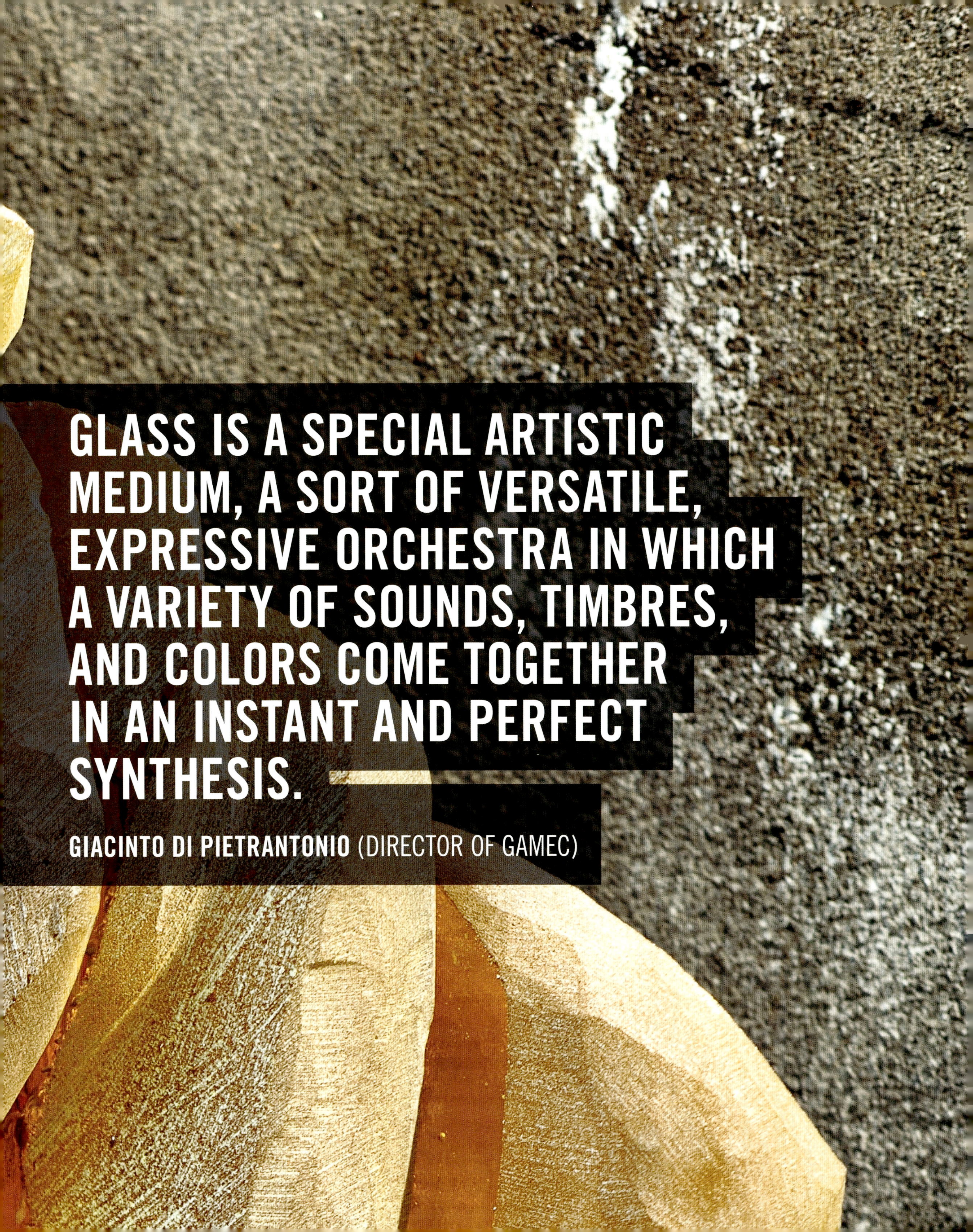
GLASS IS A SPECIAL ARTISTIC MEDIUM, A SORT OF VERSATILE, EXPRESSIVE ORCHESTRA IN WHICH A VARIETY OF SOUNDS, TIMBRES, AND COLORS COME TOGETHER IN AN INSTANT AND PERFECT SYNTHESIS.
GIACINTO DI PIETRANTONIO (DIRECTOR OF GAMEC)

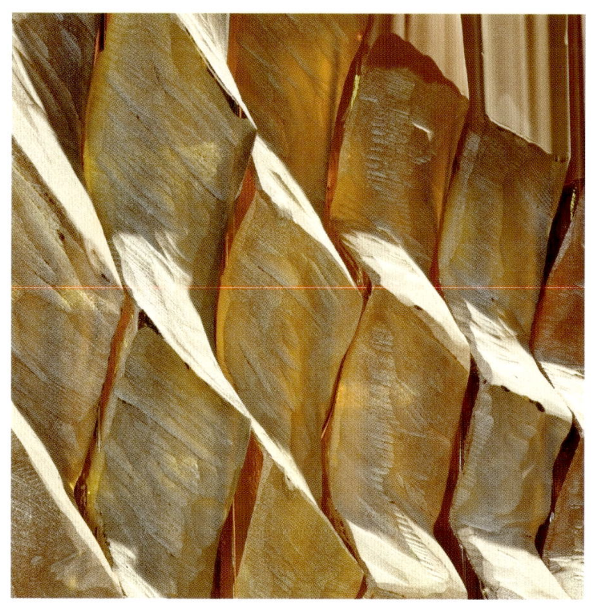

URSULA VON RYDINGSVARD

Ursula von Rydingsvard was born in Deensen, Germany, in 1942. During World War II her family, of Polish-Ukrainian origins, was enslaved and forced to work on farms. This dramatic experience has unquestionably influenced her artistic style. When the artist was nine years old, her family emigrated to the United States where she has continued to live. Von Rydingsvard studied at Columbia University, earning an MFA in 1975. Four years later, the artist received a grant from the National Endowment for the Arts, followed by a Guggenheim Fellowship. In 1991, she received an honorary doctorate from the Maryland Institute College of Art in Baltimore.

The artist is known internationally for the imposing sculptures she creates with cedar wood. Her past, marked by the continual wandering from one refugee camp to another, is relived through the choice of wood and manual labor. Each time the artist selects, cuts, shapes, and finishes the surface of the wood, she again evokes her difficult childhood: the artisanal process, linked to the real world, becomes a vehicle for her introspective, evocative, and highly personal art.

Her works have been exhibited in important museums around the world, including many in New York such as the Whitney Museum of American Art, the Metropolitan Museum of Art, the MoMA, and the Brooklyn Museum. The artist reached a high point in her career in 1997 when Microsoft commissioned her to create *Skip to My Lou*, a sculpture for the company's headquarters in Redmond, Washington. In 2006, an outdoor installation was exhibited in Madison Square Park. At this time, the artist continues to work in New York, specifically in the dynamic Brooklyn neighborhood where her studio is located.

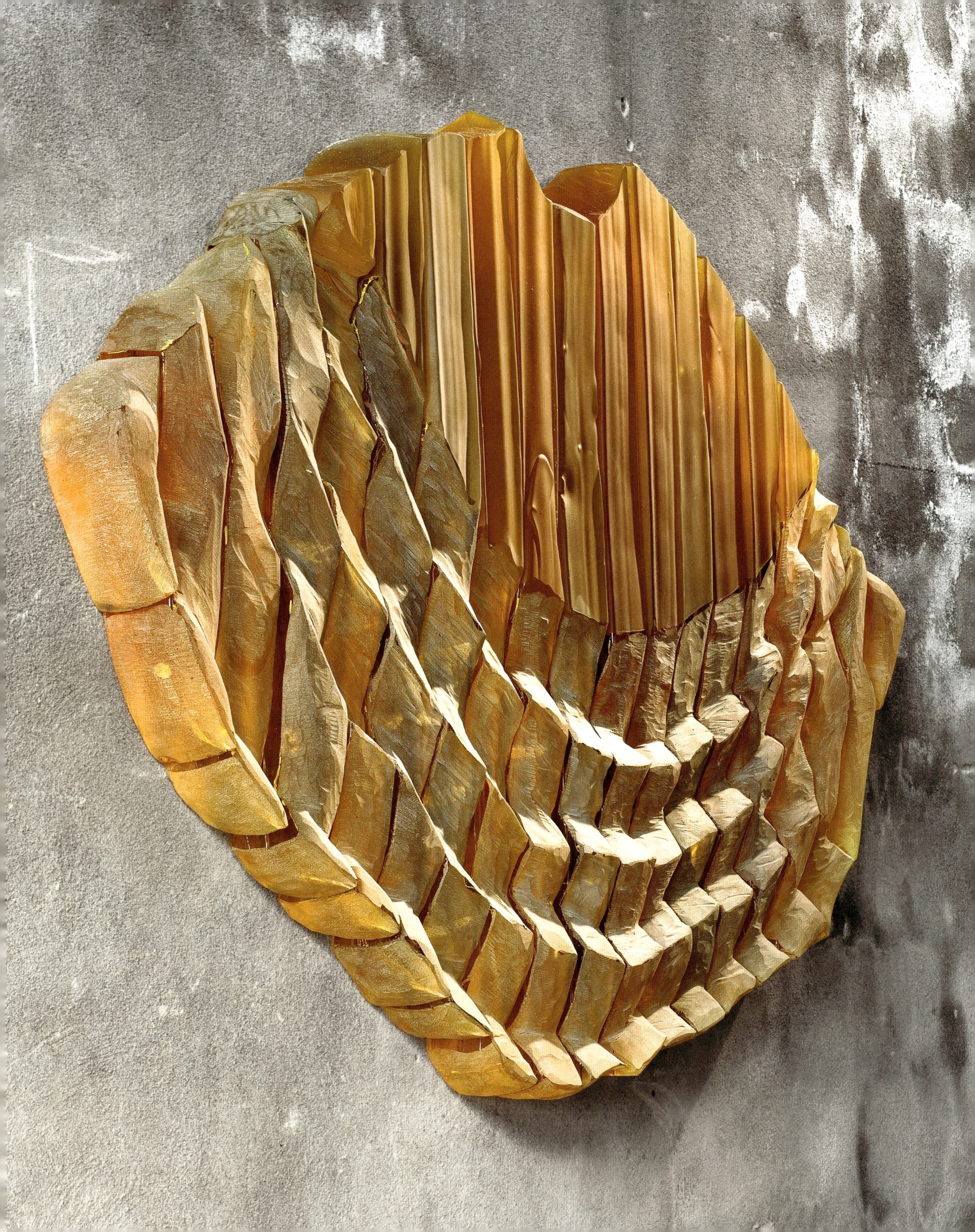

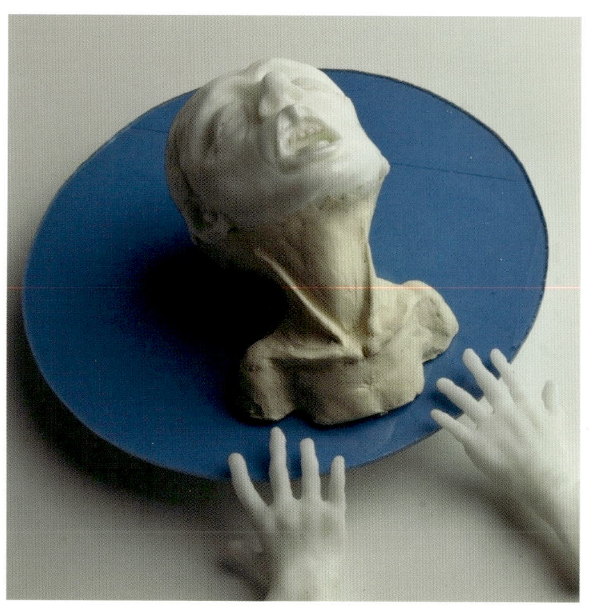

JUDITH SCHAECHTER

Judith Schaechter was born in Newton, Massachusetts, in 1961. She lives and works in Philadelphia.

Educated at Rhode Island School of Design, Schaechter discovered in stained glass her unique creative voice. In this dazzling and virtually untapped medium, Schaechter has combined high craft with the historical traditionalism of painting on canvas to create a singular voice in contemporary art.

The artist graduated in 1983 and has since worked to overcome the conventions of stained glass, adopting innovative techniques to maximize the medium's potential. Her graphic leaded line, signature, doe-eyed figures, and inventive layering systems have made her a critically acclaimed artist, and she is as respected for her studio practice as well as her challenging subject matter. The artist's light boxes are comprised of multi-layered flash glass that has been cut and ground smooth, then variously painted, sandblasted, filed, and engraved, resulting in incredibly detailed yet ambiguous narratives that bridge past centuries with the present. In a field much better known for abstraction, her studio practice relies on painstaking draftsmanship and the human figure, giving new meaning to the stained glass genre by creating both spatial and narrative depth through paper-thin layers of glass. Schaechter employs traditional copper foil and soldering techniques, balancing both practice and medium that hearkens back to the Middle Ages with contemporary iconography. Schaechter is in the permanent collections of the Metropolitan Museum of Art, New York, the Smithsonian Institute of American Art, Washington, DC, Philadelphia Museum of Art, Philadelphia, de Young Museum, San Francisco, Victoria and Albert Museum, London, Montreal Museum of Fine Arts, Quebec, the Museum of Arts and Design, New York, Corning Museum, Corning, New York, Carnegie Museum of Art, Pittsburgh, and many other prestigious institutions. The artist's work was included in the 2000 Whitney Biennial and the 2011 Venice Biennale. She is the recipient of a 2005 Guggenheim Fellowship, a USA Artists Fellowship, the Joan Mitchell Award, the Louis Comfort Tiffany Foundation Award, and two NEA grants.

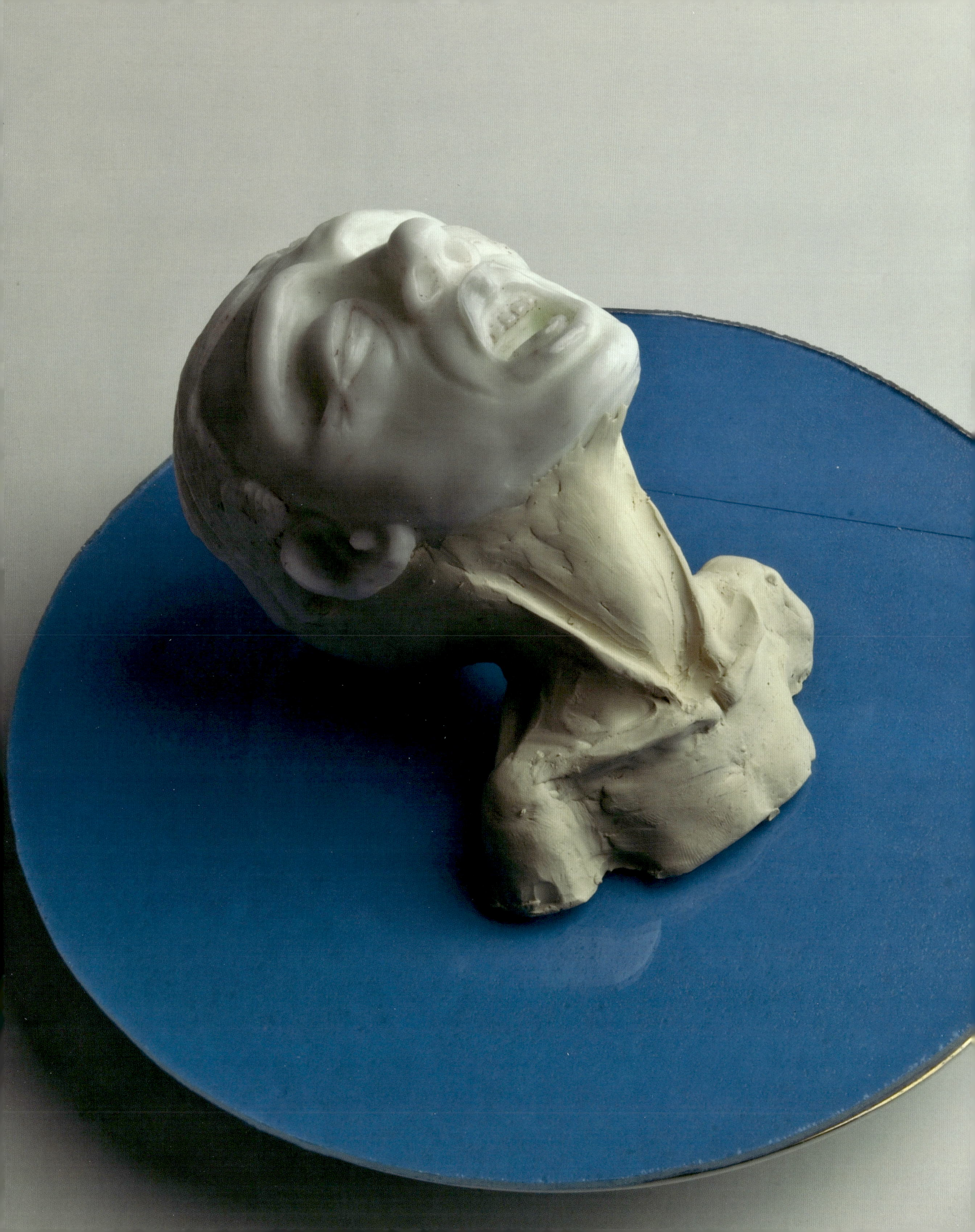

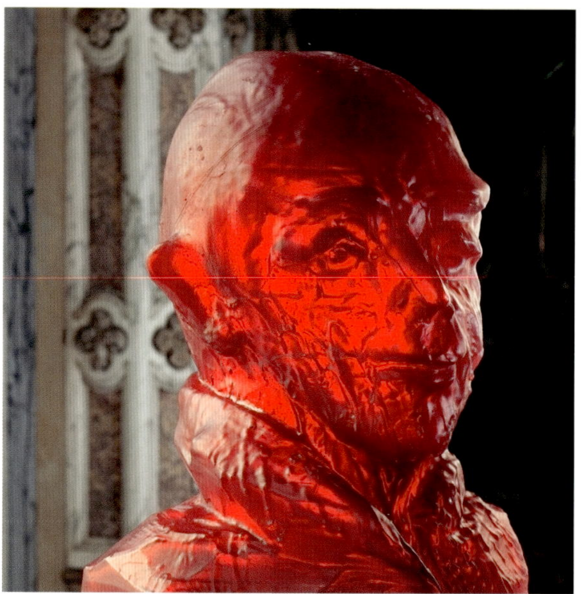

THOMAS SCHÜTTE

Thomas Schütte was born in Oldenburg, Germany, in 1954. He lives in Düsseldorf.

After studying painting with Daniel Buren, Gerhard Richter, and Blinky Palermo, he moved towards the worlds of sculpture and architecture. In the 1980s his architectural models inspired reflection on the social consequences of post-war reconstruction policies and choices in Germany. In his 1995 work *Haus das Gedenkens*, designed for the Neuengamme concentration camp, he addresses the question of the relationship between a work of art and the context in which it is placed. The theme of the artist's role in society permeates all his works. Unlike Joseph Beuys, according to whom the artist should act as a guide for civil society, Schütte believes the artist should describe reality with objective humor devoid of any foolish educational aspirations.

Architecture and such themes related to it as the concept of monumentality are other questions raised in his work. With his series of architectural models of real and imaginary buildings, he reflects on both the relationship of the structure to the surrounding space as well as the contrast between a building's grandeur and monumentality and the sometimes delicate appearance of materials that make it up, as in the work *Model for a Hotel,* 2007, on display in Trafalgar Square as part of a public art project.

His work is imbued with social and political issues, but also with such human feelings as vulnerability, isolation, and despair. The ambivalence and falsehood of modern society (*United Enemies*, 1993–1994) as well as its depravity (*Efficiency Men*, 2005) are depicted by Schütte in the iron and colored silicone sculptures that portray men with grotesque and caricatured faces, forced to stay together forever because they are tied together by lies or bent under the crushing weight of compromise.

He has exhibited in numerous museums around the world: the Van Abbemuseum, Eindhoven (1990); the Hamburger Kunsthalle, Hamburg (1994); the Württembergischer Kunstverein, Stuttgart (1994); the Musée d'Art Contemporain, Nîmes (1994); the Museu Serralves Porto, Porto (1998); the ARC, Paris 1990; the Whitechapel Art Gallery, London (1998); and the DIA Center for Contemporary Art, New York (1998–1999).

In 2005, he was awarded the Golden Lion at the Venice Biennale. In addition to having been invited three times to Documenta in Kassel, he was awarded the Düsseldorf Prize in 2010, previously given to Bruce Nauman, Marlene Dumas, and Rosemarie Trockel.

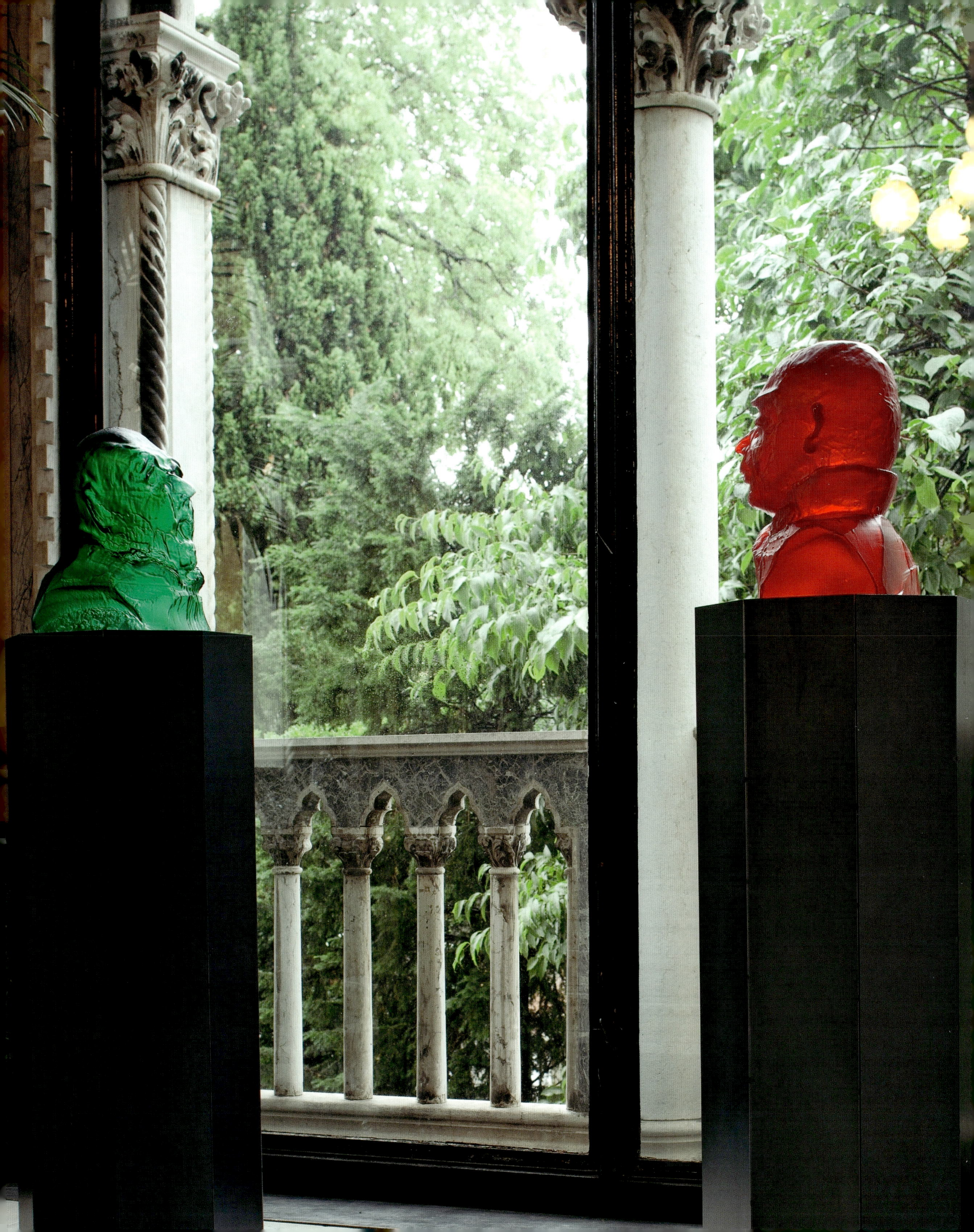

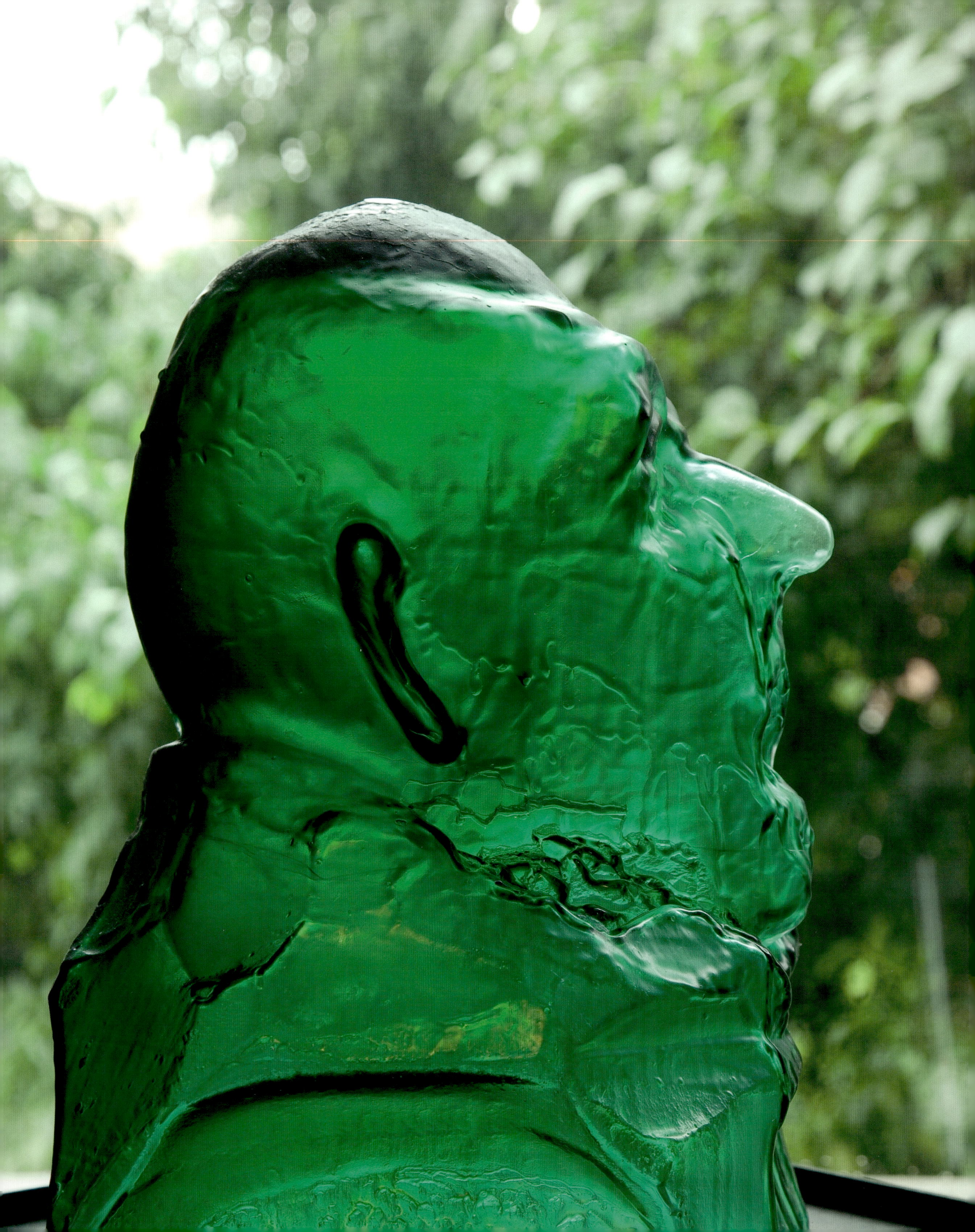

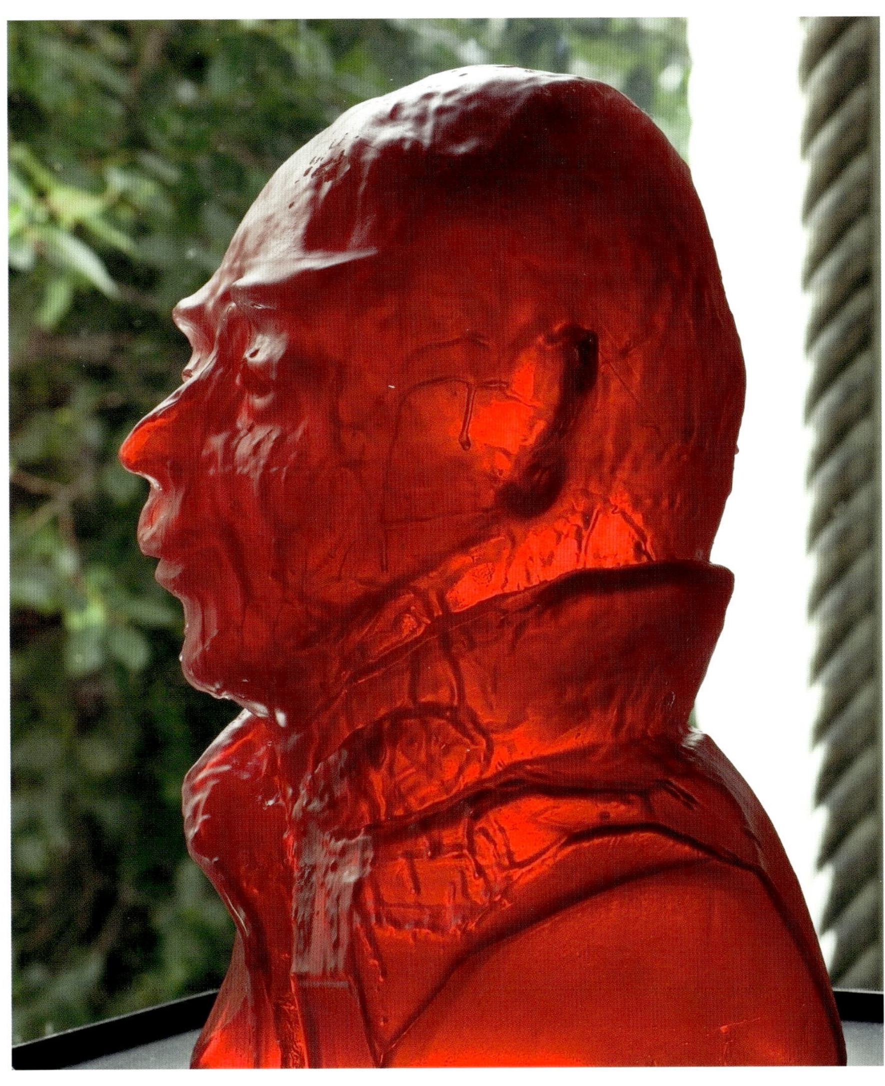

BERENGO HEAD
2011 / DETAIL
45 x 30 x 27 CM (GREEN HEAD) /
50 x 30 x 27 CM (RED HEAD)
COURTESY THE ARTIST
AND BERENGO PRIVATE COLLECTION, VENICE

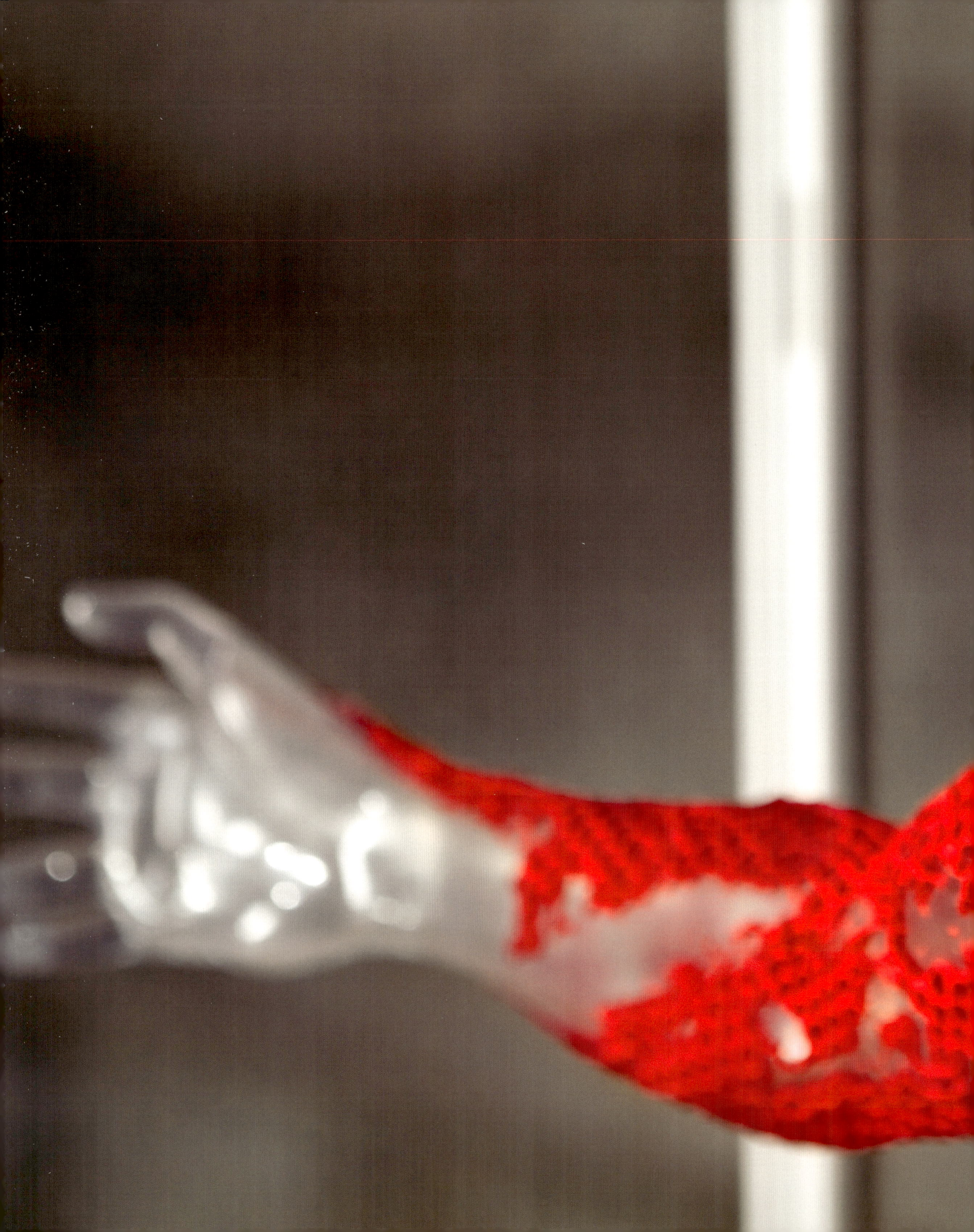

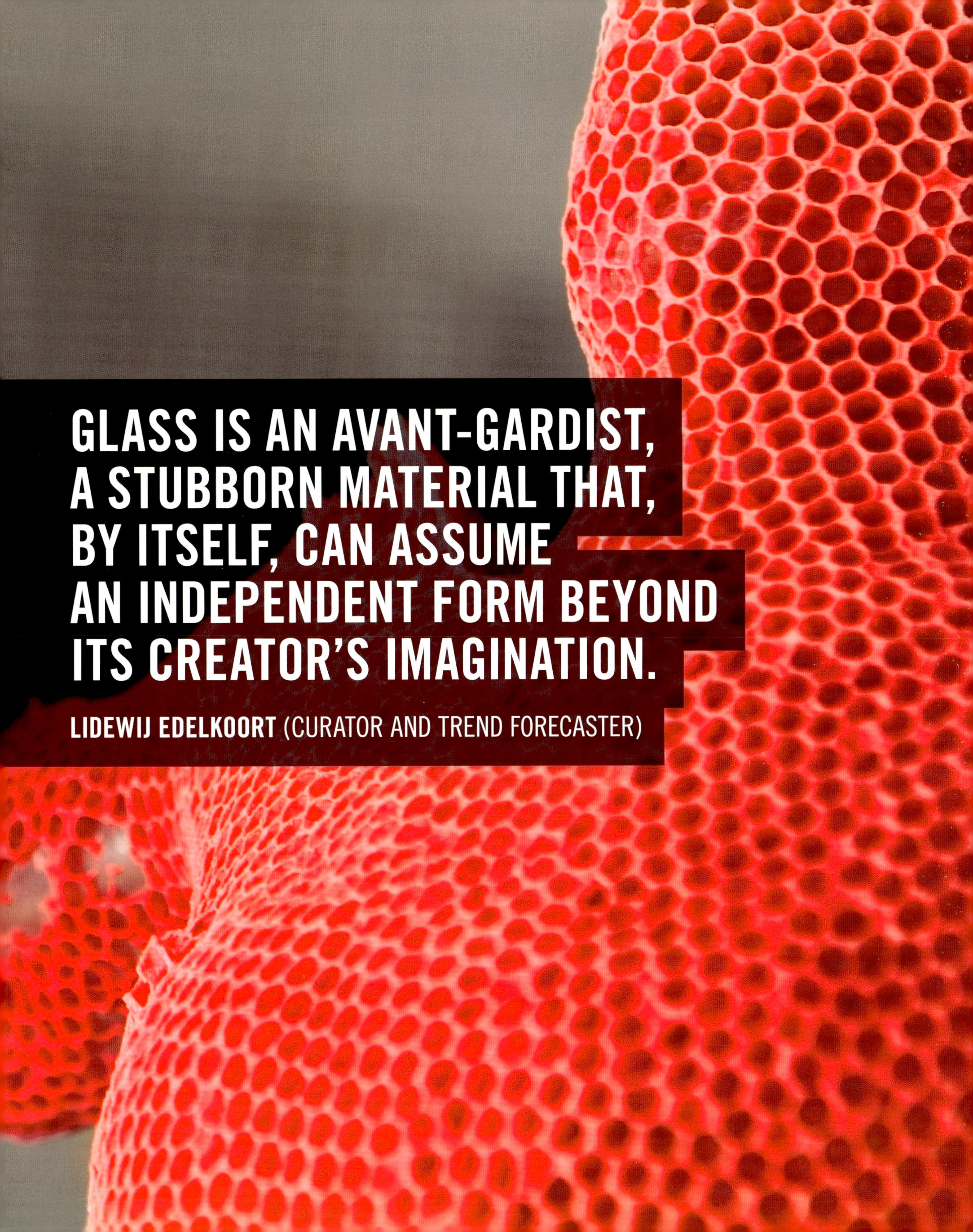

GLASS IS AN AVANT-GARDIST,
A STUBBORN MATERIAL THAT,
BY ITSELF, CAN ASSUME
AN INDEPENDENT FORM BEYOND
ITS CREATOR'S IMAGINATION.
LIDEWIJ EDELKOORT (CURATOR AND TREND FORECASTER)

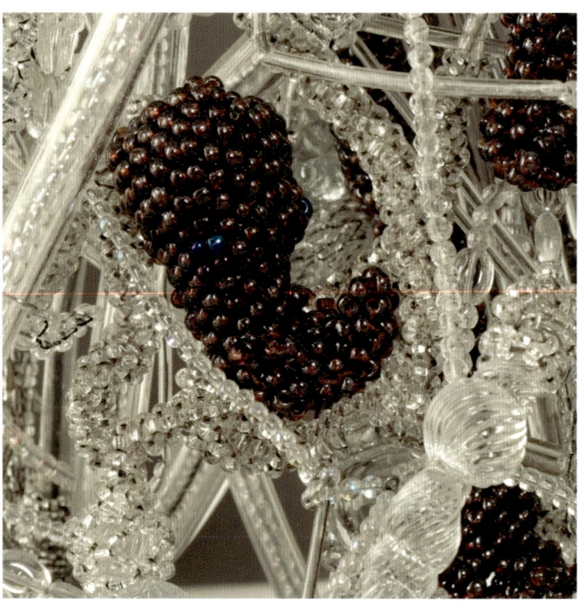

JOYCE JANE SCOTT

Joyce Jane Scott was born in 1948 in Baltimore, where she has been a lifetime resident. She descends from several generations of Southern craft artisans. Having made paintings, dolls, clothing, and jewelry in the 1960s, Scott's first artworks emerged in the early 1970s, colorful flat textiles made with her quilt-maker mother, with whom she continued to live and collaborate. Scott received a BFA degree from the Maryland Institute College of Art in 1970 and the following year an MFA in Crafts from Institute Allende in San Miguel Allende, Guanajuato, Mexico. She pursued further study at Rochester Institute of Technology in New York and then the Haystack Mountain School of Crafts in Maine. Using fiber, beads, wire, thread, and other mixed media, the strands of Joyce Jane Scott's urban, multi-ethnic African-American, female identity and experience unite in her art. Her flat weaving led to jewelry and soft sculptures that further flowered into the small standing figurative beadwork assemblages for which she is best known. Her art combines the caring humanism of craft with the intellectualism and political drive of social protest. Glass in the form of beadwork has been part of her art from its beginnings. Starting in the mid-1990s her collaborations with teams of artisans in several US glass shops and recently a Venetian glass studio have assumed a key role in her works. The resulting cast, blown, poured, and fused glass has increased the scale, sensuality, and seduction of her art. Scott's intensified fascination with and incorporation of African art and knockoffs of royal European porcelain has pushed the globalism and layered complexity of her vision. With her work now in numerous private and public collections, Scott's much increased importance and visibility connects with the broader shifts in the art world; the upgrading of craft and the media associated with it; the recognition of the talents and distinct visions of women artists; the diminution of the artistic centrality of New York City and New York artists; and the ascending acknowledgement and centrality of African-American artists. The first thirty years of Scott's art was surveyed in *Joyce J. Scott: Kicking' It With the Old Masters*, at The Baltimore Museum of Art, the Maryland Institute College of Art, and elsewhere in Baltimore. An updated, smaller solo show entitled *Kickin' It with Joyce J. Scott* toured to ten US museums from 2005 to 2007. A solo Scott museum show is currently being organized.

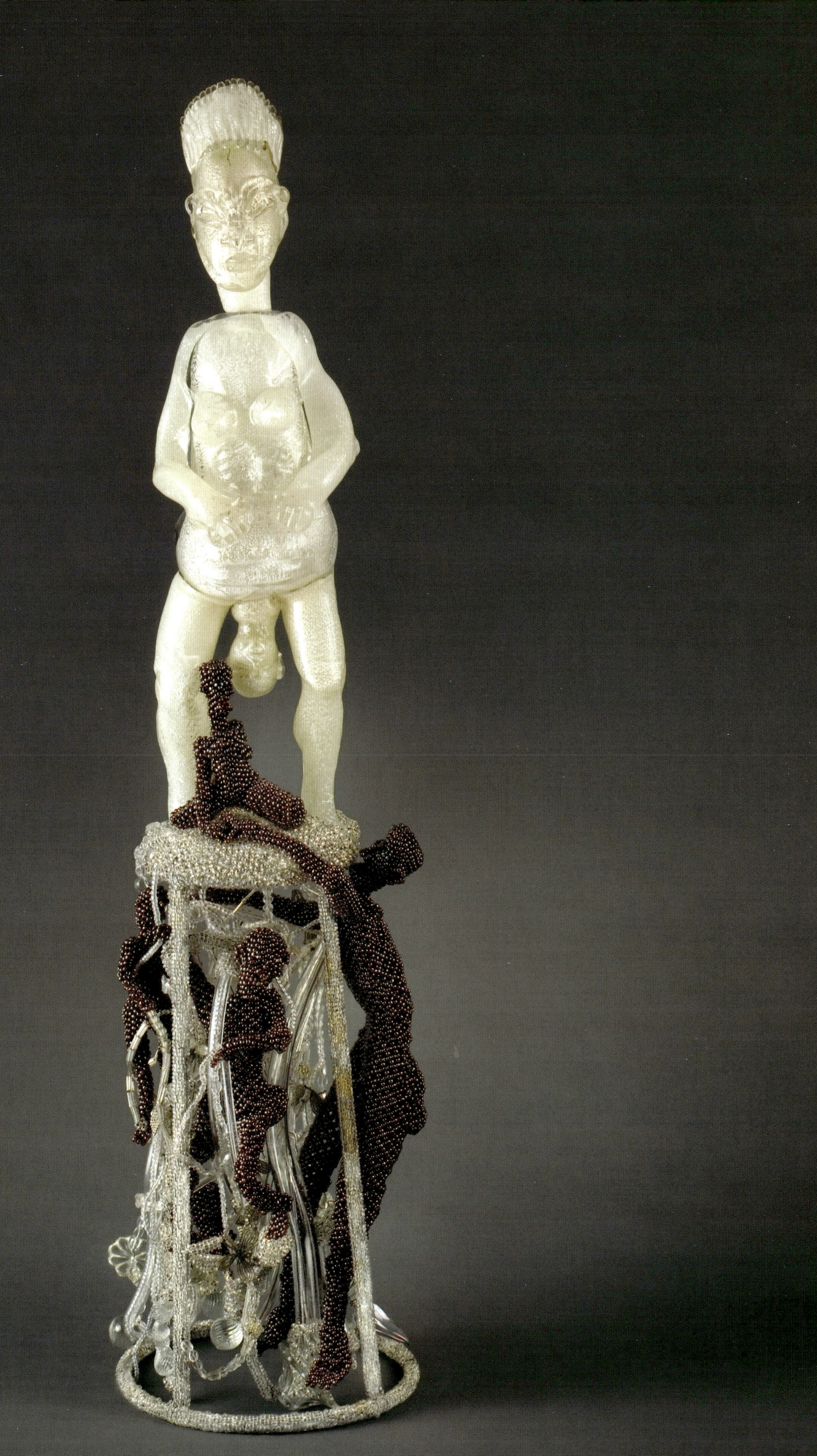

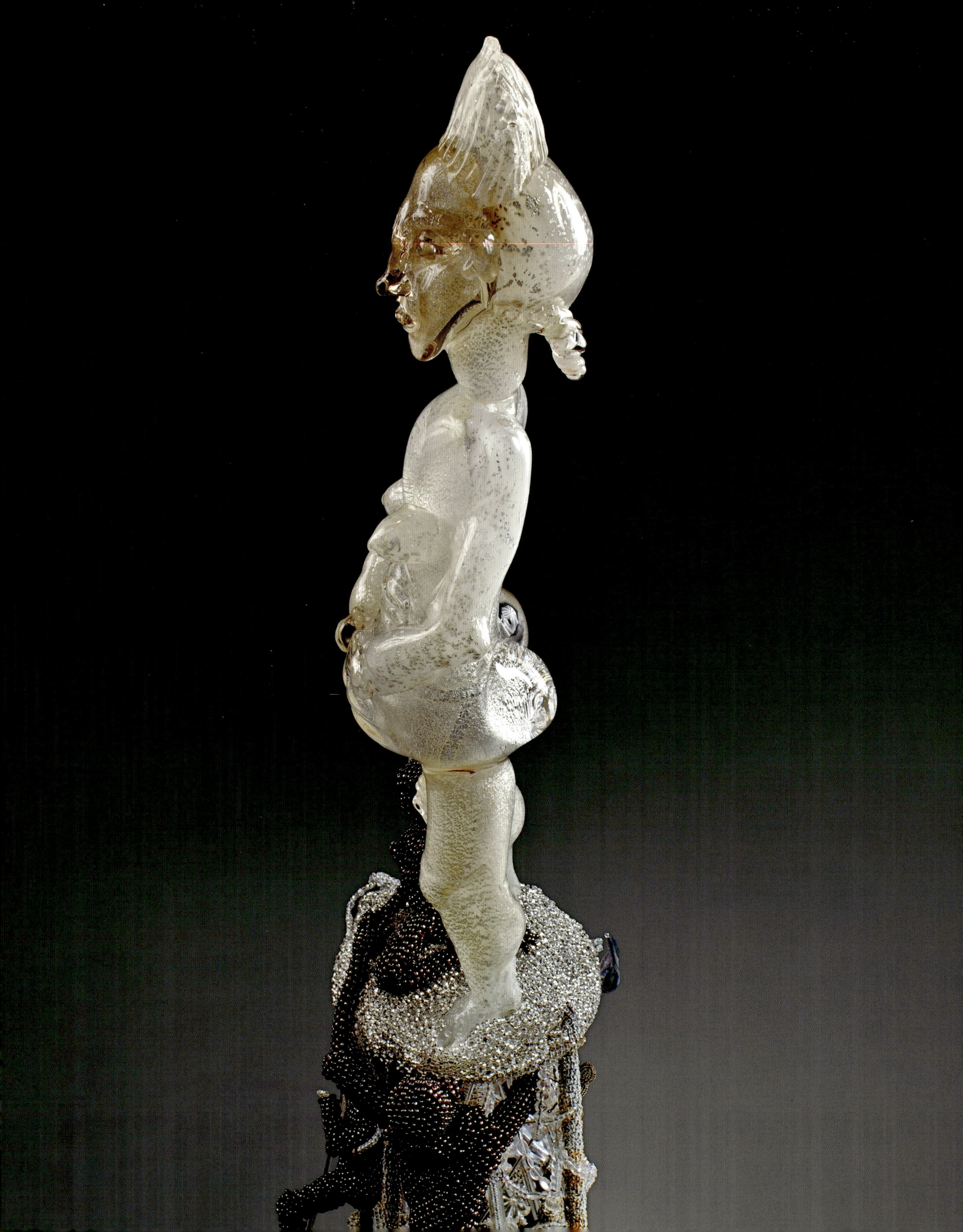

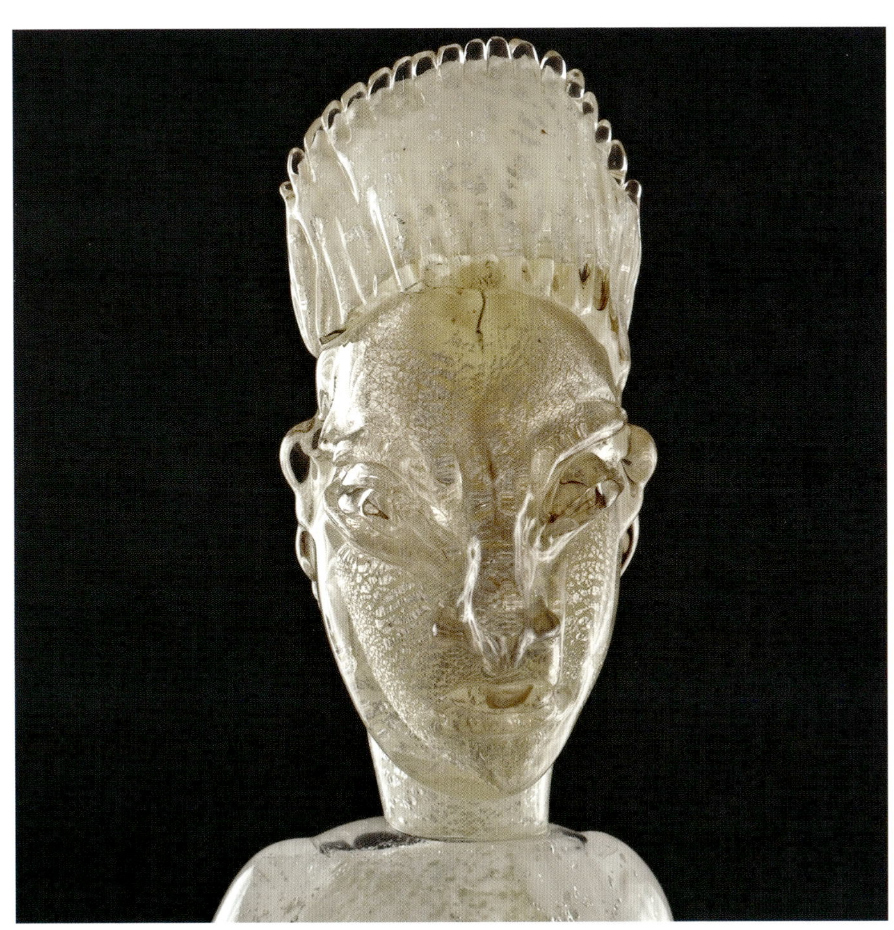

MILK MAMMY 1
2012 / *DETAIL*
113 x 30.5 x 27 CM
COURTESY GOYA CONTEMPORARY, BALTIMORE,
AND BERENGO STUDIO, VENICE

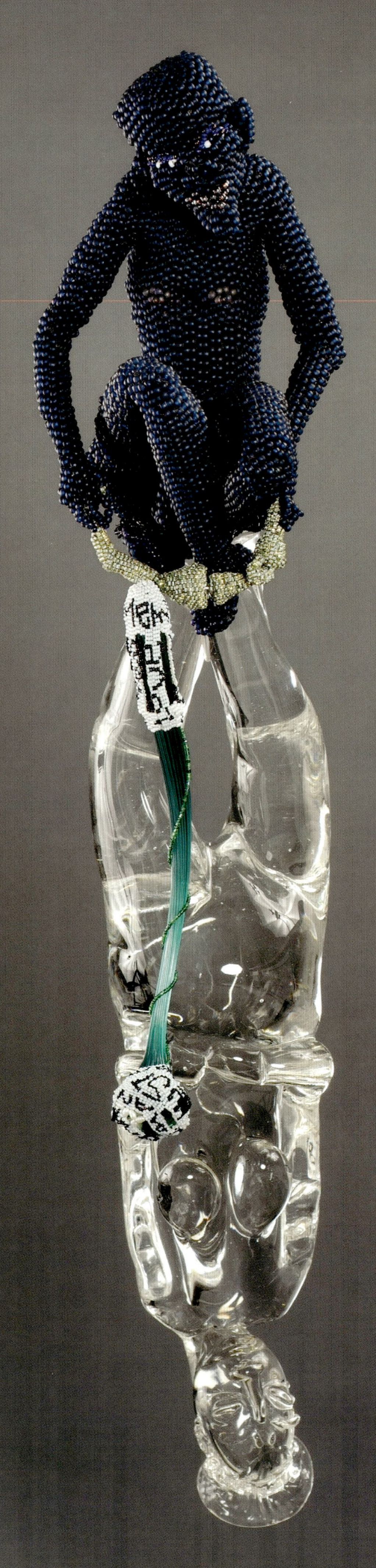

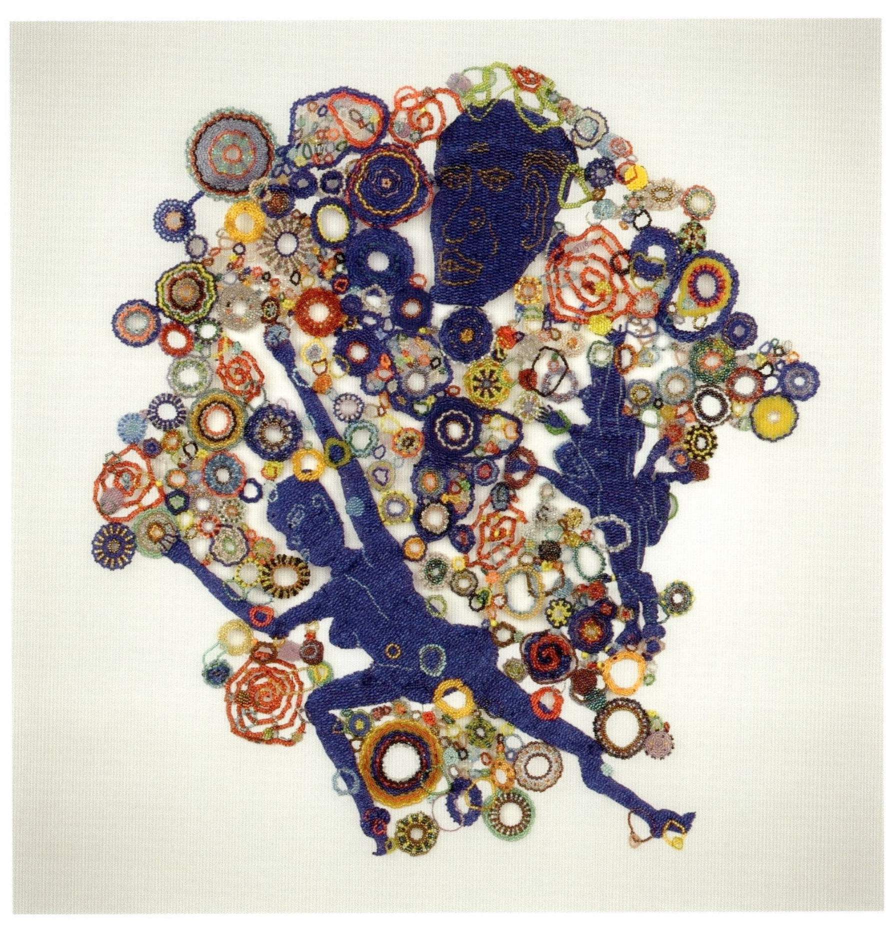

WATER MAMMY 1
2012
89 x 16.5 x 25.5 CM
COURTESY GOYA CONTEMPORARY, BALTIMORE,
AND BERENGO STUDIO, VENICE

COBALT, YELLOW CIRCLES
2010
53 x 49 CM
COURTESY PRIVATE COLLECTION, BALTIMORE,
AND GOYA CONTEMPORARY, BALTIMORE

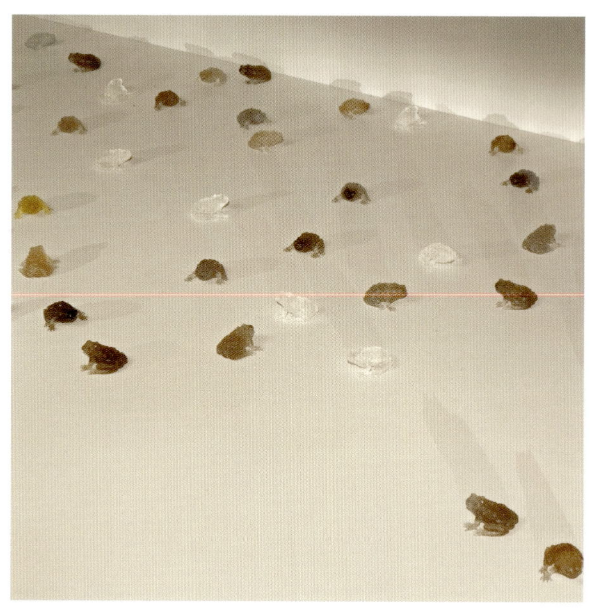

KIKI SMITH

Kiki Smith was born in Nuremberg, Germany, in 1954. She lives and works in New York.

The daughter of the sculptor Tony Smith, she began as a young girl by helping her father make cardboard models for his sculptures. Her work consists of sculptures, prints, and installations. In the 1980s, she abandoned the figurative tradition and produced objects and drawings based on organs, cells, and the human nervous system. Soon her work included animals, domestic objects, elements from folk tales and classical mythology. She is concerned with human nature and its philosophical, social, and spiritual aspects and her works also include a wide-ranging series of self-portraits. She deals with life, death, and resurrection, a legacy of her upbringing in the Catholic Church. Furthermore, she has always had a deep passion for working and collaborating with people in shared environments like universities, foundries, and print workshops which drove her to work in different countries.

Recently her work has been inspired by the life of St. Genevieve. She represents the saint along with a wolf, thus investigating the symbolic relationships between humans and animals. In 2003, a retrospective of her prints was held at MoMA in New York, followed by exhibitions at the Fondazione Querini Stampalia in Venice in 2005, the San Francisco Museum of Modern Art in 2006, and the Whitney Museum of American Art in 2007. In 2005, she was awarded the prestigious Showhegan Medal for Sculpture and in 2009 the Brooklyn Museum Women In The Arts Award.

Smith's work can be found in prestigious international museum collections such as the Metropolitan Museum of Art, New York, the Tate Modern, London, the Victoria and Albert Museum, London, and the Museum of Fine Arts, Boston.

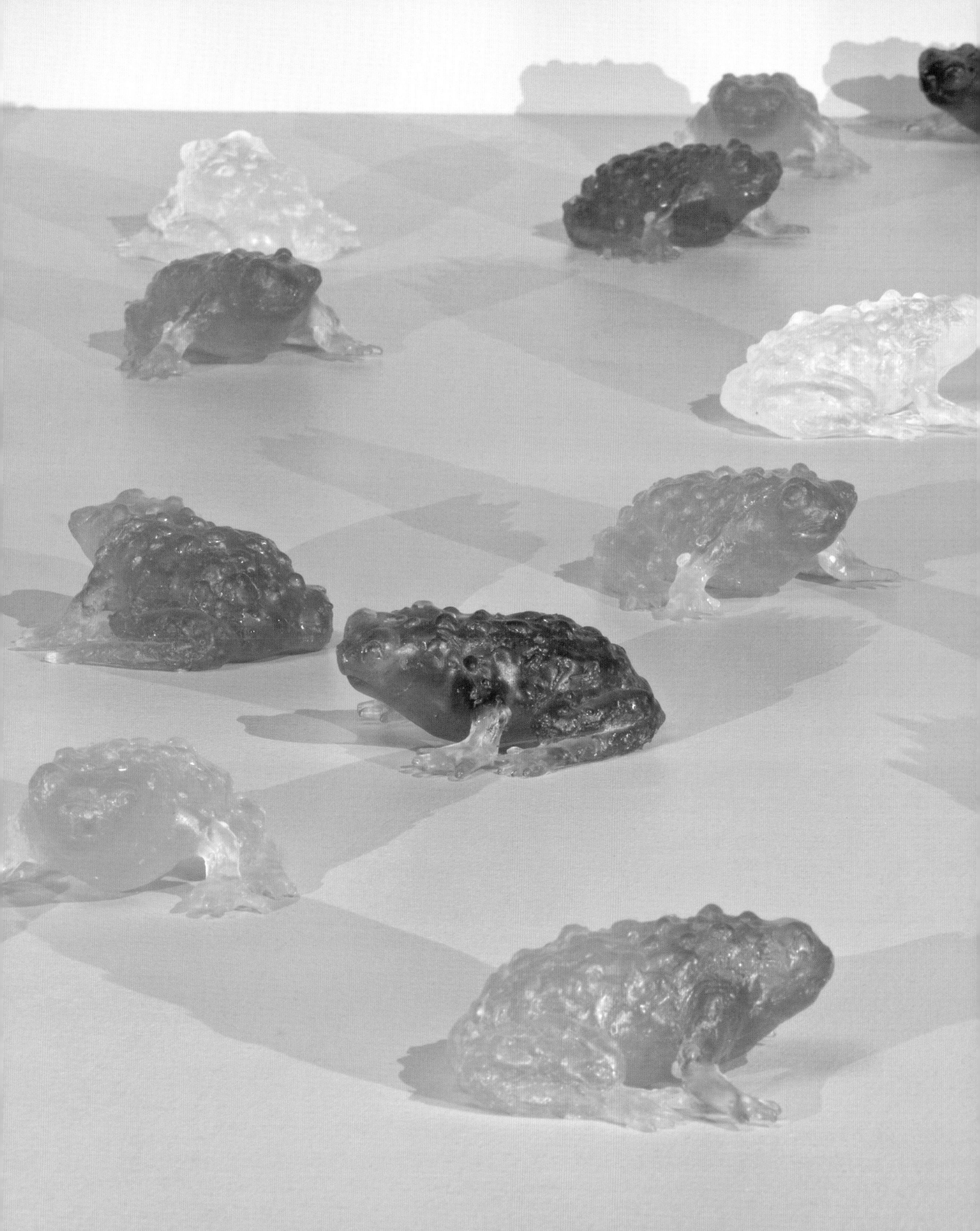

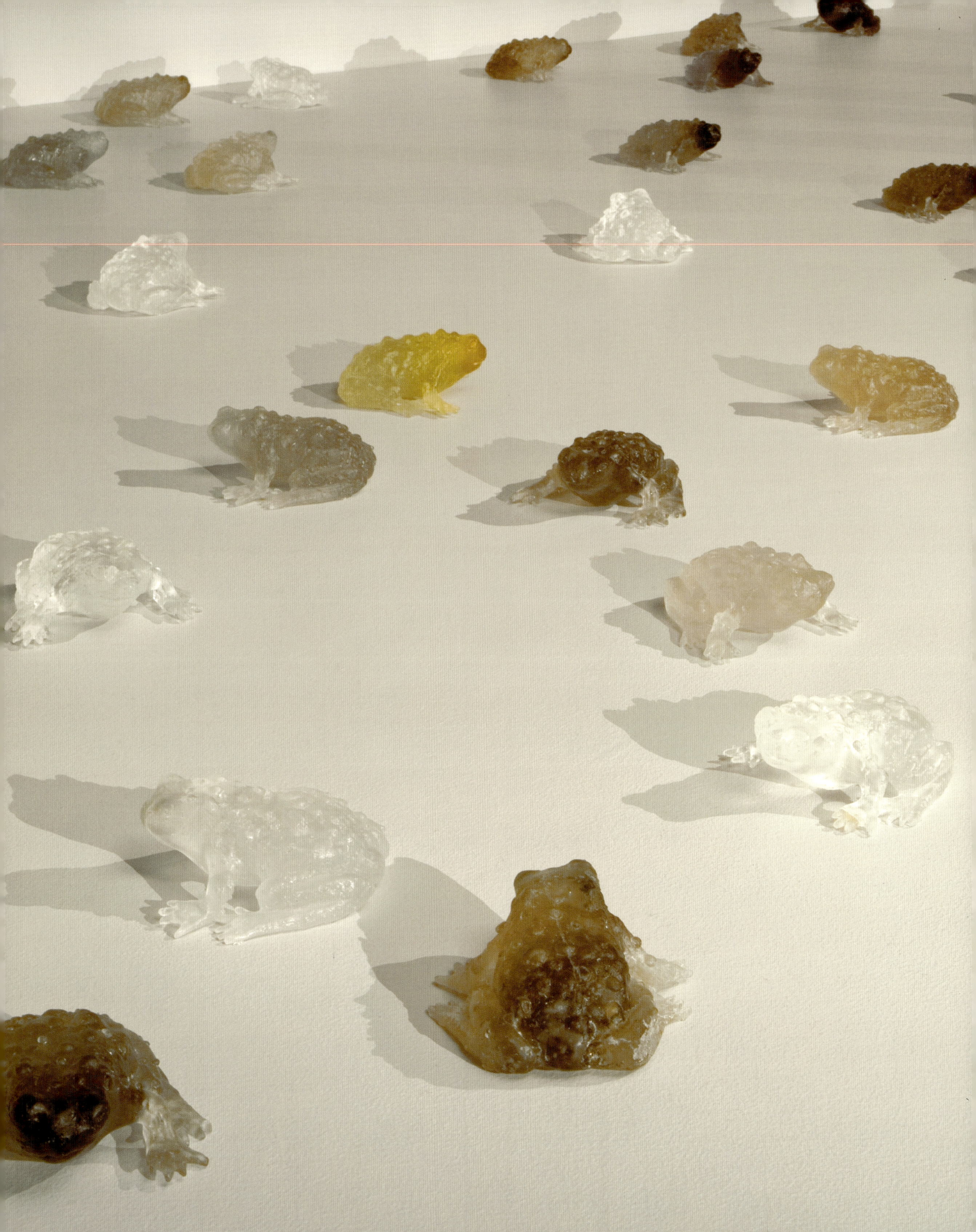

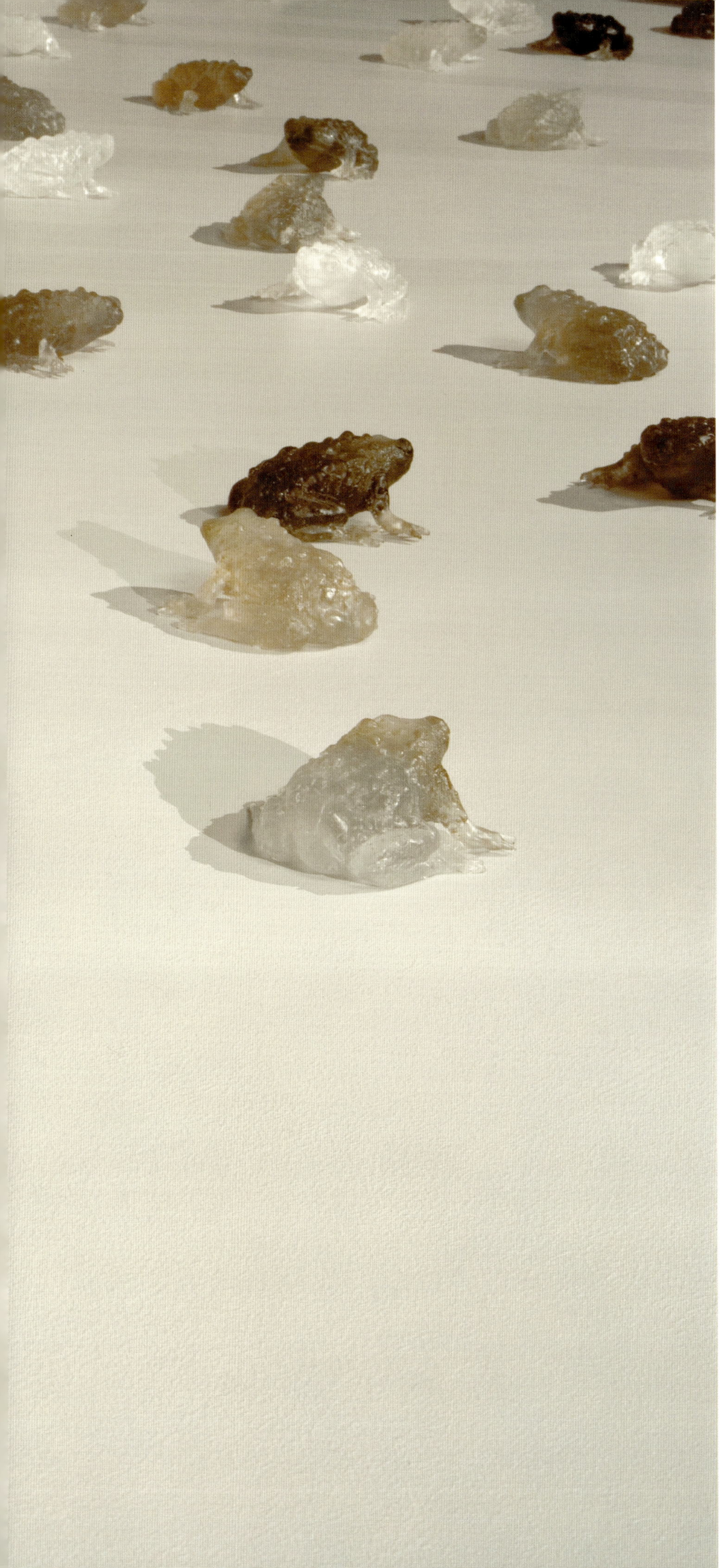

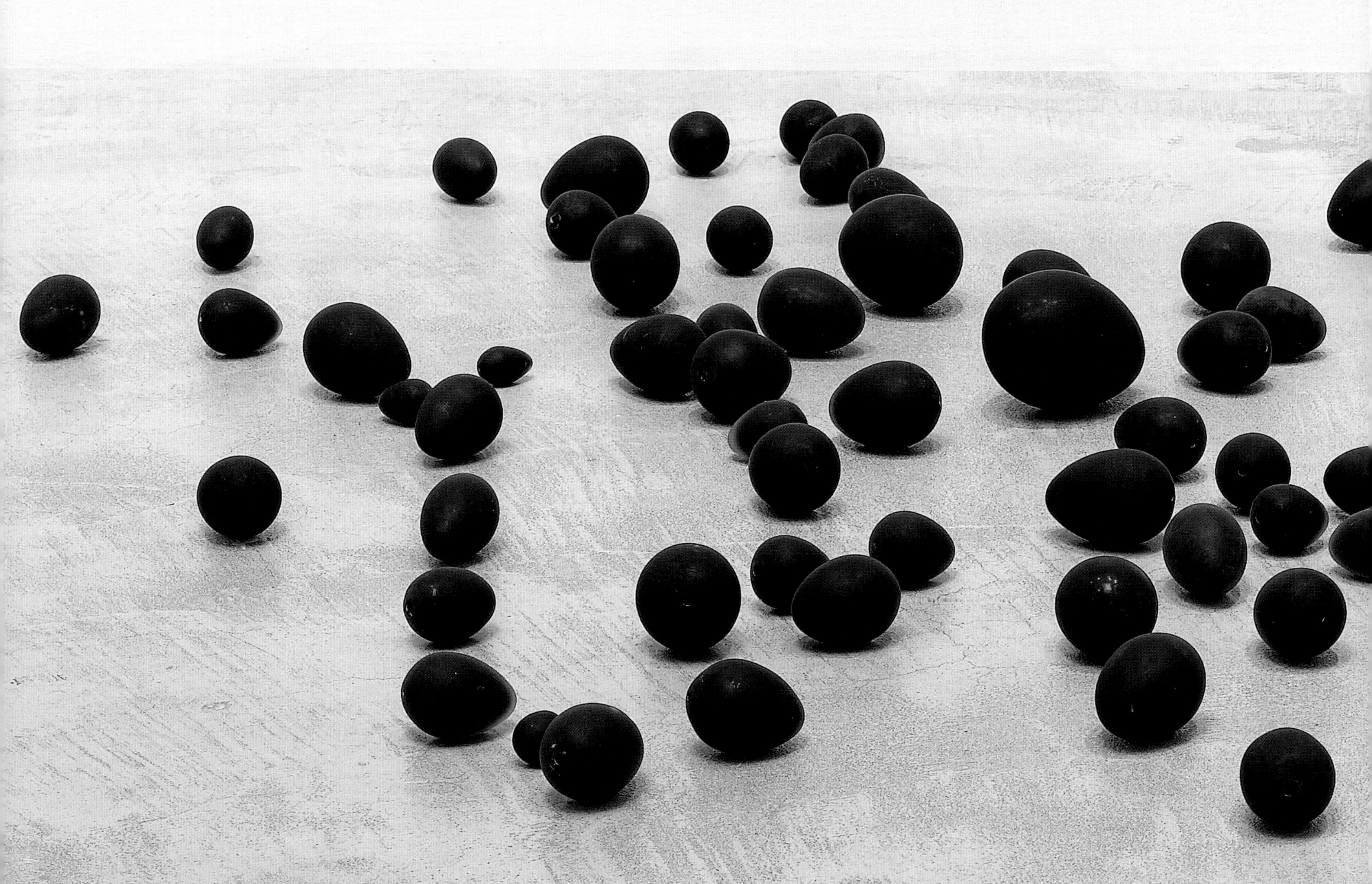

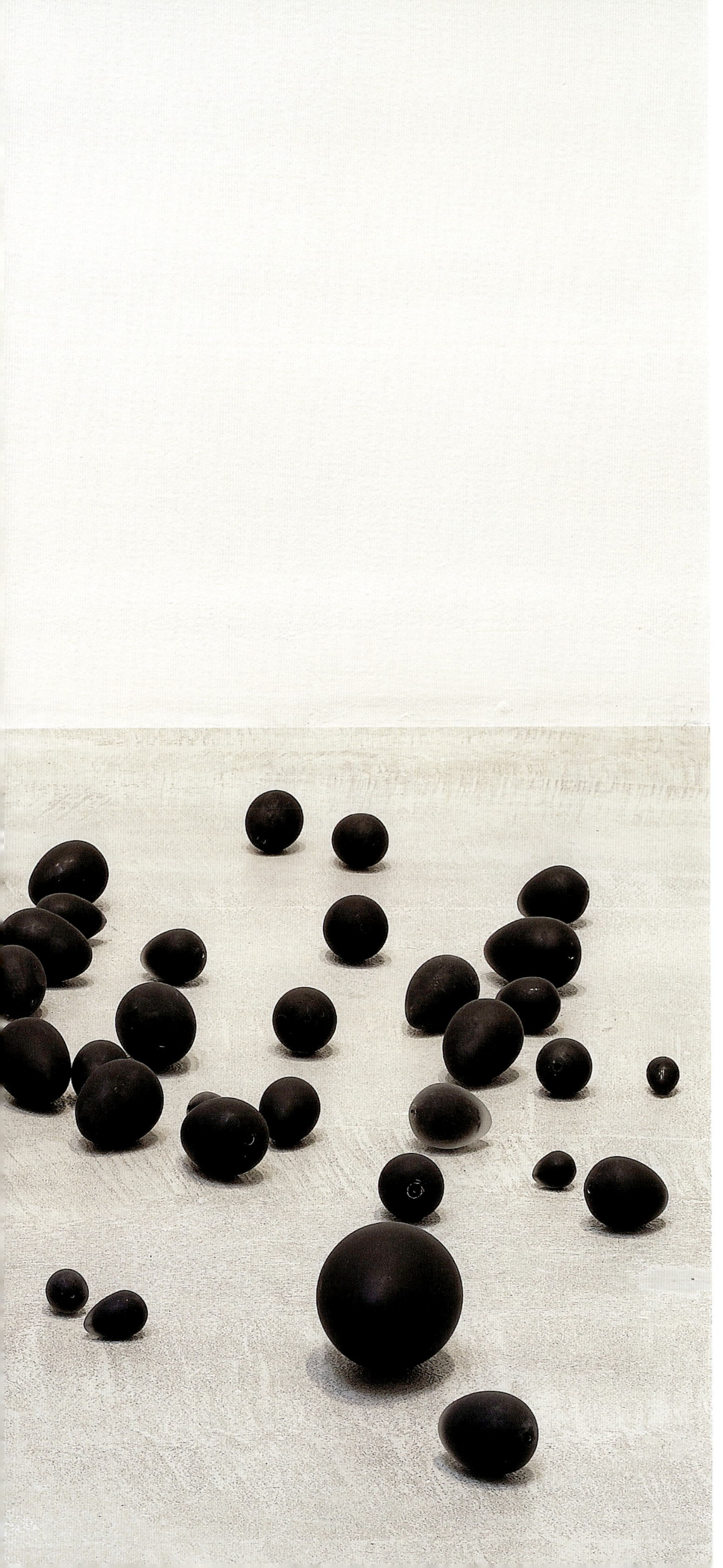

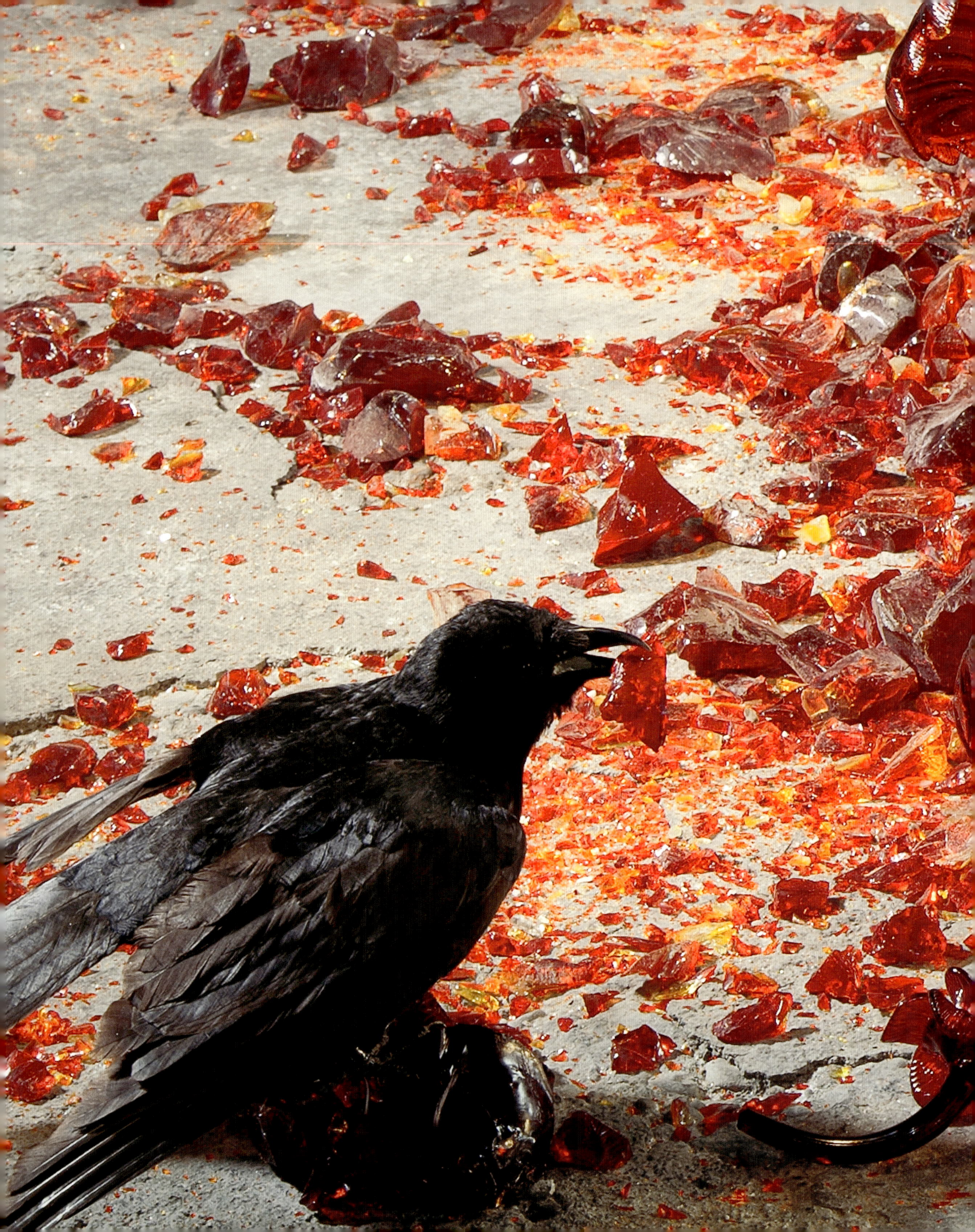

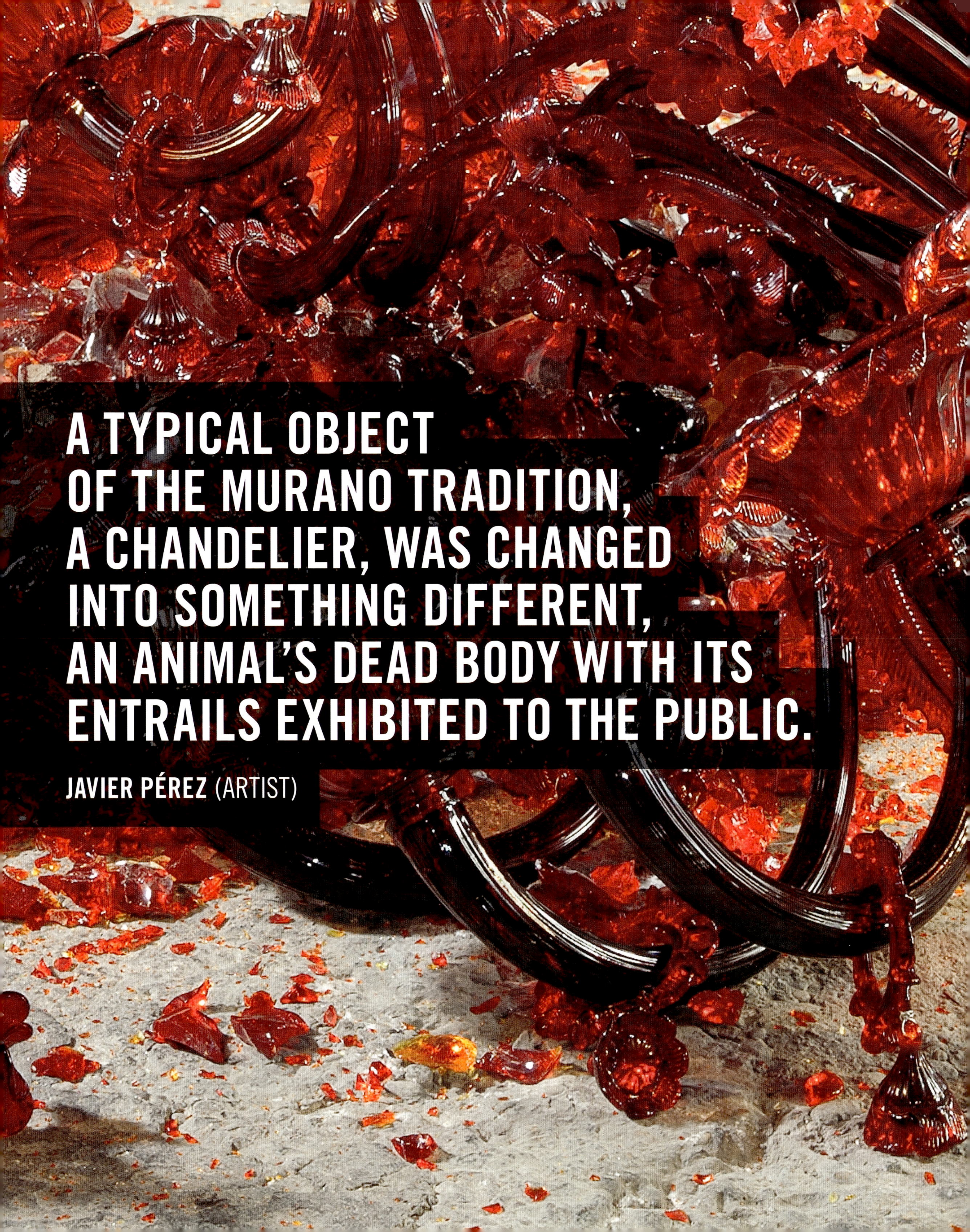
A TYPICAL OBJECT
OF THE MURANO TRADITION,
A CHANDELIER, WAS CHANGED
INTO SOMETHING DIFFERENT,
AN ANIMAL'S DEAD BODY WITH ITS
ENTRAILS EXHIBITED TO THE PUBLIC.
JAVIER PÉREZ (ARTIST)

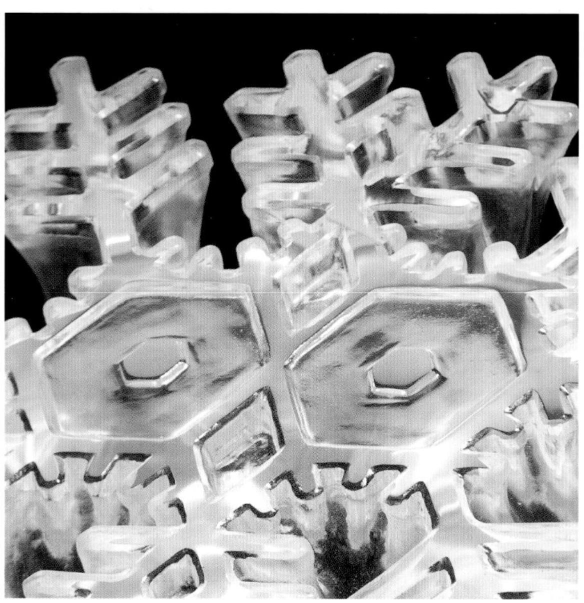

YUTAKA SONE

Sone was born in 1965 in Shizuoka, Japan, and currently lives and works in Los Angeles.

The artist's architectural training has had a profound effect on his subsequent artistic output, which is marked by an almost obsessive attention to detail and by the structural-volumetrical construction of his pieces.

Yutaka Sone is primarily a sculptor, but he has often resorted to painting, drawing, photography, video, and performance.

Known for his love of nature, that which truly characterizes his work is found in his rejection of the dialectical and in the contrast between nature and artifice. Sone concerns himself with micro- and macrocosms, the natural and the artificial, without distinction. His works are created by combining organic and synthetic materials and by contrasting the city's image with that of the jungle. It was in this sense that *Little Manhattan*, 2007–2009, was created, a depiction of the city laboriously carved, in minute detail, from a block of marble and worked out using photographs, Google Earth, and helicopter flights over the city.

A particular interest in the utopian aspects of language and narrative emerges from his artwork, with the island being, in this sense, a recurring theme.

His most recent solo exhibitions include *Baby Banana Tree* at the Boone Sculpture Garden in Pasadena, California, (2009); *Yutaka Sone: Snow* at the Maison Hermès Le Forum in Tokyo (2010); and *Yutaka Sone: Perfect Moment* at the Tokyo Opera City Art Gallery (2011).

He has also exhibited at the Museum of Contemporary Art in Los Angeles (2003); the 50th Venice Biennale (2003), representing Japan, together with Motohiko Odan; the Kunsthalle in Bern, Switzerland; the Aspen Art Museum in Colorado (2006); and the Parasol Unit Foundation for Contemporary Art in London (2007).

Among his major exhibitions are the 7th Istanbul Biennial (2001); the 25th Bienal de São Paulo (2003); the 2004 Whitney Biennial at the Whitney Museum of American Art (2004); and *Badlands: New Horizons in Landscape* at the Massachusetts Museum of Contemporary Art (2008).

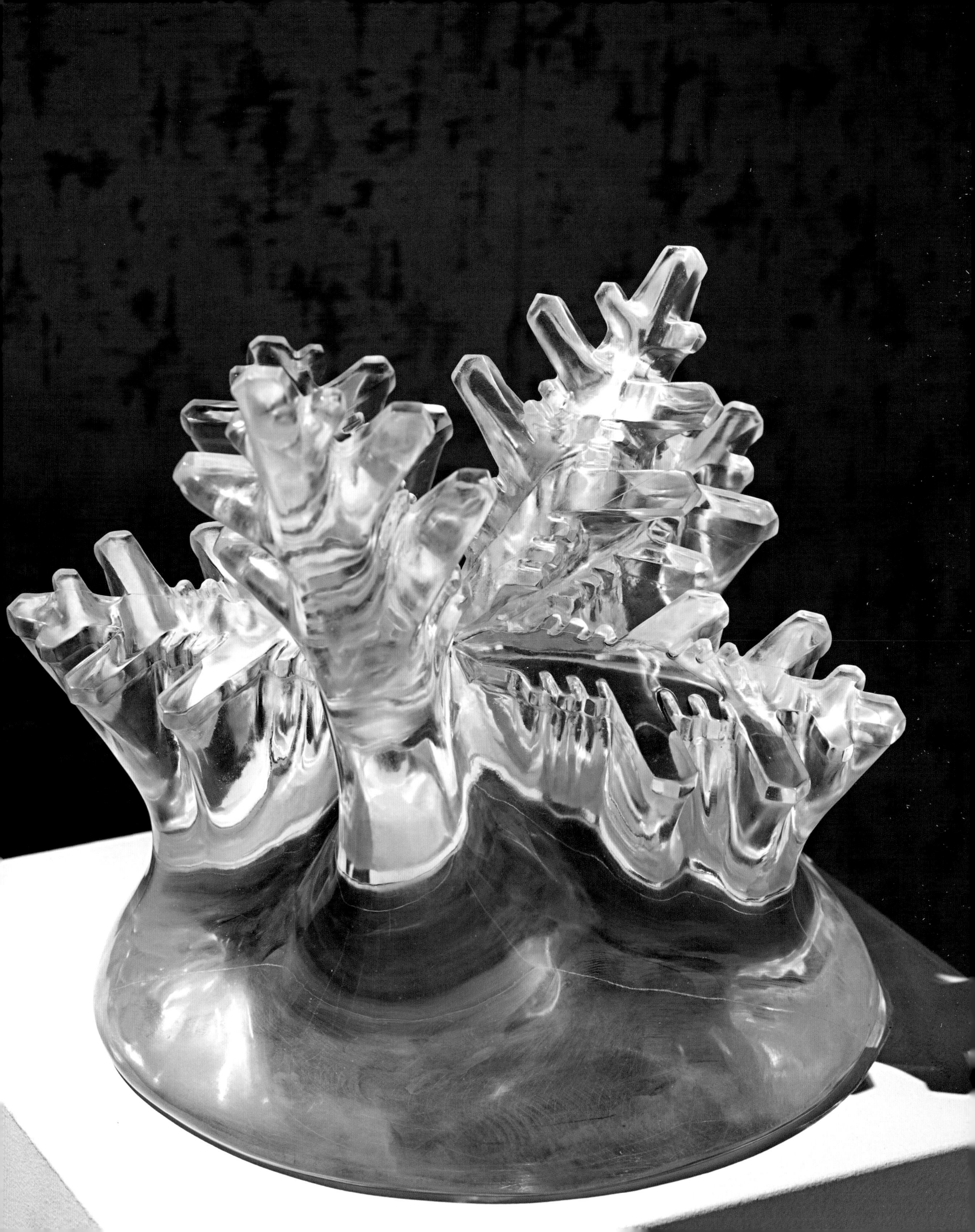

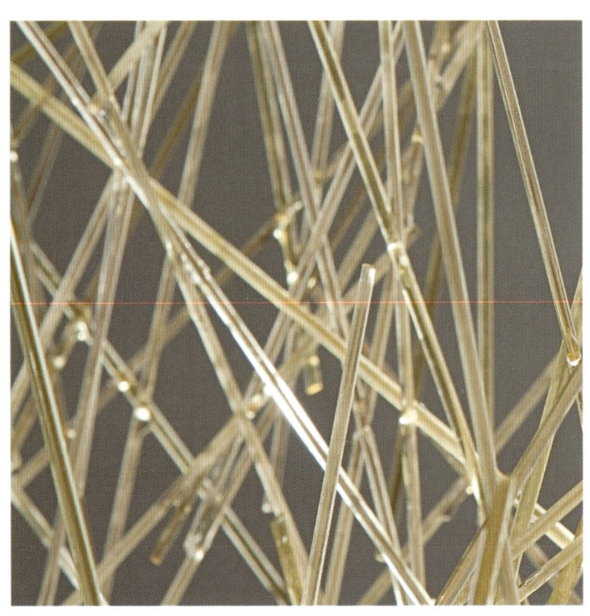

MIKE + DOUG STARN

Mike and Doug Starn were born in New Jersey in 1961. At present, they live and work in New York.

In the 1980s they began to challenge categorization, working with photography in combination with sculpture, painting, video, and installation.

Their most recent work is entitled *Big Bambù*, 2008, a monumental bamboo structure made by combining different creative and design skills in a single installation. The large-scale work (15 meters high) was made possible with the help of a group of climbers who built the structure, whose size, like a living organism, grows in spring and shrinks in autumn. The installation is a work in progress that adapts to the exhibition space and the season, growing and developing with the passage of time.

This recent work is closely related to their early work in which the artists once filled trees, insects, and leaves with a particular symbolic and metaphorical importance.

Even light, for the Starn Brothers, assumes a central role at both a technical and a symbolic level. Indeed, it represents a cycle of time and change and it interests them also as a work tool. Their artistic explorations have revolved around light absorption techniques and old carbon-printing techniques.

Their works include *Sphere of Influence*, 1994, *Behind Your Eye*, 2004, *Absorption + Transmission*, 2005/2006, and *Gravity of Light*, 2004/2008.

The Starns have received arts grants (1987 and 1995) and the Infinity Award for Fine Art Photography (1992). In the 1990s they received an artistic commission from NASA.

Their principal works are found in such private and public collections as those of the Museum of Modern Art, the Solomon R. Guggenheim Museum, and the Whitney Museum of American Art, New York; the Museum of Modern Art in San Francisco; The National Gallery of Victoria in Melbourne; and La Maison Européenne de la Photographie in Paris.

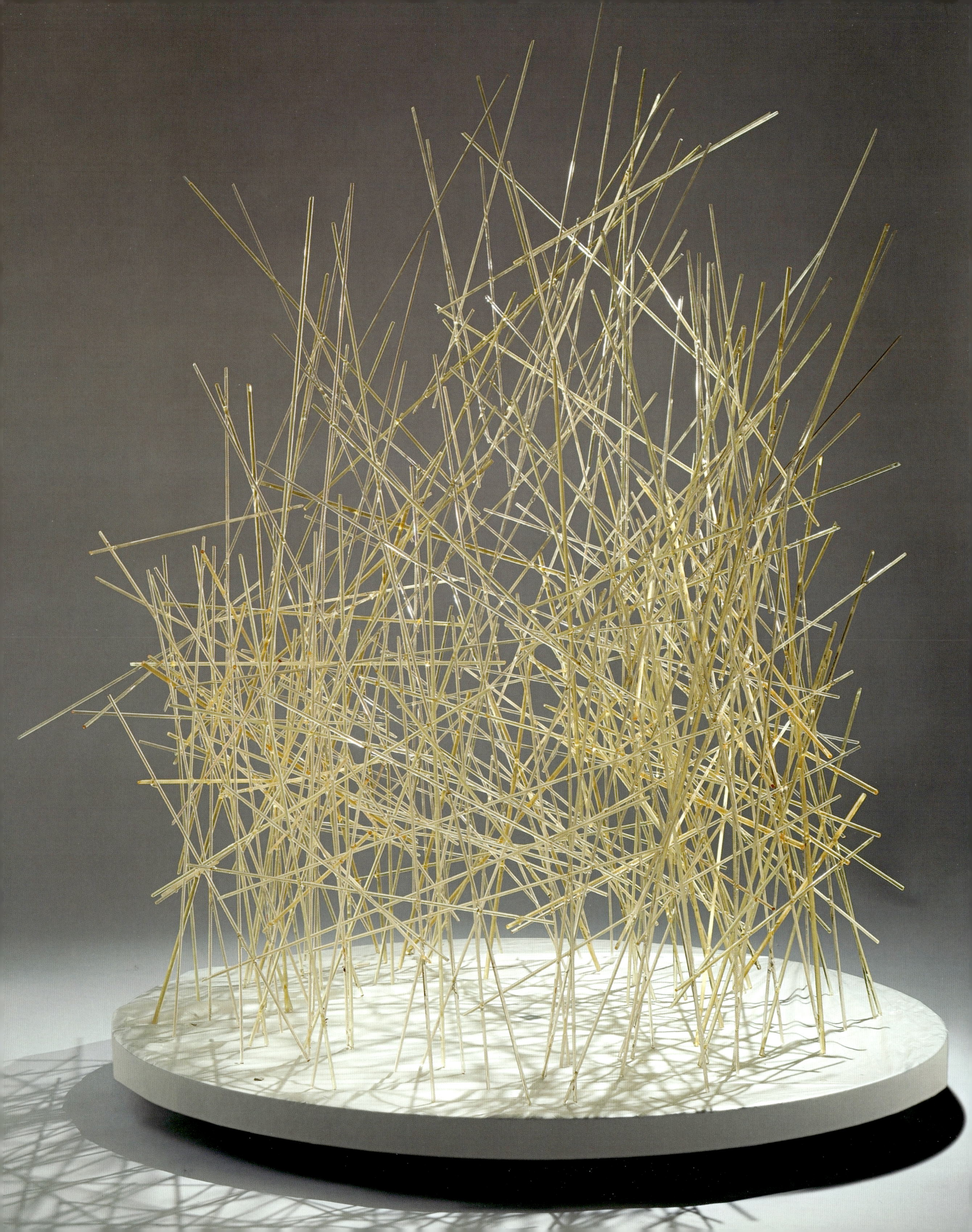

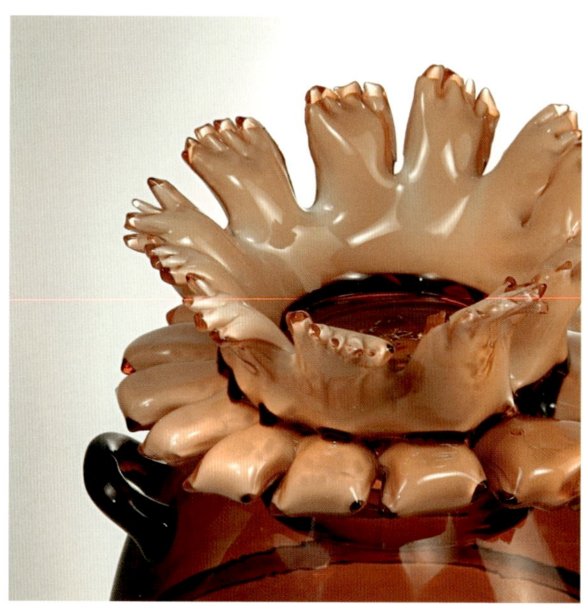

PATRICIA URQUIOLA

Patricia Urquiola was born in 1961 in Oviedo, Spain. She attended the Department of Architecture at the Universidad Politécnica de Madrid and then moved to Italy to attend the Politecnico di Milano. In the early 1990s, she became the assistant of Eugenio Bettinelli and Achille Castiglioni.

As a teacher, she began a series of lessons at both the Politecnico and the ENSCI in Paris. She then undertook a series of collaborations: she opened an architecture and design firm, worked with Vico Magistretti, managed the firm of Lissoni Associati, worked with such prestigious brands as Alessi, Artelano, Kartell, Cappellini, Cassina and, at the same time, with De Vecchi, Fasem, MDF Italia, Moroso, and B & B for whom she created three collections: Canasta, Crinoline, and Ravel, between 2007 and 2009.

Patricia Urquiola's works are a perfect combination of minimalism and femininity, especially admired for her harmonious use of form and light. Her works are characterized by a continuous experimentation with new forms and styles. She gained international recognition in 2001 and opened her first studio of design and architecture. That same year some of her works were selected for the Italian Design and the International Design Yearbook exhibitions. She was chosen as the jury president for the 19th CDIM Design Award and has held conferences at the Domus Academy. In recent years, she has received numerous awards including Designer of the Year and Design Prize Cologne. At present, Patricia Urquiola continues her many activities in her Milano studio. In 2011, she enthusiastically accepted the invitation to the *Glasstress* exhibition, a collateral event of the 54th International Art Exhibition, Venice Biennale, from Adriano Berengo, the event's originator and organizer, for which she created a highly original collection of blown glass, a material with which she had not yet experimented and which was greatly appreciated by the public and the press.

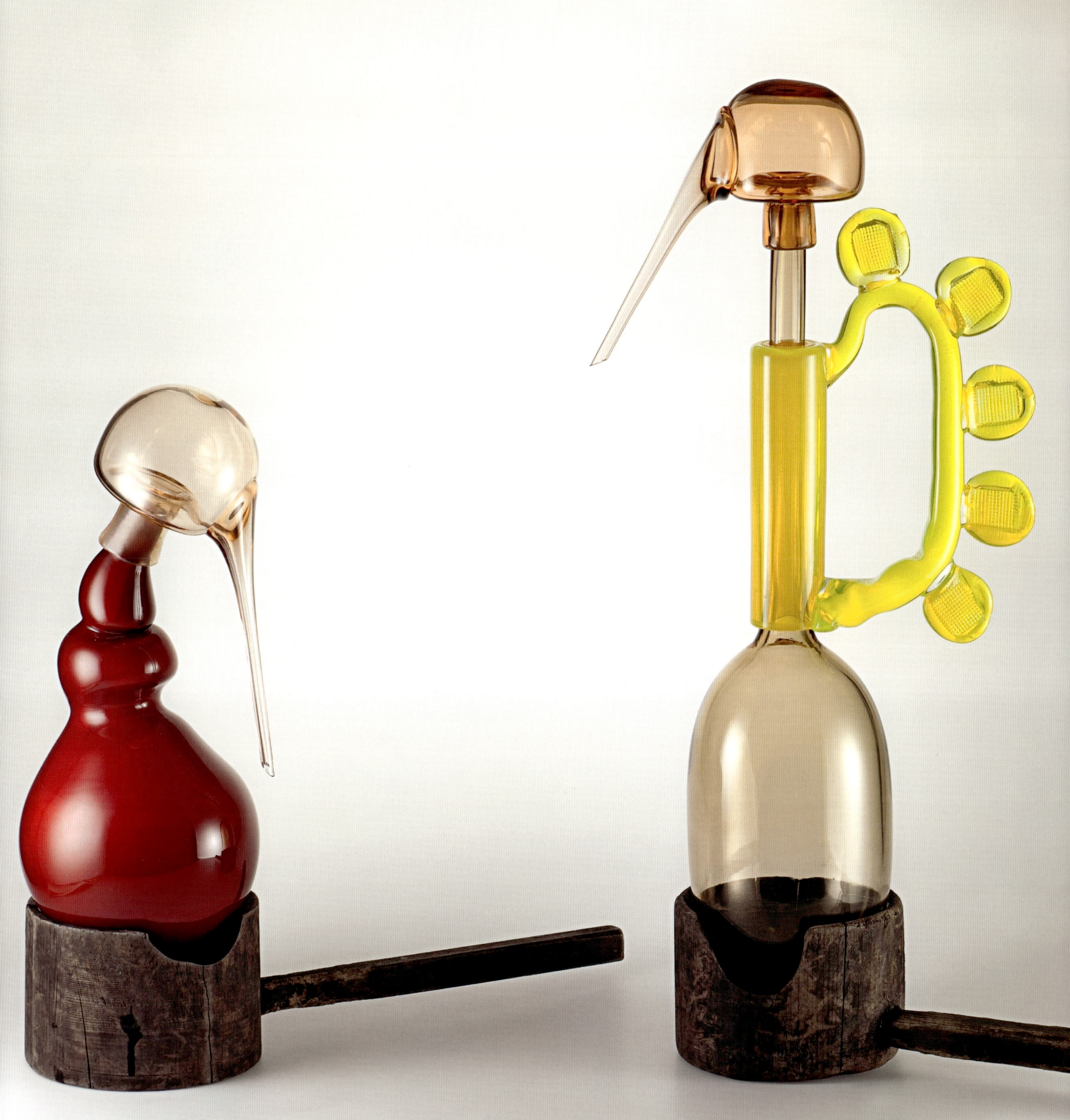

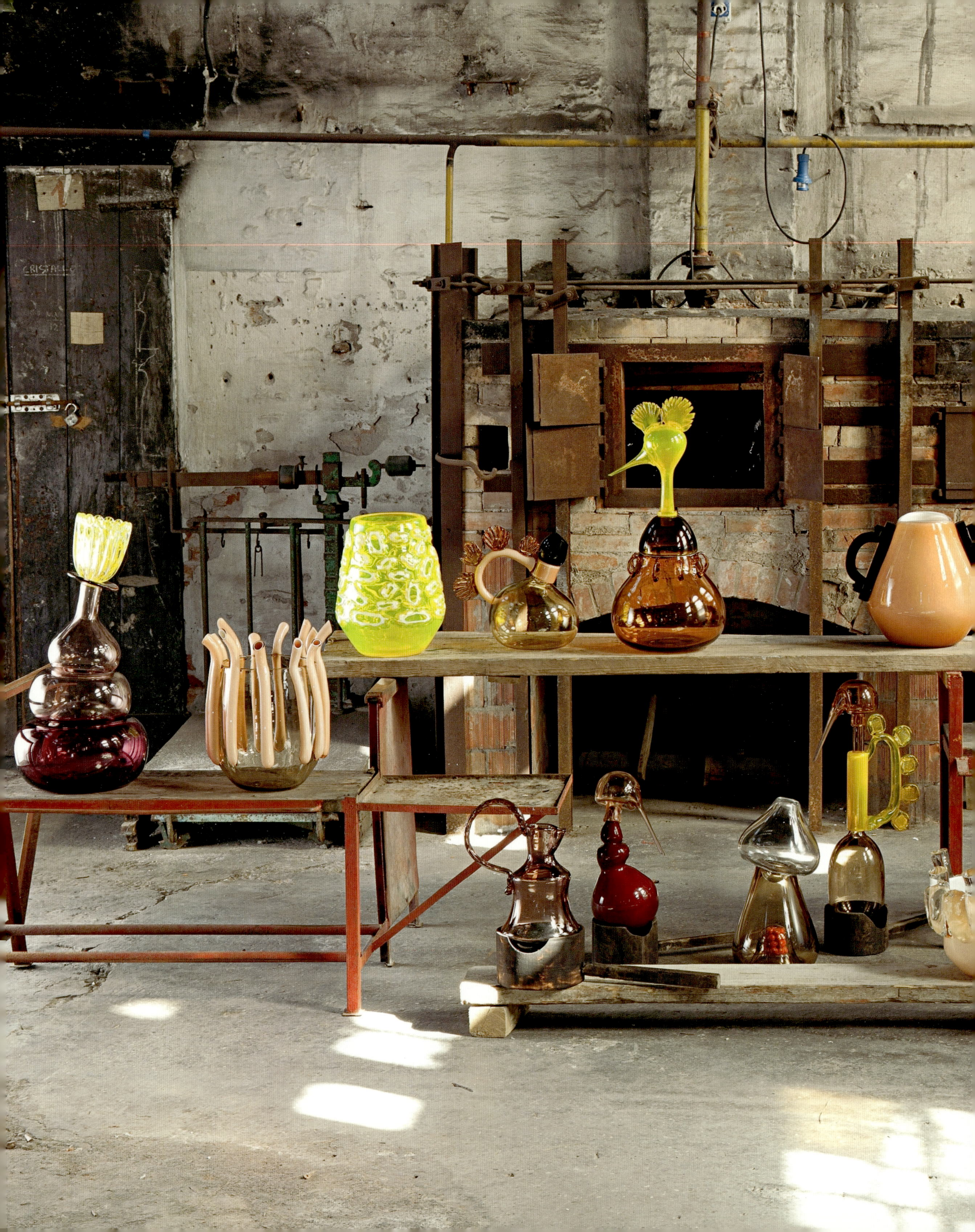

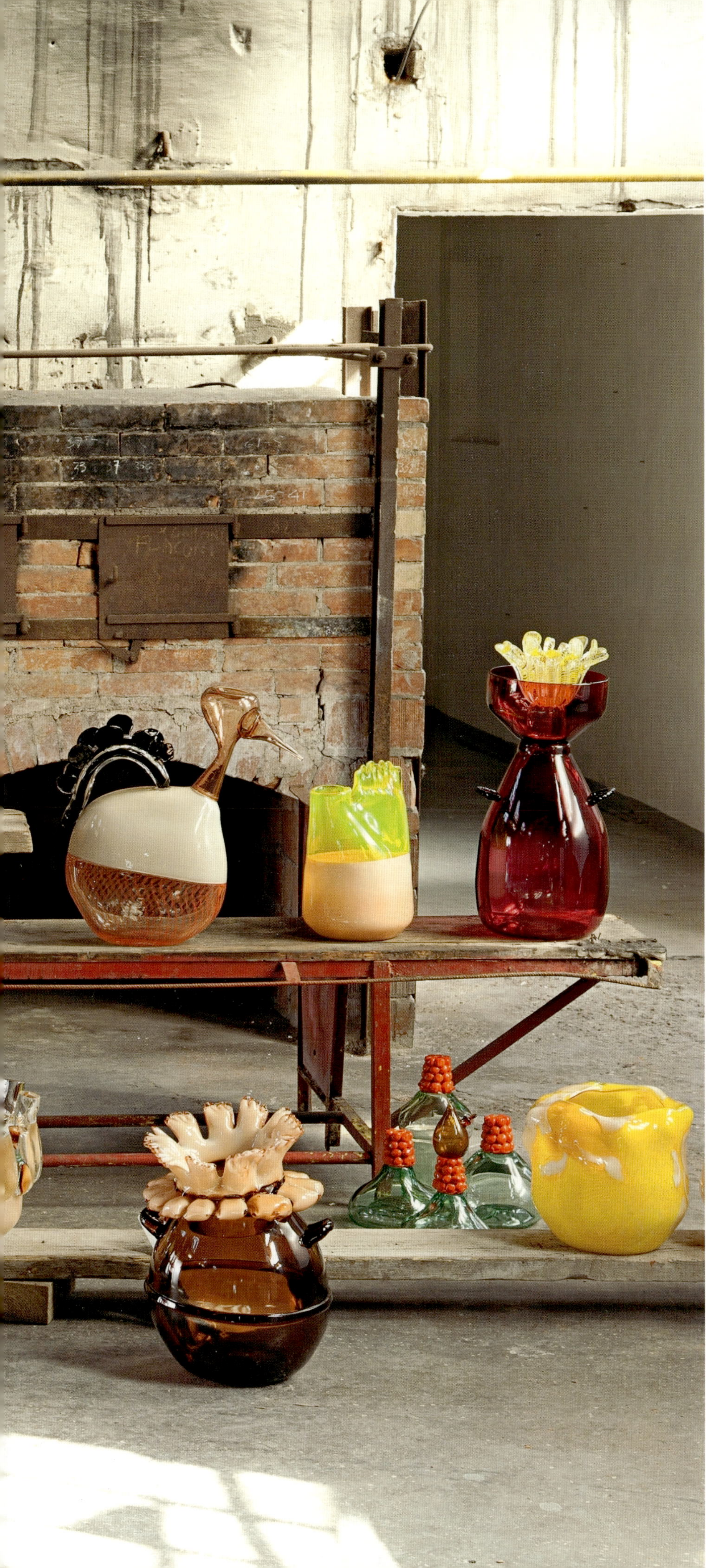

ALL AMBIQ
2011
150 x 430 x 180 CM / VARIABLE DIMENSIONS
COURTESY STUDIO URQUIOLA, MILAN,
AND BERENGO PRIVATE COLLECTION, VENICE

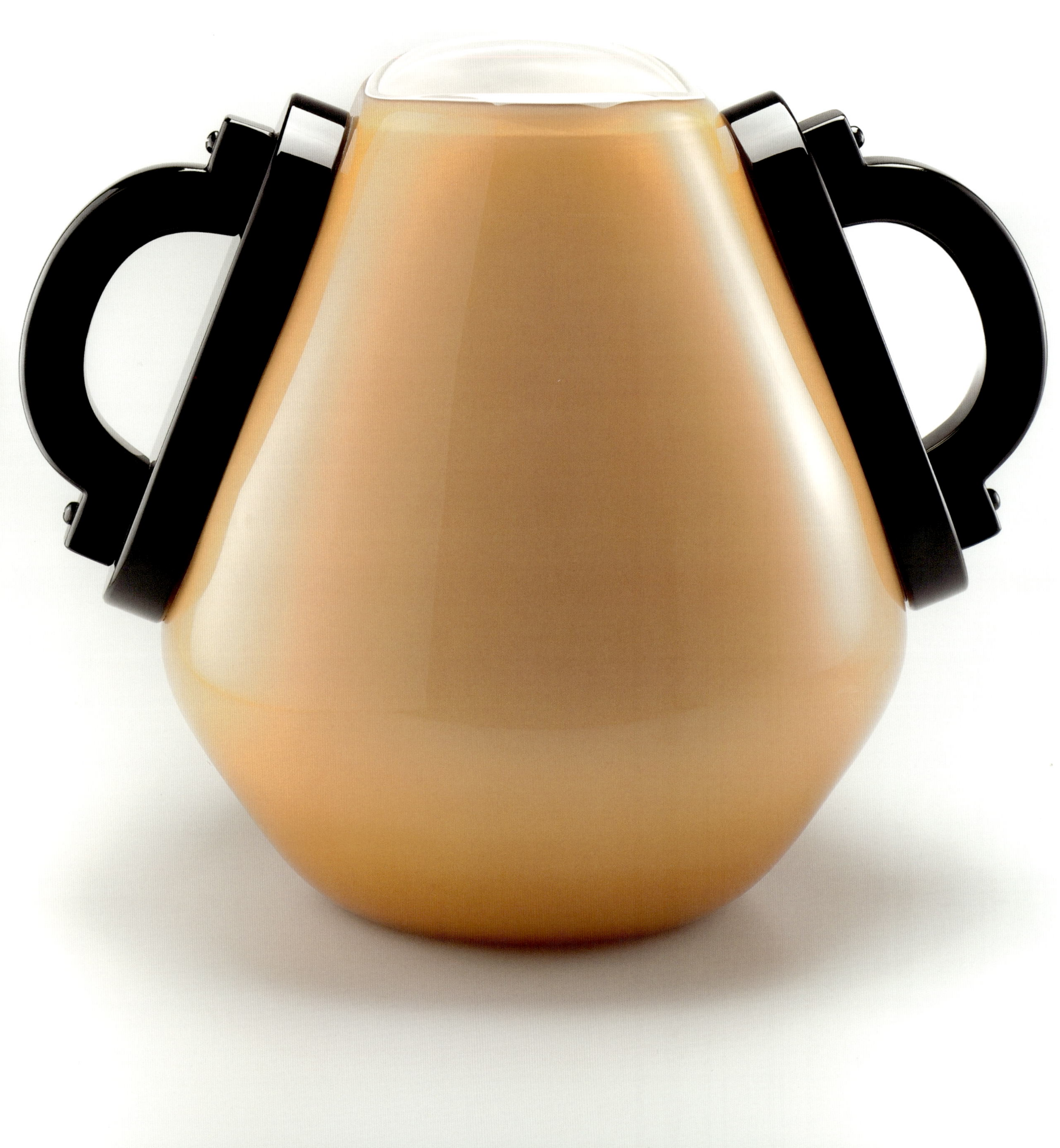

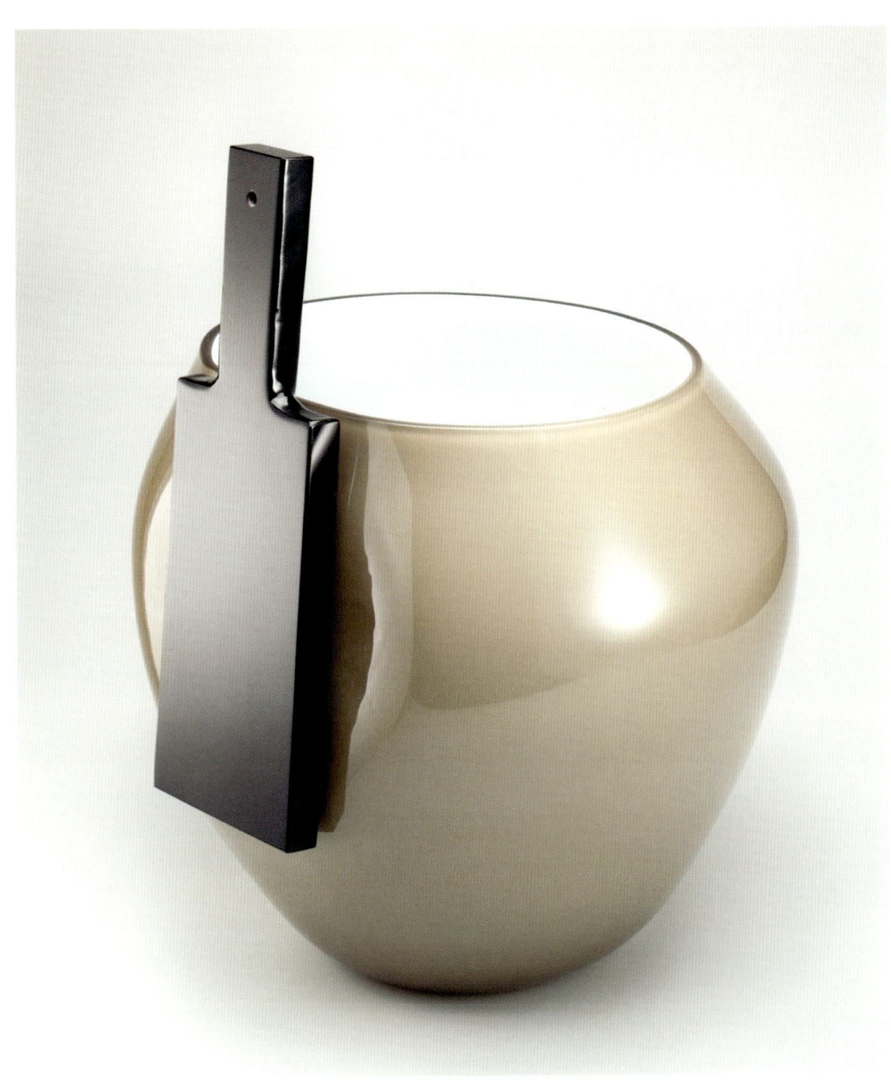

ALL AMBIQ
2011 / *DETAIL*
150 x 430 x 180 CM / VARIABLE DIMENSIONS
COURTESY STUDIO URQUIOLA, MILAN,
AND BERENGO PRIVATE COLLECTION, VENICE

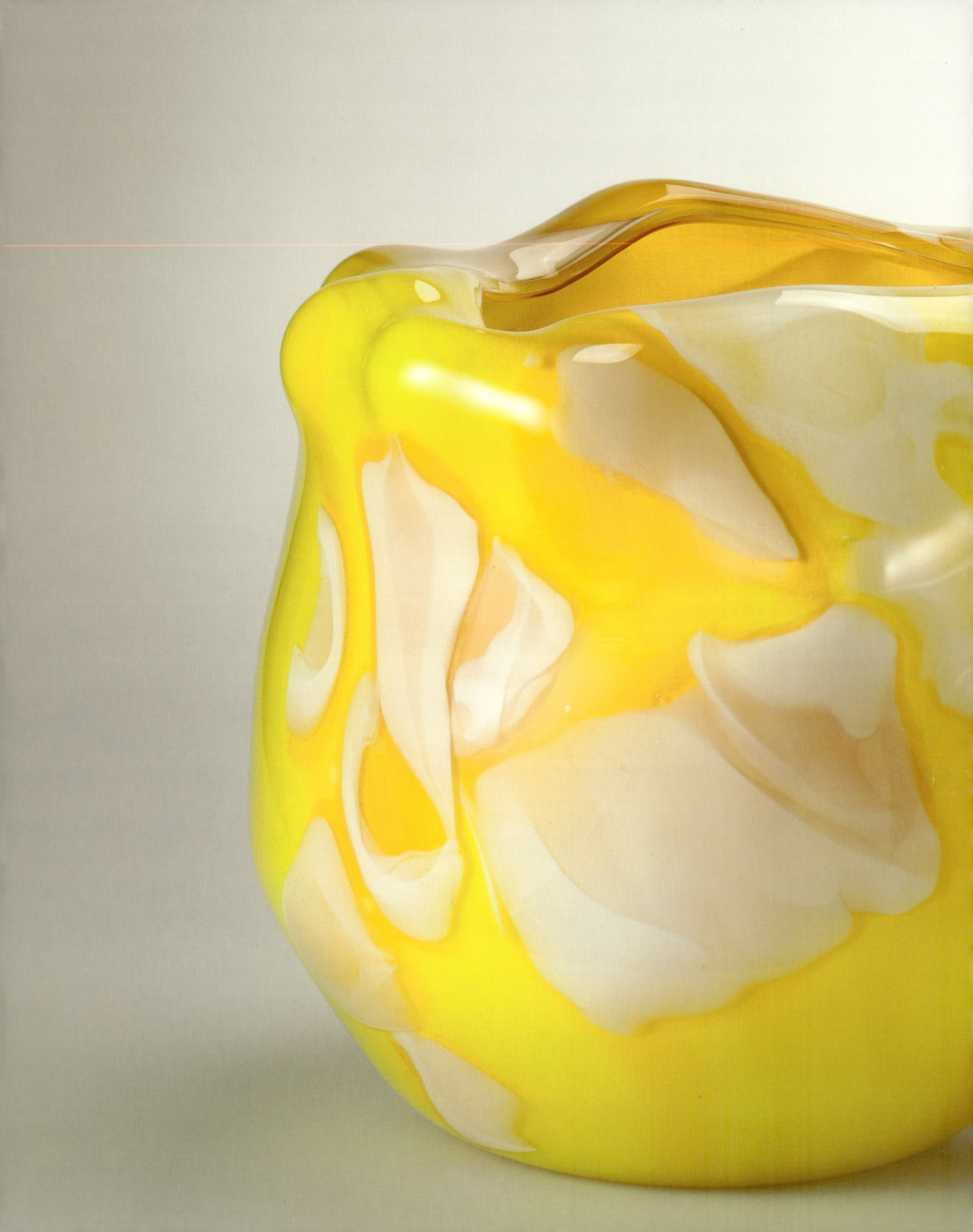

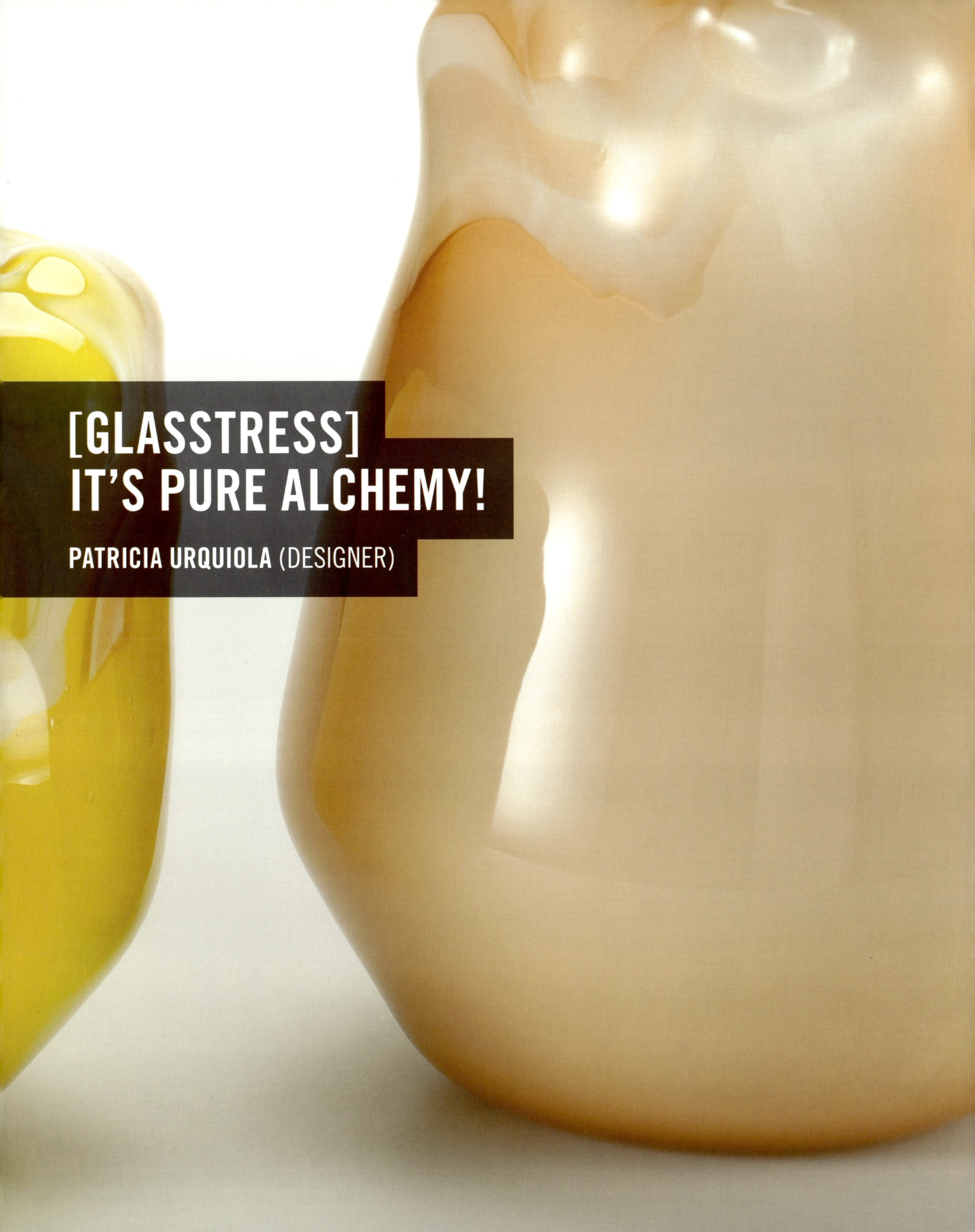
[GLASSTRESS]
IT'S PURE ALCHEMY!
PATRICIA URQUIOLA (DESIGNER)

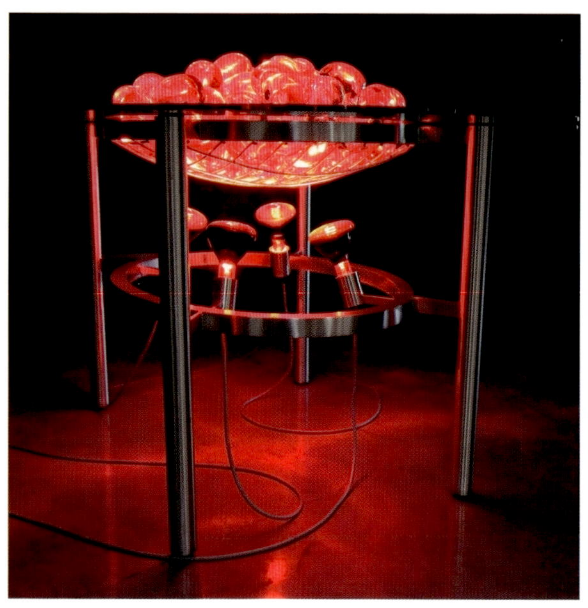

SPAWN – C.C.P.
2011
2 x 140 x 110 CM
COURTESY THE ARTIST

THE ACCIDENT
2005
60 x 35 x 45 CM
COURTESY MOSS PRIVATE COLLECTION, MIAMI

KOEN VANMECHELEN

Koen Vanmechelen was born in Sint-Truiden, Belgium, in 1965; he lives
and works in Meeuwen, Belgium.
His works range from highly expressive paintings and drawings to
photography, video, installations, works in glass, and a recurring wooden
sculpture, all dealing with the theme of the chicken and the egg. These
important symbols connect Koen's art to scientific, political, philosophical, and
ethical issues, the subject of debates and lectures. His work can be defined by
three main categories: The Cosmogolem, a powerful, wooden sculpture adopted
around the world as a symbol for children's rights. Golem, the principle of man
as creator, was the starting point of all his work and still is an important pillar
for him; The Cosmopolitan Chicken Project (CCP), the core of his extensive
breeding program with chicken breeds from all over the world, meant to merge
into a new species, a universal chicken or Superbastard; and Medusa, where
art meets science, the scientific part that used to be called The Walking Egg
and can be considered the think tank behind the CCP. "Cross-breeding is the
only thing," says Vanmechelen. "We need to cross-breed across boundaries
if we want the world not to perish. We need to think cosmopolitical. Nothing
is as beautiful as joining with other cultures and taking energy from this."
He has held conferences all over the world and participated in the most
important events of contemporary art.

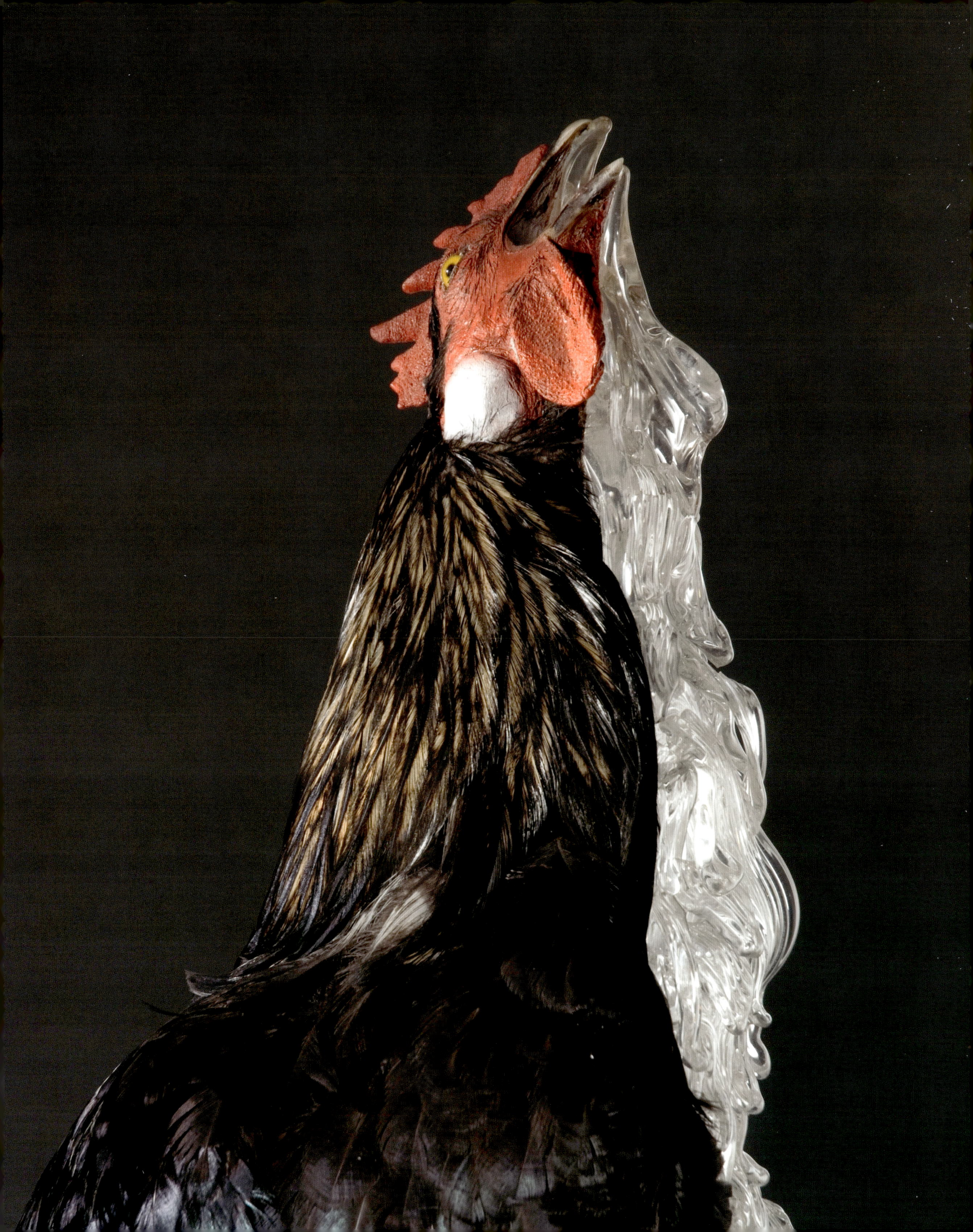

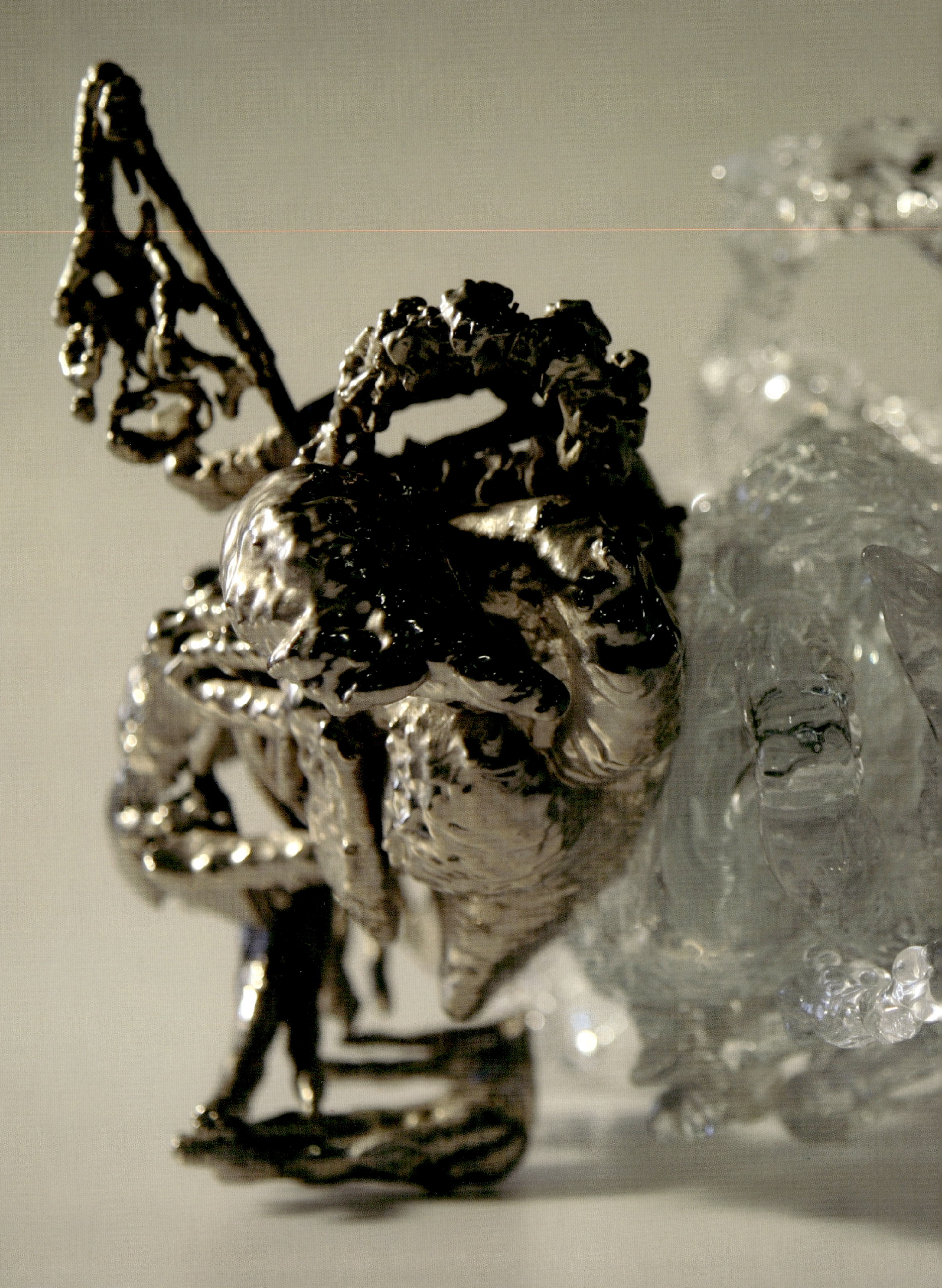

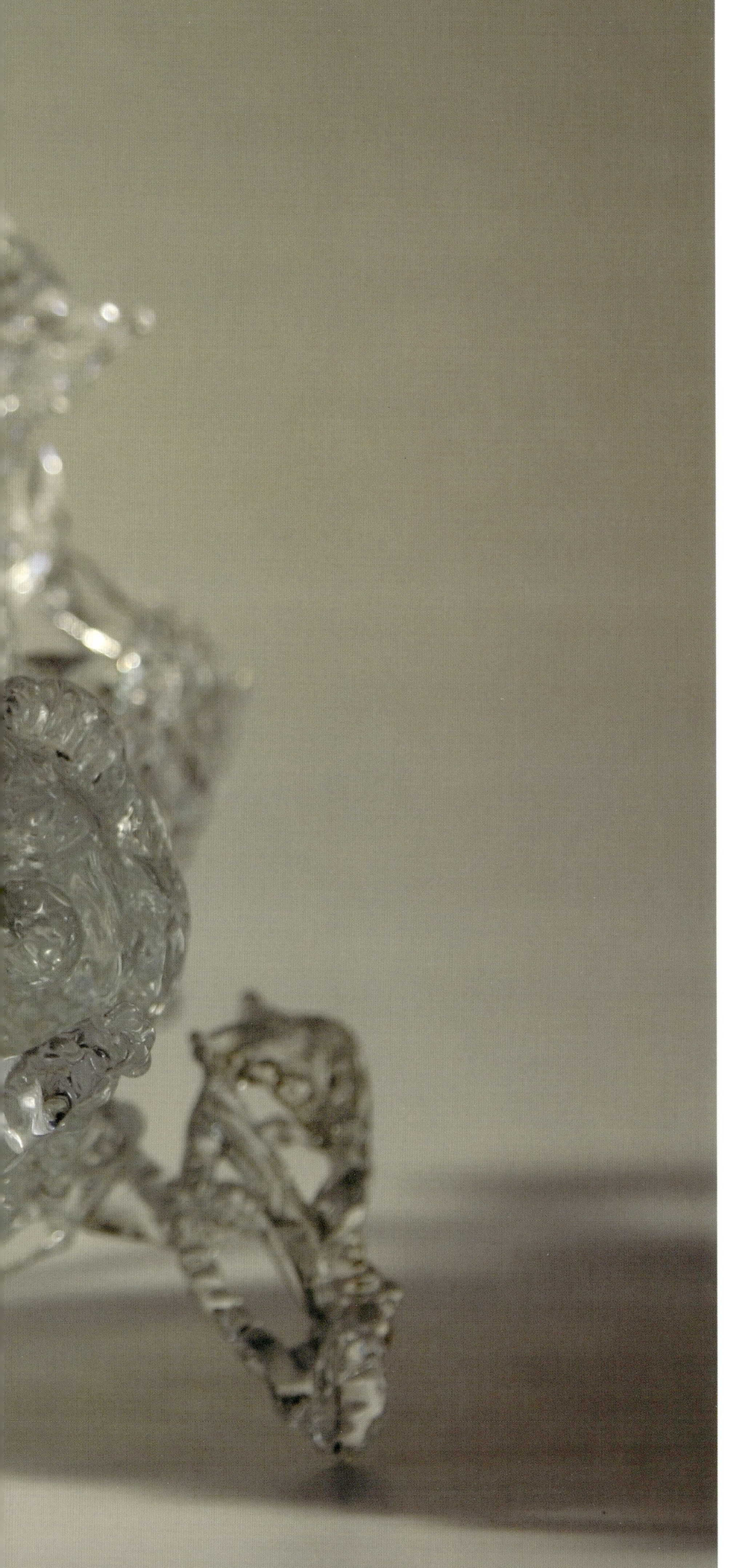

ENTWINED
2011
20 x 30 x 25 CM
COURTESY THE ARTIST

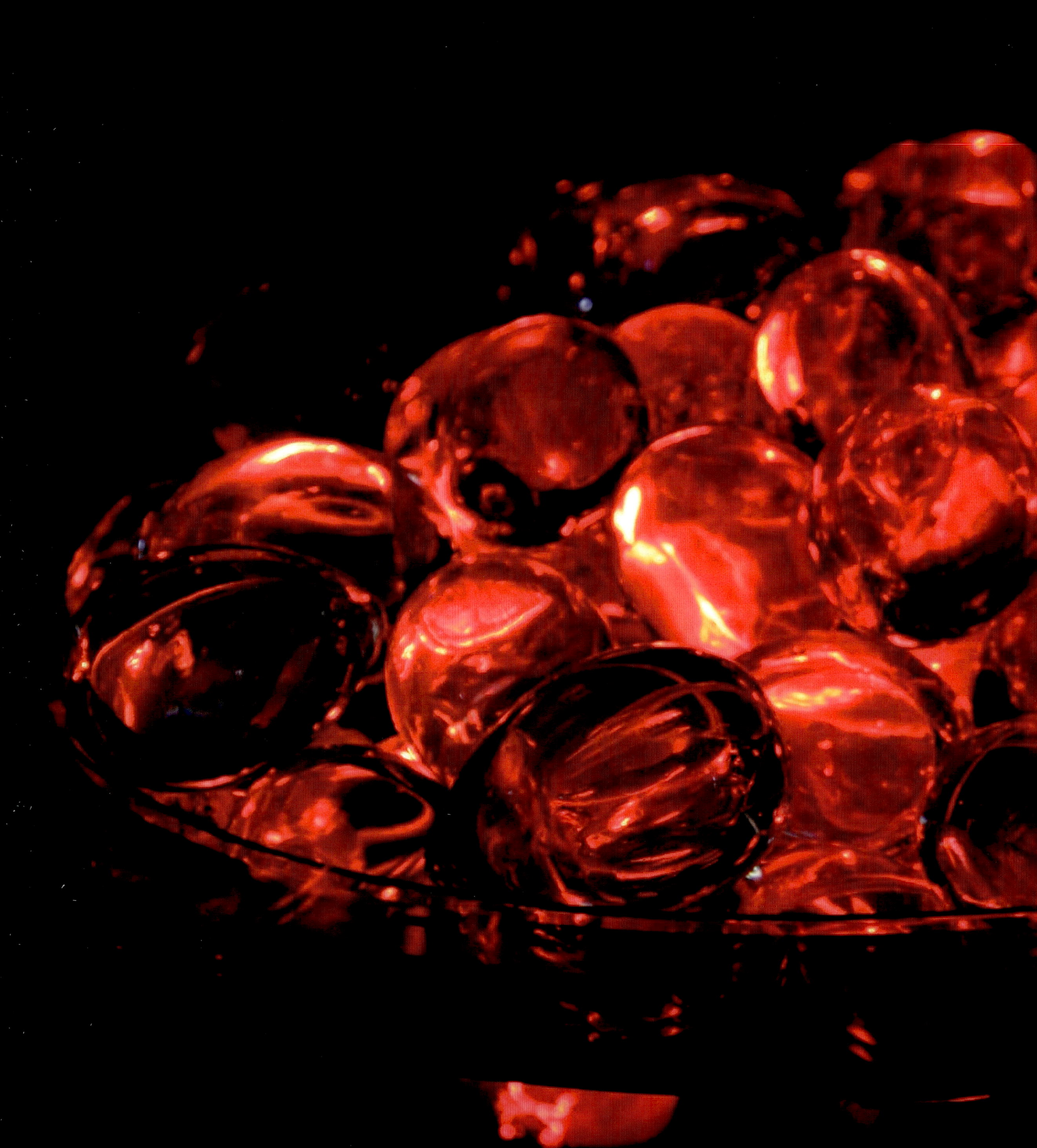

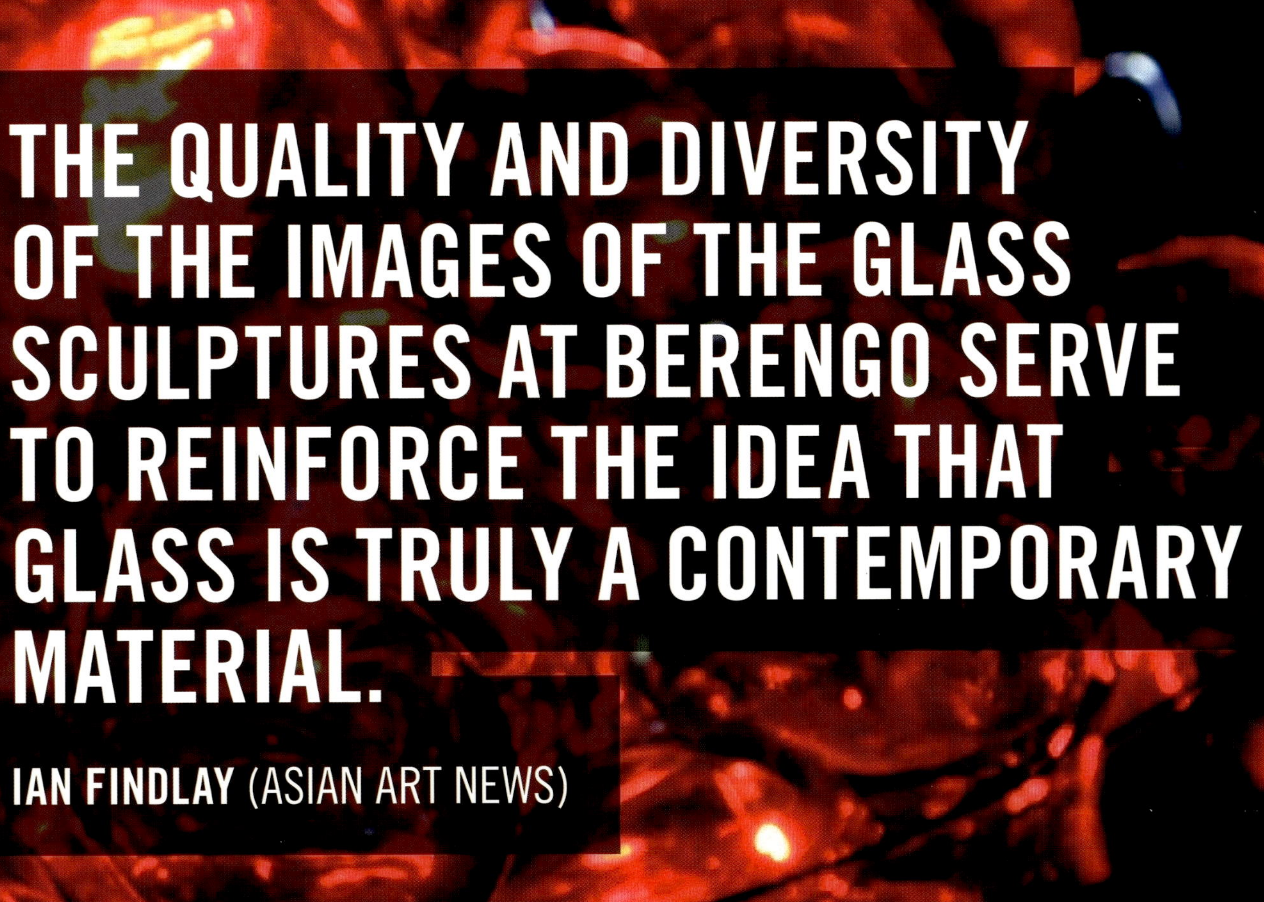

THE QUALITY AND DIVERSITY OF THE IMAGES OF THE GLASS SCULPTURES AT BERENGO SERVE TO REINFORCE THE IDEA THAT GLASS IS TRULY A CONTEMPORARY MATERIAL.

IAN FINDLAY (ASIAN ART NEWS)

Those intent on retracing the history and development of
Murano glass in the twentieth century cannot help but focus
their attention on the 1950s and 1960s. Over the course of these
decades, an extraordinary woman nurtured incredible sensitivity
towards art, cultivating the idea of inviting modern artists to
create works in glass. That woman was Peggy Guggenheim.
She can be credited for launching a glass Renaissance of
sorts, drawing in names like Max Ernst, Marc Chagall, Le
Corbusier, Mark Tobey, Oskar Kokoschka, and Lucio Fontana.
Despite expectations, her powerful sense of intuition was not
fully developed in the years to follow; nonetheless, her insight
became the inspiring principle behind the ambitious cultural
project championed by Adriano Berengo: *Glasstress.*
The Venice Biennale, a Venetian institution boasting over 110
years of activities, has shown striking interest in *Glasstress* since
its first edition in 2009, thanks to the distinct "Glocal" nature
of the initiative. Designed to enhance the artistic production

GLASSTRESS
ANTHOLOGY

LAURA BRESOLIN

of Murano, a landmark in the history of Venice, the event has
succeeded in contextually pervading the contemporary art
world's most avant-garde scene.
The two editions, *Glasstress* 2009 and *Glasstress 2011*, were
both official side events for the International Exhibition of Art at
Venice's Biennale. Though different, each event shared the same
goal: to demonstrate how glass continues to increasingly prove
itself as a material capable of expressing the artistic needs of
contemporary art and design. To reach this aim, the first event
in 2009 strove to document how glass was employed in the
past by leading artists such as Josef Albers, Man Ray, Anton
Pevsner, Lucio Fontana, César, and Robert Rauschenberg.

In fact, the show primarily focused on pre-existing art from large established collections, with the exception of new works by artists like Fred Wilson, Tony Cragg, Jan Fabre, and Koen Vanmechelen, which spotlighted the potential of glass, focusing on its use in the future. Thanks to contributions by its four curators, *Glasstress 2011* also achieved its objective, showcasing a sensational selection of new creations by renowned artists and designers including Michael Joo, Vik Muniz, Javier Pérez, Jaume Plensa, Thomas Schütte, Patricia Urquiola, Fred Wilson, and Zhang Huan.

Berengo Studio, with Venice Projects, offers the opportunity to create and promote works that other studios are not likely to develop. The uniqueness of its approach lies in inviting artists that have never worked with glass before, guaranteeing results that prove totally released from the traditional canons of glassmaking. At the same time, it creates these works with the support of expert glass masters who are highly skilled in the sector's most complex techniques.

The artists' overall cultural diversity is an integral part of the project designed to involve them in the first person, spurring a creative process characterized by collaboration and the exchange of know-how. It also fostered connections with a new material whose essence conveys a dynamic relationship between volume and empty space, density and fragility, fluidity, crystallization, reflections and transparency. By absorbing surrounding experiences and energies, participants freed glass from its material nature, restoring it to a brand of lightness capable of expressing the full significance of their quest. Never before has matter been so molded or "stressed," brought to its very limit by challenging the skills of masters and their time-tested techniques.

In 2011, *Glasstress* became a worldwide traveling exhibition. In fact, a selection of its works has journeyed from Venice to Riga's National Museum of Latvian Art and Stockholm's Millesgården Museum, bringing together contemporary artists from diverse geographical areas and cultural contexts.

Today, *Glasstress* is debuting at MAD in New York with a noteworthy exhibition that officially marks the grand entrance of glass into the world of contemporary art and design, foreshadowing the beginning of a new era for glass.

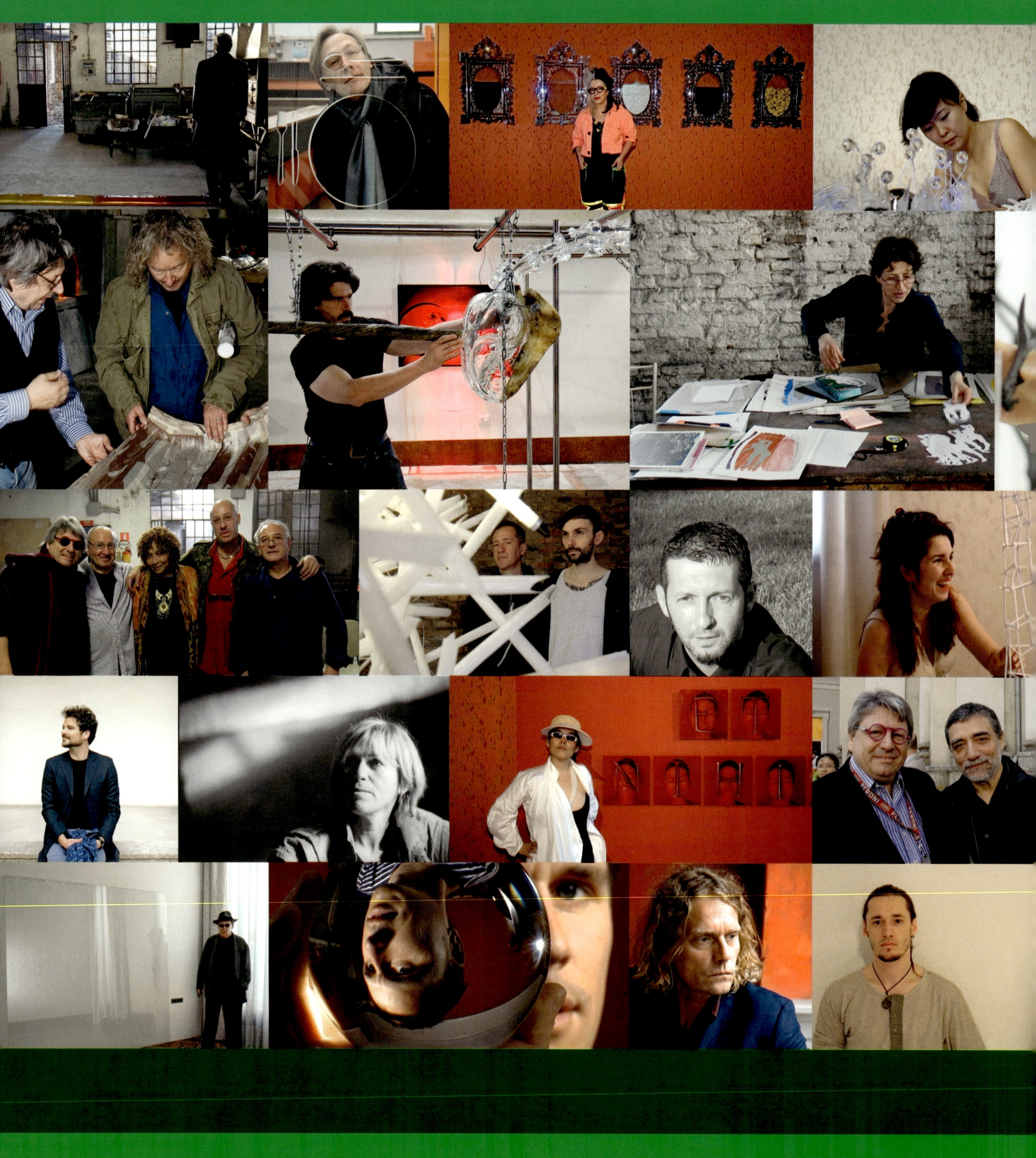

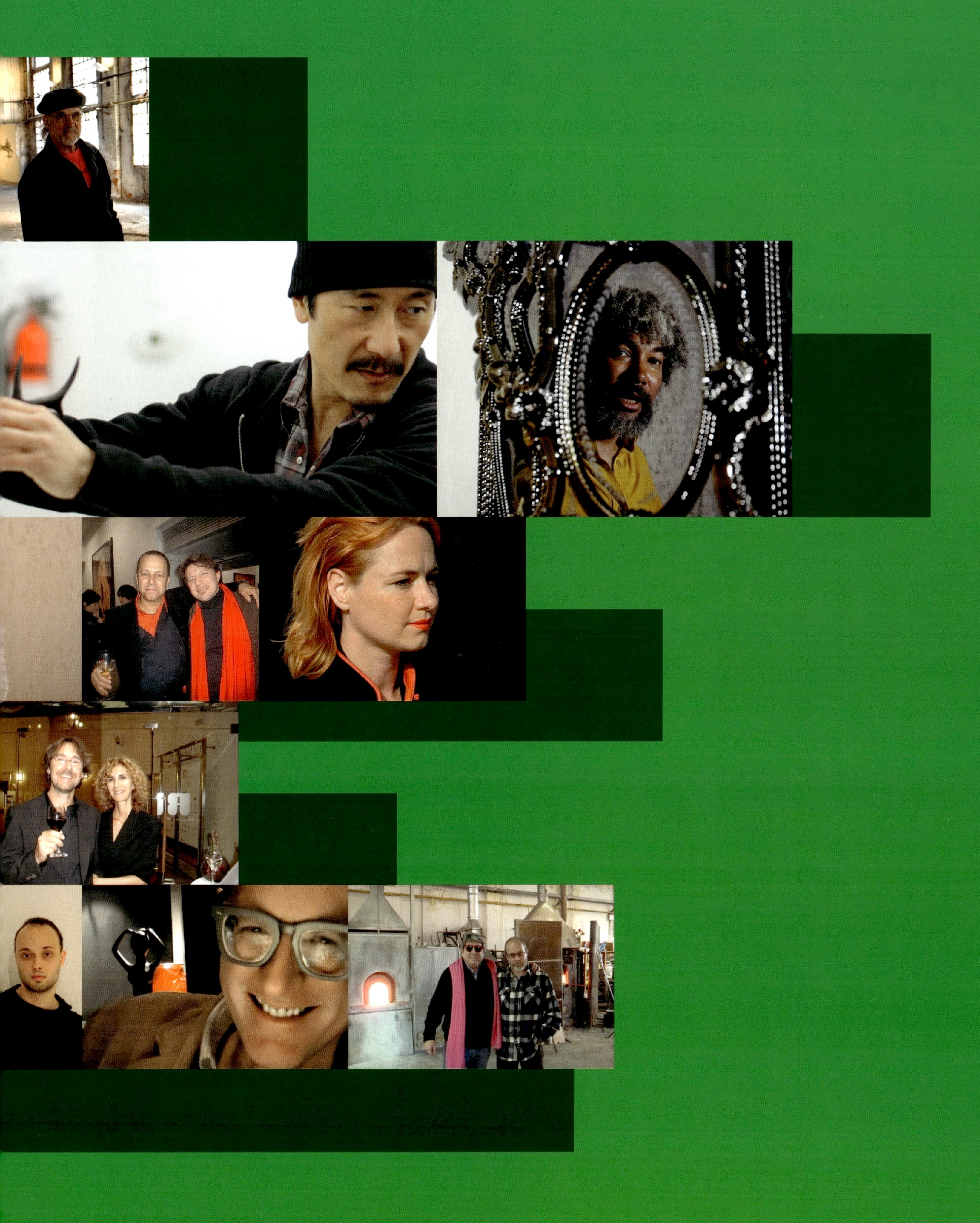

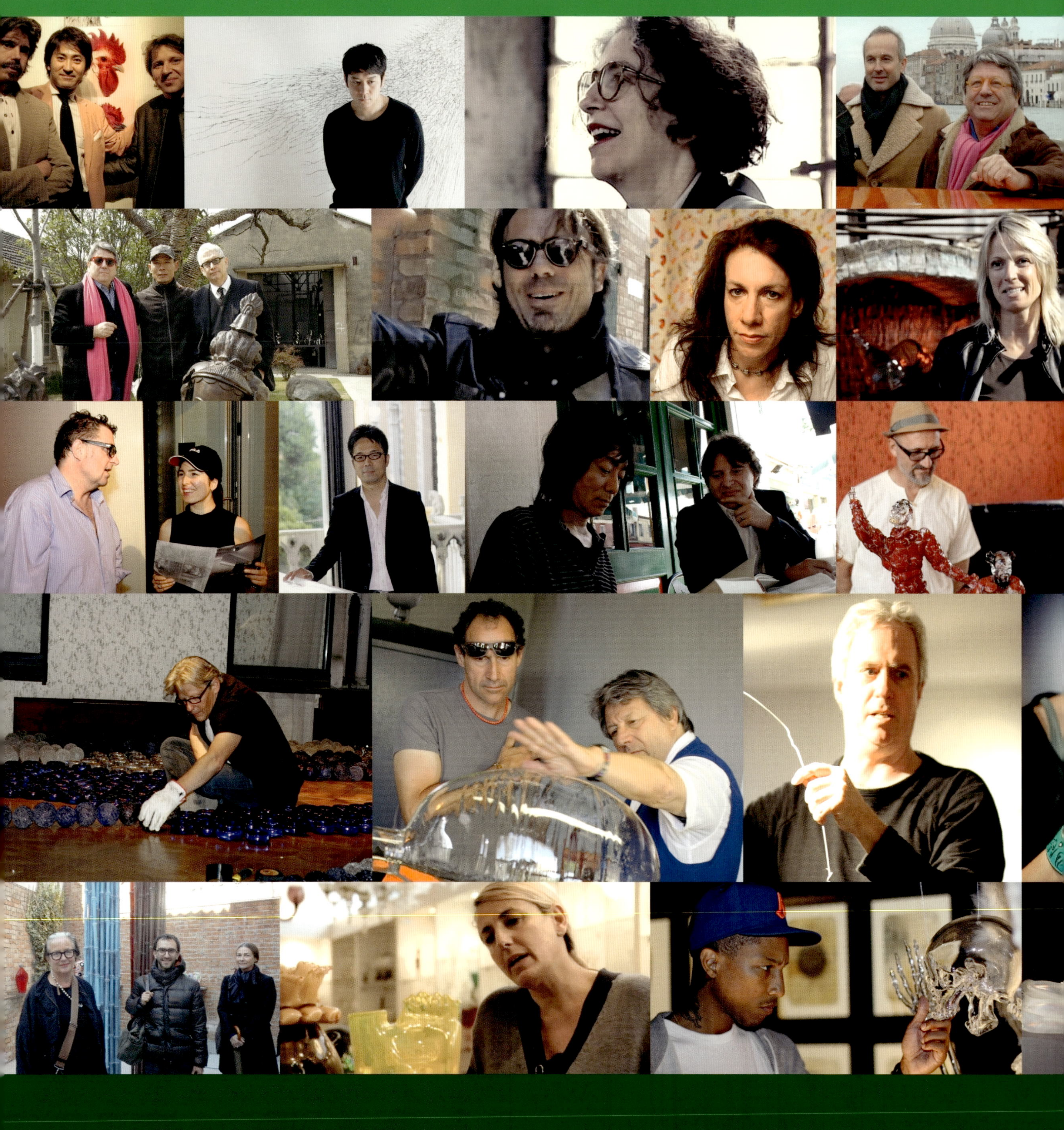

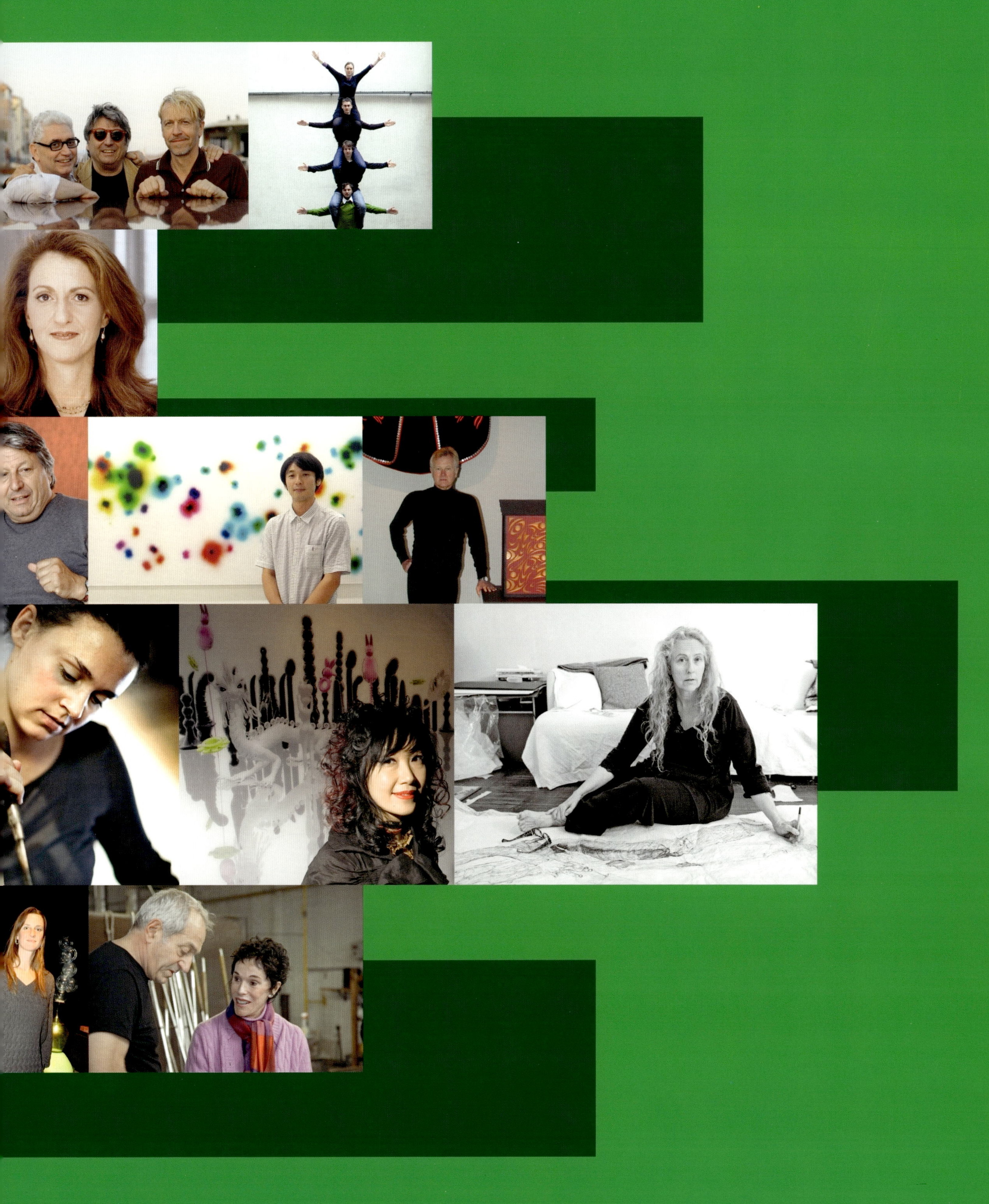

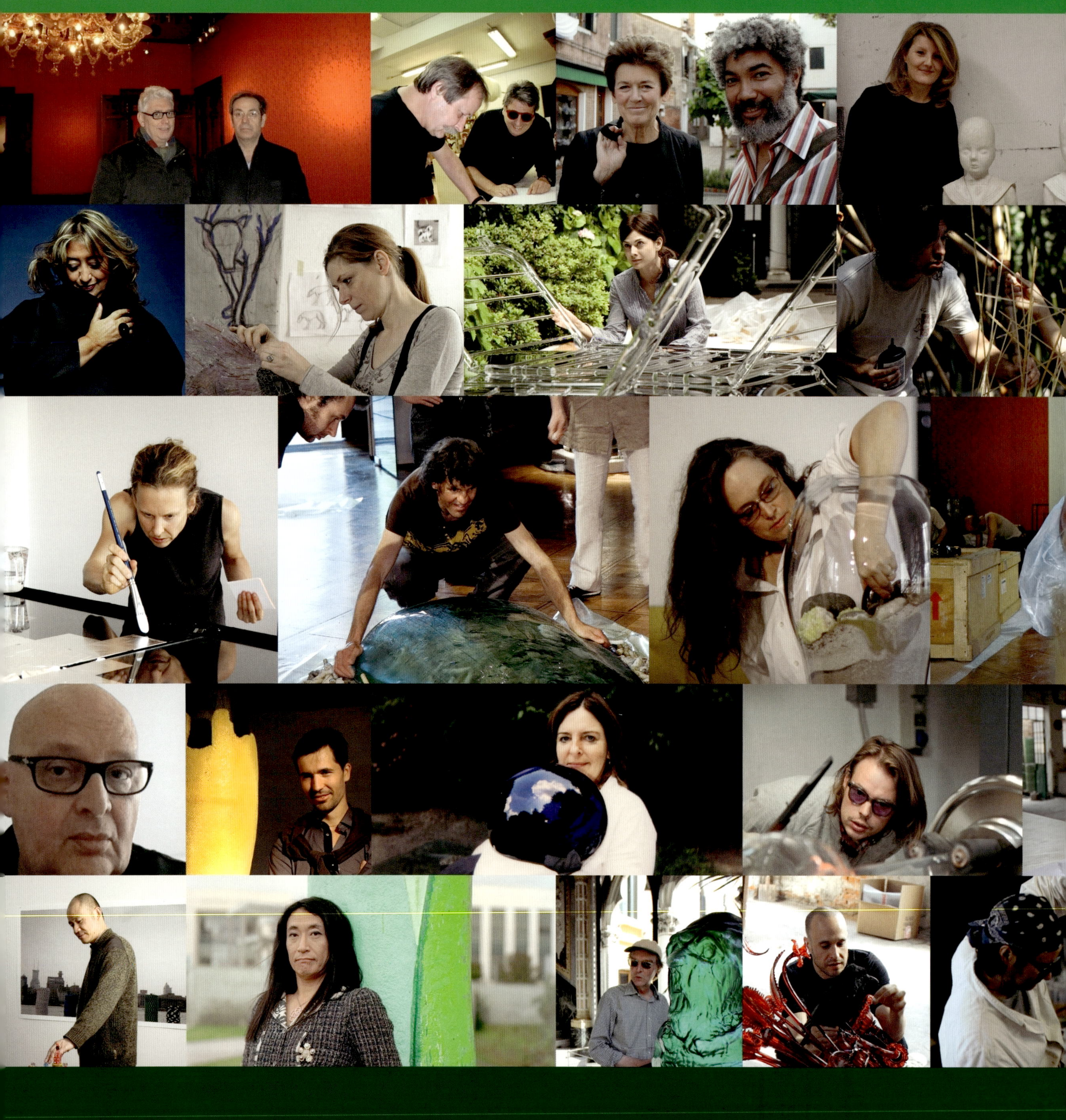

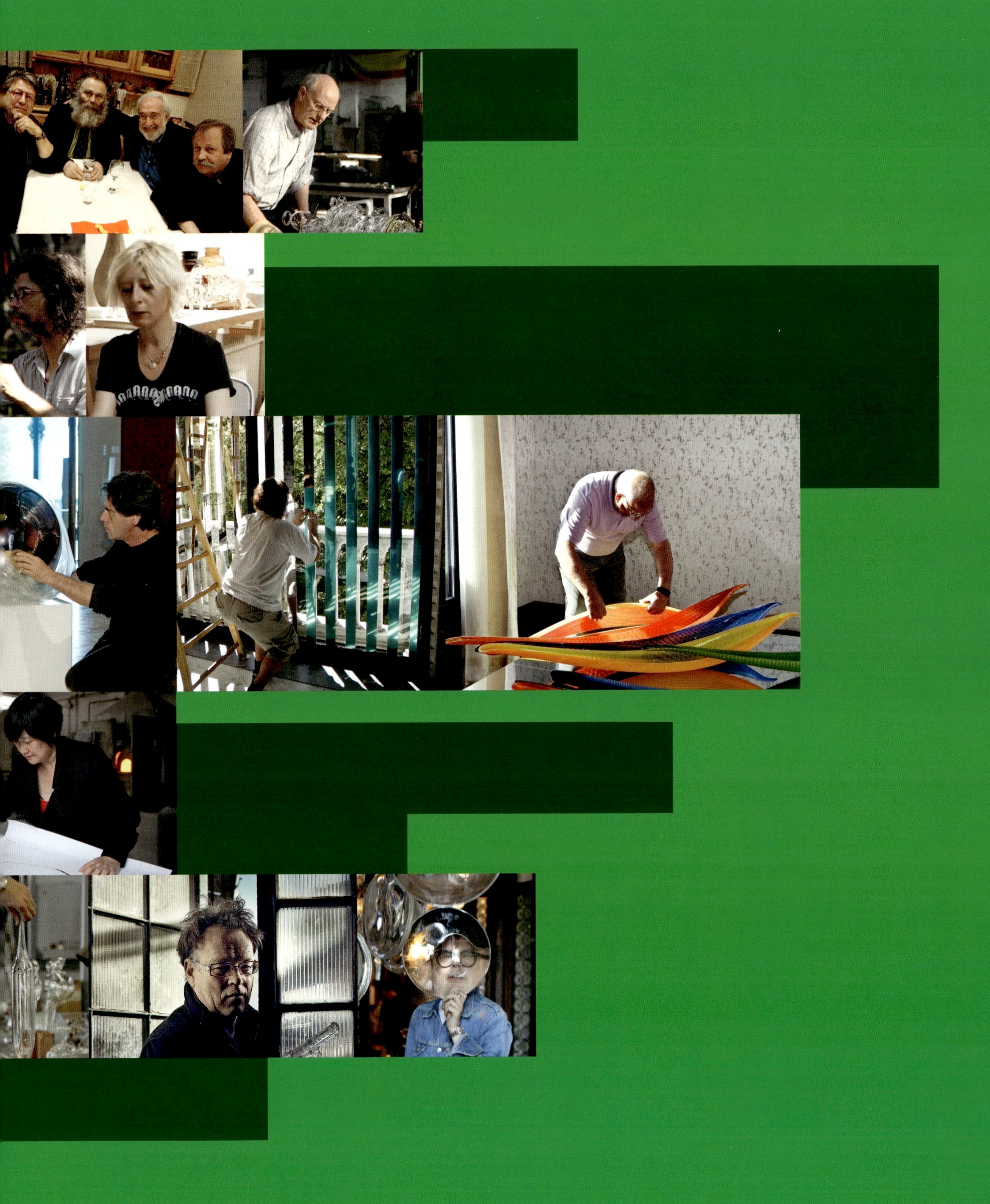

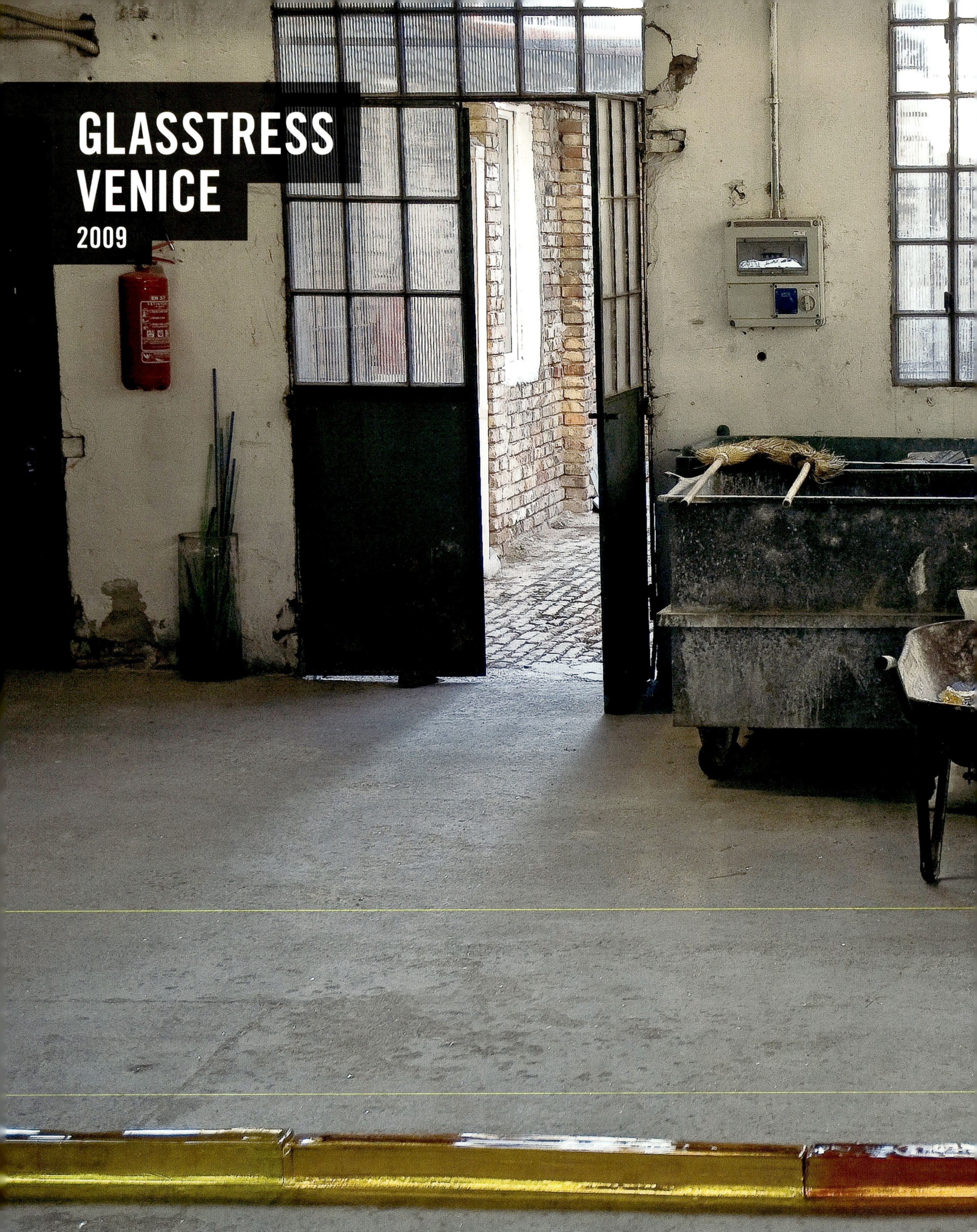

GLASSTRESS
VENICE
2009

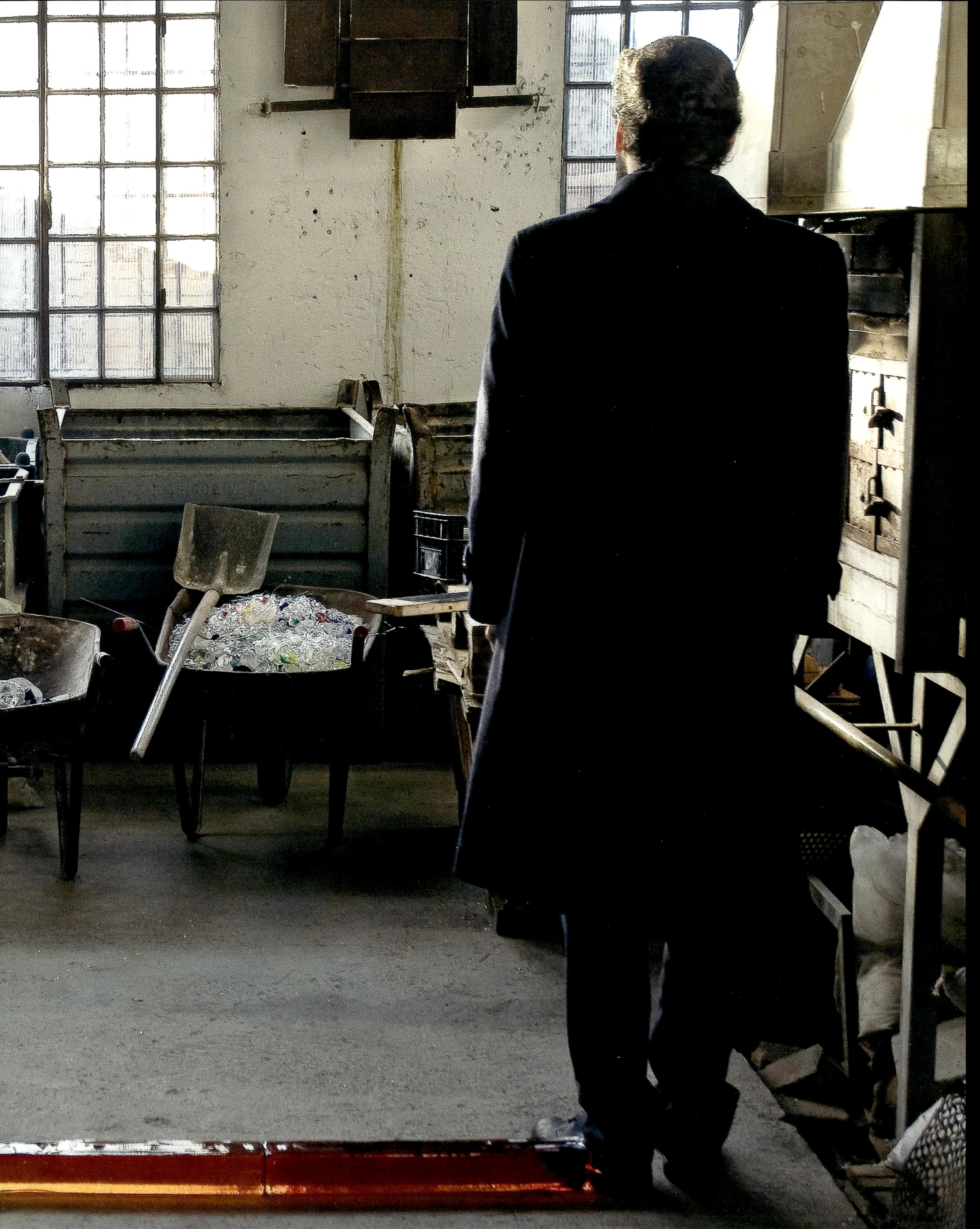

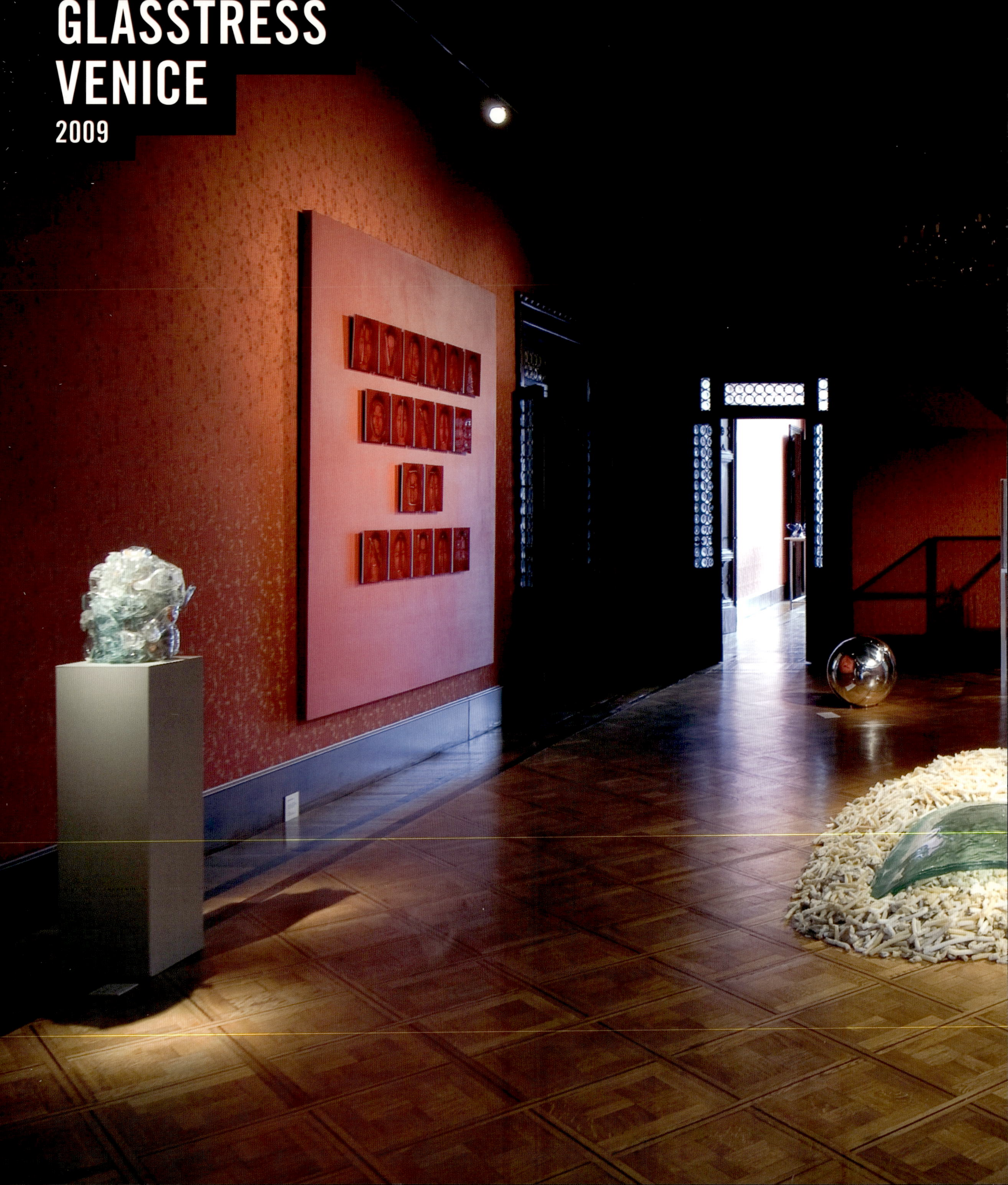

GLASSTRESS
VENICE
2009

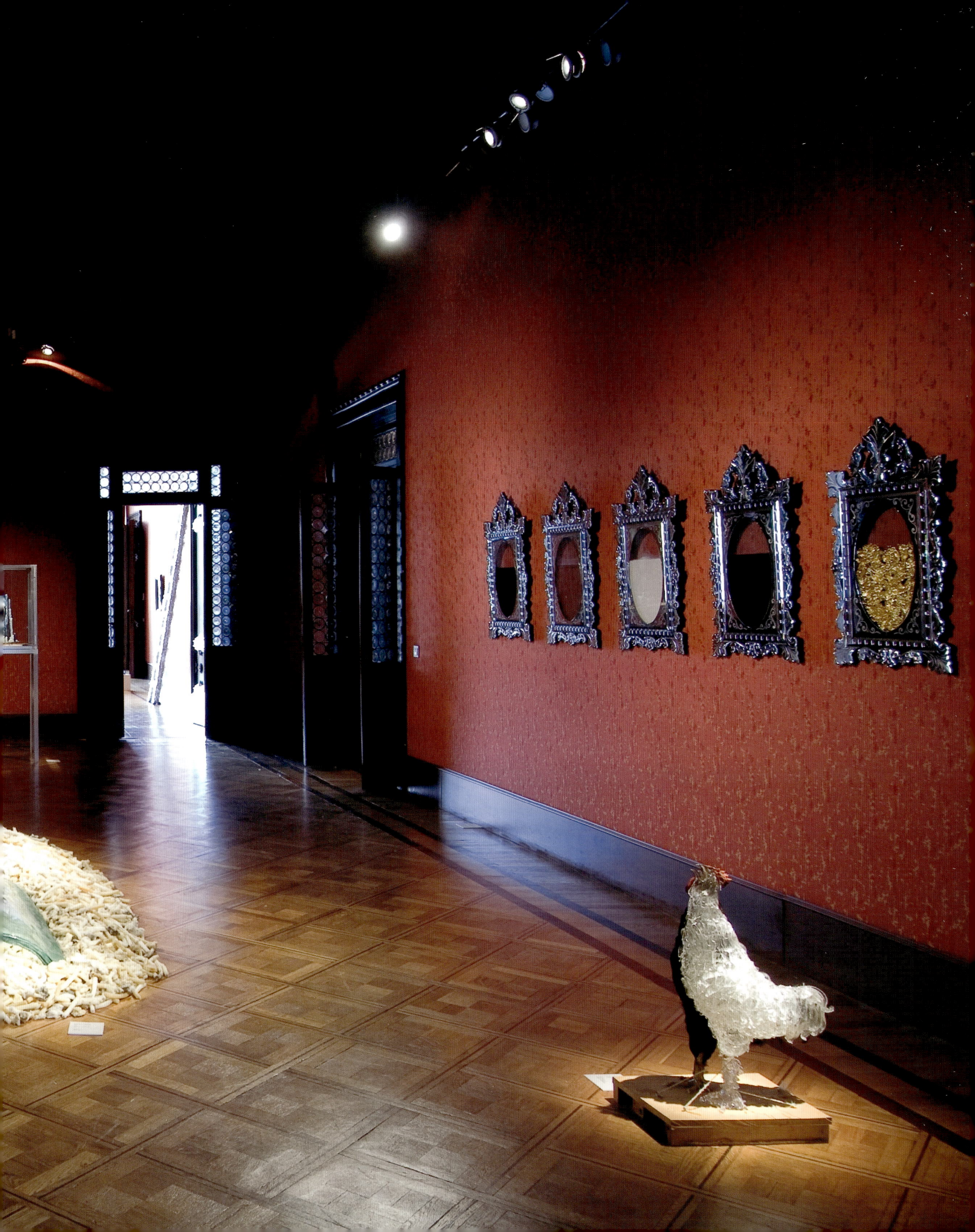

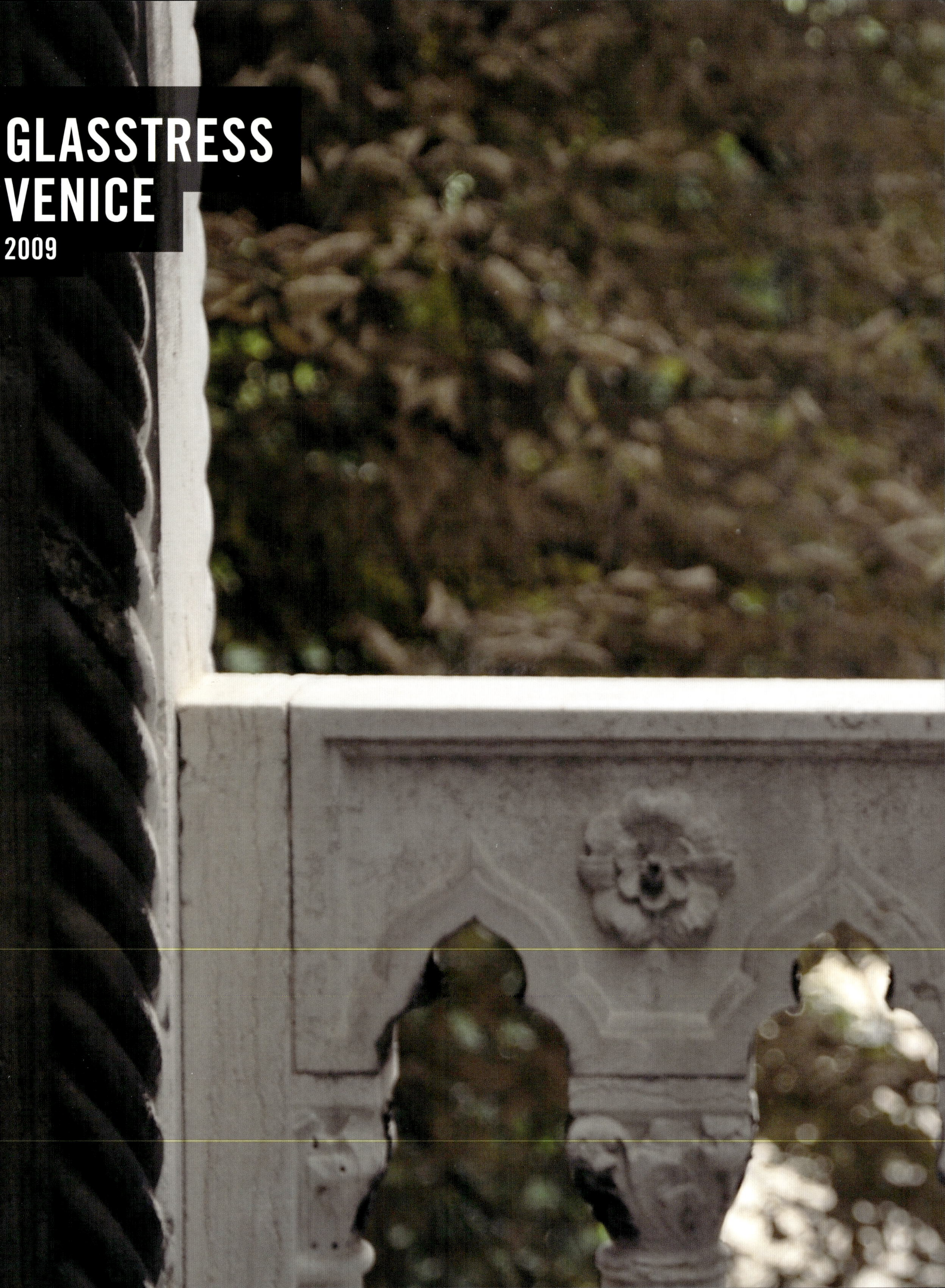
GLASSTRESS
VENICE
2009

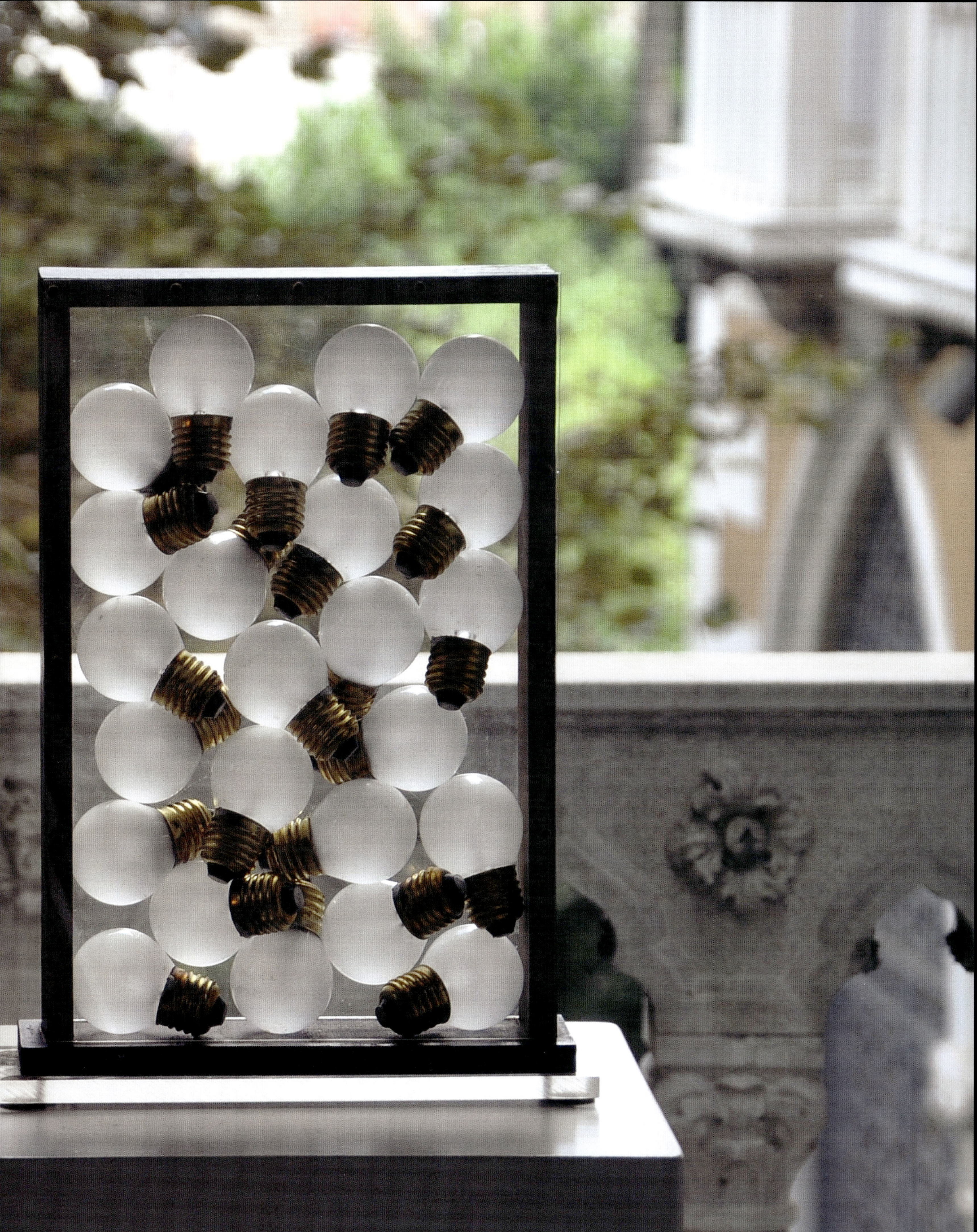

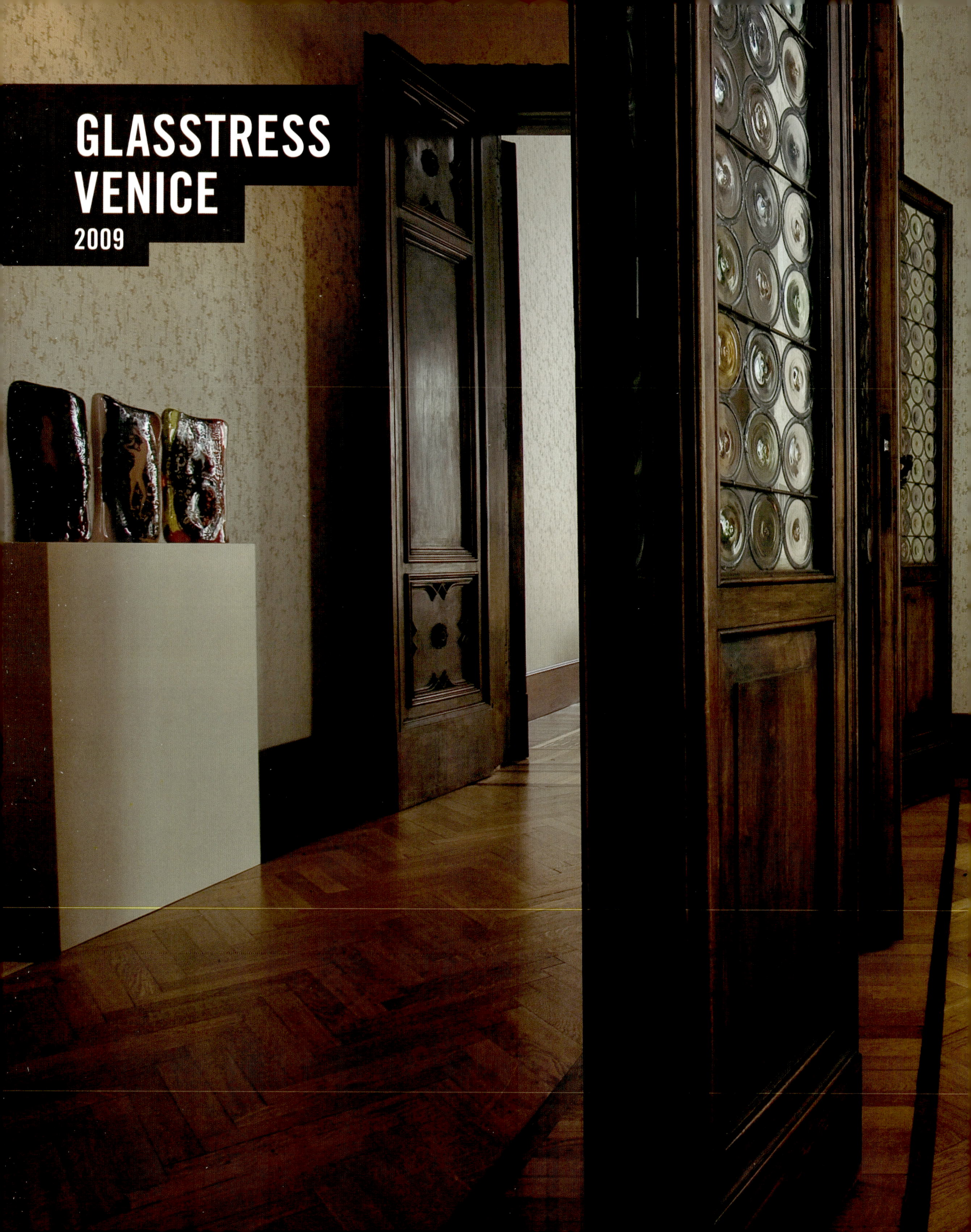

GLASSTRESS
VENICE
2009

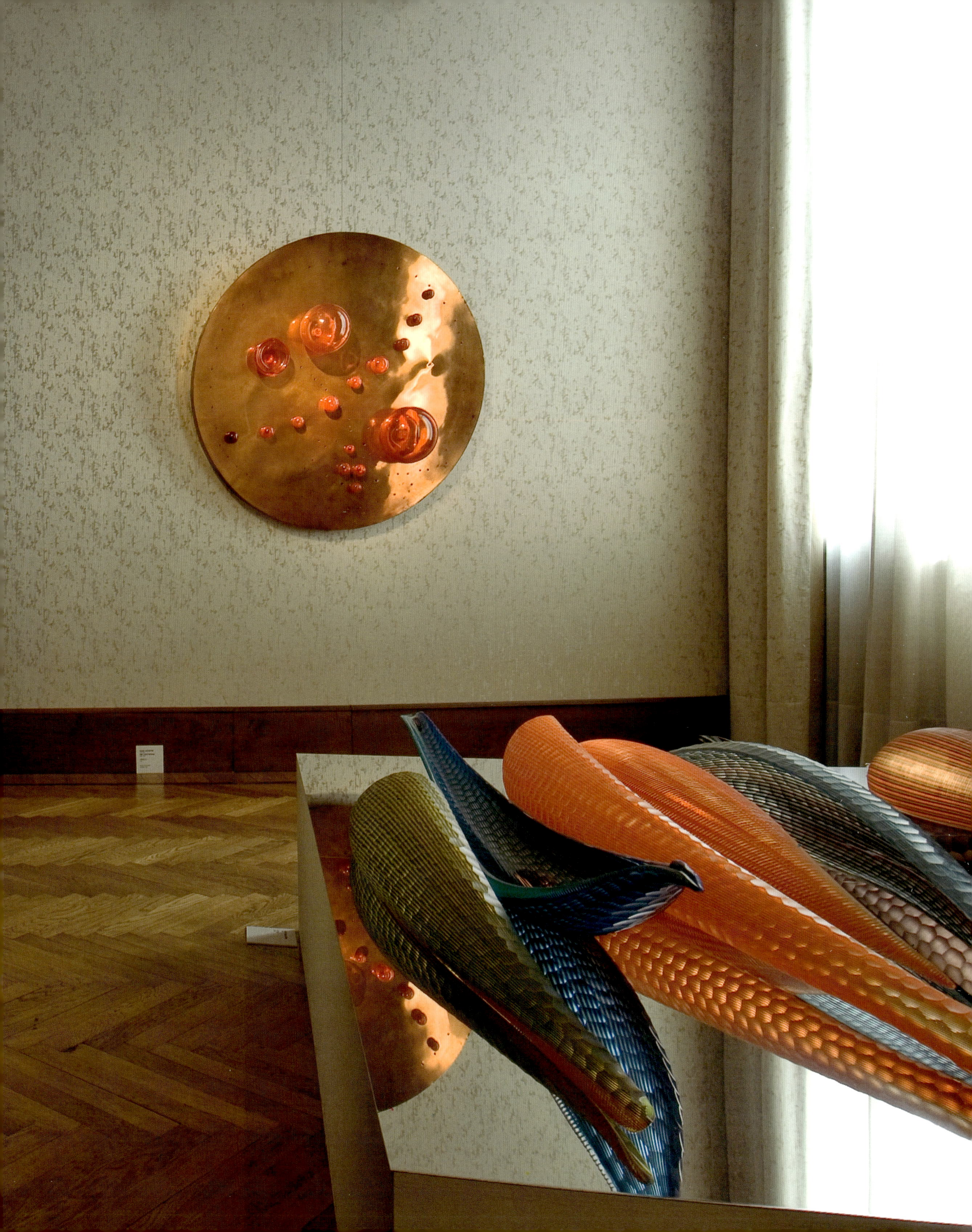

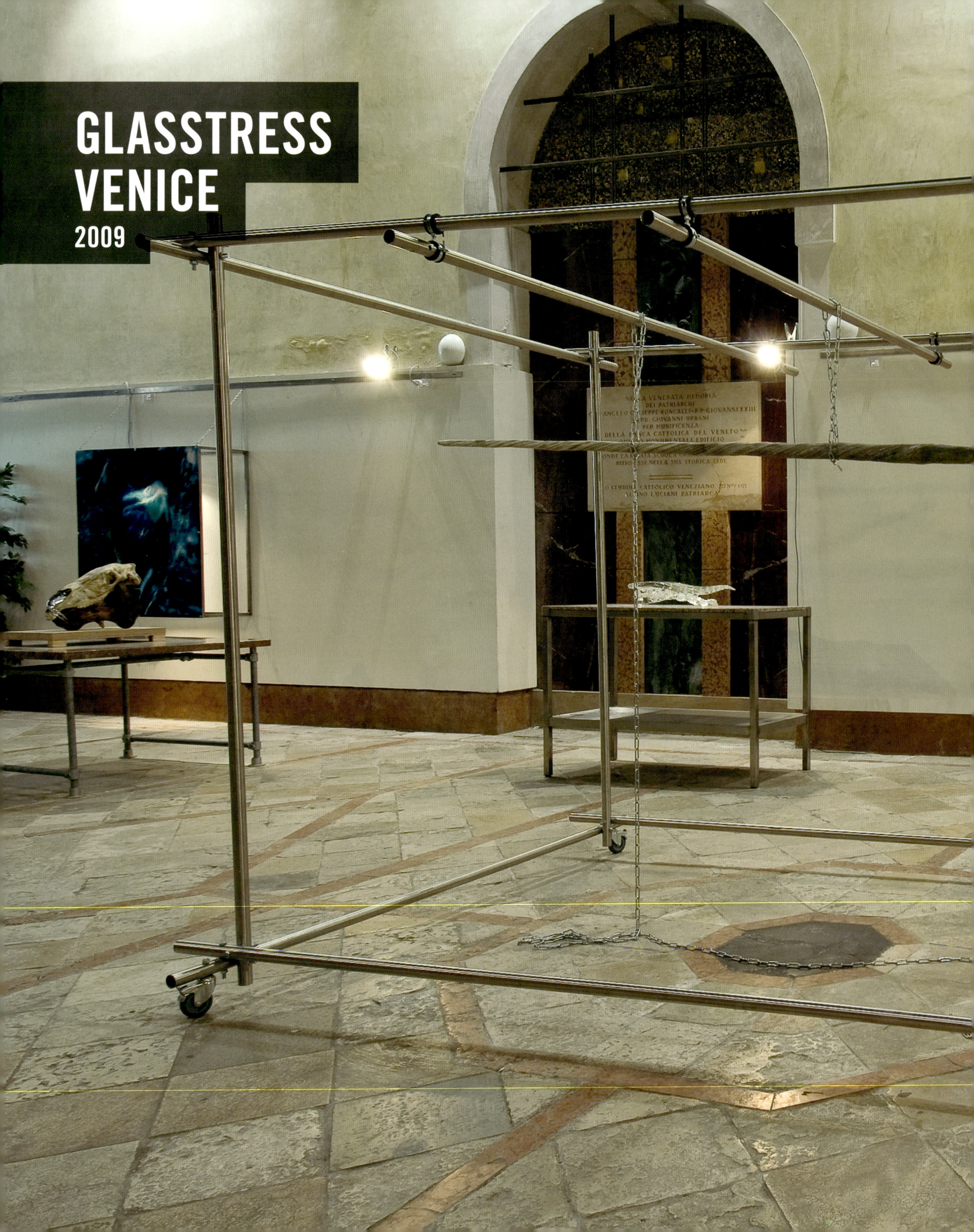
GLASSTRESS
VENICE
2009

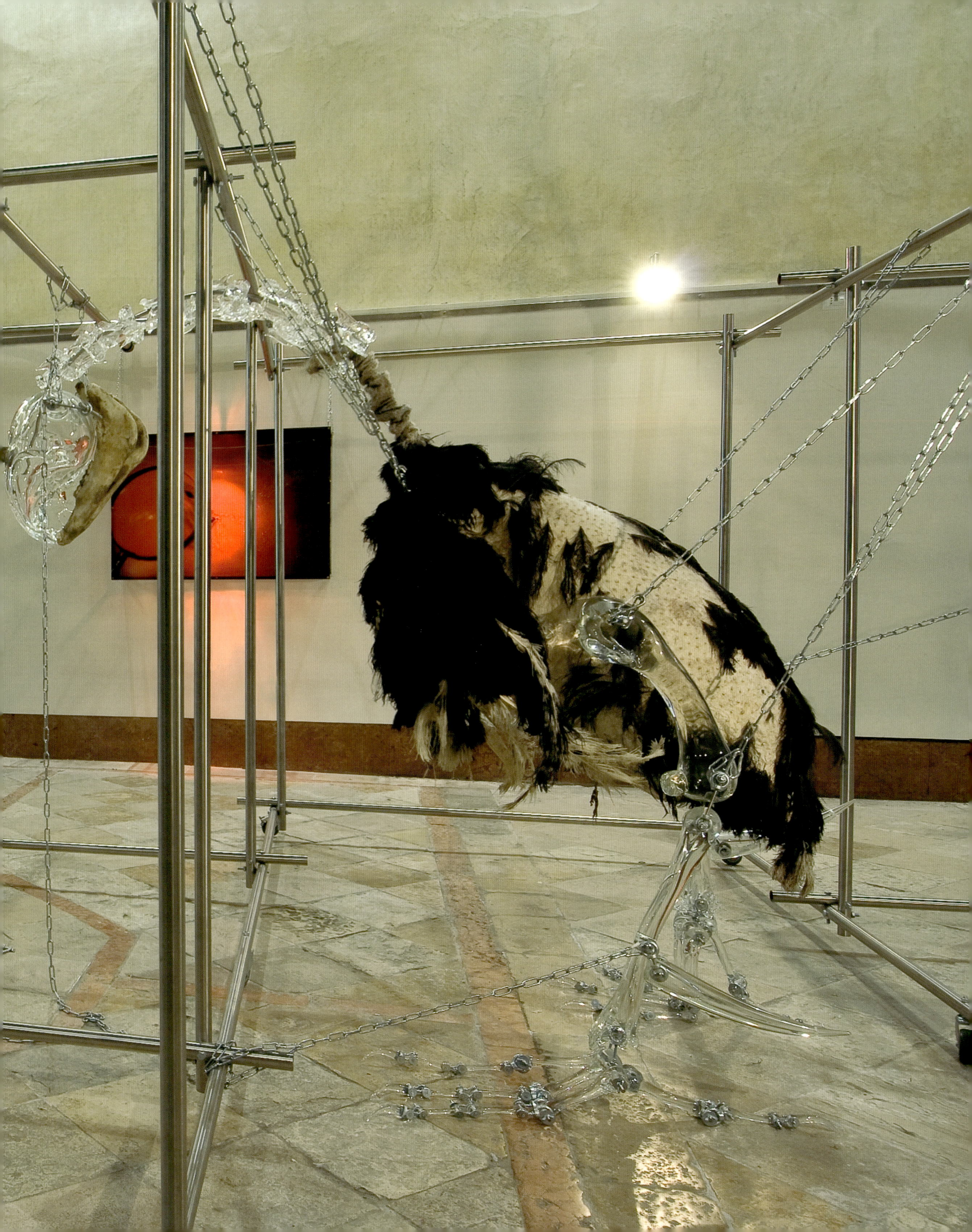

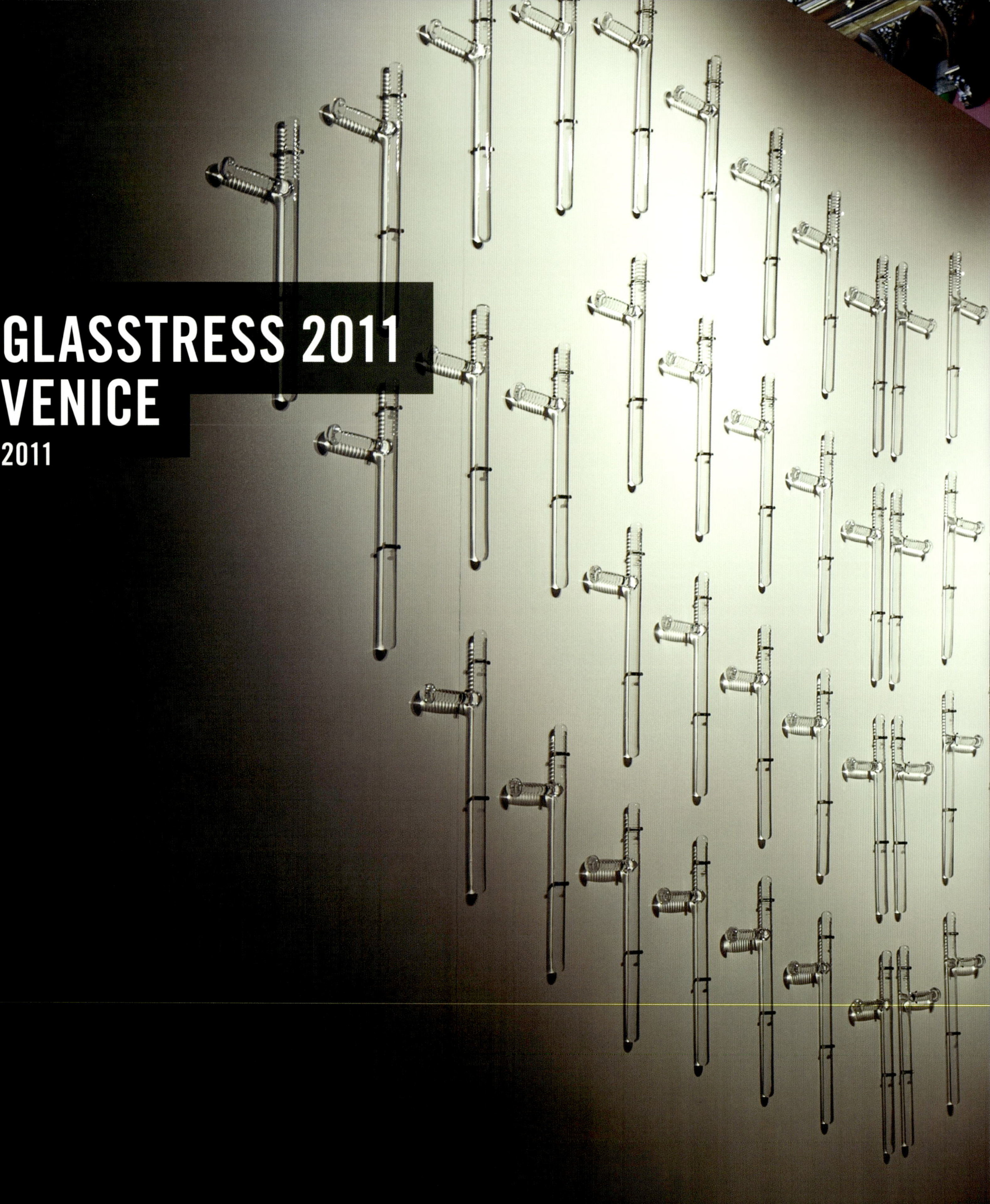

GLASSTRESS 2011
VENICE
2011

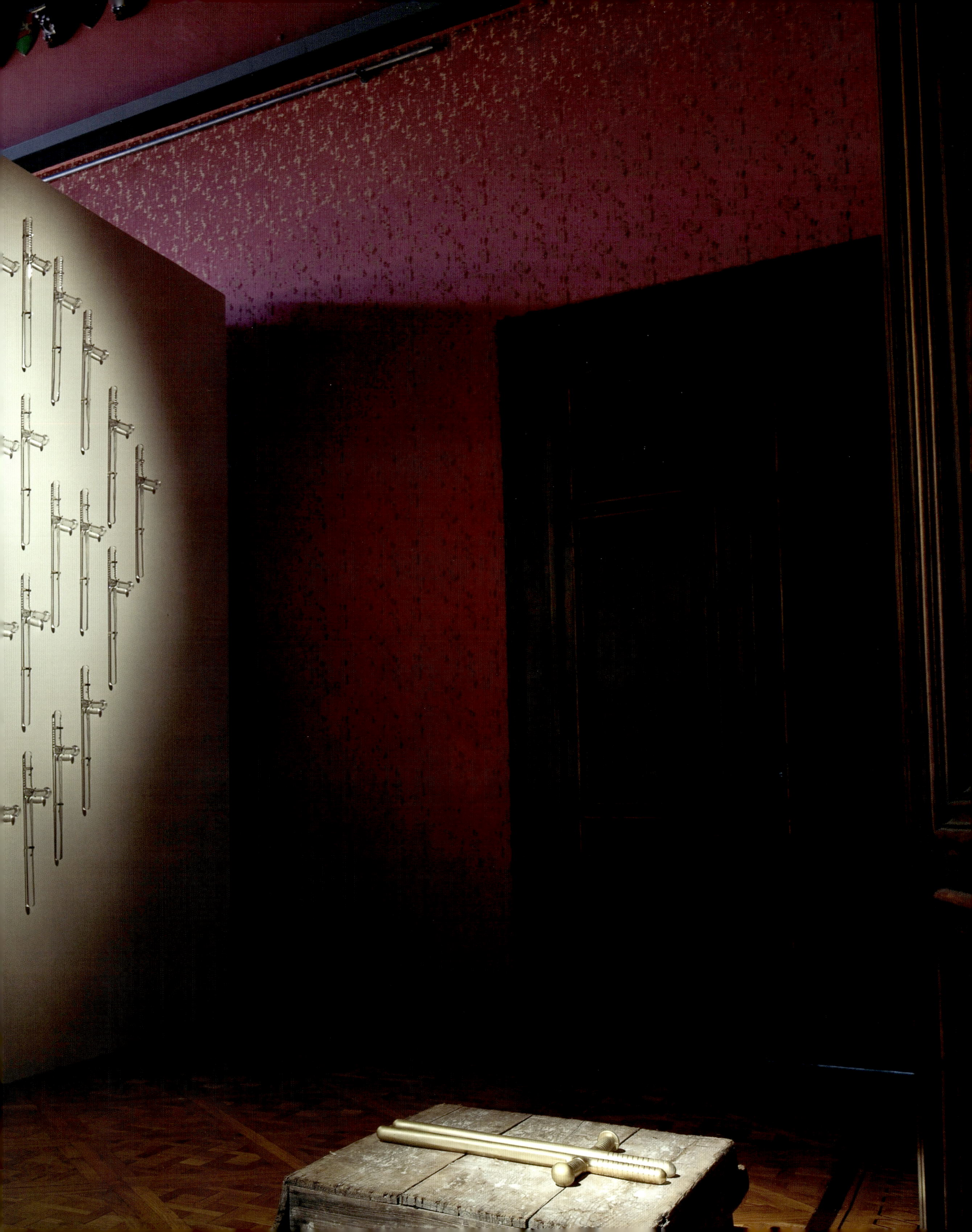

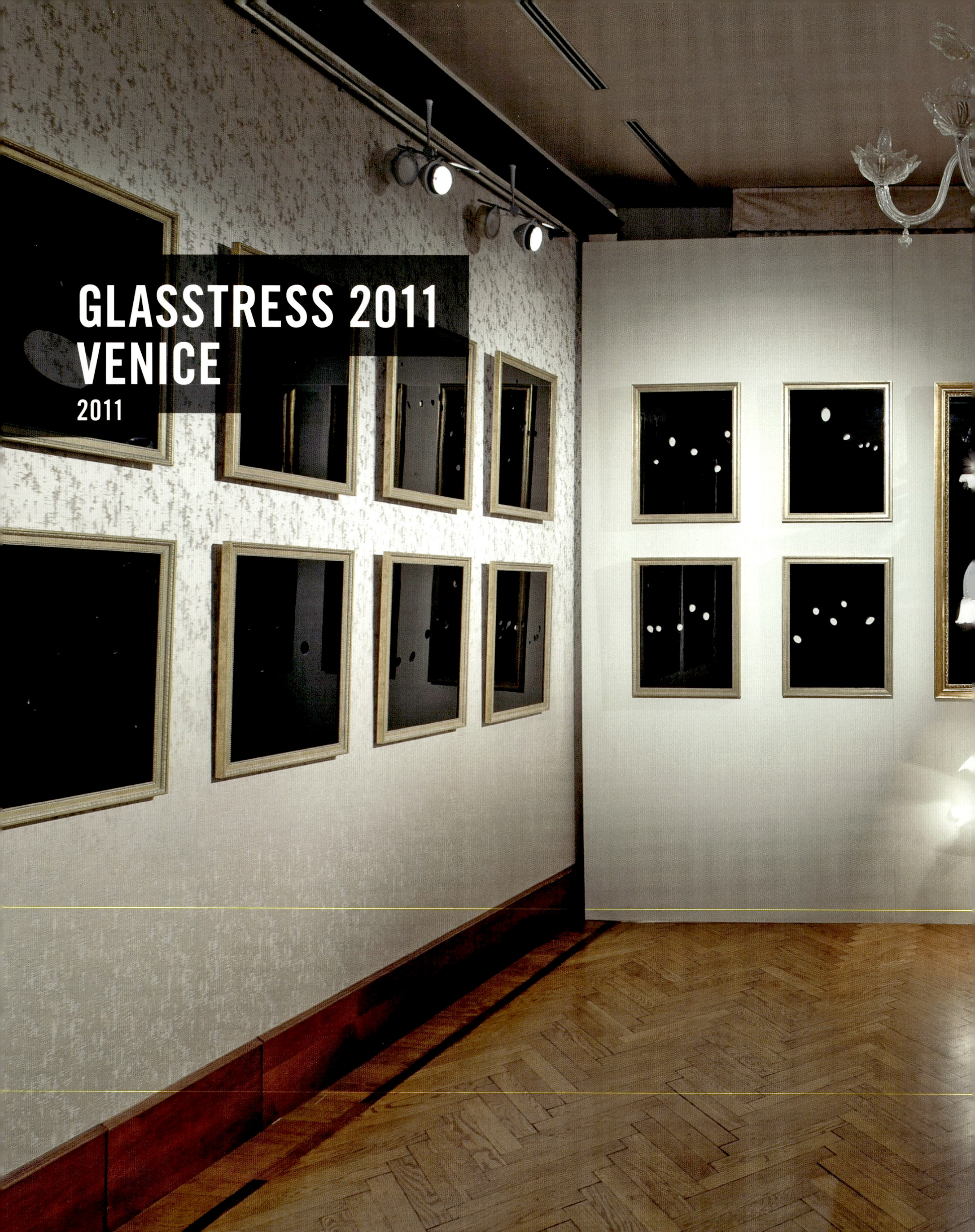
GLASSTRESS 2011
VENICE
2011

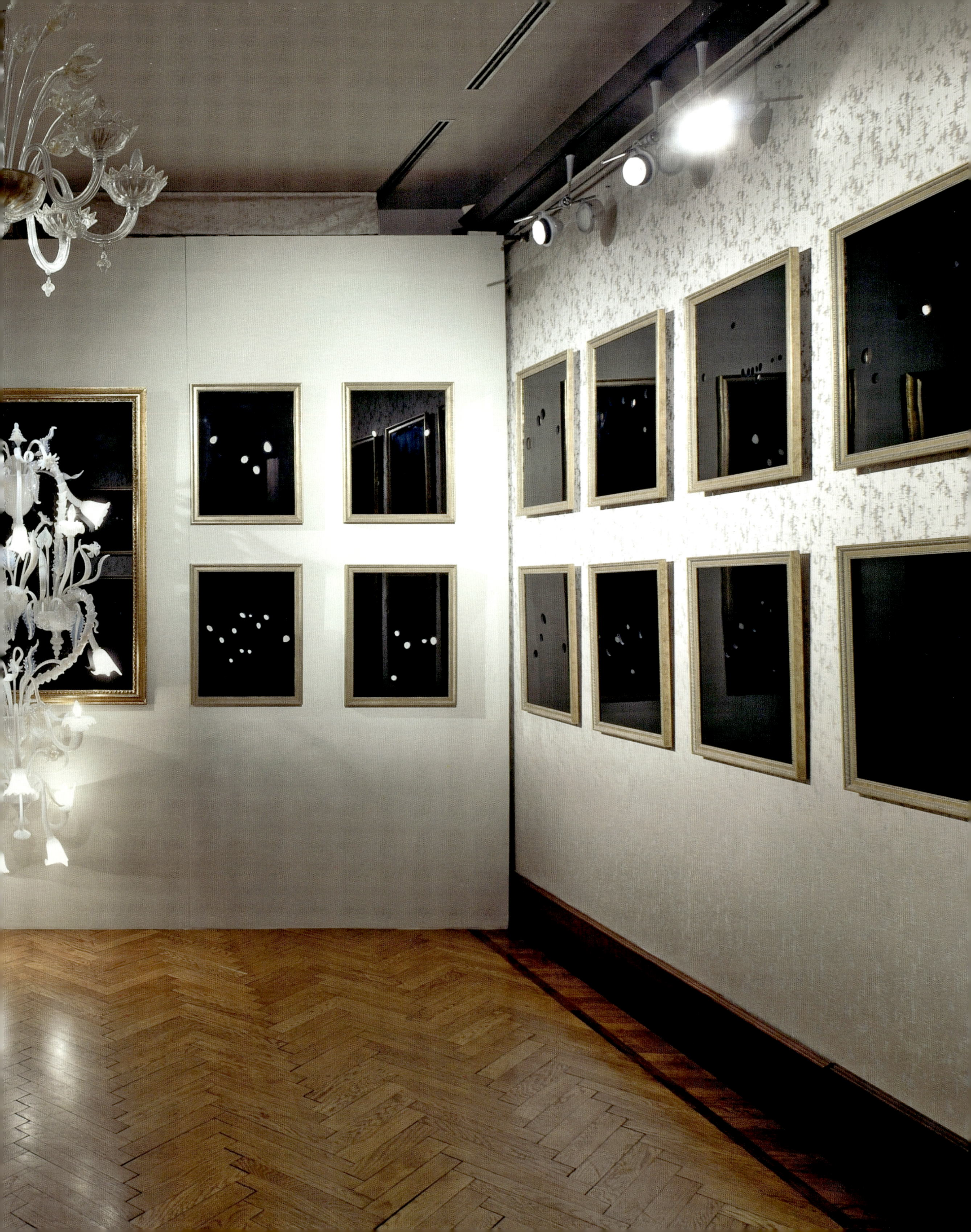

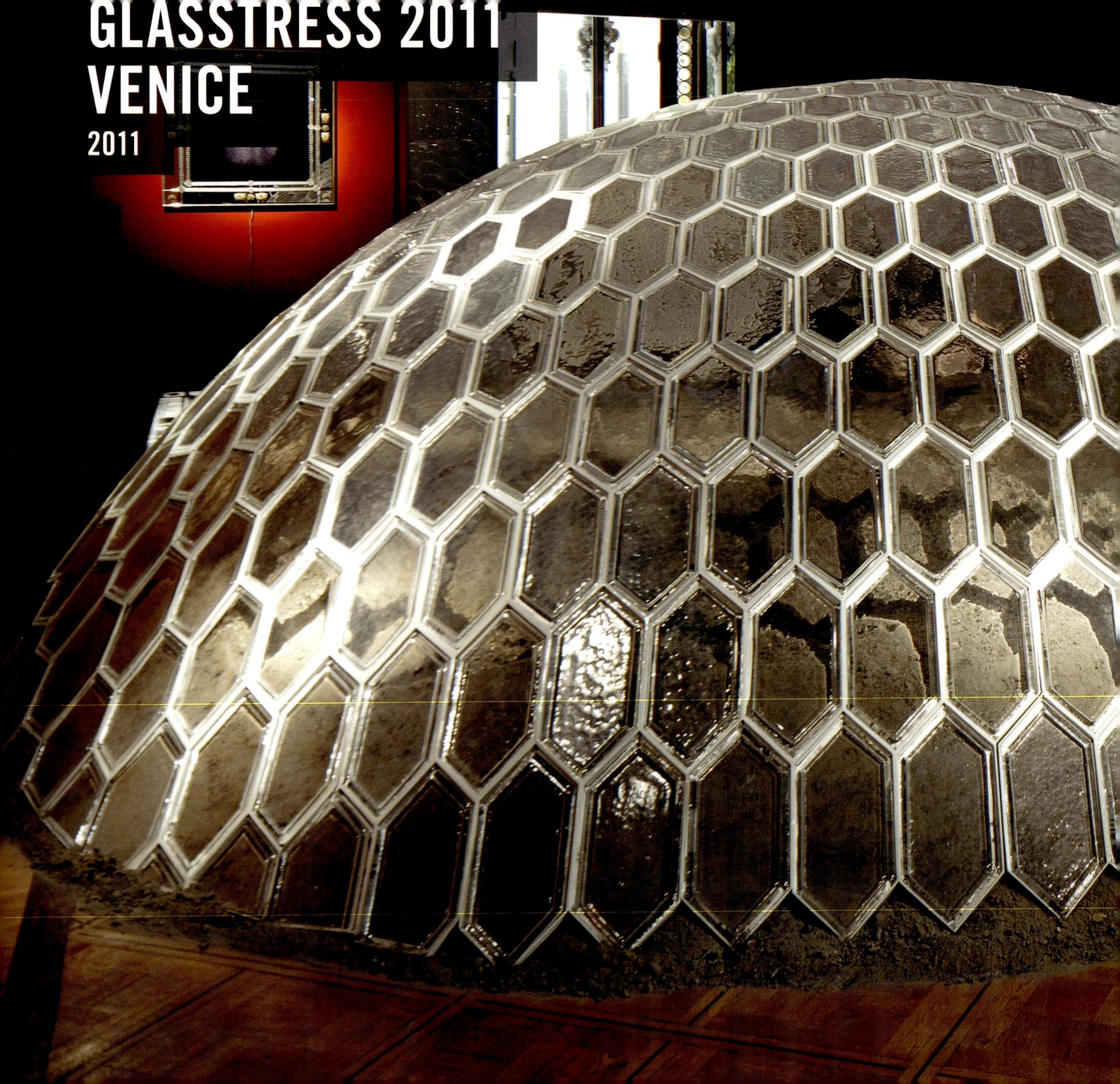
GLASSTRESS 2011
VENICE
2011

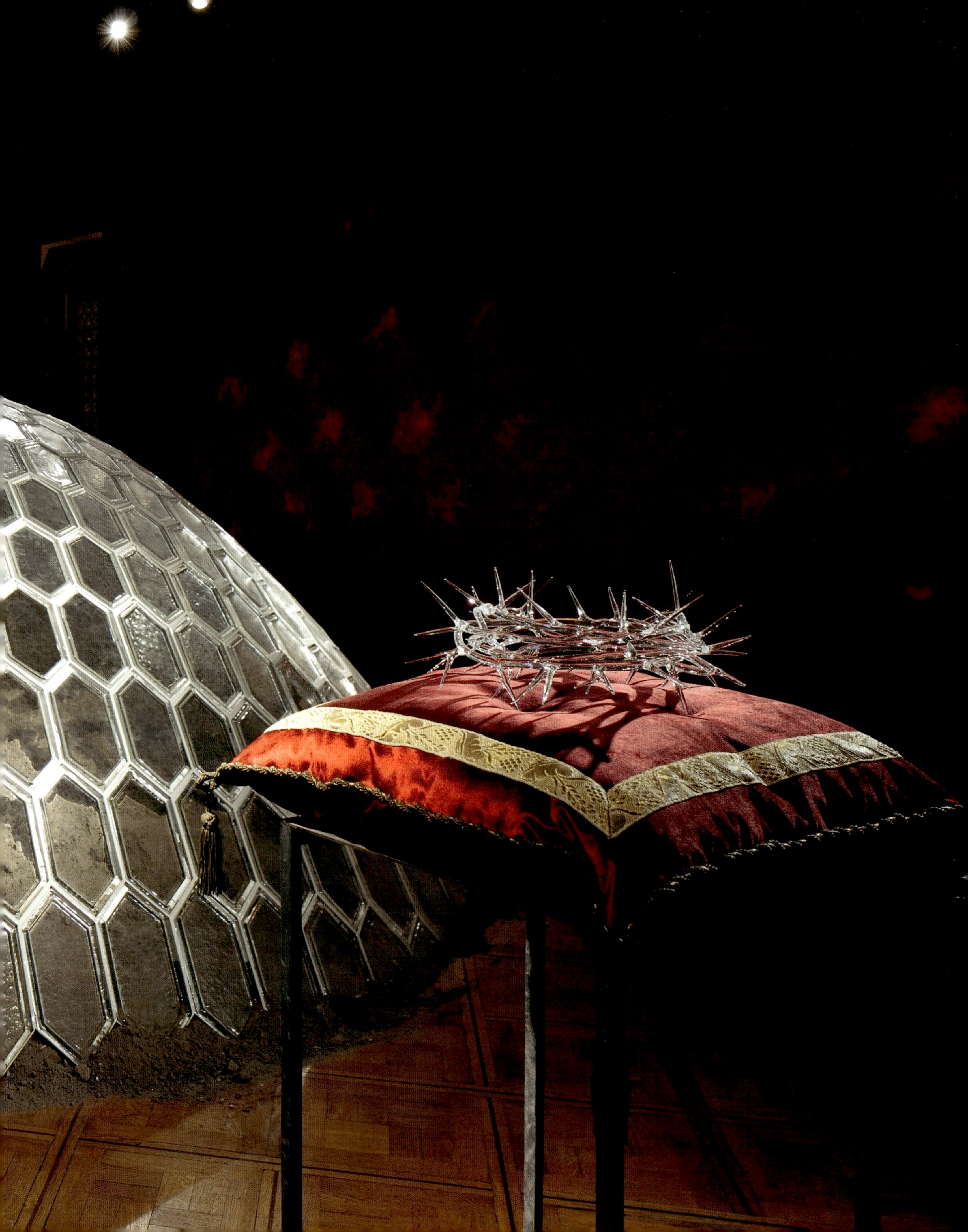

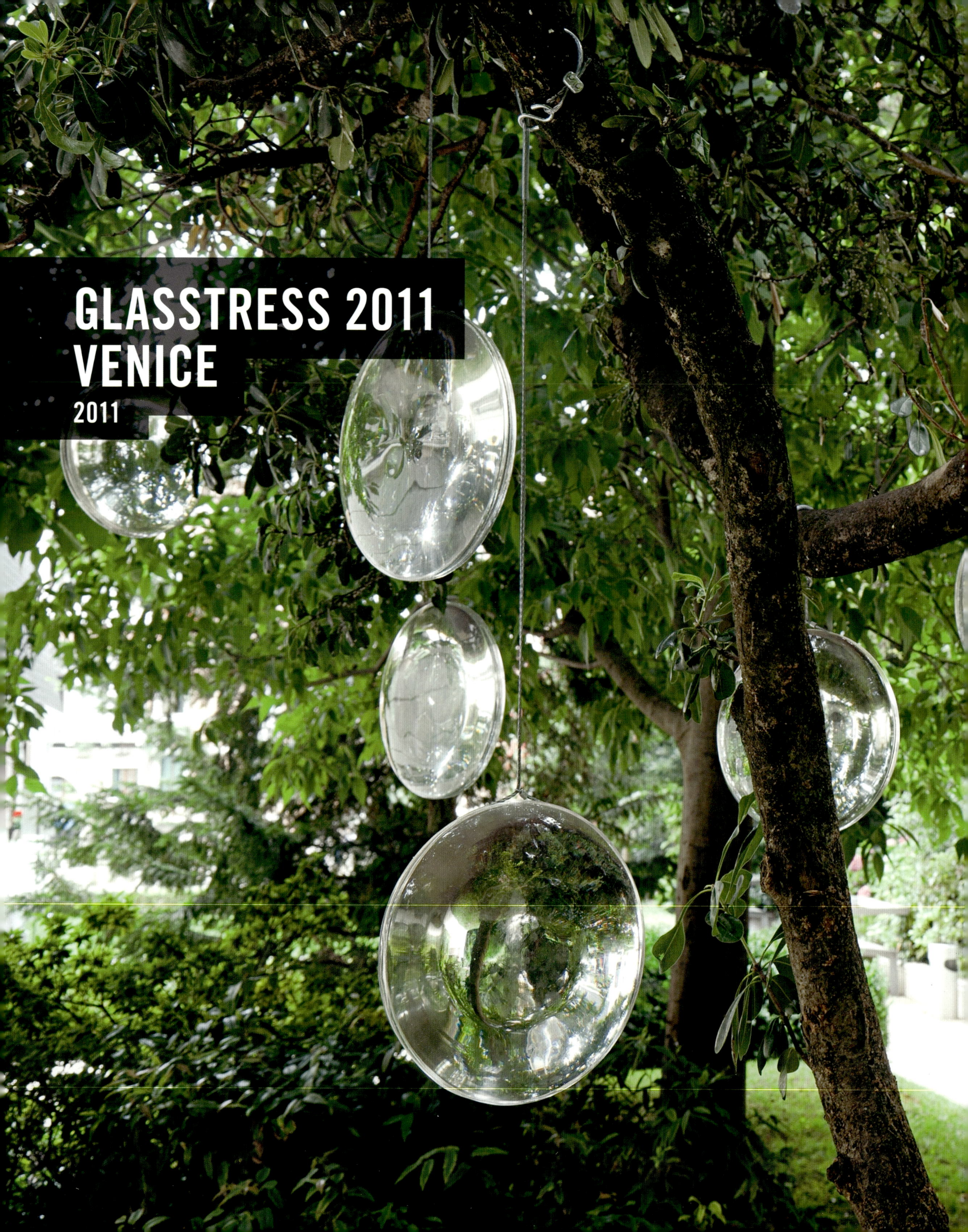

GLASSTRESS 2011
VENICE
2011

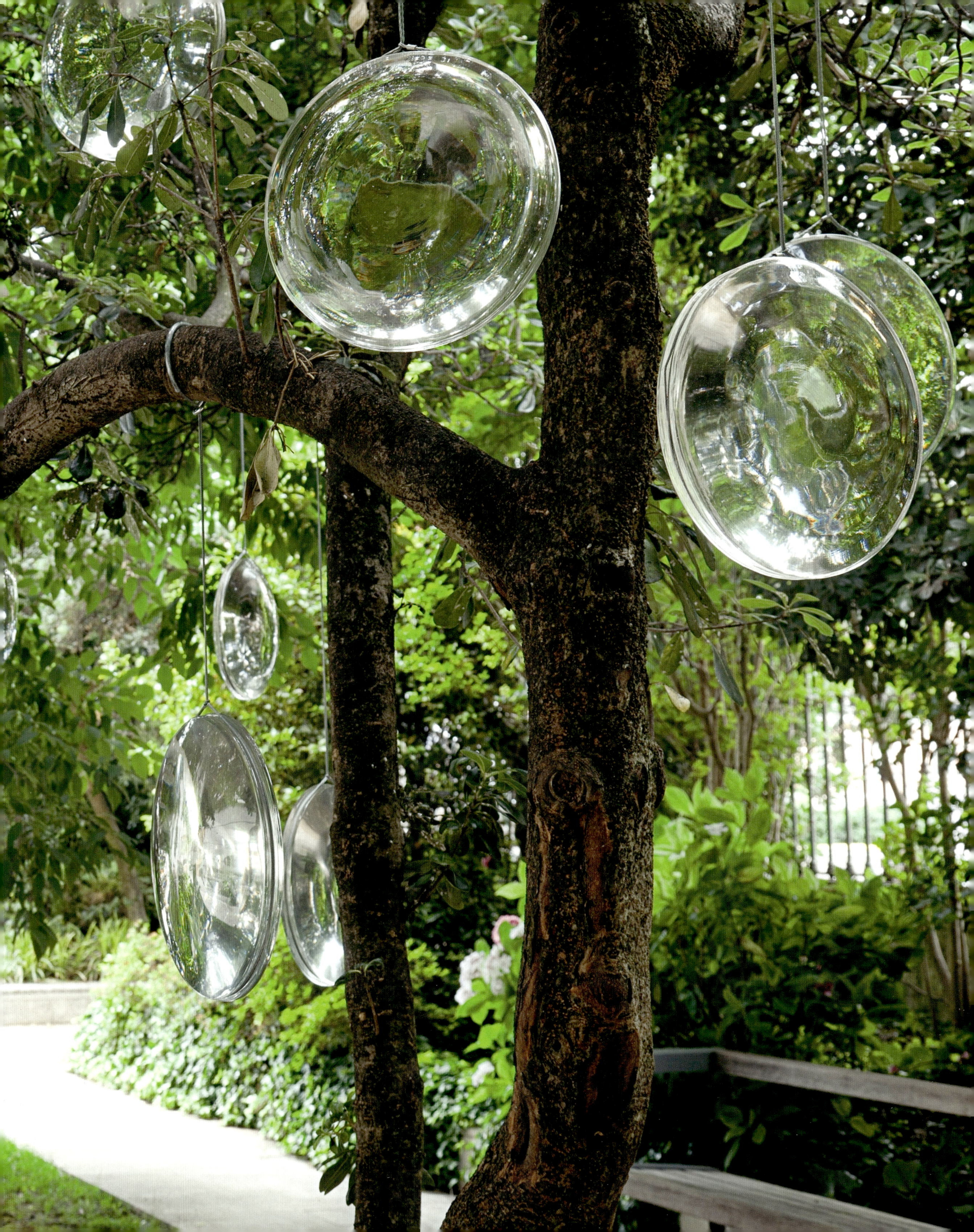

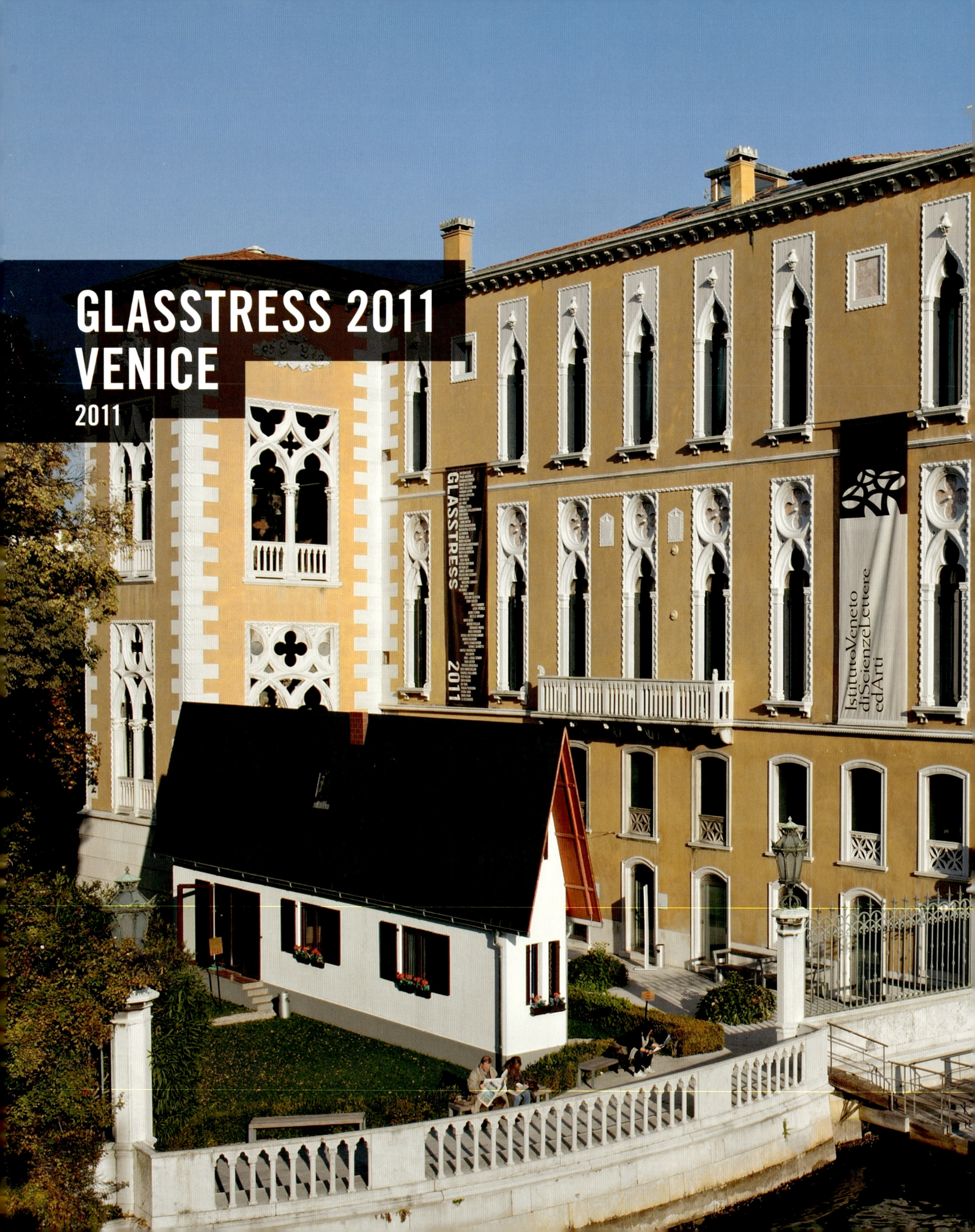

GLASSTRESS 2011
VENICE
2011

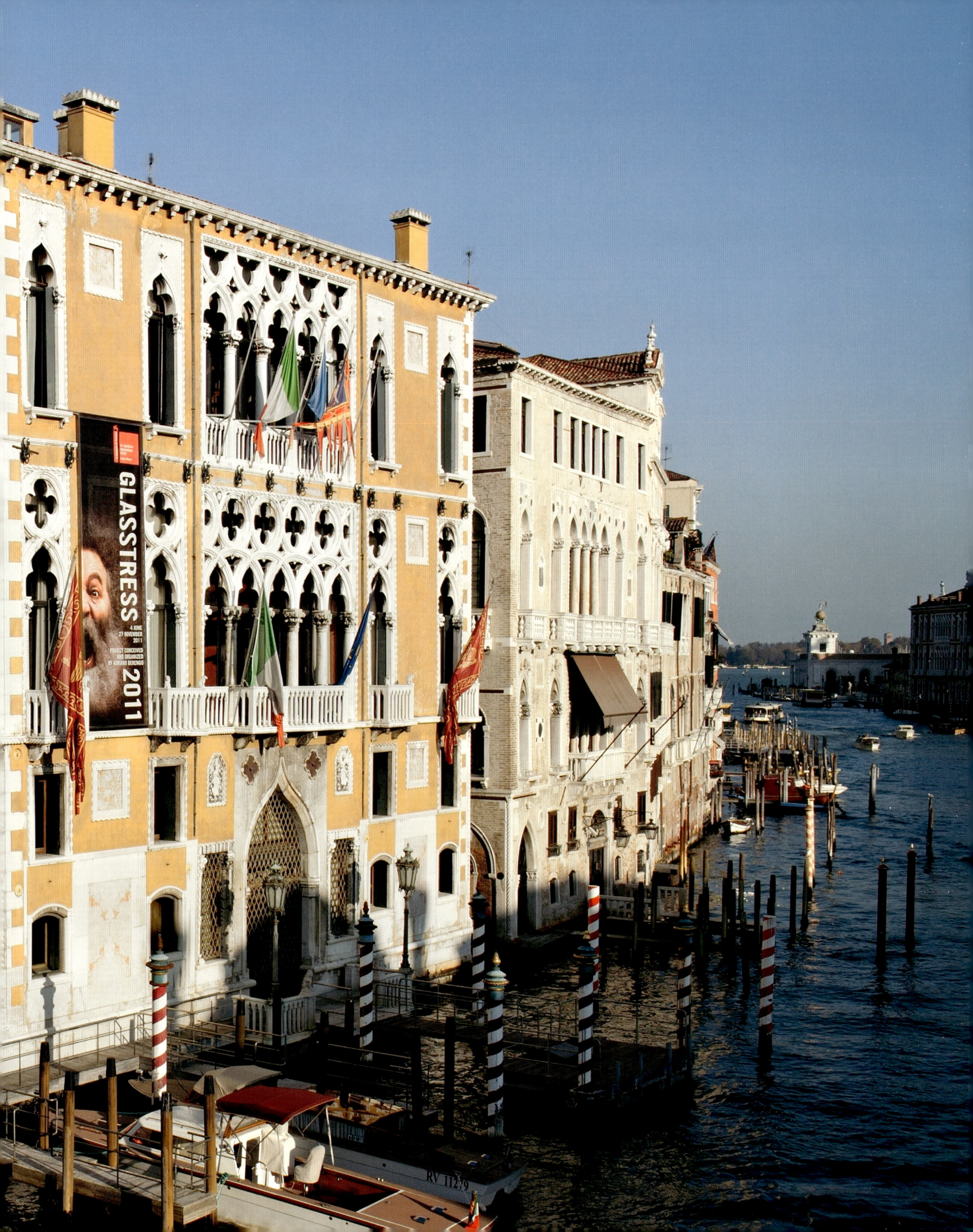
GLASSTRESS
4 JUNE
27 NOVEMBER
2011
PROJECT CONCEIVED
AND ORGANIZED
BY ADRIANO BERENGO
2011

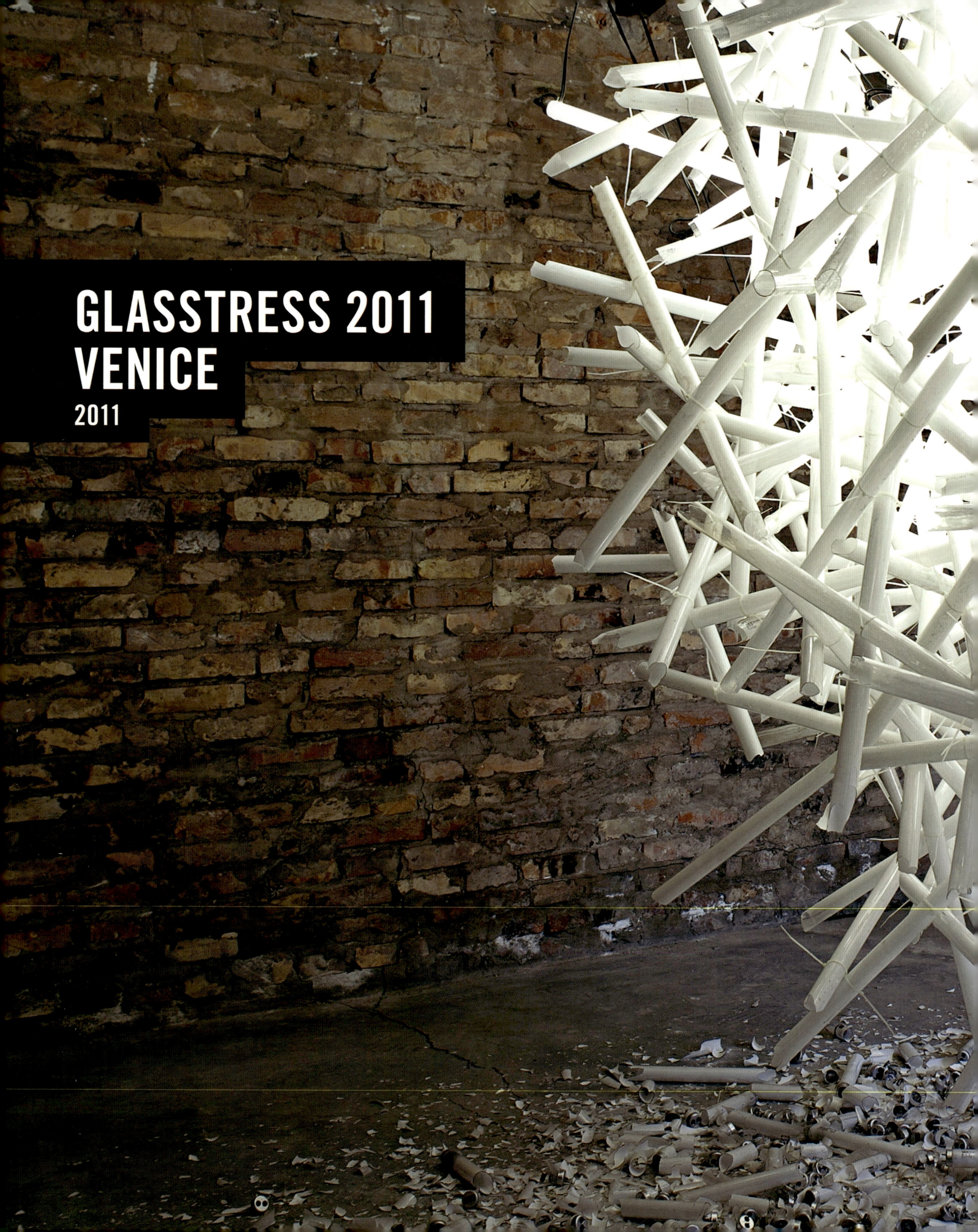

GLASSTRESS 2011
VENICE
2011

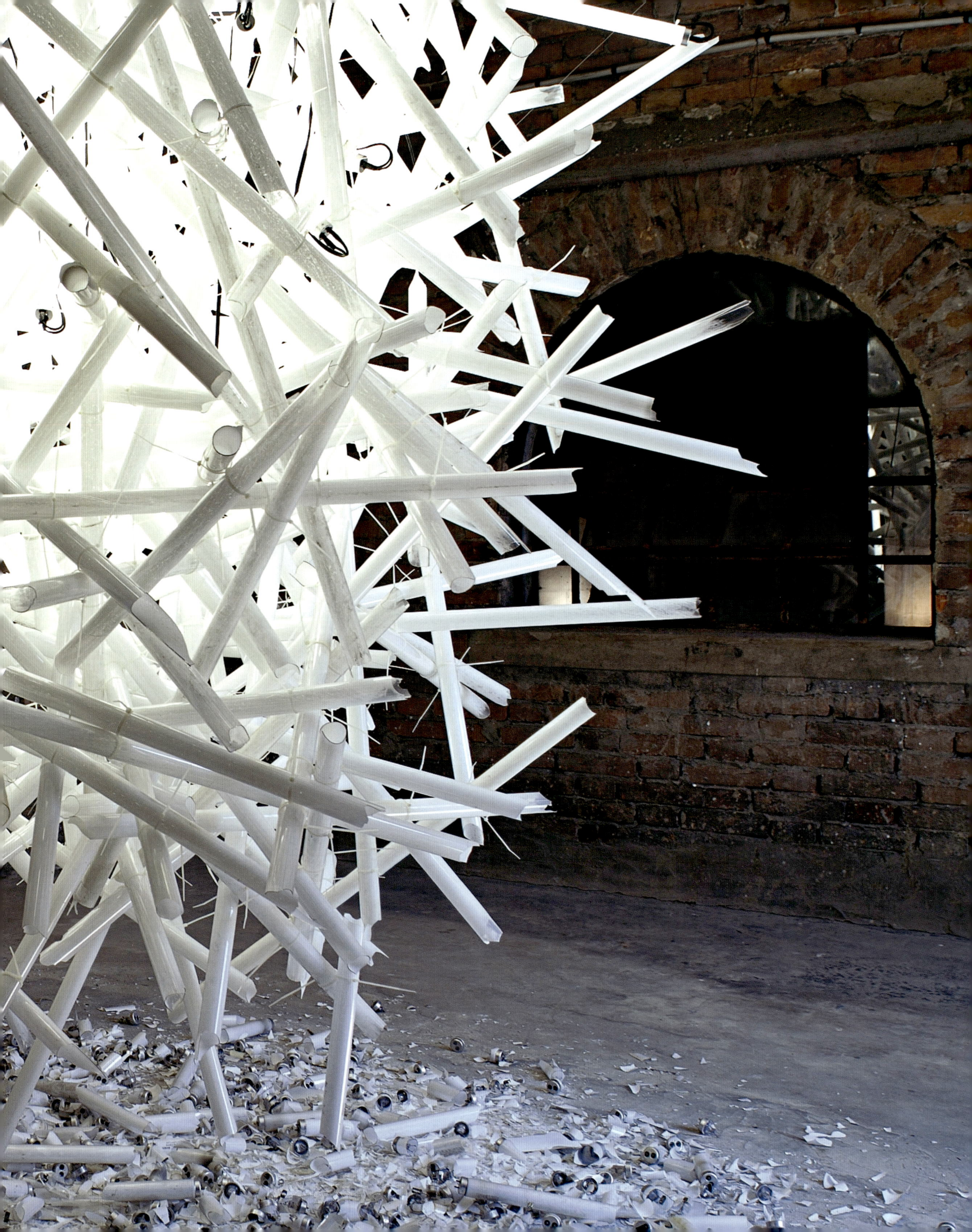

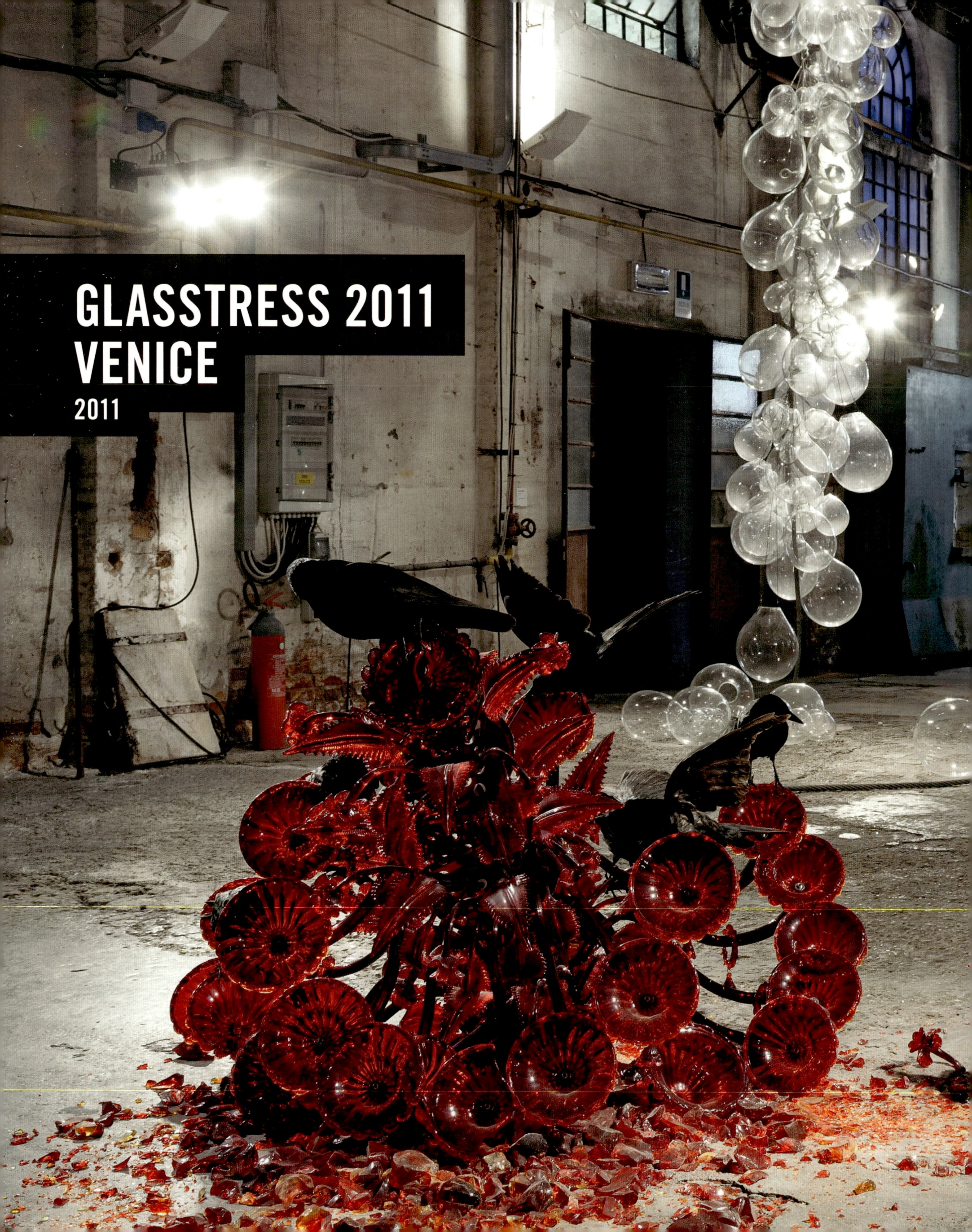
GLASSTRESS 2011
VENICE
2011

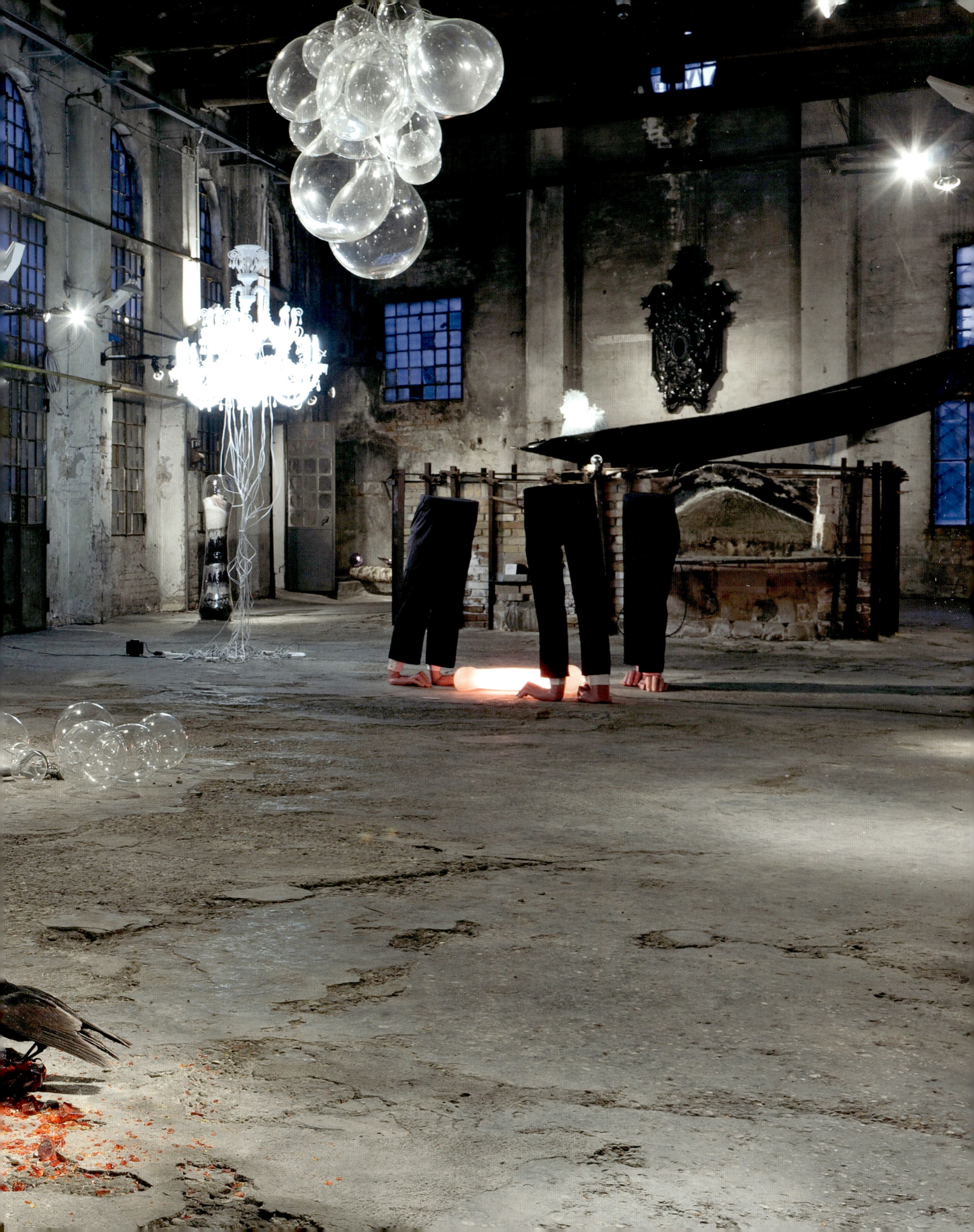

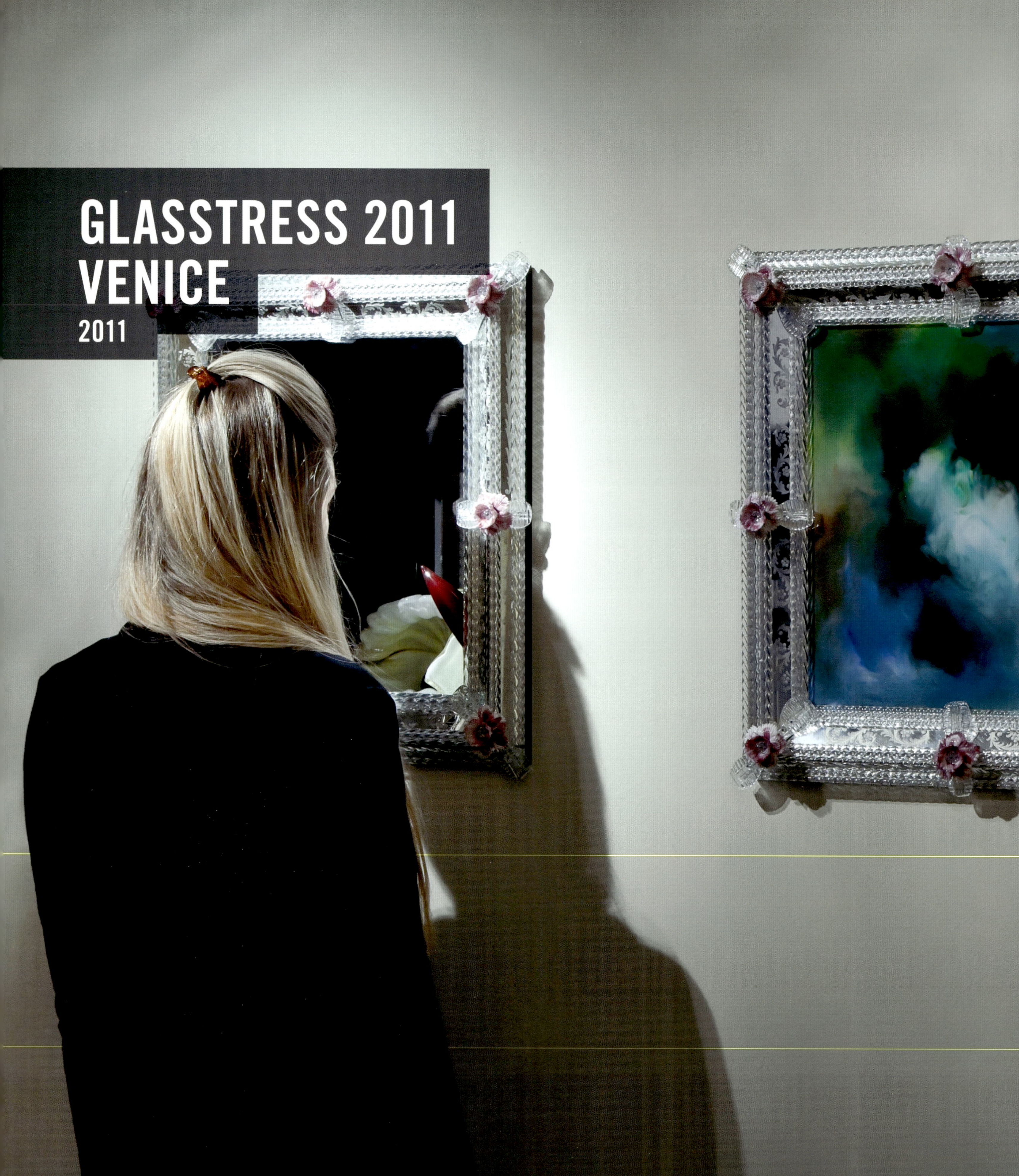
GLASSTRESS 2011
VENICE
2011

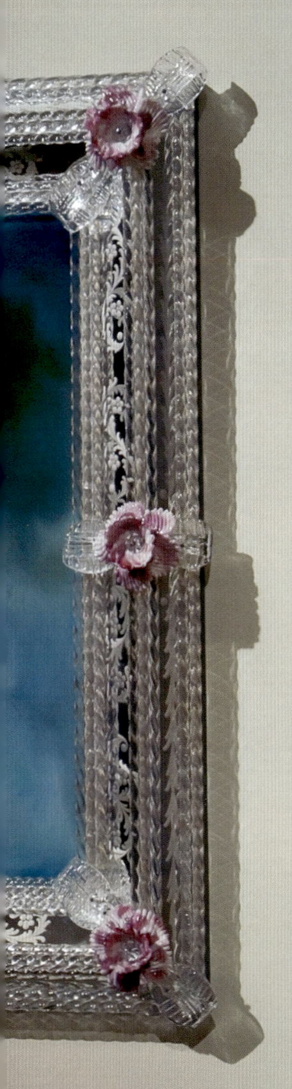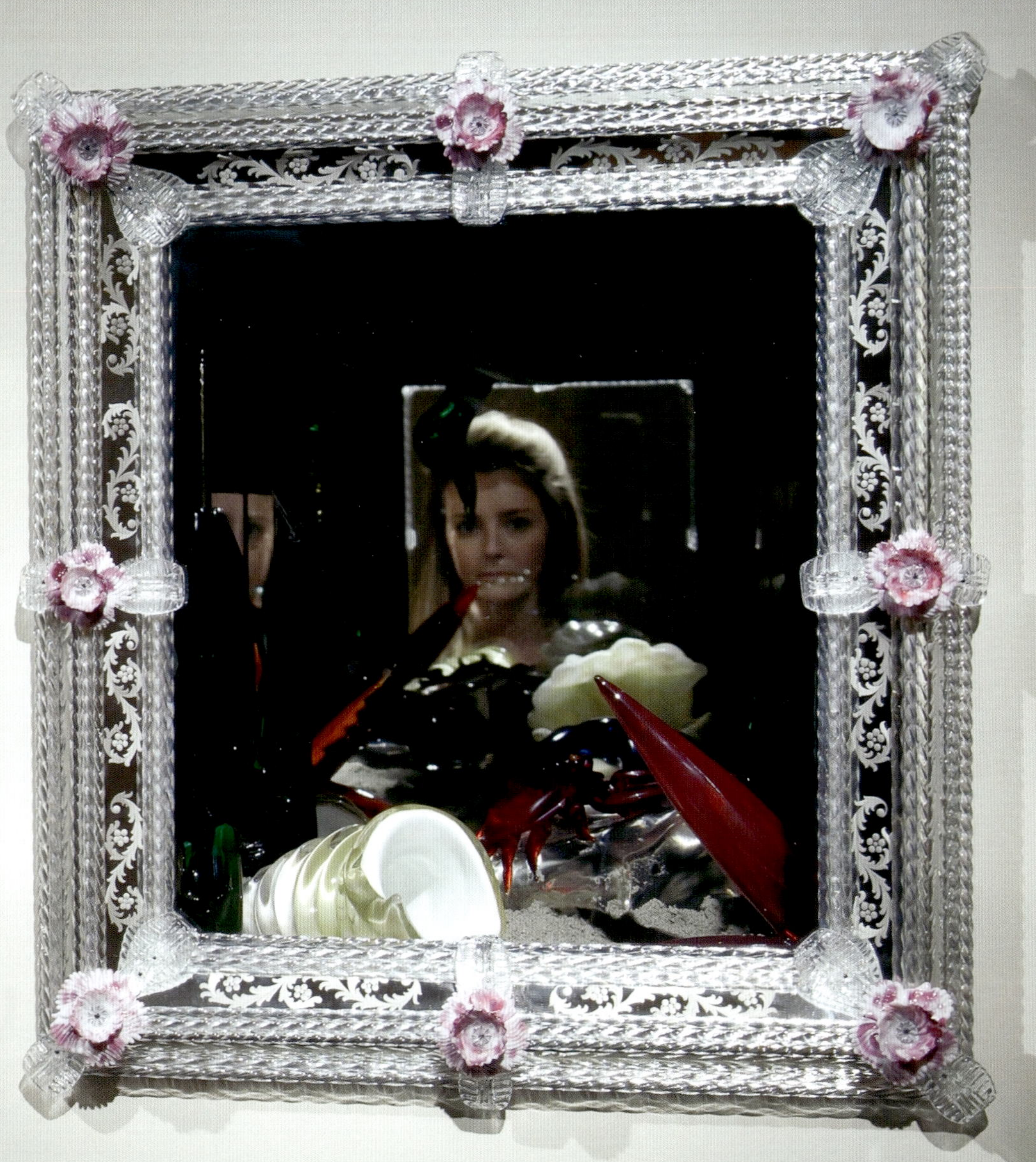

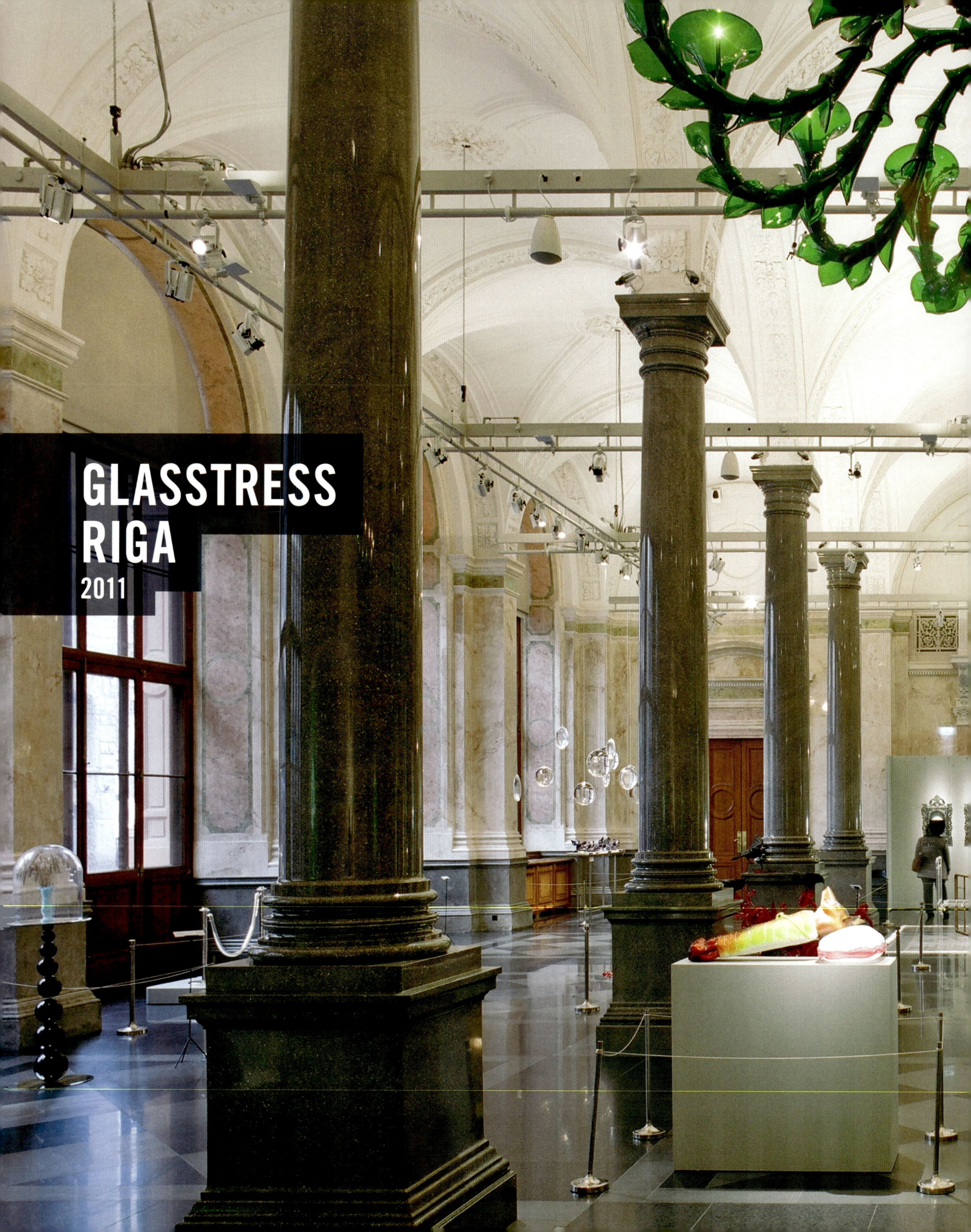

GLASSTRESS
RIGA
2011

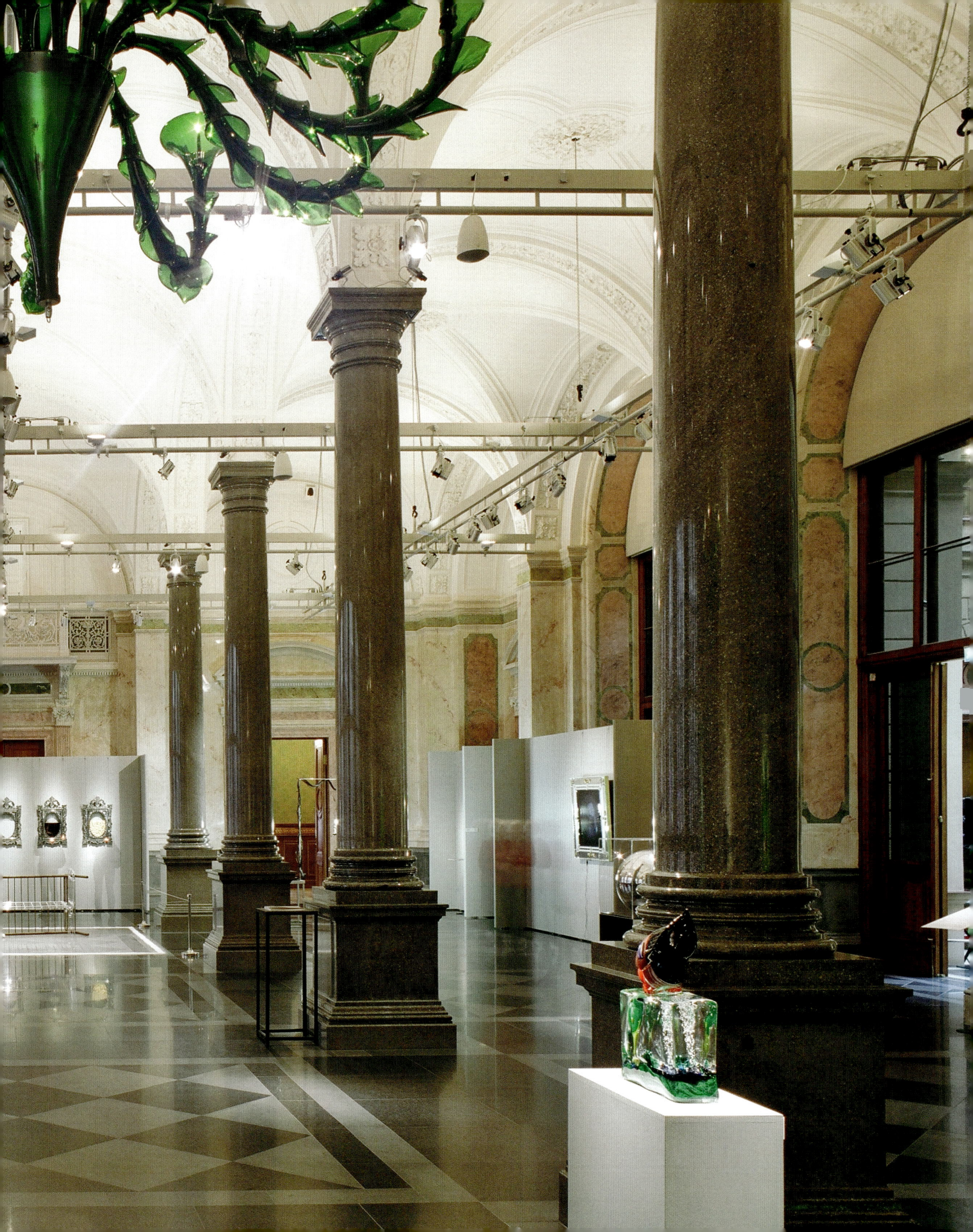

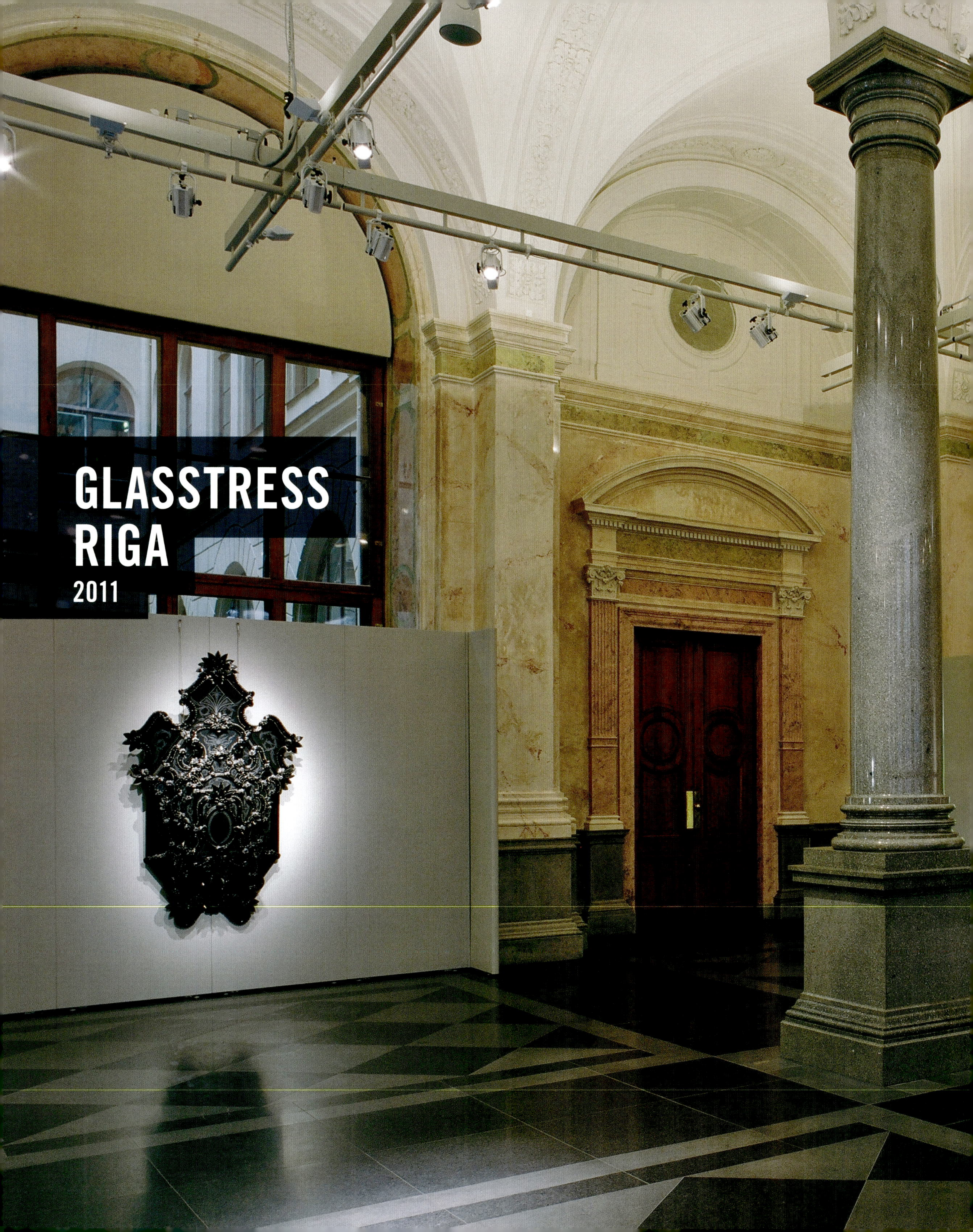

GLASSTRESS
RIGA
2011

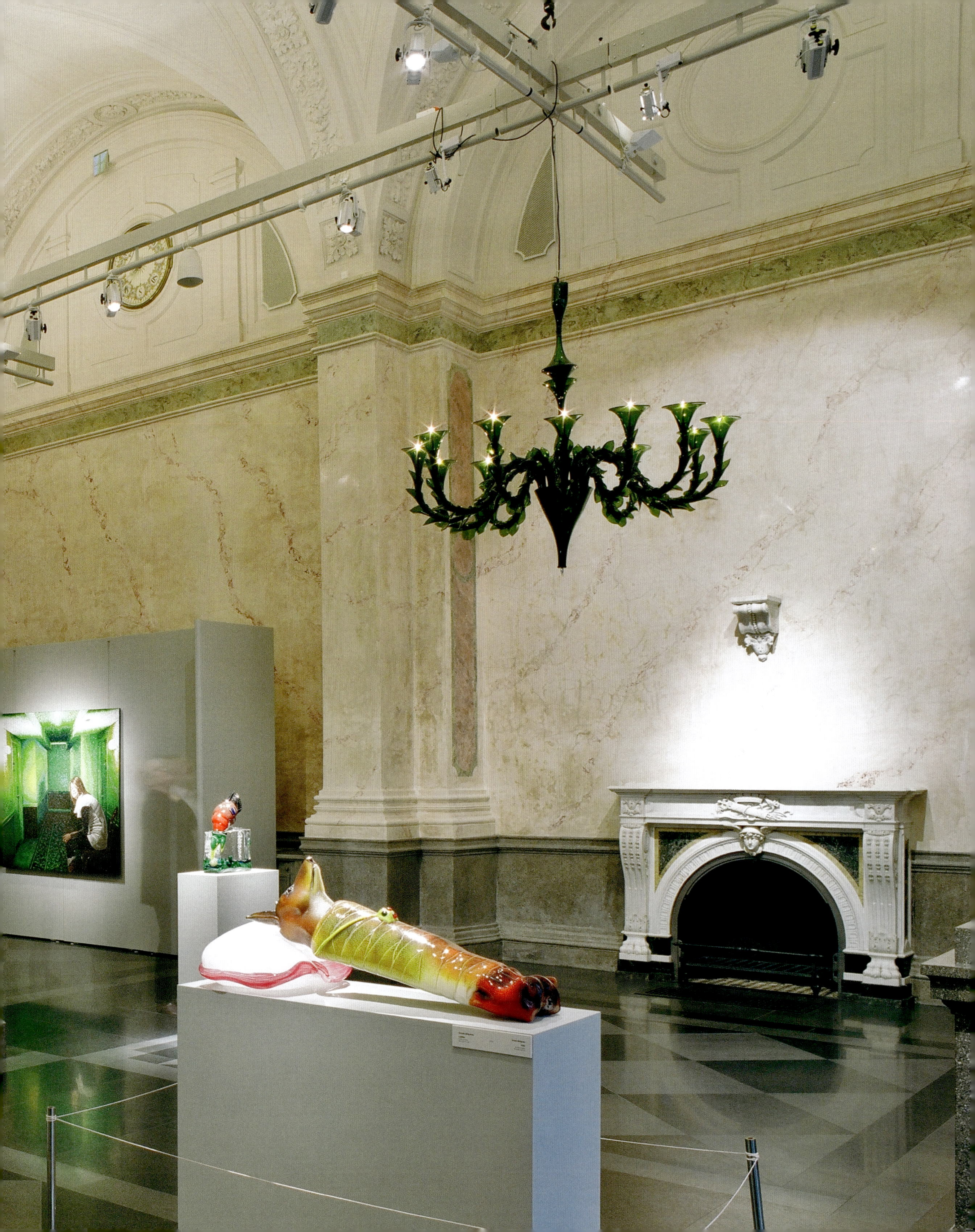

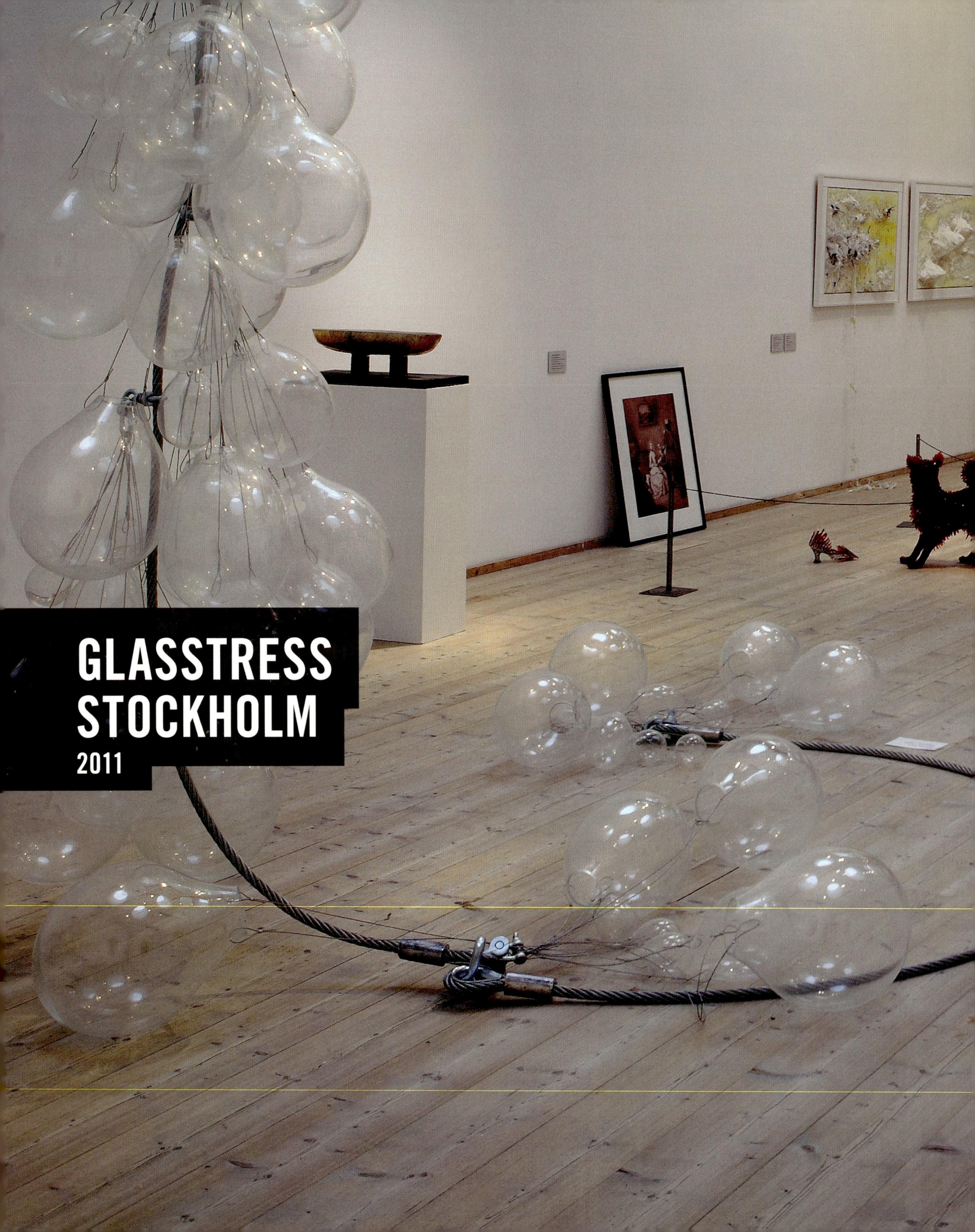

GLASSTRESS
STOCKHOLM
2011

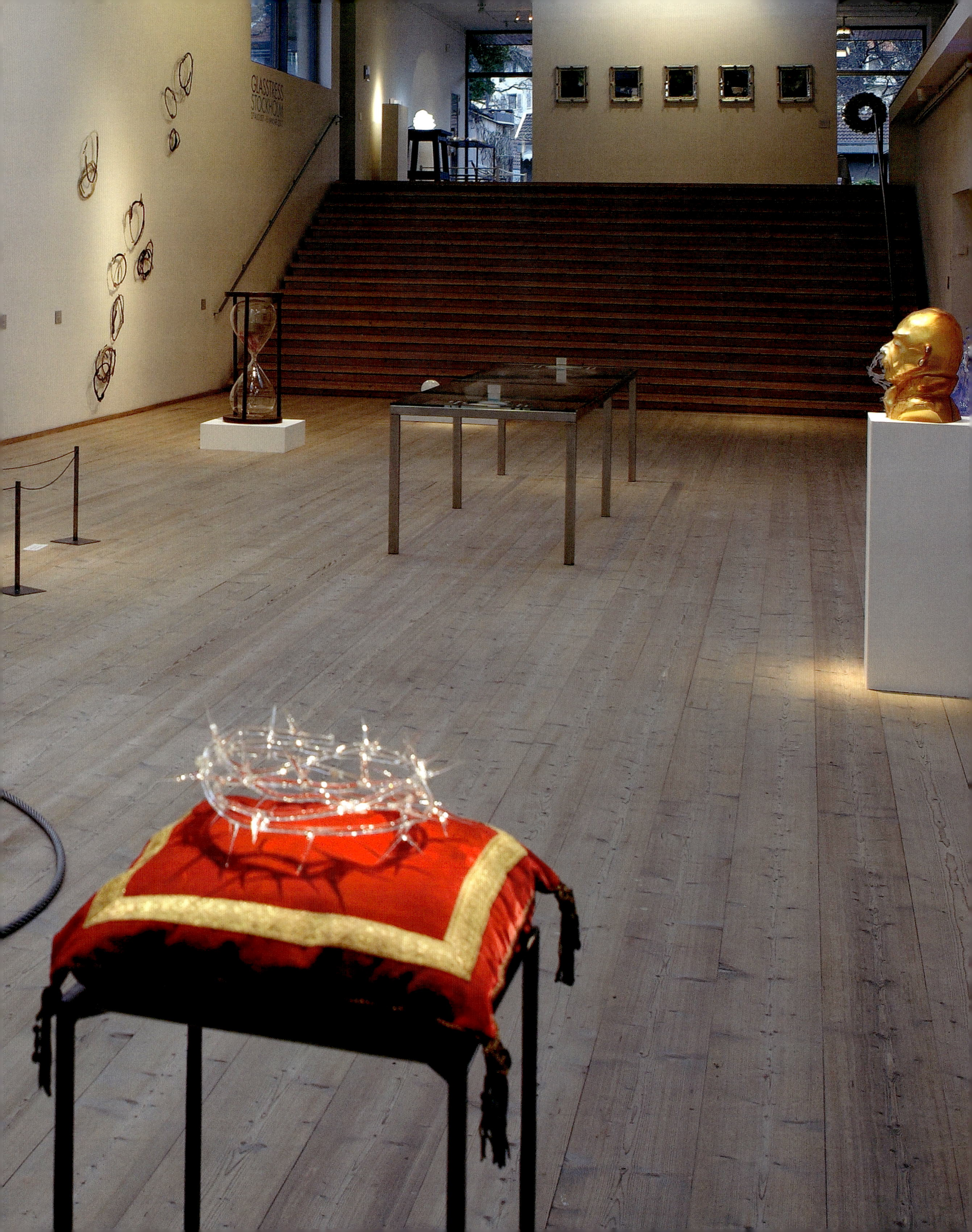

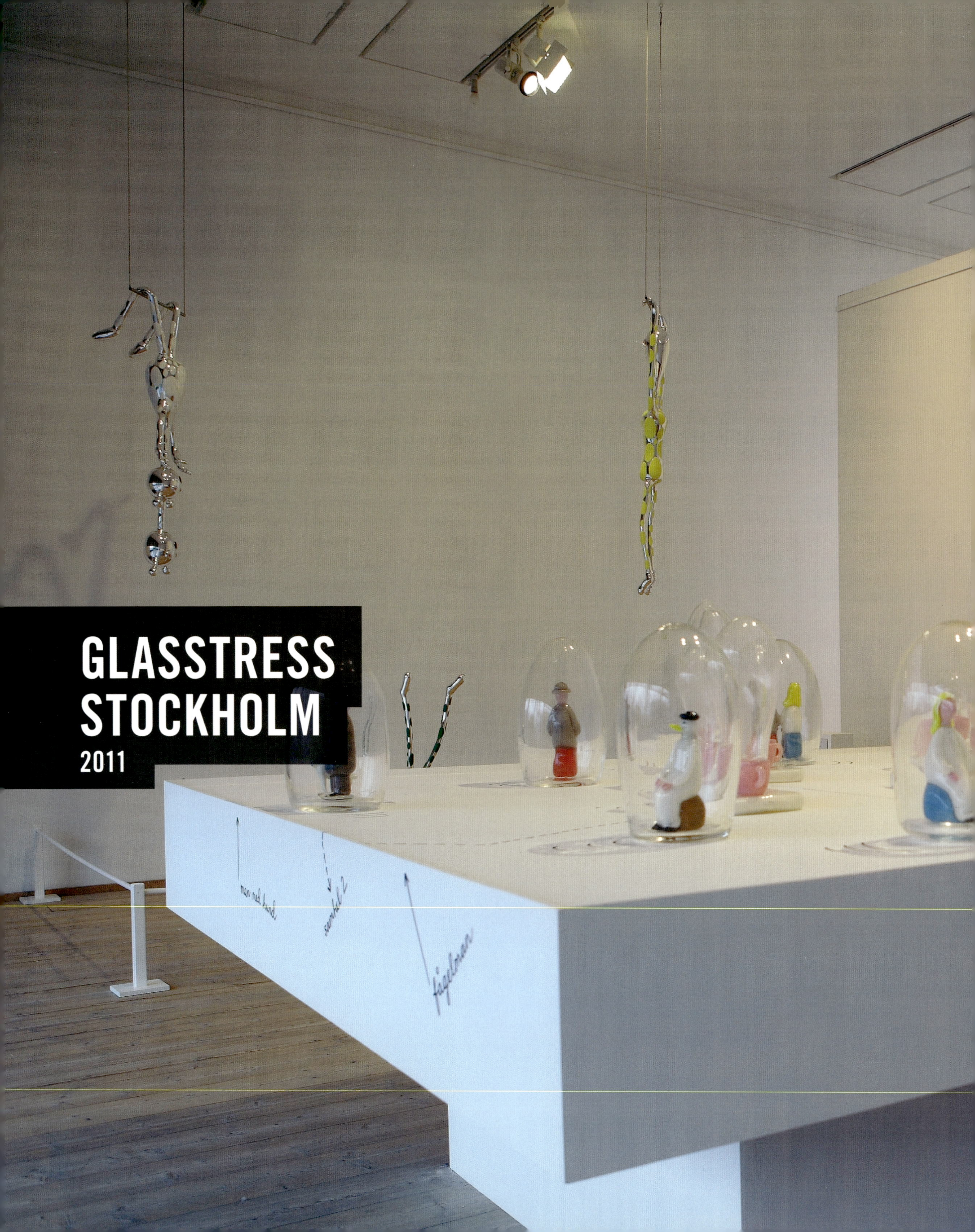
GLASSTRESS
STOCKHOLM
2011

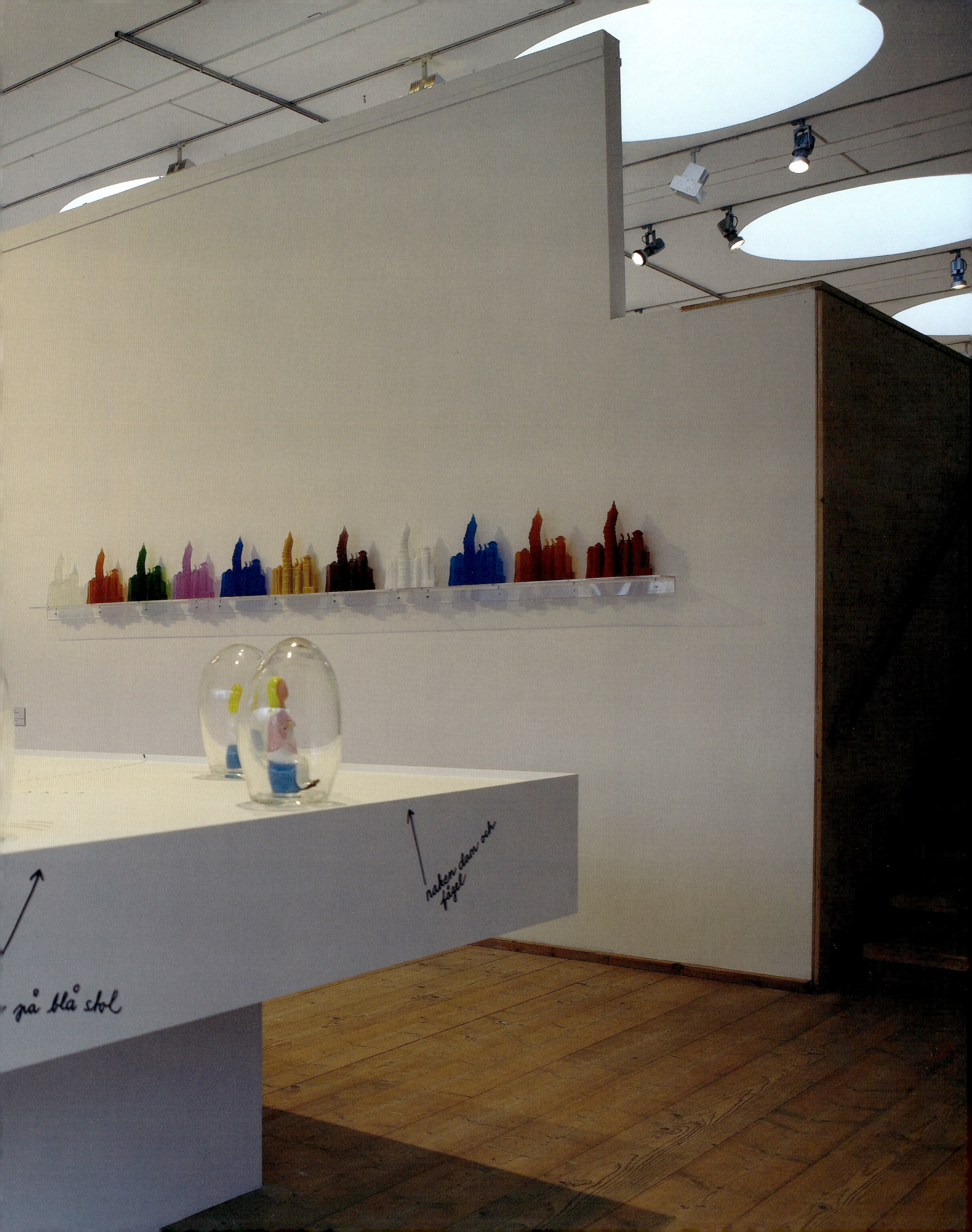

naken dan och
fågel
på blå stol

GLASSTRESS WORKS

GLASSTRESS 2009
    AT THE 53RD VENICE BIENNALE
GLASSTRESS 2011
    AT THE 54TH VENICE BIENNALE
GLASSTRESS RIGA 2011
GLASSTRESS STOCKHOLM 2011
GLASSTRESS NEW YORK 2012

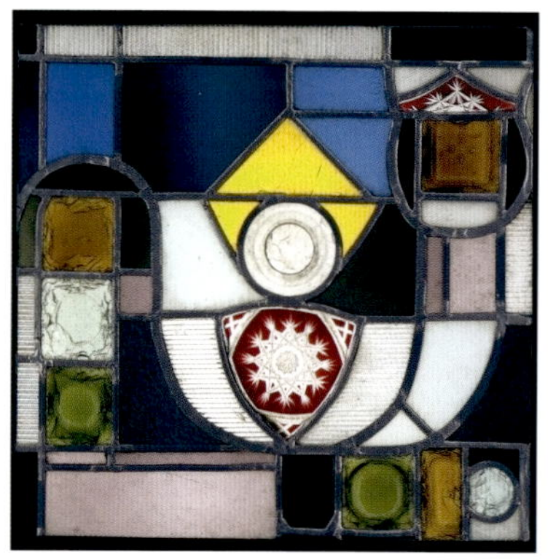

JOSEF ALBERS
Kaiserlich (Imperial),
ca. 1923
48 x 49 x 4.4 cm /
72 x 72 x 16.4 cm
(with frame)

Courtesy Josef Albers Museum
Quadrat Bottrop, Bottrop
Exhibited at *Glasstress 2009*,
Venice (IT)

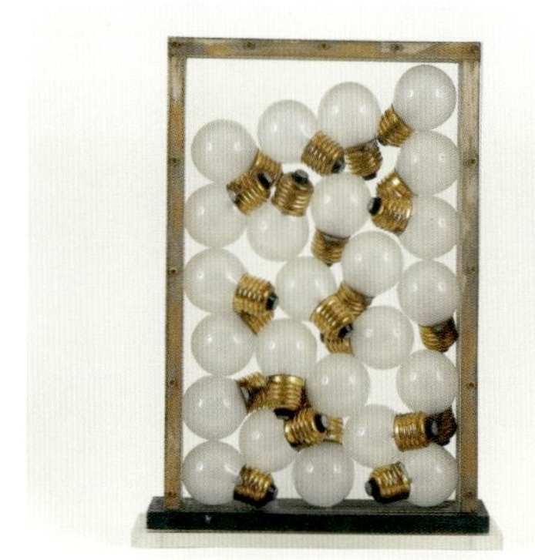

ARMAN
**Accumulation of Light
Bulbs,** 1962
33.5 x 22 x 5.5 cm

Courtesy Private Collection,
Bassano
Exhibited at *Glasstress 2009*,
Venice (IT)

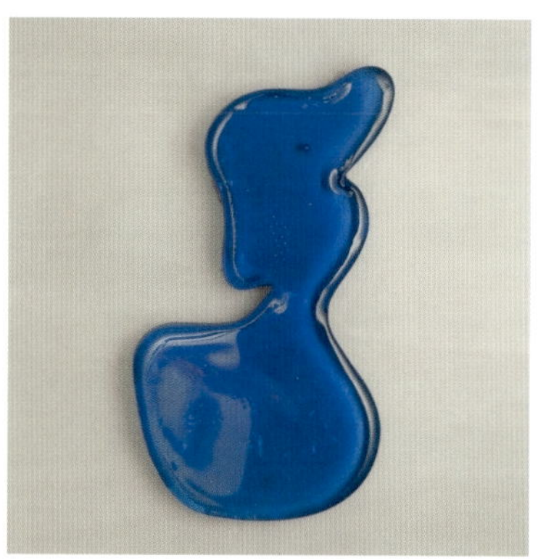

JEAN ARP
Collage n.2 (glass object),
1964
Ed. 2/3
50 x 34.7 x 3 cm

Courtesy Berengo Private
Collection, Venice
Exhibited at *Glasstress 2009*,
Venice (IT)
Exhibited at *Glasstress Stockholm*
2011, Stockholm (SE)

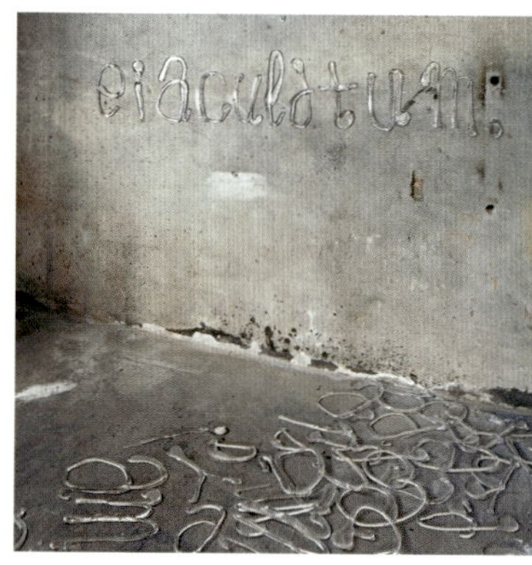

ANTHON BEEKE
Eiaculatum,
2009 / *detail*
variable dimensions

Courtesy the artist
Exhibited at *Glasstress 2011*,
Venice (IT)

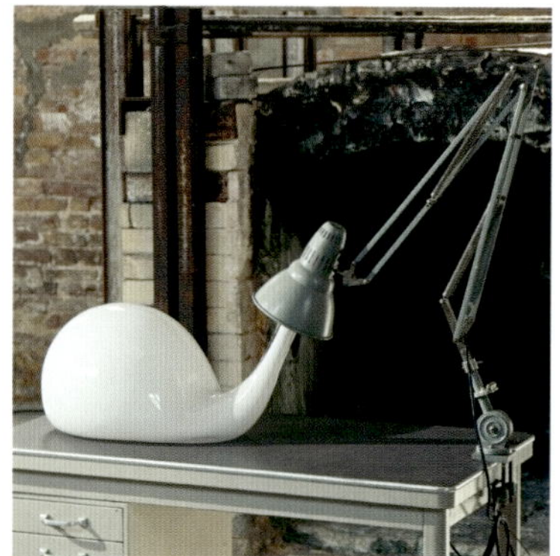

PIEKE BERGMANS
Desk Light Bulb, 2009
125 x 125 x 50 cm

Courtesy Pieke Bergmans –
Design Virus, Amsterdam
Exhibited at *Glasstress 2011*,
Venice (IT)

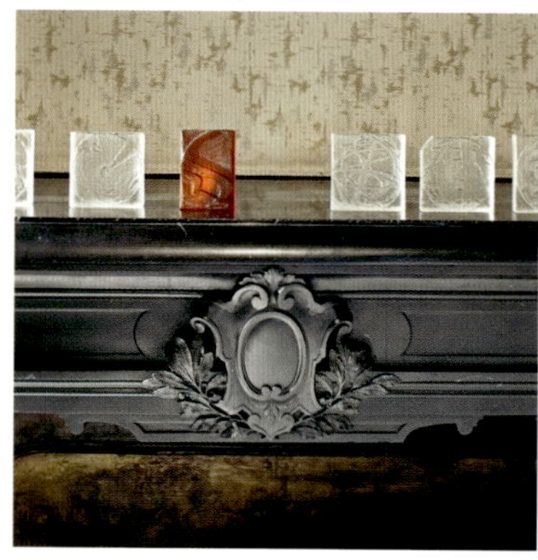

DOMENICO BIANCHI
Untitled, 2011
9 x 9 x 3 cm (white) /
9 x 6 x 3 cm (amber)

Courtesy the artist and Berengo
Private Collection, Venice
Exhibited at *Glasstress 2011*,
Venice (IT)
Exhibited at *Glasstress Stockholm*
2011, Stockholm (SE)

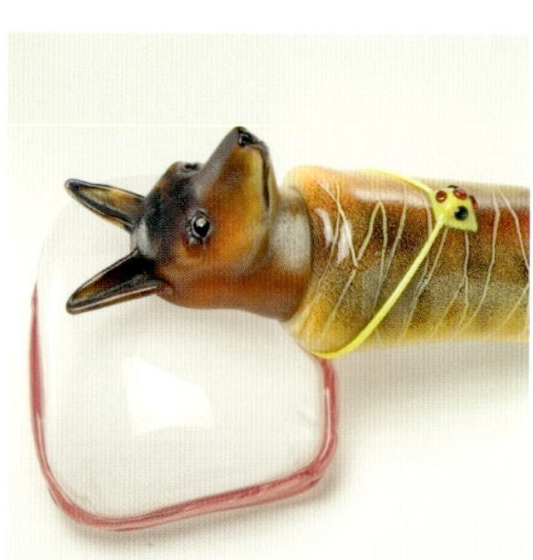

ERNST BILLGREN
Fox,
2000 / *detail*
25 x 90 x 27 cm

Courtesy Berengo Private
Collection, Venice
Exhibited at *Glasstress Riga* 2011,
Riga (LV)

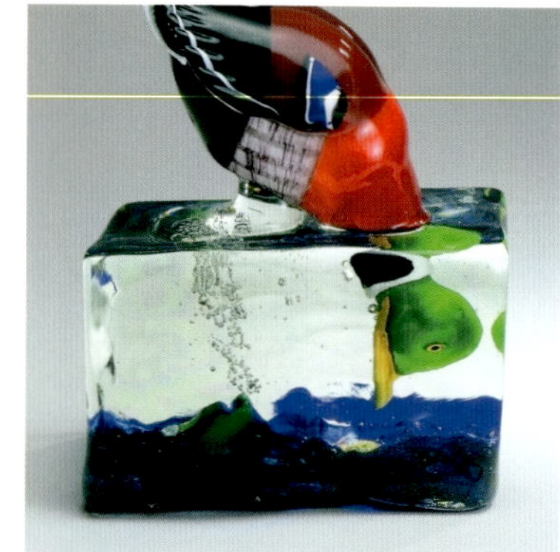

ERNST BILLGREN
Golden Coin,
1999 / *detail*
40 x 29 x 16 cm

Courtesy Berengo Private
Collection, Venice
Exhibited at *Glasstress Riga* 2011,
Riga (LV)

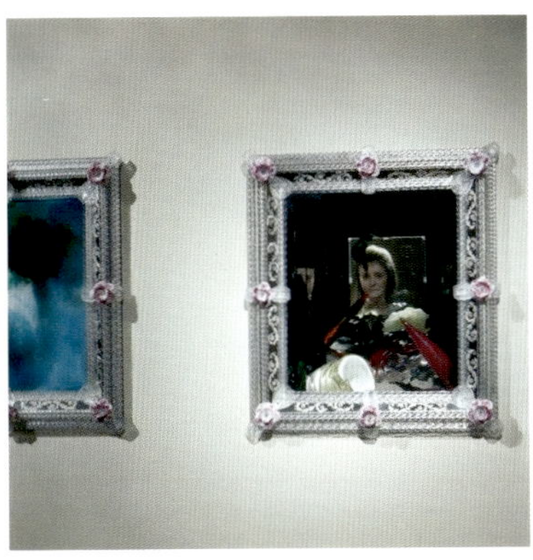

ERNST BILLGREN
Mermaid's View,
2011 / *detail*
57 x 51 x 3 cm
(flat frames) /
57 x 51 x 110 cm
(3D frames)

Courtesy the artist and Berengo
Private Collection, Venice
Exhibited at *Glasstress 2011*,
Venice (IT)
Exhibited at *Glasstress Stockholm*
2011, Stockholm (SE)

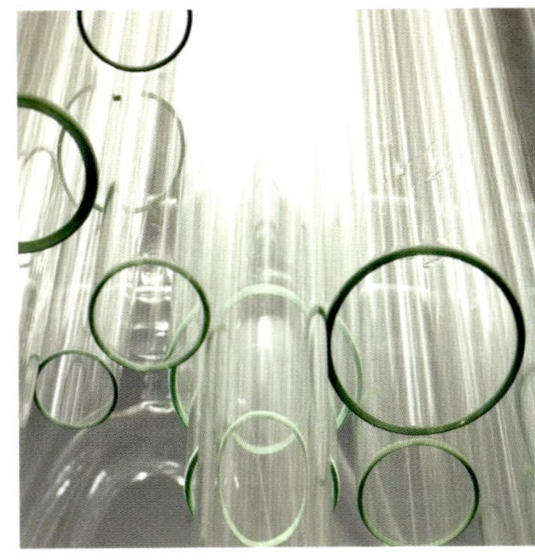

JOOST VAN BLEISWIJK
**Fragile Factory/Heavy Duty
Trestles,** 2011 / *detail*
98 x 180 x 75 cm

Courtesy Venice Projects, Venice
Exhibited at *Glasstress 2011*,
Venice (IT)

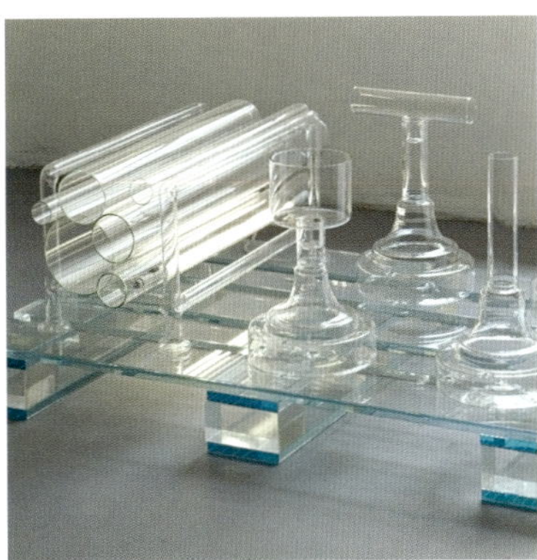

JOOST VAN BLEISWIJK
**Fragile Factory/Industry
Pallet,** 2011 / *detail*
50 x 120 x 80 cm

Courtesy Venice Projects, Venice
Exhibited at *Glasstress 2011*,
Venice (IT)

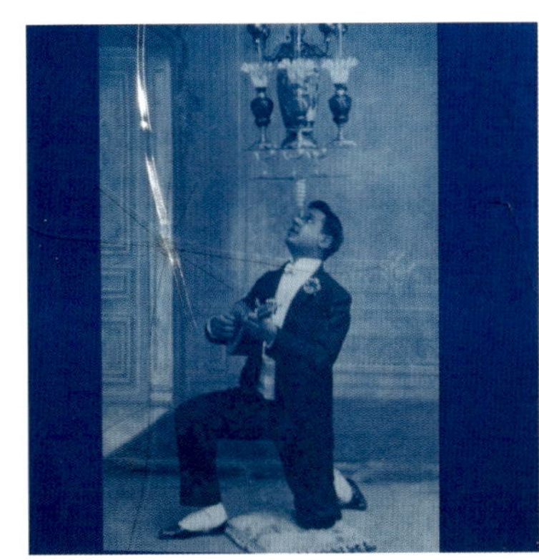

BARBARA BLOOM
Balance: Blue Gentleman,
2011 / *detail*
103 x 75 x 5 cm

Courtesy Galleria Raffaella Cortese,
Milan, Tracy Williams ltd., New
York, and Galerie Gisela Capitain,
Cologne
Exhibited at *Glasstress 2011*,
Venice (IT)

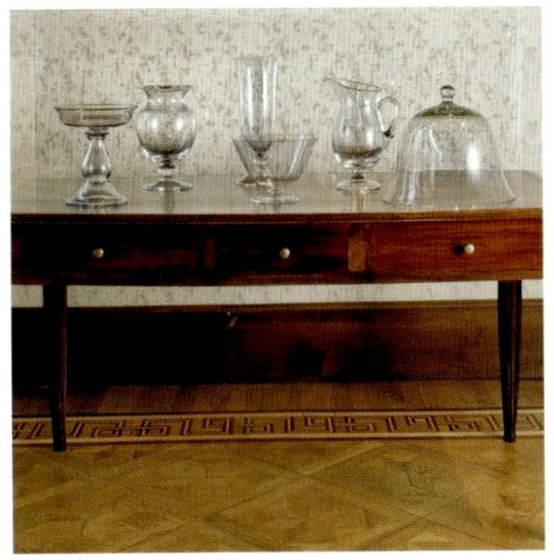

BARBARA BLOOM
Flaubert Letters II,
1987–2008
Ed. 2/3 three versions,
each unique
variable dimensions

Courtesy Private Collection,
Piacenza
Exhibited at *Glasstress 2009*,
Venice (IT)
Exhibited at *Glasstress New York*,
New York (USA)

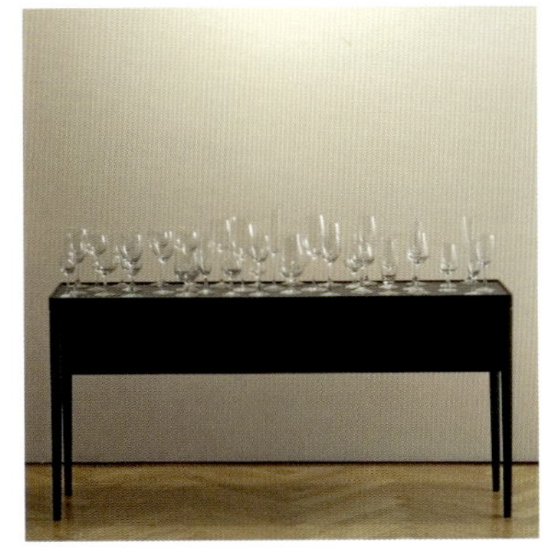

BARBARA BLOOM
**To Allan McCollum, from
Each and Every One of Us
(Together in Harmony) II,**
2010
70 x 150 x 38 cm

Courtesy E. Righi Collection and
Galleria Raffaella Cortese, Milan
Exhibited at *Glasstress 2011*,
Venice (IT)

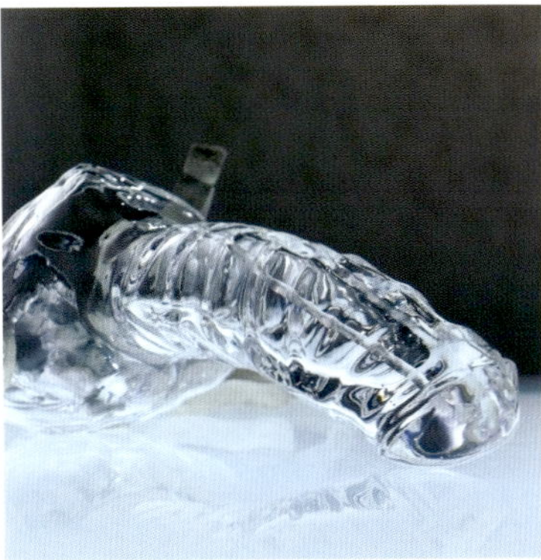

MONICA BONVICINI
Tears, 2011
10 x 24 x 12 cm /
11 x 8 x 8 cm /
100 x 50 x 50 cm
(pedestal)

Courtesy the artist, Max Hetzler
Gallery, Berlin, and Berengo
Private Collection, Venice
Exhibited at *Glasstress 2011*,
Venice (IT)
Exhibited at *Glasstress Stockholm*
2011, Stockholm (SE)

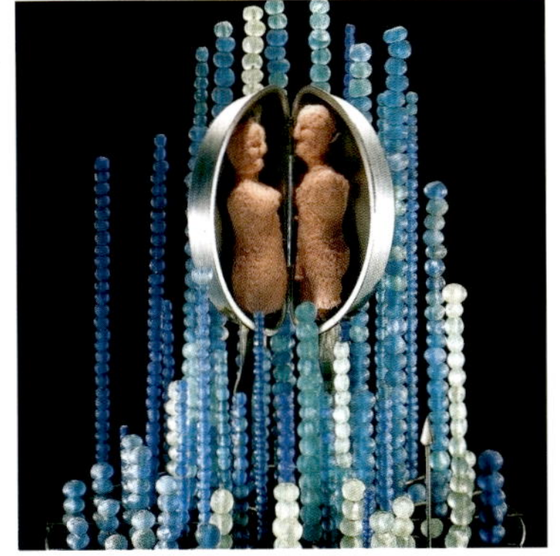

LOUISE BOURGEOIS
The Couple, 2002
54.6 x 44.5 x 44.5 cm /
177.8 x 76.2 x 76.2 cm
(vitrine)

Courtesy Karsten and Claudia
Greve, St. Moritz
Exhibited at *Glasstress 2009*,
Venice (IT)

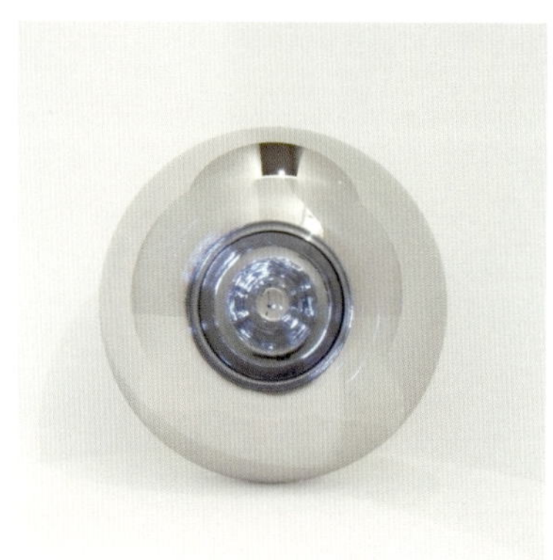

SERGIO BOVENGA
Spazio, 2009
Ed. 1/6
55 cm diameter

Courtesy Berengo Private
Collection, Venice
Exhibited at *Glasstress* 2009,
Venice (IT)
Exhibited at *Glasstress Riga* 2011,
Riga (LV)

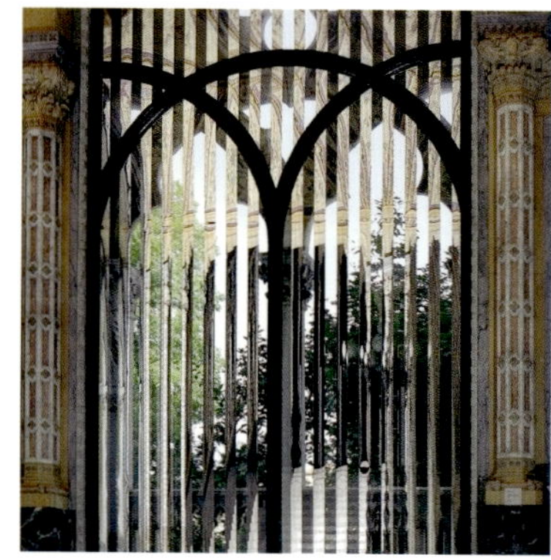

DANIEL BUREN
**Photo-souvenir:
Transparence vénitienne
avec reflets travail in
situ, in Glasstress, Istituto
Veneto di Scienze, Lettere
ed Arti-Palazzo Cavalli
Franchetti, Venice,**
1972–2009 / *detail*
611 x 270 cm

Courtesy Buchmann Galerie,
Berlin/Lugano / Exhibited
at *Glasstress* 2009, Venice (IT)

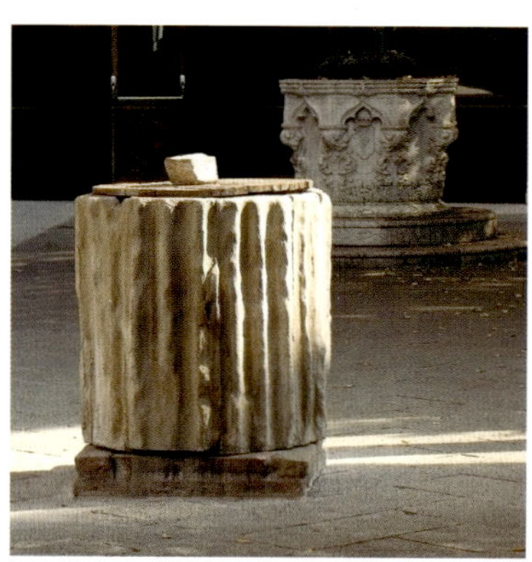

LAWRENCE CARROLL
Untitled, 2009
Ed. 1/5
100 x 90 cm diameter

Courtesy Buchmann Galerie,
Berlin/Lugano, and Berengo
Private Collection, Venice
Exhibited at *Glasstress* 2009,
Venice (IT)

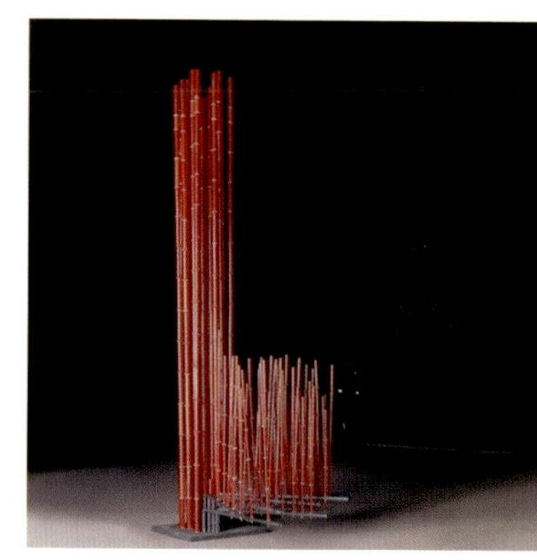

PINO CASTAGNA
Bamboo, 2011
430 x 100 cm

Courtesy Berengo Private
Collection, Venice
Exhibited at *Glasstress Stockholm*
2011, Stockholm (SE)

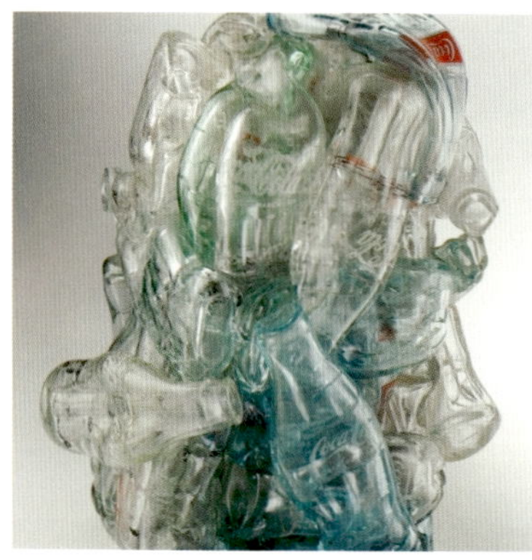

CÉSAR
Compression,
1992 / *detail*
37 x 23 x 24 cm

Courtesy Berengo Private
Collection, Venice
Exhibited at *Glasstress* 2009,
Venice (IT)

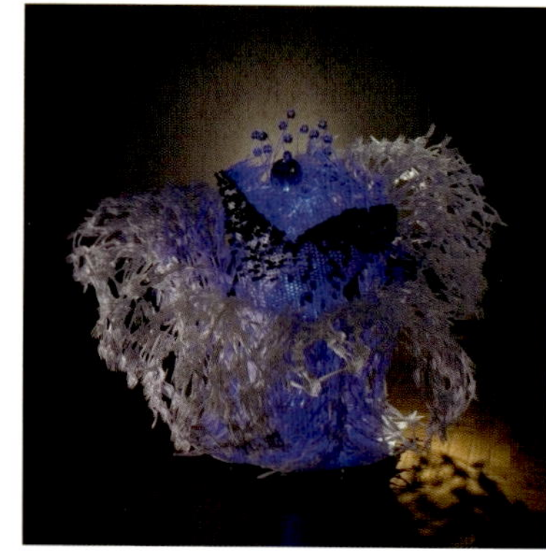

SOYEON CHO
In Bloom, 2009
150 x 150 x 110 cm

Courtesy Berengo Private
Collection, Venice
Exhibited at *Glasstress* 2009,
Venice (IT)
Exhibited at *Glasstress Stockholm*
2011, Stockholm (SE)

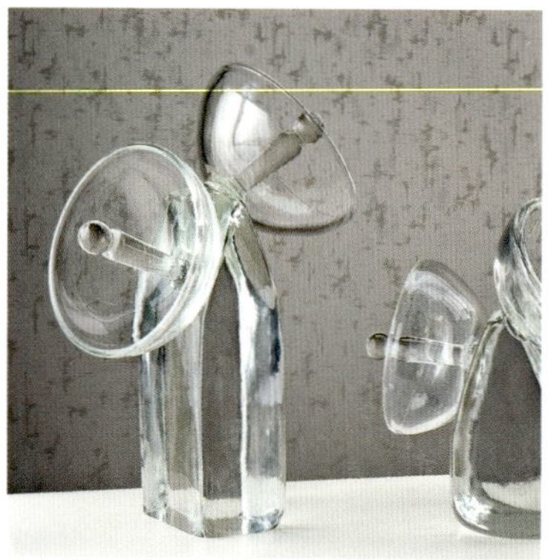

TONY CRAGG
Sensory Devices,
2009 / *detail*
47 x 15 x 10 cm /
37.5 x 19 x 11.5 cm

Courtesy Buchmann Galerie,
Berlin/Lugano
Exhibited at *Glasstress* 2009,
Venice (IT)

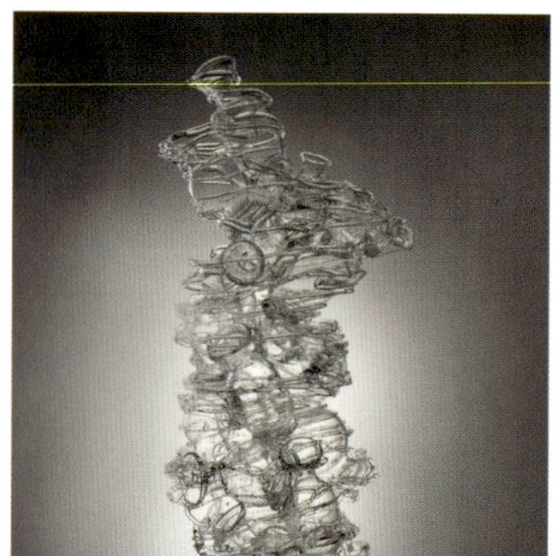

TONY CRAGG
Visible Men,
2009 / *detail*
47 x 16 cm

Courtesy Buchmann Galerie,
Berlin/Lugano
Exhibited at *Glasstress* 2009,
Venice (IT)

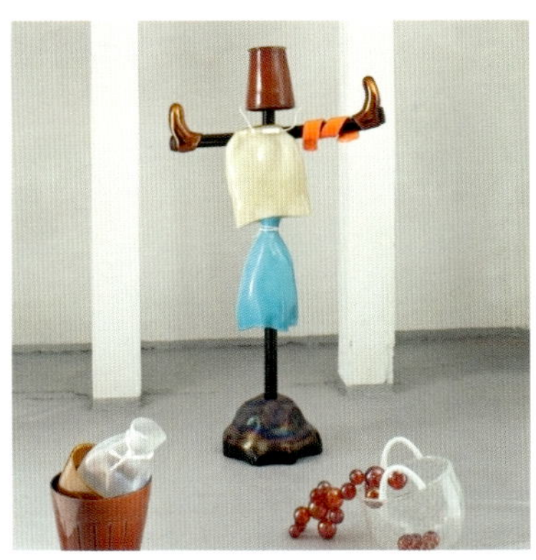

KIKI VAN EIJK
Allotment / Harvest Red
Fruit Bucket, Scarecrow,
Sowing Time-Pots, 2011
37 x 70 x 38 cm /
199 x 110 x 54 cm /
63 x 33 cm diameter

Courtesy Venice Projects, Venice
Exhibited at *Glasstress 2011*,
Venice (IT)

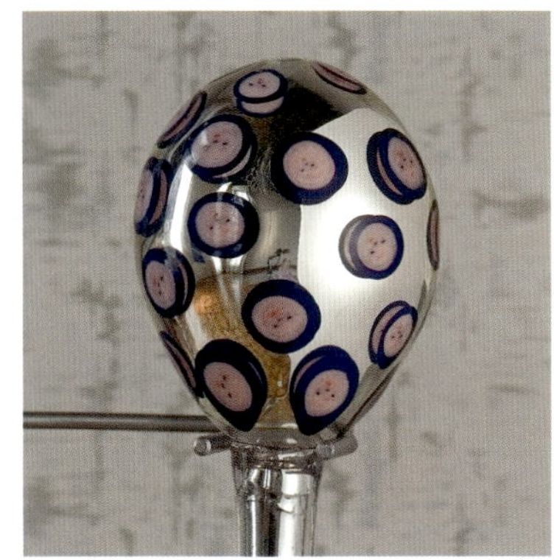

MARIE-LOUISE EKMAN
Termometri, 2005–2007 /
detail **(from the *Hospital***
series) Ed. 6
Height 100 cm /
height 90 cm /
11 cm diameter

Courtesy Angelika Knapper
Gallery, Stockholm, and Berengo
Private Collection, Venice
Exhibited at *Glasstress* 2009,
Venice (IT)

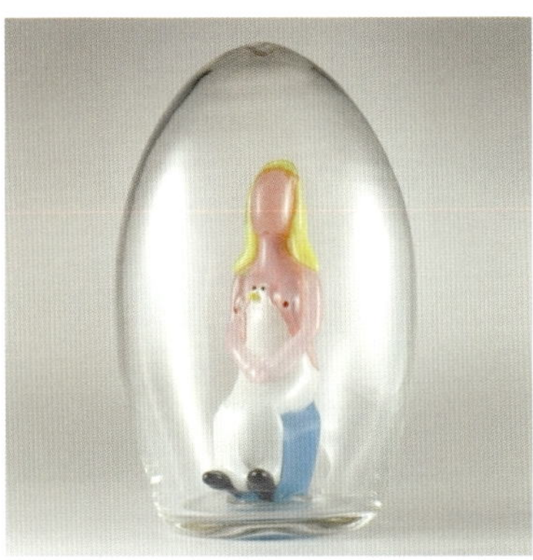

MARIE-LOUISE EKMAN
The Transparent Family,
2007/2011
100 x 260 x 260 cm

Courtesy the artist and Berengo
Private Collection, Venice
Exhibited at *Glasstress Stockholm*
2011, Stockholm (SE)

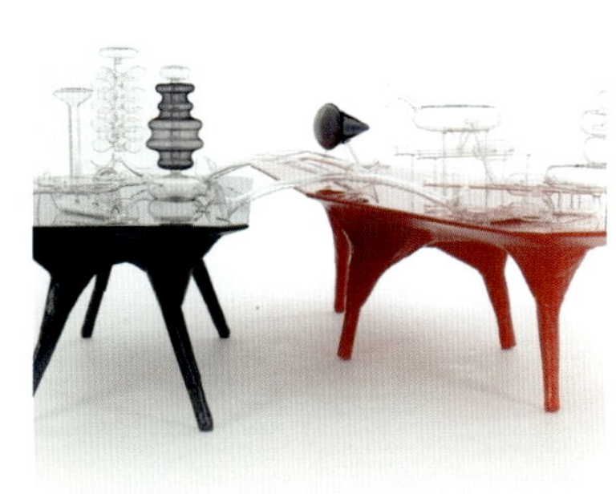

EL ULTIMO GRITO
Imaginary Architectures,
2011 / *detail*
variable dimensions

Courtesy Spring Projects, London
Exhibited at *Glasstress New York*,
New York (USA)

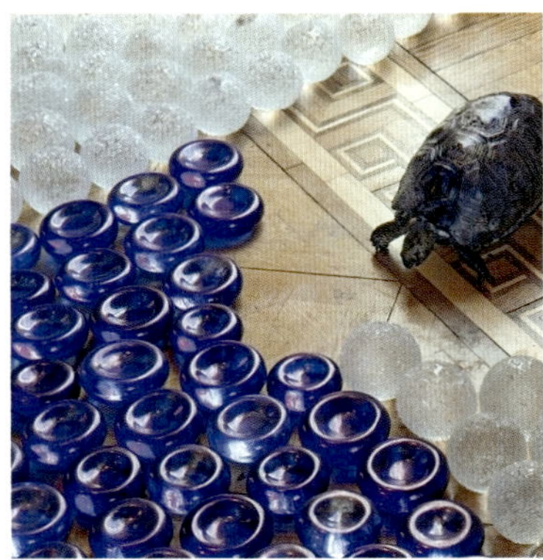

JAN FABRE
Greek Gods in a Body-
Landscape (Griekse Goden
in Ean Lichaa-Landaschap),
2011 / *detail*
variable dimensions

Courtesy Angelos Bvba Collection,
Antwerp
Exhibited at *Glasstress 2011*,
Venice (IT)

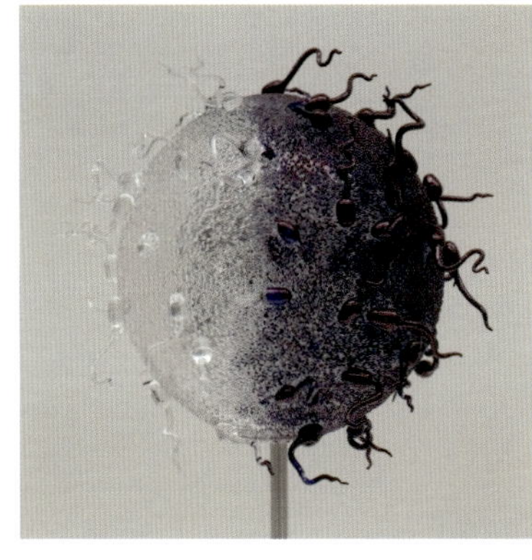

JAN FABRE
Planet VII from the Series
Planets I-IX, 2011
32 cm diameter (glass),
58 cm (planet with stand)

Courtesy Angelos Bvba Collection,
Antwerp, and Berengo Private
Collection, Venice
Exhibited at *Glasstress 2011*,
Venice (IT), and Kröller-Müller
Museum 2011, The Netherlands

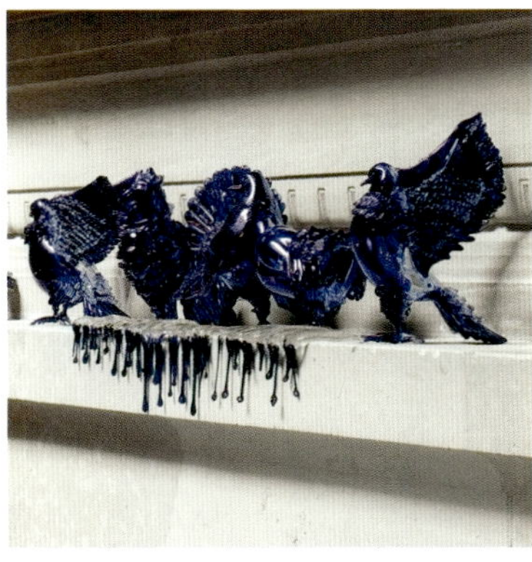

JAN FABRE
Shitting Doves of Peace
and Flying Rats, 2008
25 x 260 x 25 cm /
variable dimensions

Courtesy Berengo Private
Collection, Venice / Exhibited
at *Glasstress* 2009, Venice (IT)
Exhibited at *Glasstress Riga* 2011,
Riga (LV)
Exhibited at *Glasstress Stockholm*
2011, Stockholm (SE)
Exhibited at *Glasstress New York*,
New York (USA)

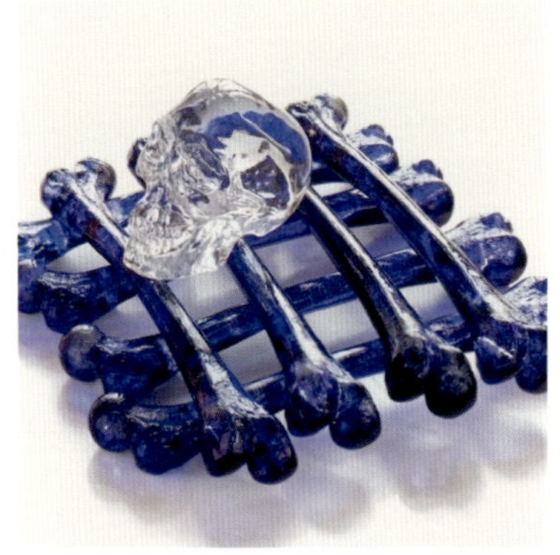

JAN FABRE
Untitled, 2009
Ed. 6 + 2 AP
22 x 44 x 43 cm

Courtesy Berengo Private
Collection, Venice
Exhibited at *Glasstress* 2009,
Venice (IT)

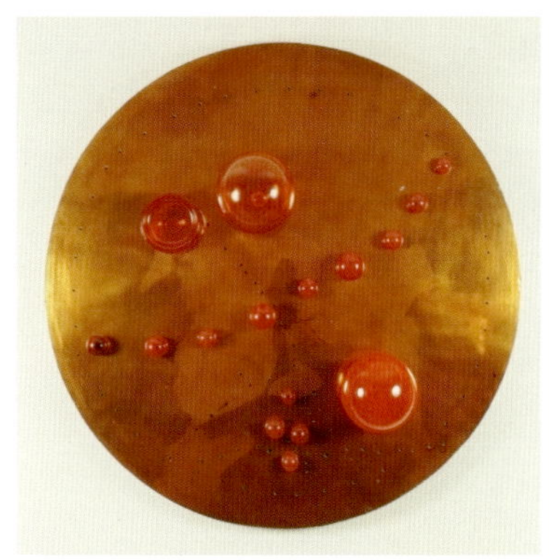

**LUCIO FONTANA
AND EGIDIO COSTANTINI**
Pannello, 1965
124.5 x 6 cm diameter

Courtesy Private Collection,
Bassano
Exhibited at *Glasstress 2009*,
Venice (IT)

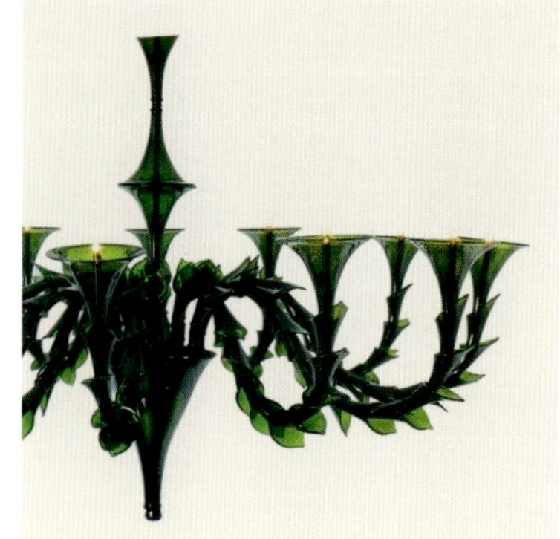

FABIO FORNASIER
Recycled Chandelier,
2007 / *detail*
200 x 200 cm

Courtesy Berengo Private
Collection, Venice
Exhibited at *Glasstress Riga 2011*,
Riga (LV)

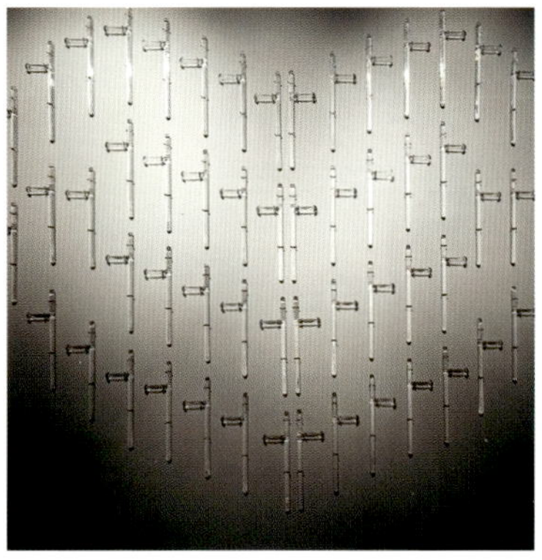

KENDELL GEERS
Cardiac Arrest VIII, 2011
310 x 420 x 3 cm

Courtesy the artist, Galleria
Continua, San Gimignano, Beijing,
Le Moulin, Gallery Stephen
Friedman, London, Galerie
Rodolphe Janssen, Brussels,
Goodman Gallery, Johannesburg,
Cape Town, and Berengo Private
Collection, Venice
Exhibited at *Glasstress 2011*,
Venice (IT)

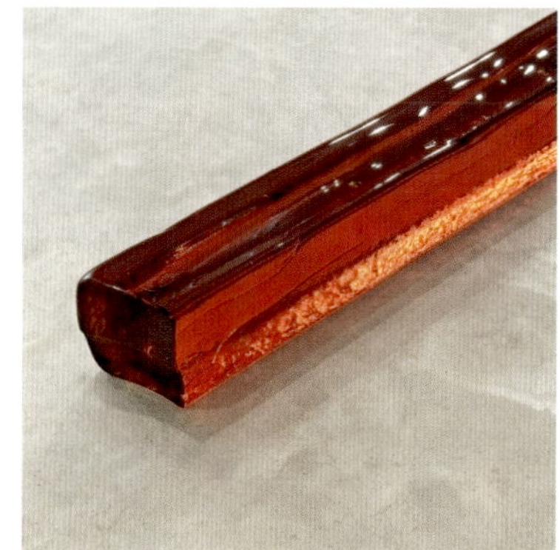

FRANCESCO GENNARI
**Autoritratto come rotazione
della terra (con loden
e scarpe clarks),**
2008 / *detail*
471 x 6.5 x 7 cm

Courtesy the artist and Tucci
Russo Studio per l'Arte
Contemporanea, Torre Pellice,
Turin
Exhibited at *Glasstress 2009*,
Venice (IT)

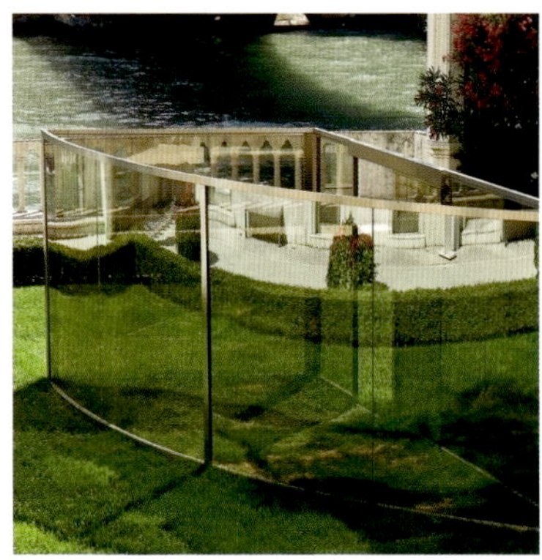

DAN GRAHAM
Sagitarian Girls, 2008
230 x 550 x 250 cm

Courtesy Francesca Minini, Milan
Exhibited at *Glasstress 2009*,
Venice (IT)

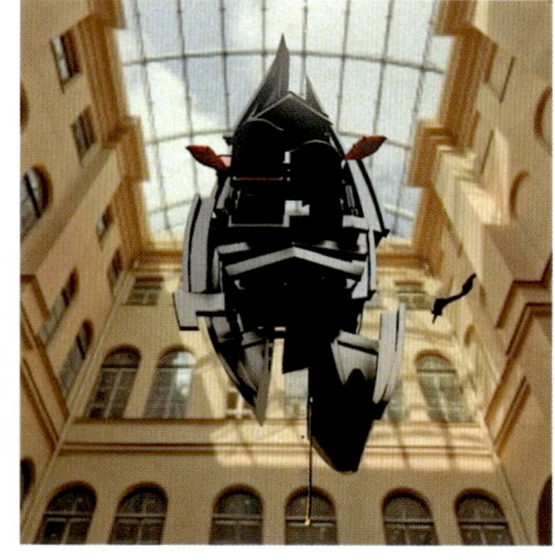

DMITRY GUTOV
Gondola, 2011
1200 x 280 x 280 cm
(3D rendering)

Courtesy Berengo Private
Collection, Venice
Exhibited at *Glasstress Riga* 2011,
Riga (LV)

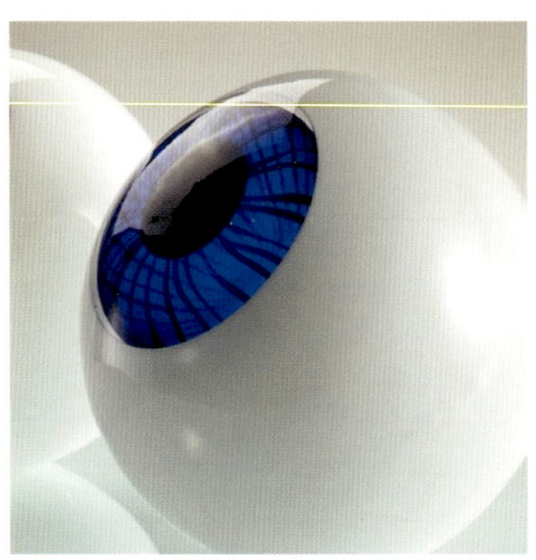

**CHARLOTTE
GYLLENHAMMAR**
Don't Look,
2011 / *detail*
18 x 60 x 60 cm

Courtesy the artist and Berengo
Private Collection, Venice
Exhibited at *Glasstress Stockholm*
2011, Stockholm (SE)

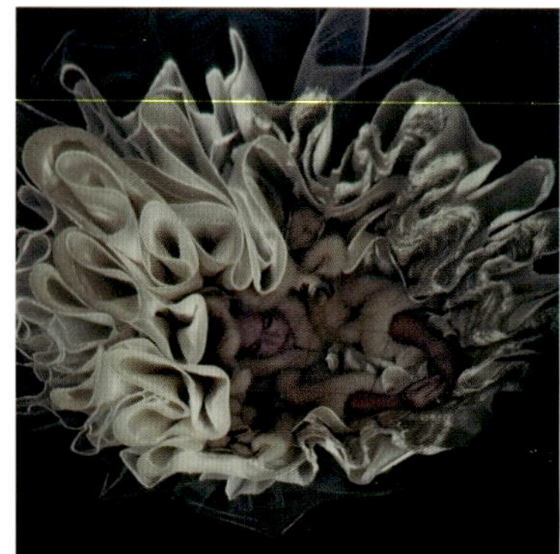

**CHARLOTTE
GYLLENHAMMAR**
Hang, 2006/2011
variable dimensions
(video projection)

Courtesy Collection Orsi, Segrate,
Milan
Exhibited at *Glasstress 2011*,
Venice (IT)

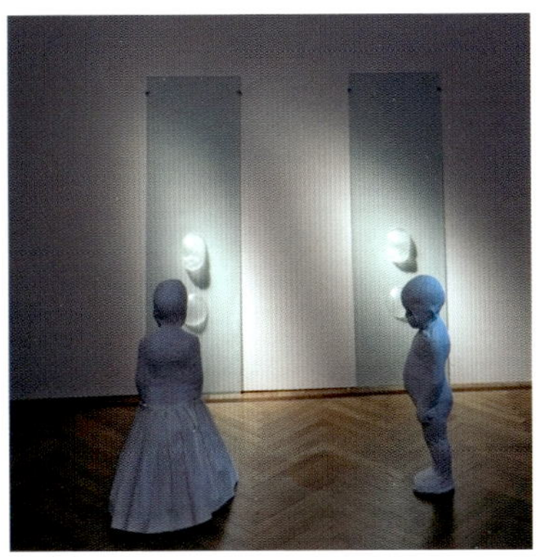

CHARLOTTE GYLLENHAMMAR
Wait, The Smallest of Us is Dead, 2011
165 x 50 x 10 cm (glass) /
84 x 28 cm (boy) /
44 x 20 cm (girl)

Courtesy the artist and Berengo
Private Collection, Venice
Exhibited at *Glasstress 2011*,
Venice (IT)

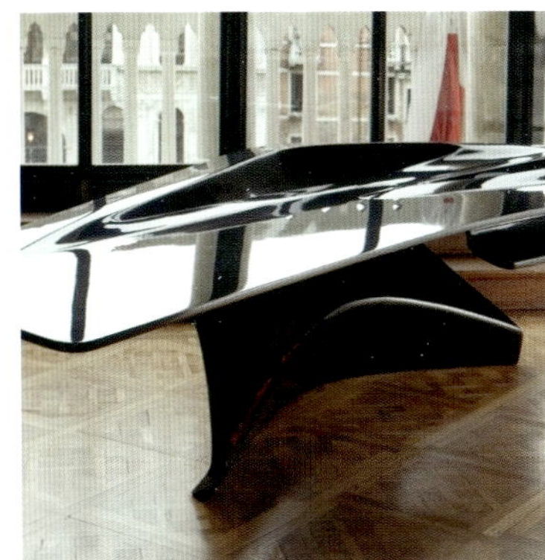

ZAHA HADID
Seoul Desk, 2008
86 x 420 x 134 cm

Courtesy Zaha Hadid Architects,
London
Exhibited at *Glasstress 2011*,
Venice (IT)

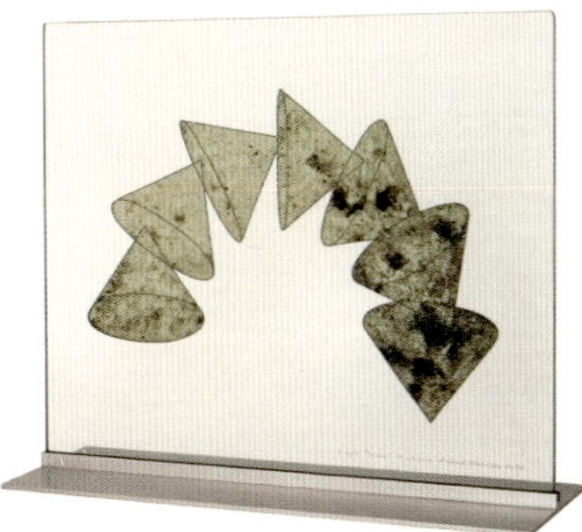

RICHARD HAMILTON
Sieves (with Marcel Duchamp), 1971
Ed. 50 + 7 AP
52 x 63.5 x 20.4 cm

Courtesy Fondazione Marconi,
Milan
Exhibited at *Glasstress 2009*,
Venice (IT)

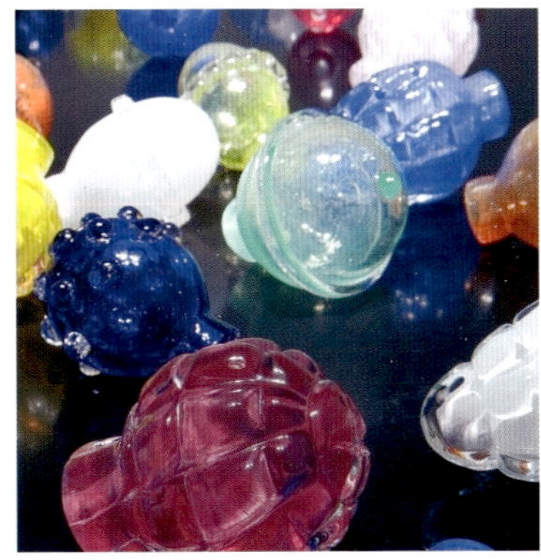

MONA HATOUM
Nature morte aux grenades,
2006/2007 / *detail*
95 x 208 x 70 cm

Private Collection, Bassano
Courtesy Galleria Continua, San
Gimignano, Beijing, Le Moulin
Exhibited at *Glasstress 2009*,
Venice (IT)
Exhibited at *Glasstress Stockholm*
2011, Stockholm (SE)

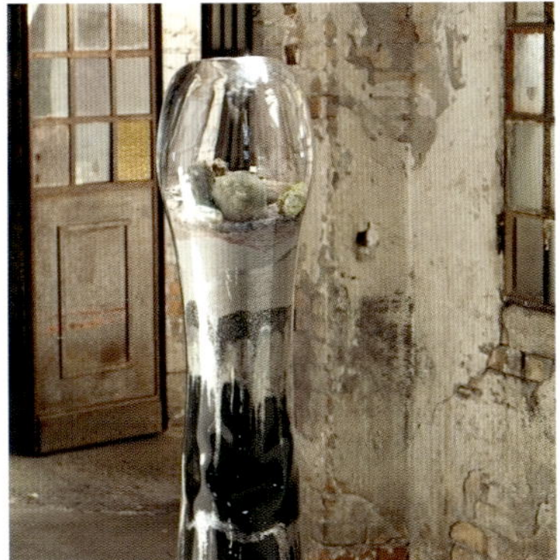

PAULA HAYES
Vertical Giant Terrarium,
2008/2009 / *detail*
147.3 x 35.6 cm

Courtesy R 20th Century Gallery,
New York
Exhibited at *Glasstress 2011*,
Venice (IT)

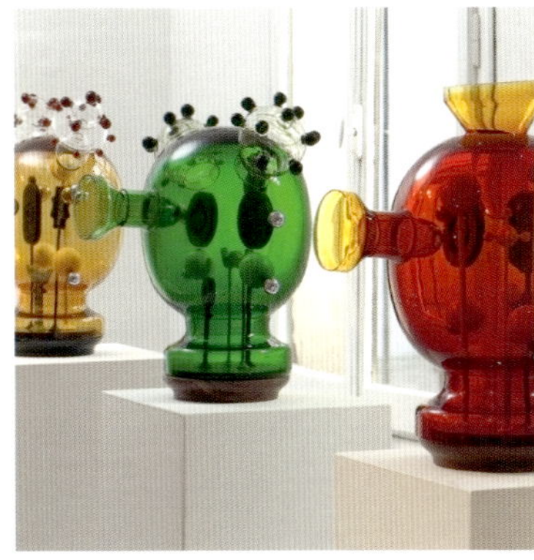

JAIME HAYON
Testa Mecanica, 2011
55 x 52 x 43 cm (green) /
53 x 35 x 43 cm (red) /
55 x 52 x 43 cm (yellow)

Courtesy the artist and Berengo
Private Collection, Venice
Exhibited at *Glasstress 2011*,
Venice (IT)
Exhibited at *Glasstress New York*,
New York (USA)

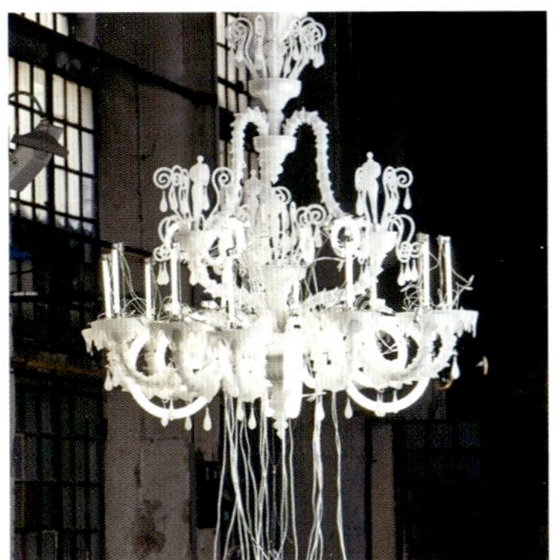

YUICHI HIGASHIONNA
Seta Chandelier, 2011
150 x 140 cm diameter

Courtesy Keith Johnson
Exhibited at *Glasstress 2011*,
Venice (IT)

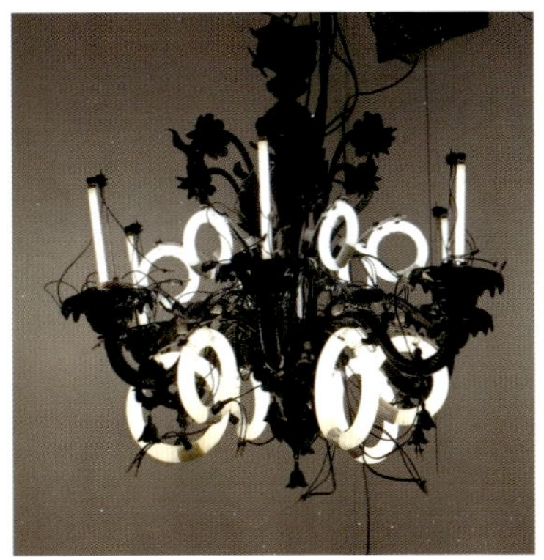

YUICHI HIGASHIONNA
Untitled (v.c.1), 2010
Ed. 3/8
85 x 85 x 90 cm

Courtesy Berengo Private
Collection, Venice, and Yumiko
Chiba Associates, Tokyo
Exhibited at *Glasstress Riga* 2011,
Riga (LV)

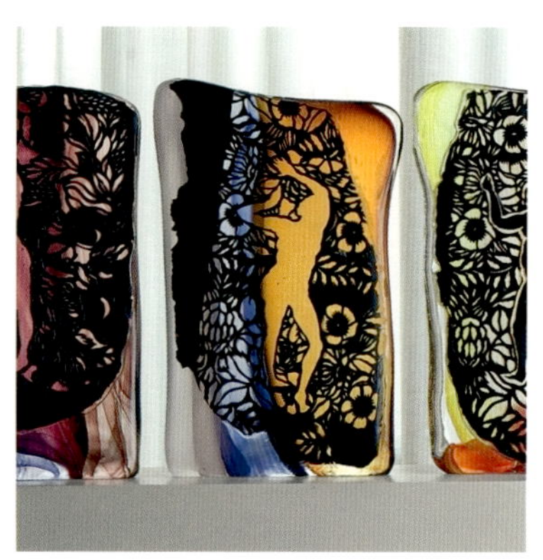

CHARLOTTE HODES
Eurydice I / II / III, 2009
40 x 22 cm / 40 x 25 cm /
40 x 26 cm

Courtesy Marlborough Gallery,
London, and Berengo Private
Collection, Venice
Exhibited at *Glasstress 2009*,
Venice (IT)

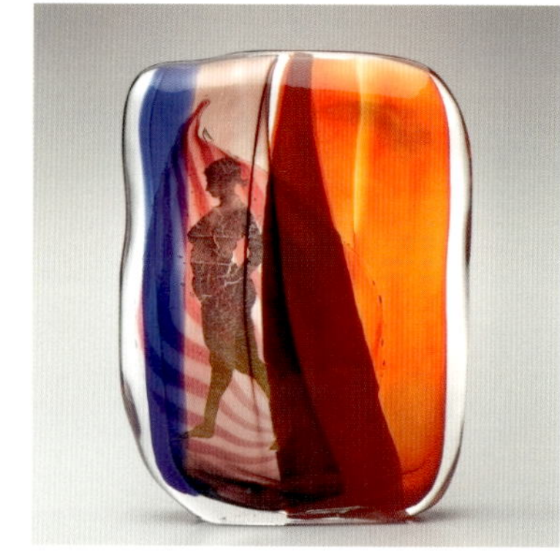

CHARLOTTE HODES
Revealed In Pink, 2011
35 x 30 x 6 cm

Courtesy Marlborough Gallery,
London, and Berengo Private
Collection, Venice
Exhibited at *Glasstress Stockholm
2011*, Stockholm (SE)

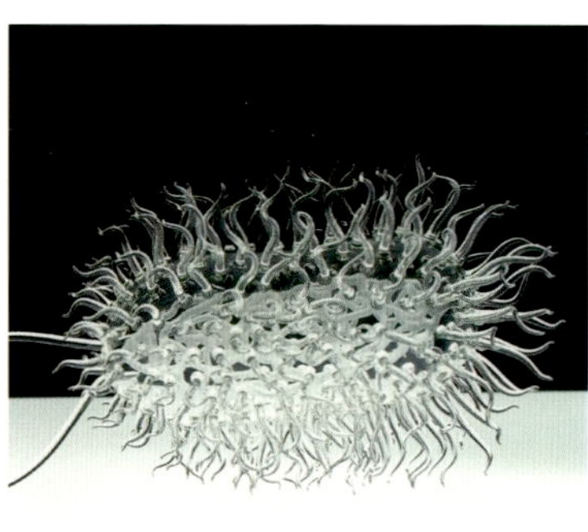

LUKE JERRAM
E. Coli, 2010
24 x 128 x 30 cm

Courtesy De Nul Collection,
Belgium
Exhibited at *Glasstress 2011*,
Venice (IT)
Exhibited at *Glasstress New York*,
New York (USA)

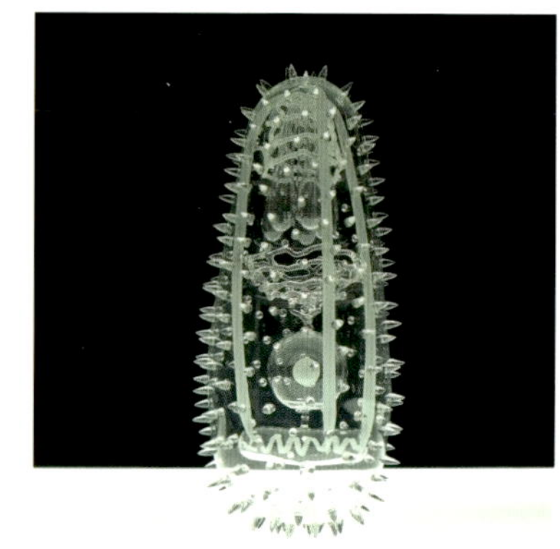

LUKE JERRAM
Large Spiky Malaria, 2010
50 x 18 cm

Courtesy the artist
Exhibited at *Glasstress New York*,
New York (USA)

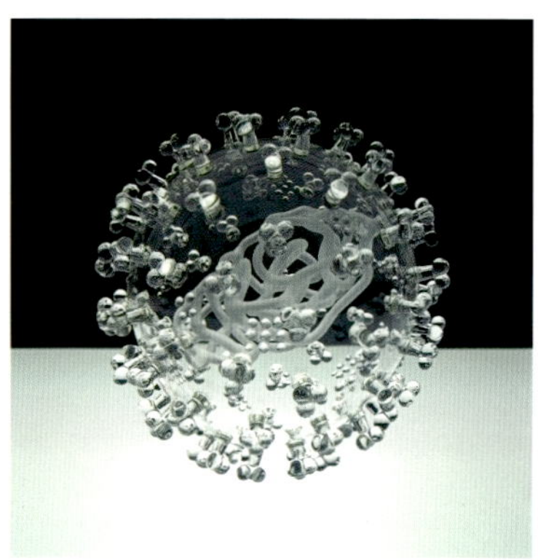

LUKE JERRAM
Round Swine Flu, 2009
20 x 20 cm

Courtesy the artist
Exhibited at *Glasstress New York*,
New York (USA)

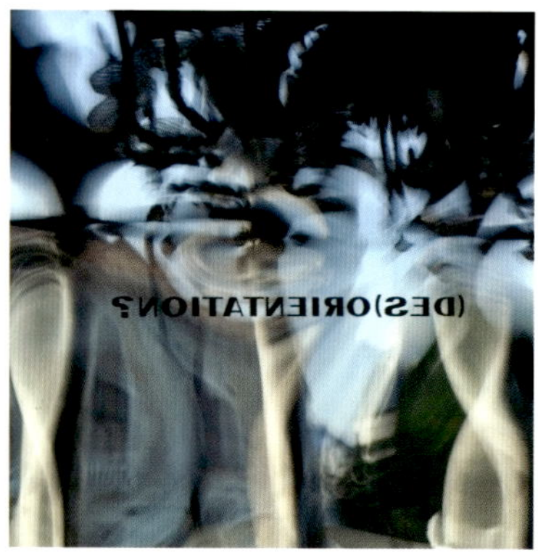

MAGDALENA JETELOVA
(Des)Orientation,
2011 / *detail*
200 x 510 x 50 cm

Courtesy the artist
Exhibited at *Glasstress 2011*,
Venice (IT)

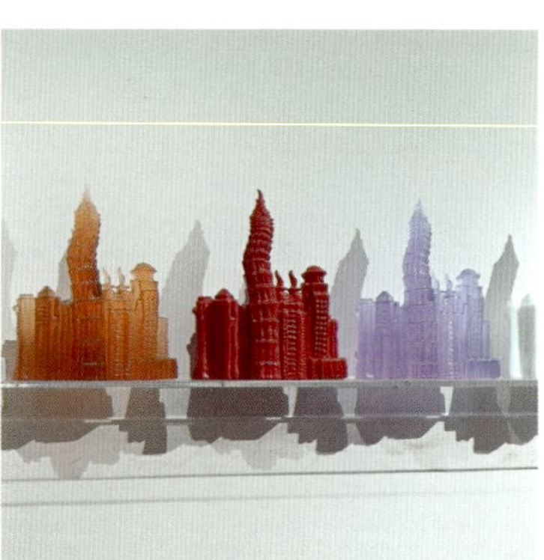

LIU JIANHUA
Shadow in the Water, 2011
32 x 230 x 7 cm /
32 x 28 x 7 cm each

Courtesy the artist and Berengo
Private Collection, Venice
Exhibited at *Glasstress 2011*,
Venice (IT)
Exhibited at *Glasstress Stockholm
2011*, Stockholm (SE)

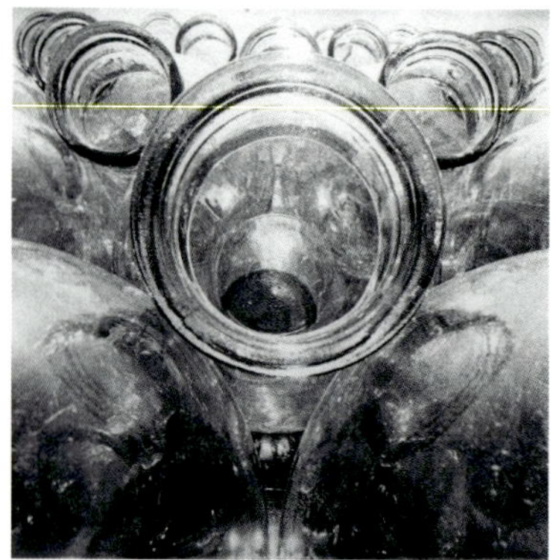

MIMMO JODICE
**Composizione, opera 1 /
opera 2 / opera 3 / opera 4 /
opera 5,** 1966 / *detail*
unique
30 x 40 cm / 60 x 60 cm
(with frame)

Courtesy the artist
Exhibited at *Glasstress 2009*,
Venice (IT)

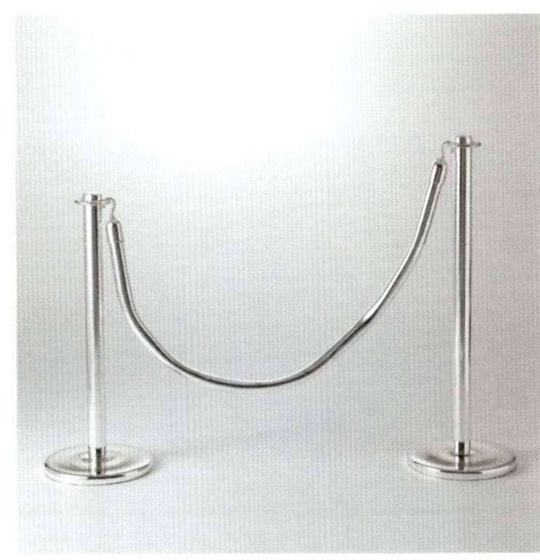

MICHAEL JOO
Access Denied, 2011
85 x 130 x 30 cm

Courtesy the artist and Berengo
Private Collection, Venice
Exhibited at *Glasstress Riga* 2011,
Riga (LV)
Exhibited at *Glasstress Stockholm*
2011, Stockholm (SE)

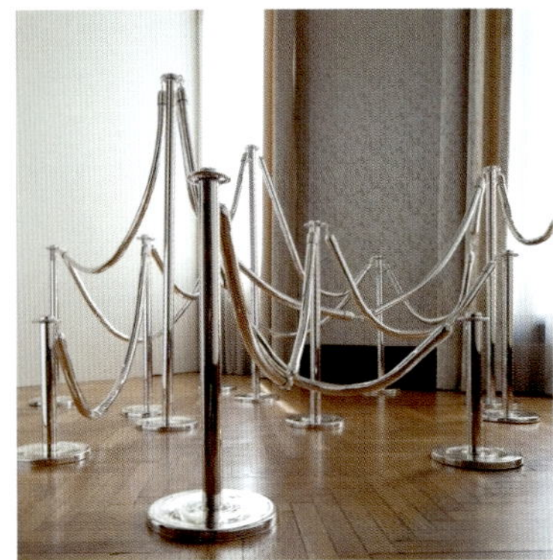

MICHAEL JOO
Expanded Access, 2011
155 x 290 x 290 cm /
85 x 67 x 8 cm

Courtesy the artist and Berengo
Private Collection, Venice
Exhibited at *Glasstress 2011*,
Venice (IT)
Exhibited at *Glasstress New York*,
New York (USA)

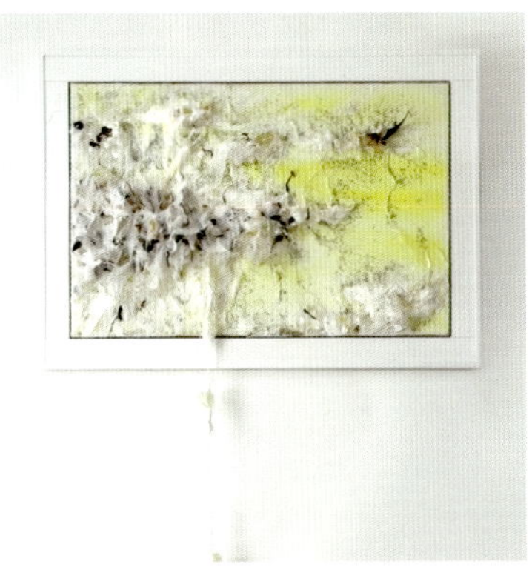

MARYA KAZOUN
Frosty Grounds:
The Beginning,
2009 / *detail*
120 x 83 x 15 cm

Courtesy the artist
Exhibited at *Glasstress Stockholm*
2011, Stockholm (SE)
Exhibited at *Glasstress New York*,
New York (USA)

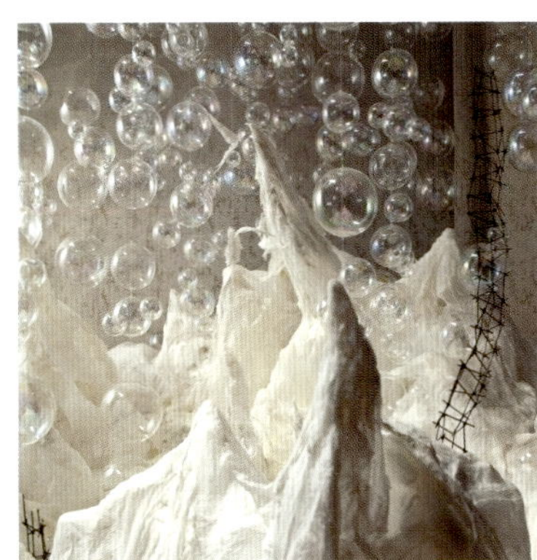

MARYA KAZOUN
Habitat: Where He Came
From, 2009 / *detail*
200 x 170 x 620 cm

Courtesy the artist
Exhibited at *Glasstress* 2009,
Venice (IT)

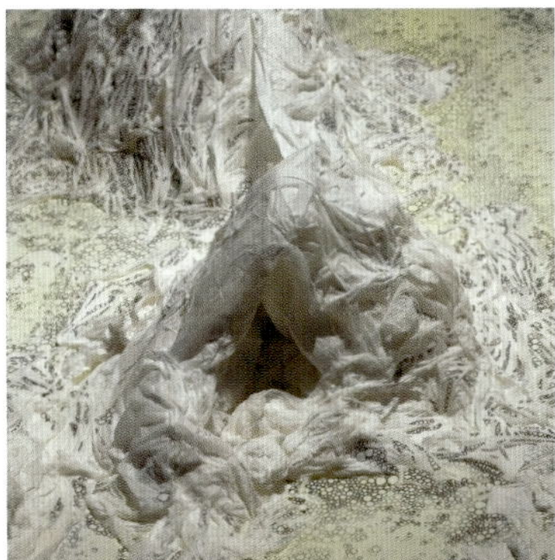

MARYA KAZOUN
The Mountains,
2009 / *detail*
120 x 83 x 25 cm

Courtesy the artist
Exhibited at *Glasstress Stockholm*
2011, Stockholm (SE)

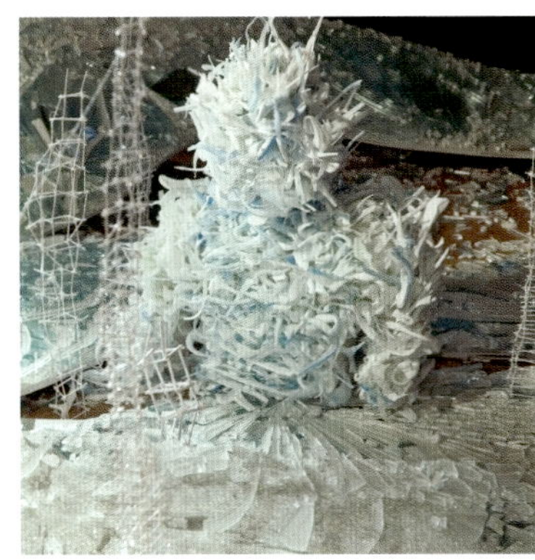

MARYA KAZOUN
They Were There,
2011 / *detail*
400 x 250 x 100 cm

Courtesy the artist
Exhibited at *Glasstress 2011*,
Venice (IT)

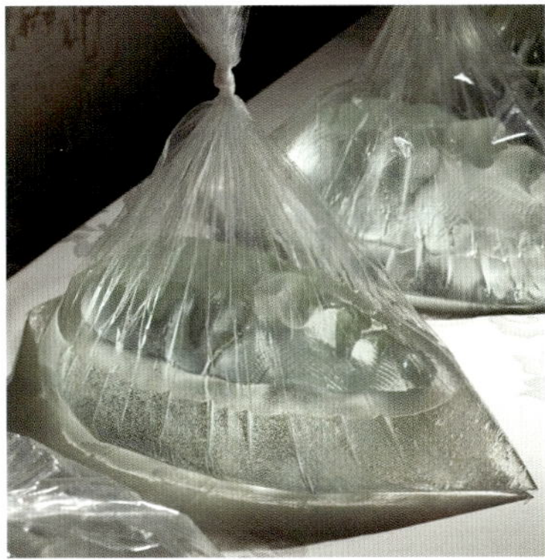

KONSTANTIN KHUDYAKOV
Last Supper,
2011 / *detail*
107 x 300 x 51 cm /
30 x 20 x 40 cm
(each head)

Courtesy the artist and Venice
Projects, Venice
Exhibited at *Glasstress 2011*,
Venice (IT)

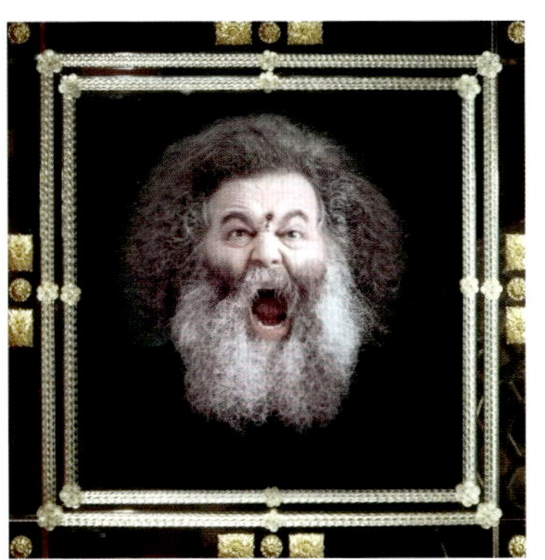

KONSTANTIN KHUDYAKOV
Mirror, 2011
108 x 108 x 20 cm

Courtesy the artist and Venice
Projects, Venice
Exhibited at *Glasstress 2011*,
Venice (IT)
Exhibited at *Glasstress Riga* 2011,
Riga (LV)
Exhibited at *Glasstress Stockholm*
2011, Stockholm (SE)

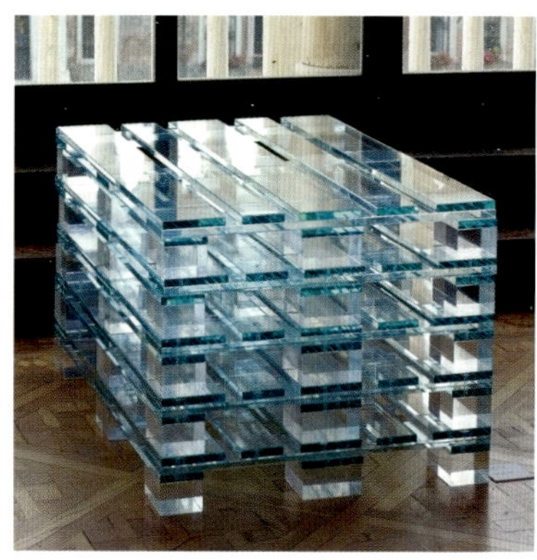

MICHAEL KIENZER
Off Order, vol. 2, 2011
65 x 82 x 120 cm

Courtesy the artist and Venice
Projects, Venice
Exhibited at *Glasstress 2011,*
Venice (IT)

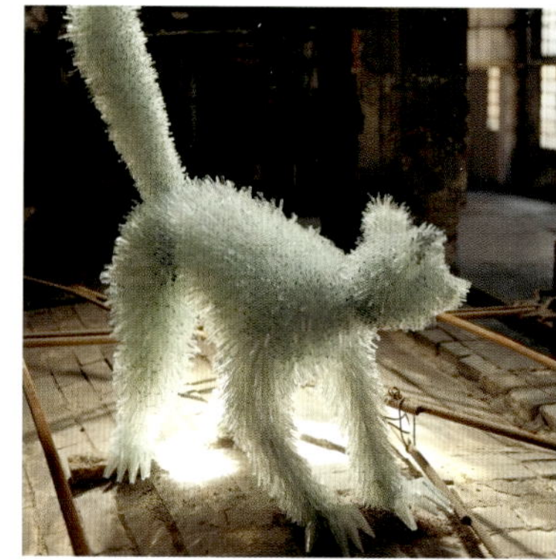

MARTA KLONOWSKA
Bestiarium: Maki, 2011
124 x 80 x 37 cm

Courtesy Susan and Fred Sanders
Exhibited at *Glasstress 2011,*
Venice (IT)
Exhibited at *Glasstress New York,*
New York (USA)

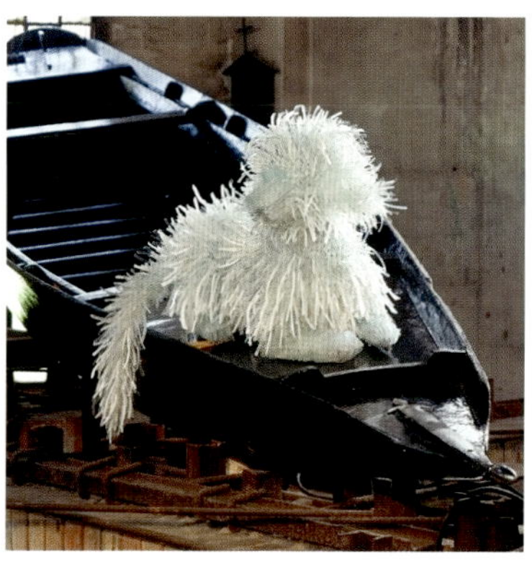

MARTA KLONOWSKA
**Il miracolo della reliquia
della Santa Croce after
Vittore Carpaccio,** 2011
48 x 58 x 35 cm

Courtesy Collection Cingoli
Exhibited at *Glasstress 2011,*
Venice (IT)

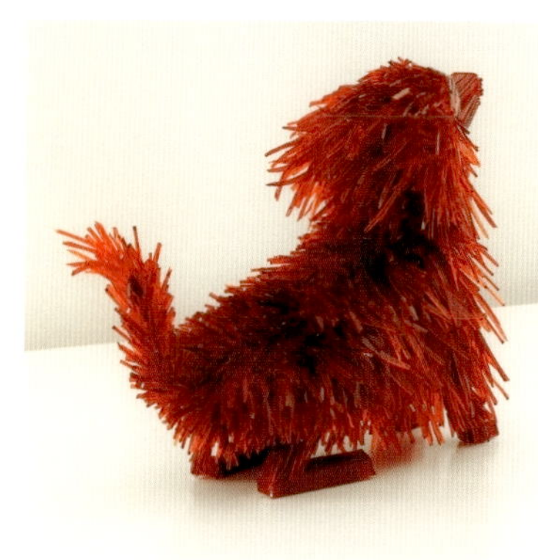

MARTA KLONOWSKA
**La presentazione after
Pietro Longhi, 1741,**
2005 / *detail*
25 x 40 x 25 cm (dog) /
66 x 55 cm
(inkjet print on paper)

Courtesy the artist and
lorch+seidel contemporary, Berlin
Exhibited at *Glasstress Stockholm*
2011, Stockholm (SE)

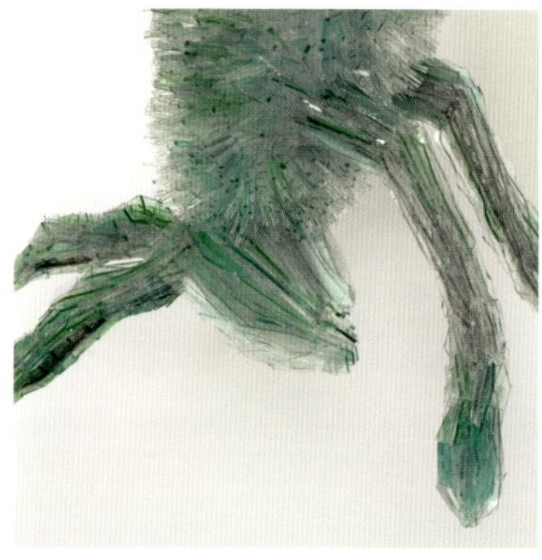

MARTA KLONOWSKA
**Large Kitchen Still Life
after Michel De Bouillon,**
2009 / *detail*
94 x 58 x 44 cm

Courtesy the artist and
lorch+seidel contemporary, Berlin
Exhibited at *Glasstress 2011,*
Venice (IT)

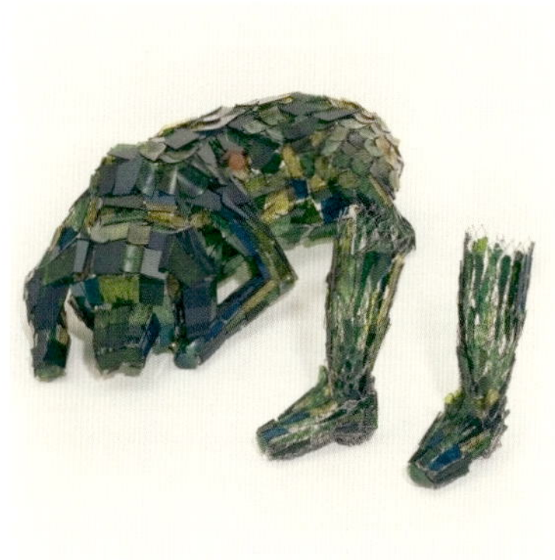

MARTA KLONOWSKA
**Prince Baltasar Carlos
as a Hunter,**
2003 / *detail*
40 x 160 x 100 cm /
variable dimensions
191 x 102 cm
(inkjet print on canvas)

Courtesy the artist and
lorch+seidel contemporary, Berlin
Exhibited at *Glasstress Riga* 2011,
Riga (LV)

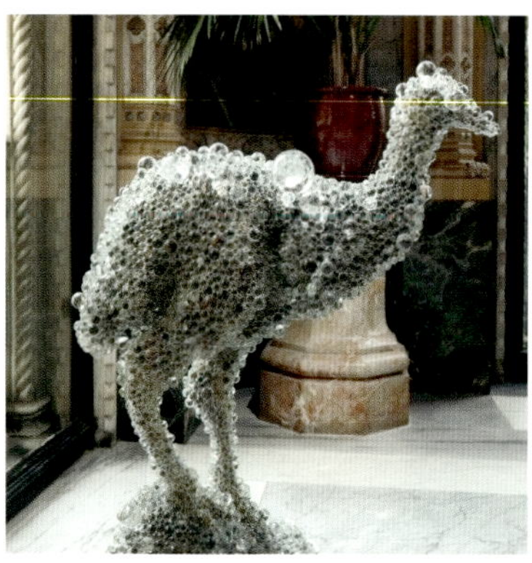

NAWA KOHEI
Pixcell Emu, 2008
116.5 x 93 x 75 cm

Courtesy Private Collection
Germany/Japan
Exhibited at *Glasstress 2011,*
Venice (IT)

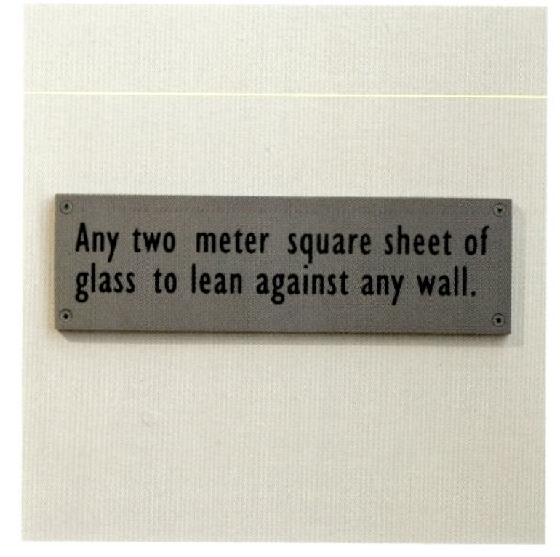

JOSEPH KOSUTH
**Any Two Meter Square
Sheet of Glass To Lean
Against Any Wall,**
1965 / *detail*
200 x 200 cm (glass) /
5.8 x 20 cm (metal plaque)

Courtesy Joseph Kosuth Studio,
Rome
Exhibited at *Glasstress 2009,*
Venice (IT)

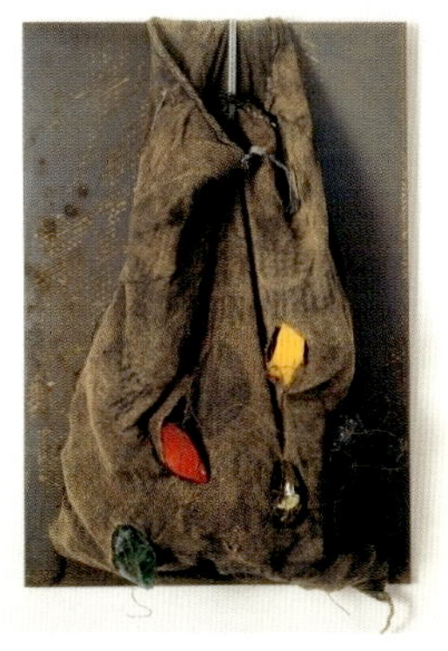

JANNIS KOUNELLIS
Senza titolo, 2005
100 x 70 cm

Courtesy Galleria Fumagalli,
Bergamo
Exhibited at *Glasstress* 2009,
Venice (IT)

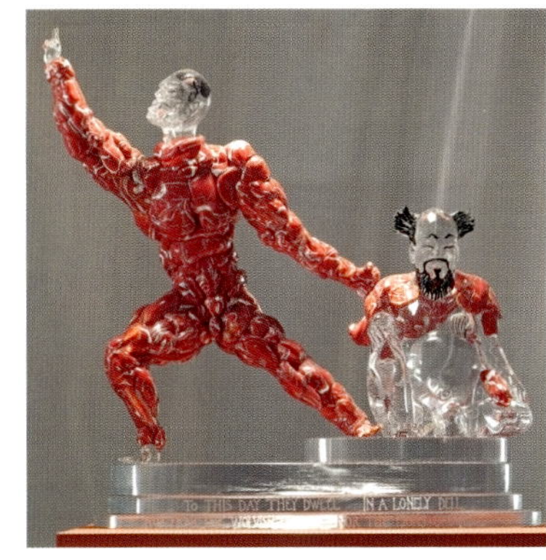

OLEG KULIK
Basta Carne, 2011
59 x 65 x 40 cm

Courtesy the artist and Berengo
Private Collection, Venice
Exhibited at *Glasstress 2011*,
Venice (IT)

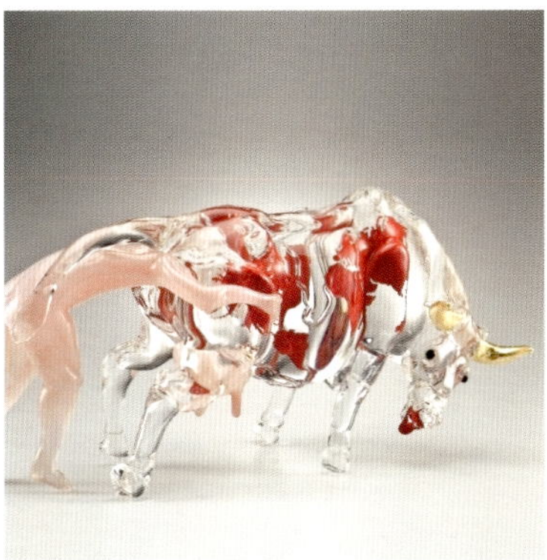

OLEG KULIK
Deep Into Russia, 2011
30 x 50 x 23 cm

Courtesy the artist and Berengo
Private Collection, Venice
Exhibited at *Glasstress 2011*,
Venice (IT)

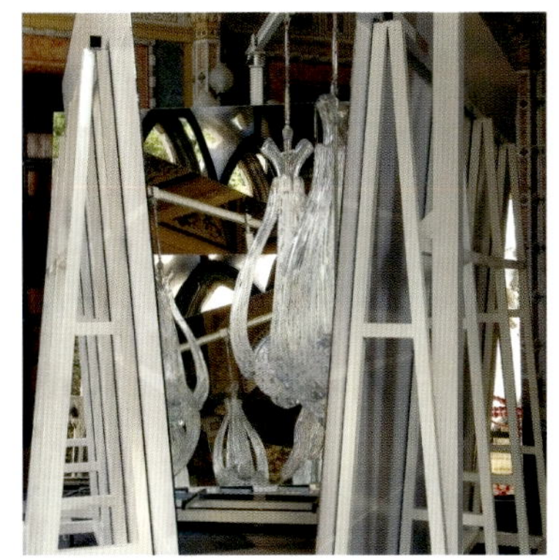

RAIMUND KUMMER
Hindsight Bias, 2007
80 x 80 x 205 cm
(glass eyes) /
240 x 300 cm
(mirror sheets)

Courtesy the artist
Exhibited at *Glasstress* 2009,
Venice (IT)

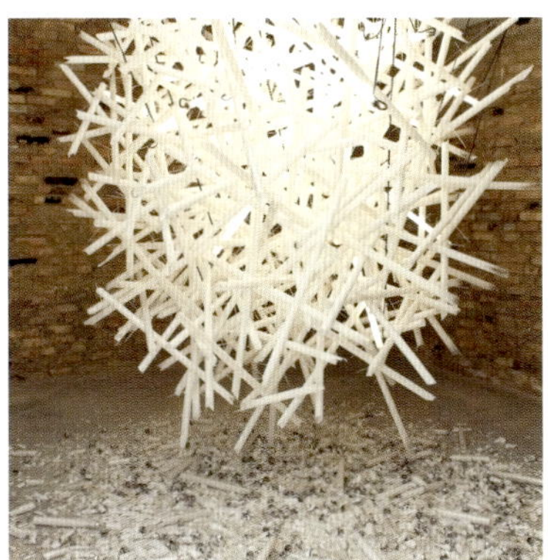

HITOSHI KURIYAMA
Life-reduction, 2010
variable dimensions

Courtesy Venice Projects, Venice
Exhibited at *Glasstress 2011*,
Venice (IT)

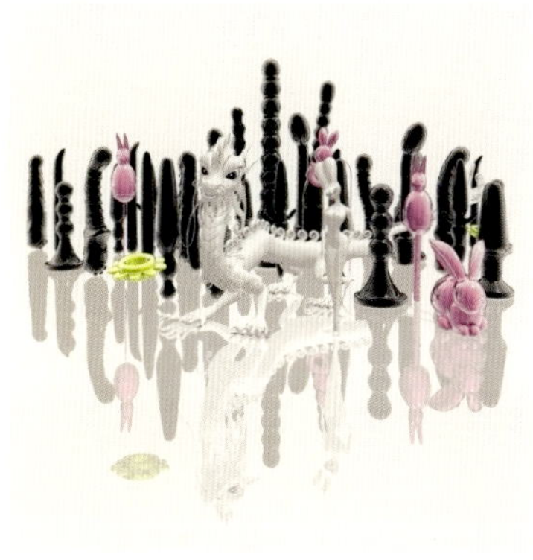

HYE RIM LEE
Crystal City Spun, 2008
variable dimensions
(3D animation)

Courtesy the artist and Kukje
Gallery, Seoul
Exhibited at *Glasstress* 2009,
Venice (IT)
Exhibited at *Glasstress Stockholm*
2011, Stockholm (SE)

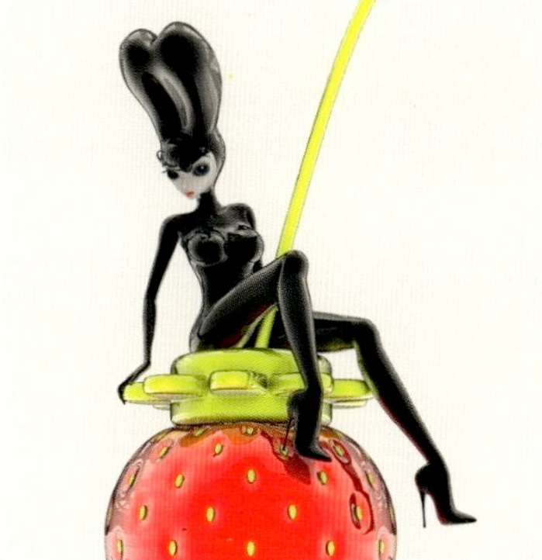

HYE RIM LEE
Strawberry Garden, 2011
variable dimensions
(3D animation)

Courtesy the artist and Kukje
Gallery, Seoul
Exhibited at *Glasstress 2011*,
Venice (IT)

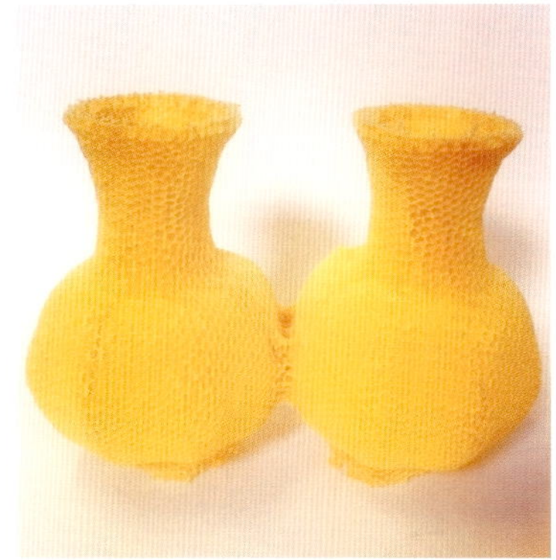

TOMÁŠ LIBERTÍNY
**Always the Years Between
Us,** 2011
26 x 30 x 14 cm (vase) /
100 x 100 x 1.5 cm
(glass and felt)

Courtesy the artist and Berengo
Private Collection, Venice
Exhibited at *Glasstress Riga* 2011,
Riga (LV)

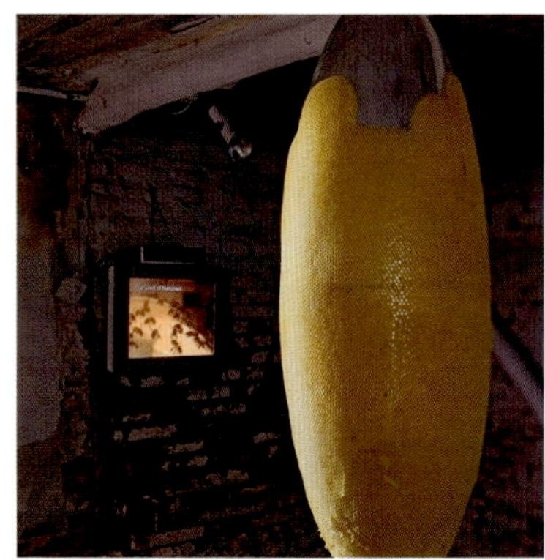

TOMÁŠ LIBERTÍNY
The Seed of Narcissus,
2011
100 x 38 cm diameter

Courtesy the artist and Venice
Projects, Venice
Exhibited at *Glasstress 2011*,
Venice (IT)
Exhibited at *Glasstress New York*,
New York (USA)

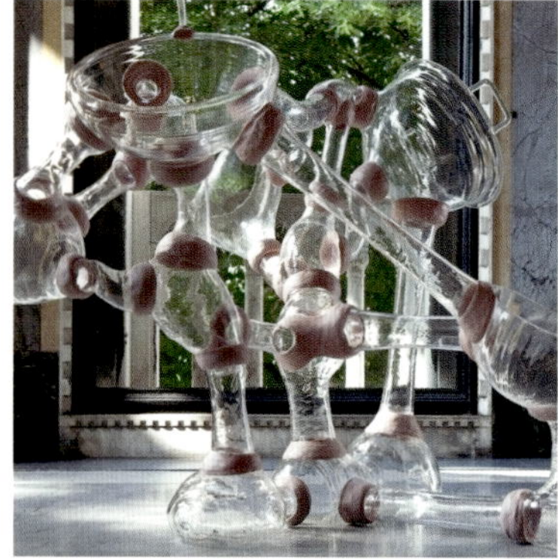

ATELIER VAN LIESHOUT
Excrementorium,
2011 / *detail*
130 x 190 x 136 cm

Courtesy the artist and Venice
Projects, Venice
Exhibited at *Glasstress 2011*,
Venice (IT)

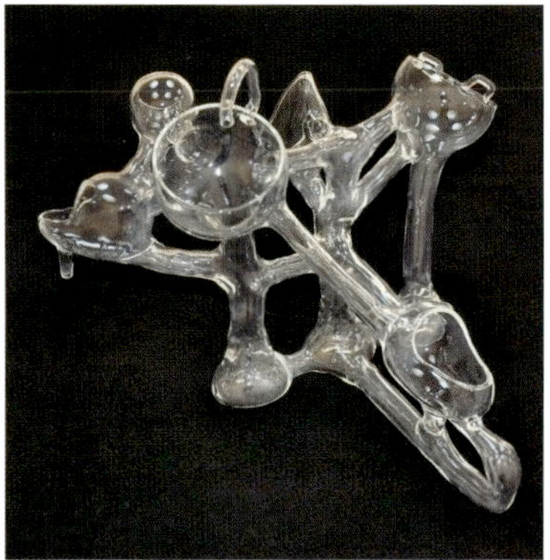

ATELIER VAN LIESHOUT
Excrementorium Small,
2011
33 x 38 x 24 cm

Courtesy the artist and Venice
Projects, Venice
Exhibited at *Glasstress Stockholm*
2011, Stockholm (SE)

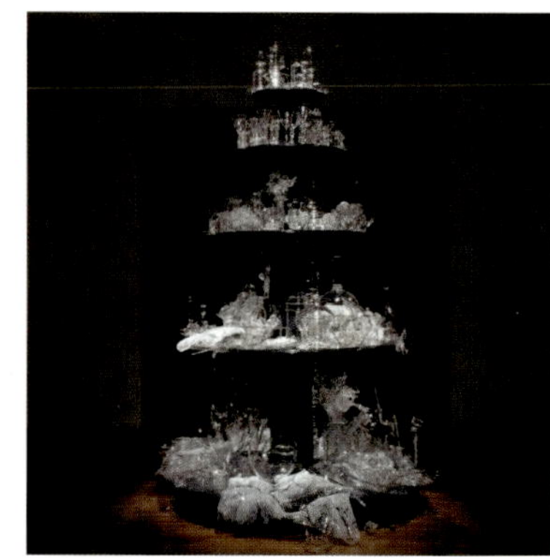

BETH LIPMAN
Bride, 2010
305 x 228 x 228 cm

Courtesy Claire Oliver Gallery,
New York
Exhibited at *Glasstress New York*,
New York (USA)

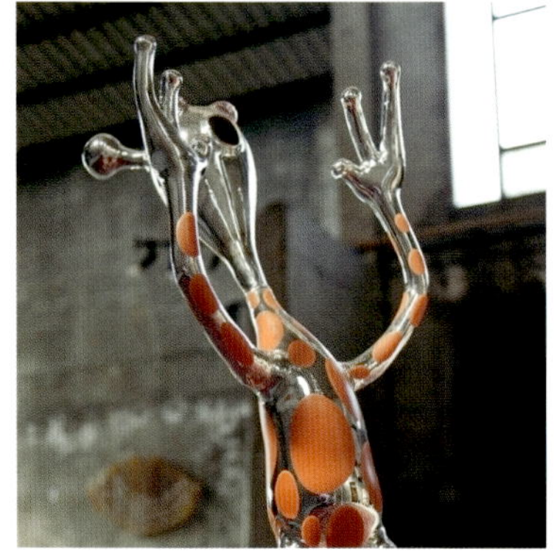

MASSIMO LUNARDON
As Is, Everywhere,
2011 / *detail*
300 x 70 x 50 cm (big) /
74 x 45 x 35 cm (small)

Courtesy Berengo Studio 1989
Exhibited at *Glasstress 2011*,
Venice (IT)

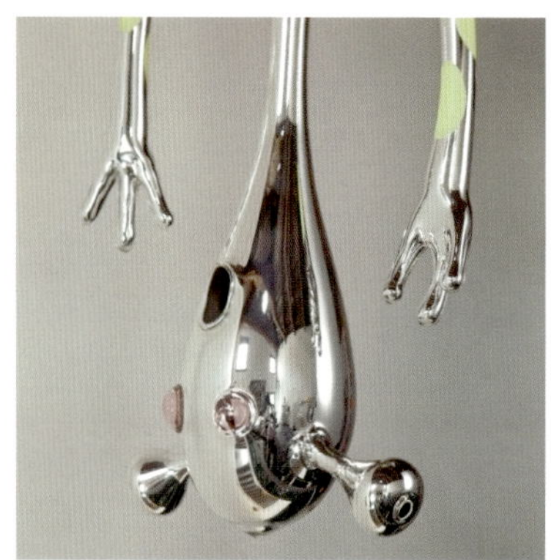

MASSIMO LUNARDON
Universo acrobatico,
2011 / *detail*
variable dimensions

Courtesy Berengo Private
Collection, Venice
Exhibited at *Glasstress Stockholm*
2011, Stockholm (SE)

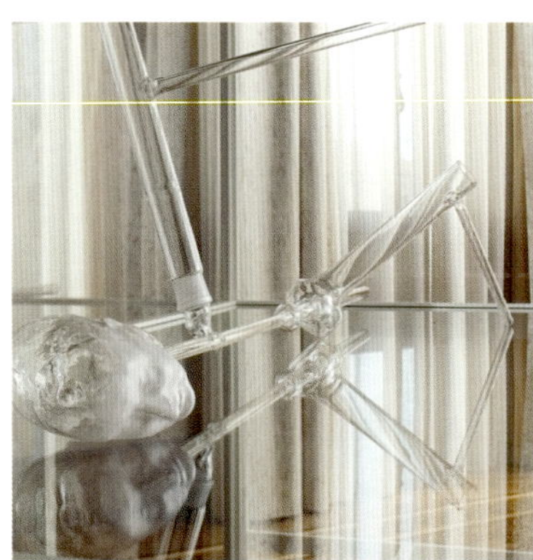

URS LÜTHI
**Ex Voto XXI from Art Is
The Better Life series,**
2010 / *detail*
174 x 236 x 105 cm

Courtesy Artbug Gallery,
Bassano
Exhibited at *Glasstress 2011*,
Venice (IT)

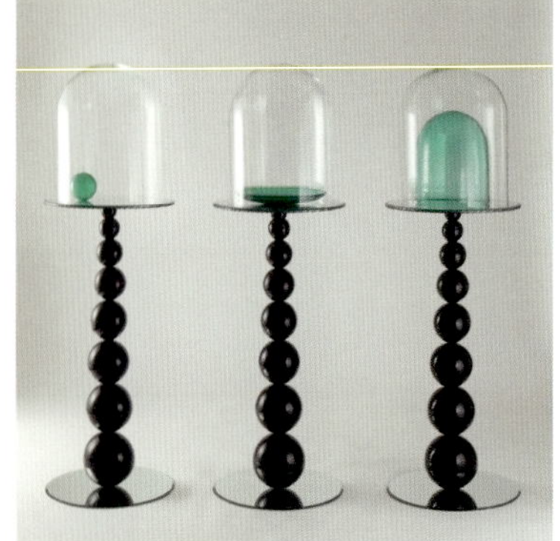

**SARMITE MALINA AND
KRISTAPS KALNS**
Don't Forget Me, 2011
150 x 50 cm diameter
each

Courtesy Berengo Private
Collection, Venice
Exhibited at *Glasstress Riga* 2011,
Riga (LV)

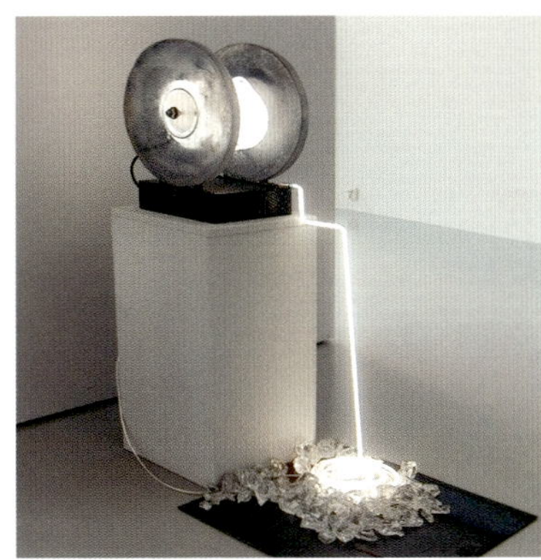

FEDERICA MARANGONI
The Thread, 2002
40 x 3.5 cm /
height 70 cm (neon)

Courtesy Berengo Private
Collection, Venice
Exhibited at *Glasstress* 2009,
Venice (IT)

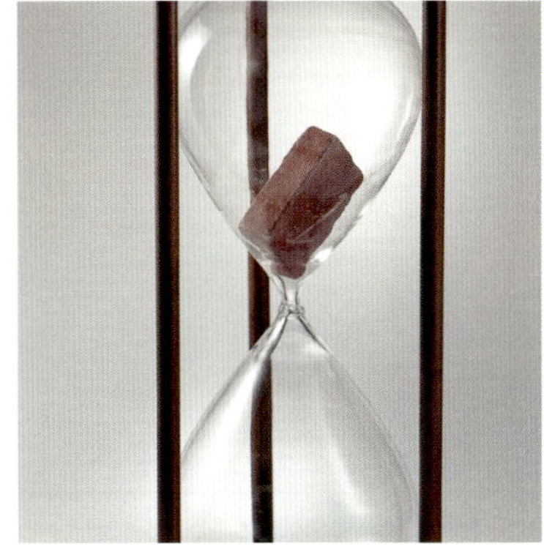

VIK MUNIZ
Untitled,
2010 / *detail*
108 x 52 cm diameter

Courtesy the artist and Venice
Projects, Venice
Exhibited at *Glasstress 2011*,
Venice (IT)
Exhibited at *Glasstress Stockholm
2011*, Stockholm (SE)
Exhibited at *Glasstress New York*,
New York (USA)

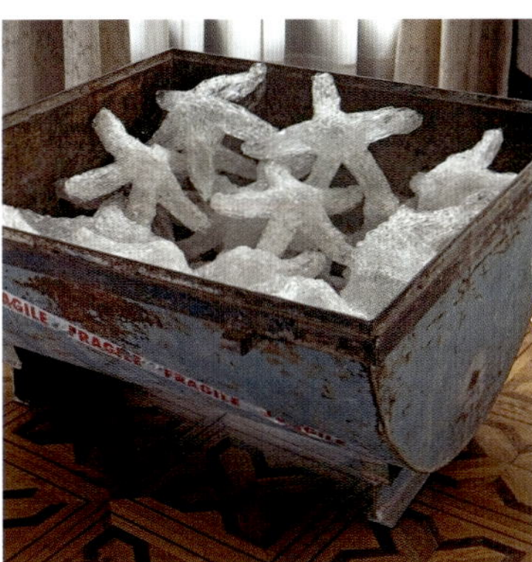

NABIL NAHAS
Untitled VP # 1, 2011
56 x 100 x 108 cm

Courtesy the artist and Venice
Projects, Venice
Exhibited at *Glasstress 2011*,
Venice (IT)

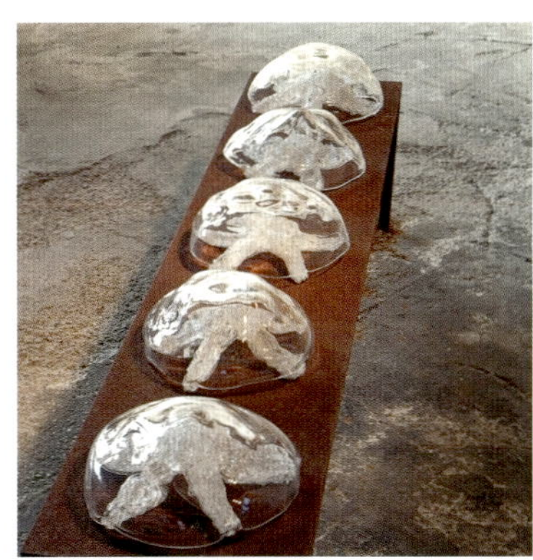

NABIL NAHAS
Untitled VP # 2, 2011
50 x 250 x 50 cm

Courtesy the artist and Venice
Projects, Venice
Exhibited at *Glasstress 2011*,
Venice (IT)

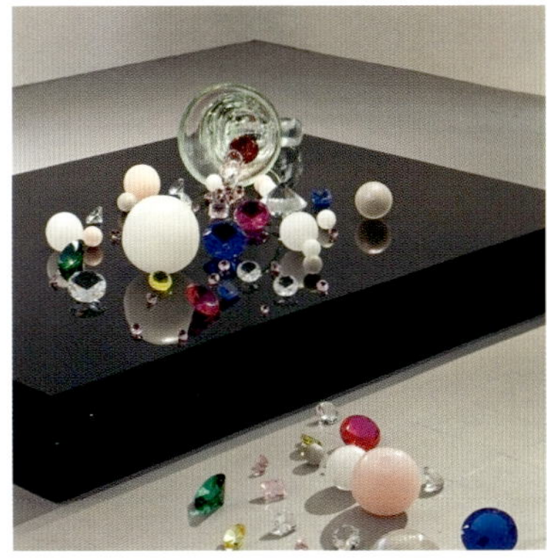

ATELIER TED NOTEN
**If You Want To Be Beautiful
You Have To Suffer,** 2011
150 x 210 cm /
variable dimensions

Courtesy the artist and Venice
Projects, Venice
Exhibited at *Glasstress 2011*,
Venice (IT)

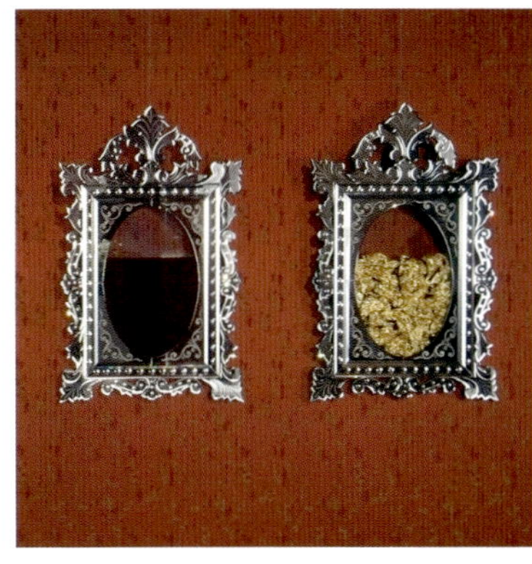

ORLAN
**Miroirs Portrait-Stress
of Our Society,**
2009 / *detail*
87 x 57 x 2 cm each

Courtesy Berengo Private
Collection, Venice
Exhibited at *Glasstress* 2009,
Venice (IT)
Exhibited at *Glasstress Riga* 2011,
Riga (LV)

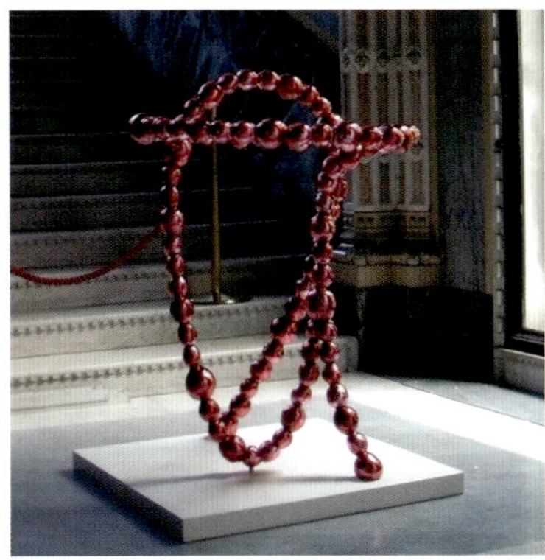

JEAN-MICHEL OTHONIEL
Ricochet Rouge, 2009
unique
110 x 110 x 110 cm

Courtesy Galerie Karsten Greve
AG, St. Moritz
Exhibited at *Glasstress* 2009,
Venice (IT)

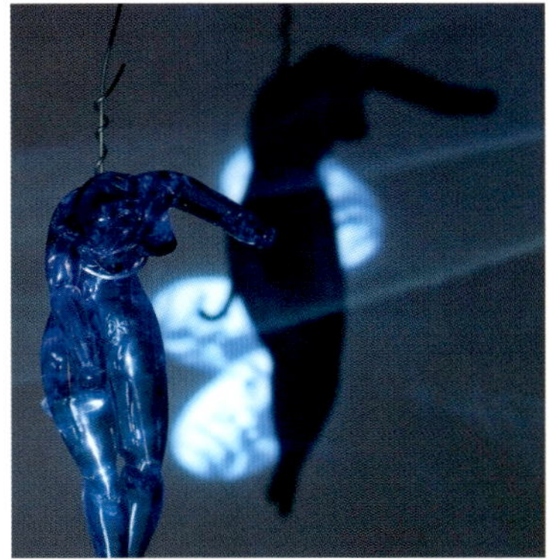

TONY OURSLER
Blue Double Negative,
1999 / *detail*
30.5 x 30.5 x 48.2 cm /
variable dimensions

Courtesy the artist
Exhibited at *Glasstress 2011*,
Venice (IT)
Exhibited at *Glasstress New York*,
New York (USA)

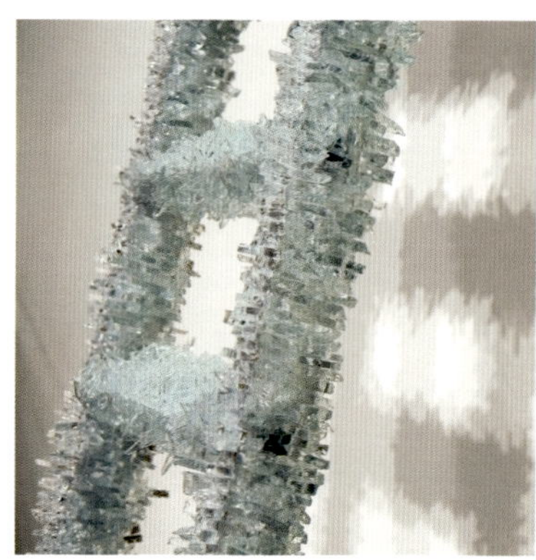

LUCA PANCRAZZI
Scala,
2008 / *detail*
Height 350 cm

Courtesy Galleria Continua,
San Gimignano, Beijing, Le Moulin
Exhibited at *Glasstress 2009*,
Venice (IT)

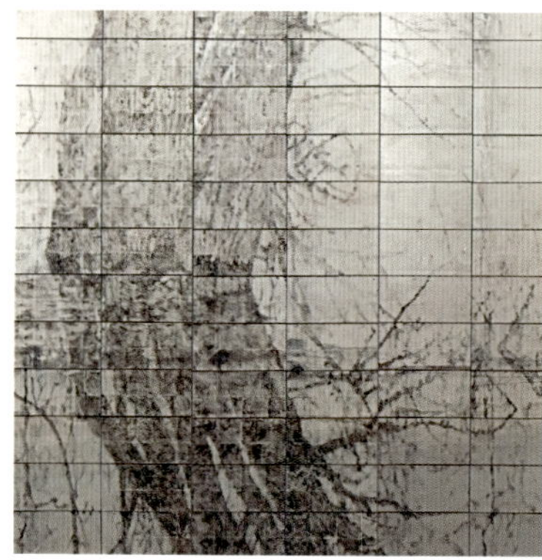

ANNE PEABODY
Alluvion Myth,
2011 / *detail*
213 x 182 x 7.6 cm

Courtesy Venice Projects, Venice
Exhibited at *Glasstress 2011*,
Venice (IT)

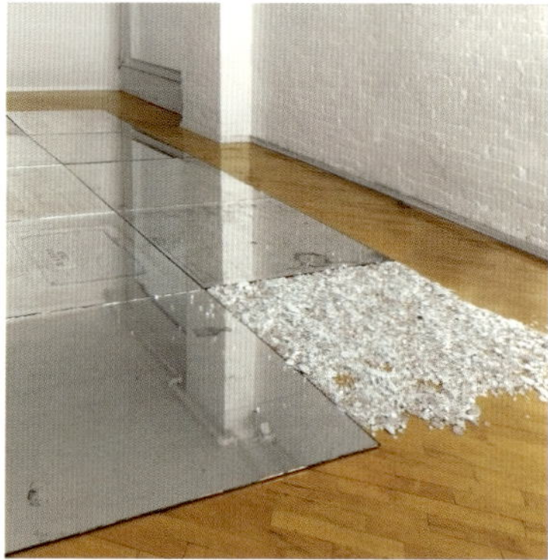

ANNE PEABODY
My Sidewalk,
2004 / *detail*
533.4 x 213.6 x 1 cm

Courtesy Venice Projects, Venice
Exhibited at *Glasstress 2009*,
Venice (IT)

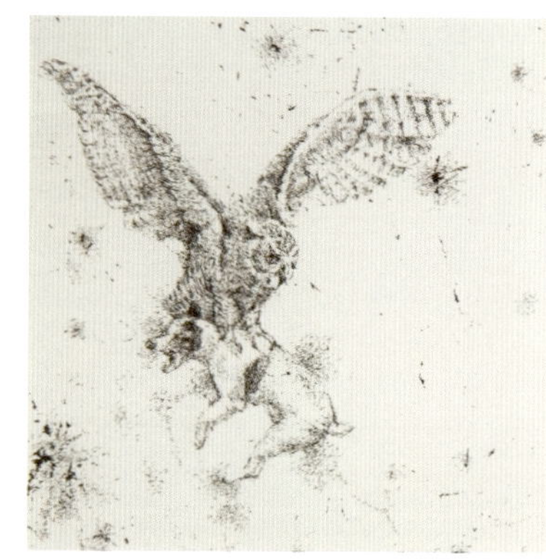

ANNE PEABODY
Owl With Dog,
2011 / *detail*
7.6 x 10.1 cm

Courtesy the artist and Venice
Projects, Venice
Exhibited at *Glasstress Stockholm
2011*, Stockholm (SE)

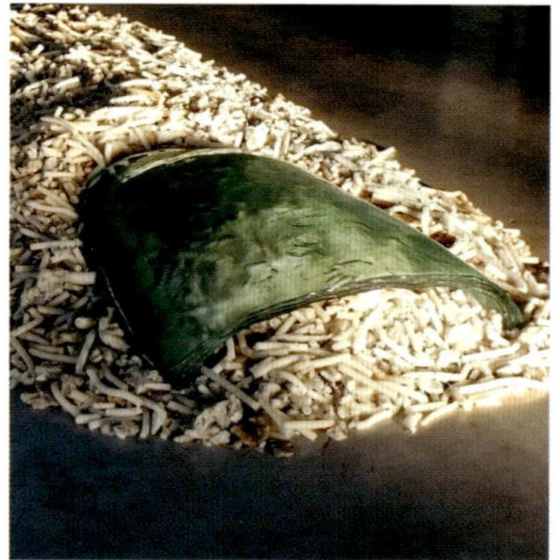

GIUSEPPE PENONE
Unghia e candele,
1994 / *detail*
30 x 300 x 150 cm

Courtesy Private Collection
Exhibited at *Glasstress 2009*,
Venice (IT)

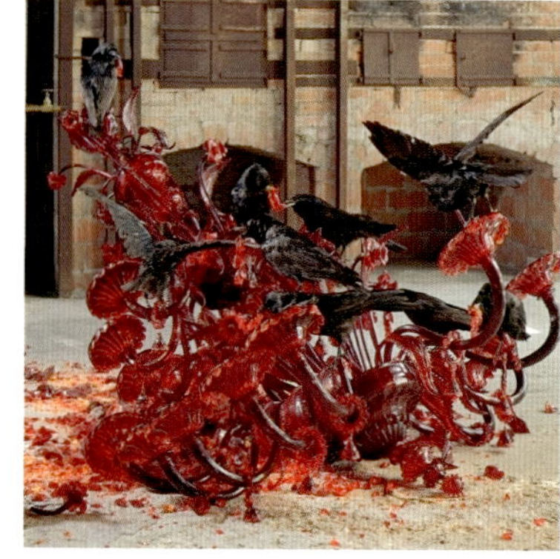

JAVIER PÉREZ
Carroña, 2011
120 x 235 x 300 cm /
variable dimensions

Courtesy Venice Projects, Venice
Exhibited at *Glasstress 2011*,
Venice (IT)
Exhibited at *Glasstress Riga* 2011,
Riga (LV)
Exhibited at *Glasstress New York*,
New York (USA)

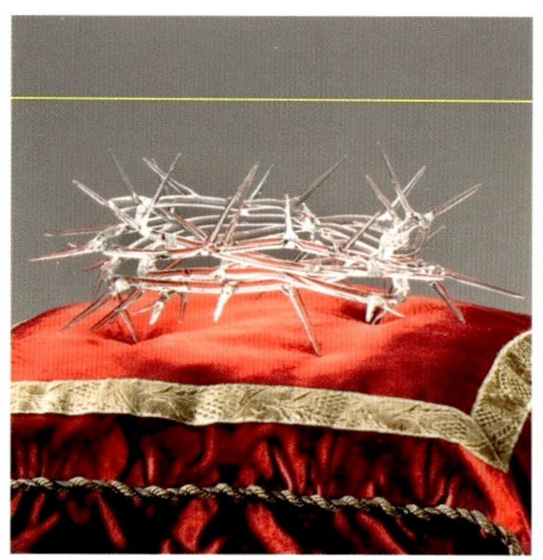

JAVIER PÉREZ
Corona, 2011
12 x 33 cm diameter

Courtesy the artist and Venice
Projects, Venice
Exhibited at *Glasstress 2011*,
Venice (IT)
Exhibited at *Glasstress Stockholm*
2011, Stockholm (SE)

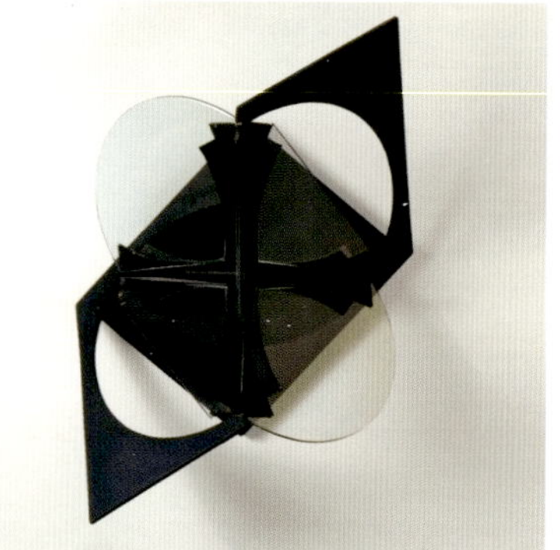

ANTON PEVSNER
**Croce ancorata
(La Croix ancrée),** 1993
84.6 cm (diagonal length)

Courtesy Peggy Guggenheim
Collection, Venice
Exhibited at *Glasstress 2009*,
Venice (IT)

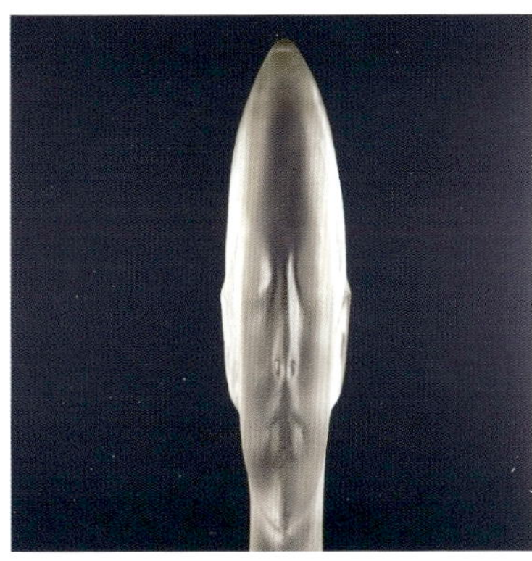

JAUME PLENSA
Cristina's Frozen Dreams,
2010
Ed. 8
52 x 40 x 40 cm

Courtesy Berengo Private
Collection, Venice, and Galerie
Lelong, Paris
Exhibited at *Glasstress 2011*,
Venice (IT)
Exhibited at *Glasstress Stockholm*
2011, Stockholm (SE)
Exhibited at *Glasstress New York*,
New York (USA)

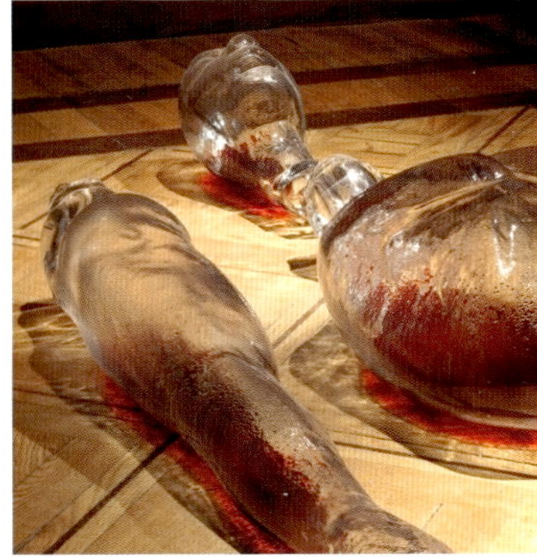

JAUME PLENSA
Glassman II,
2004 / *detail*
30 x 250 x 90 cm

Courtesy the artist and Galerie
Lelong, Paris
Exhibited at *Glasstress 2011*,
Venice (IT)

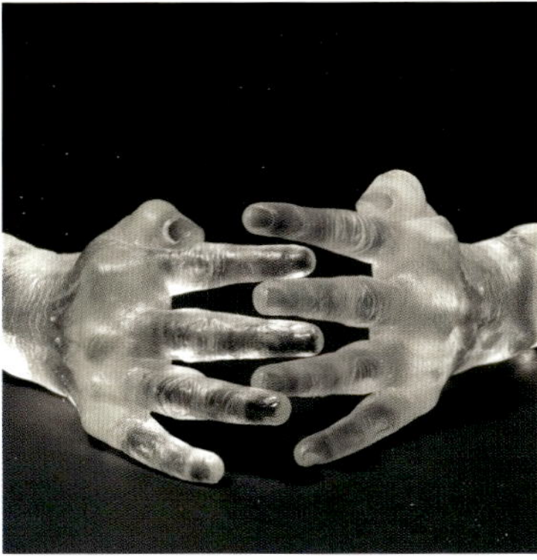

JAUME PLENSA
Laura's Hands,
2011 / *detail*
Ed. 25
6 x 19 x 10 cm each /
variable dimensions

Courtesy Berengo Private
Collection, Venice, and Galerie
Lelong, Paris
Exhibited at *Glasstress 2011*,
Venice (IT)
Exhibited at *Glasstress New York*,
New York (USA)

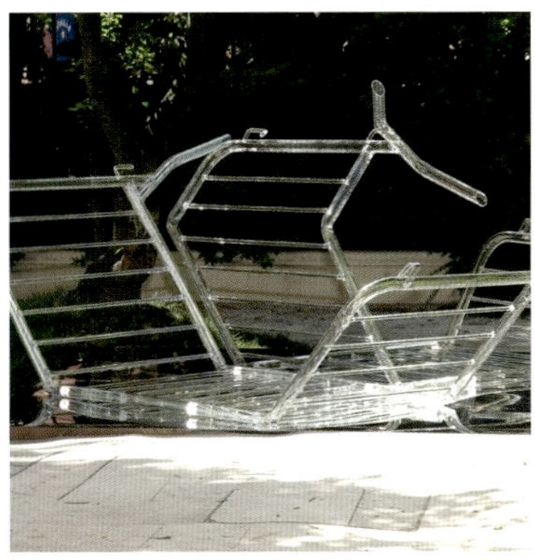

BETTINA POUSTTCHI
Cleared, 2009
150 x 200 x 220 cm

Courtesy Buchmann Galerie,
Berlin/Lugano
Exhibited at *Glasstress* 2009,
Venice (IT)

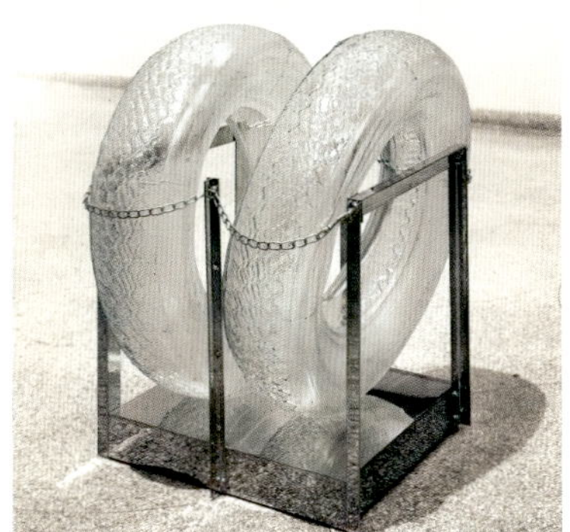

ROBERT RAUSCHENBERG
Untitled [Glass Tires], 1997
76.2 x 71.1 x 61 cm

Courtesy Estate of Robert
Rauschenberg, New York
Exhibited at *Glasstress* 2009,
Venice (IT)

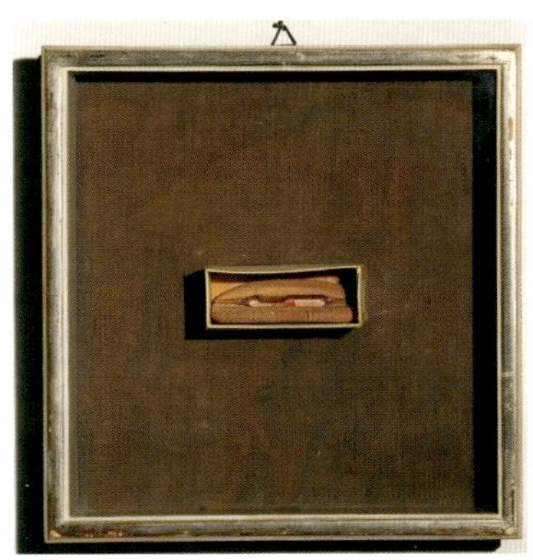

MAN RAY
Pandora's Box, 1963
4 x 11 x 4 cm

Courtesy Fondazione Marconi,
Milan
Exhibited at *Glasstress* 2009,
Venice (IT)

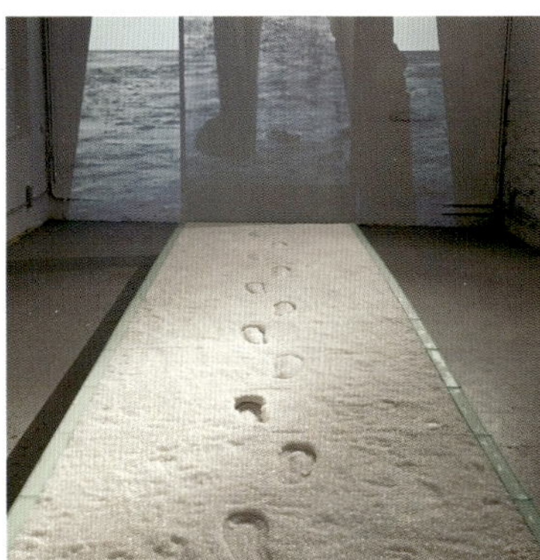

RECYCLE GROUP
Way, 2011
29 x 154 x 600 cm

Courtesy the artist, Venice
Projects, Venice, and Triumph
Gallery, Moscow
Exhibited at *Glasstress 2011*,
Venice (IT)

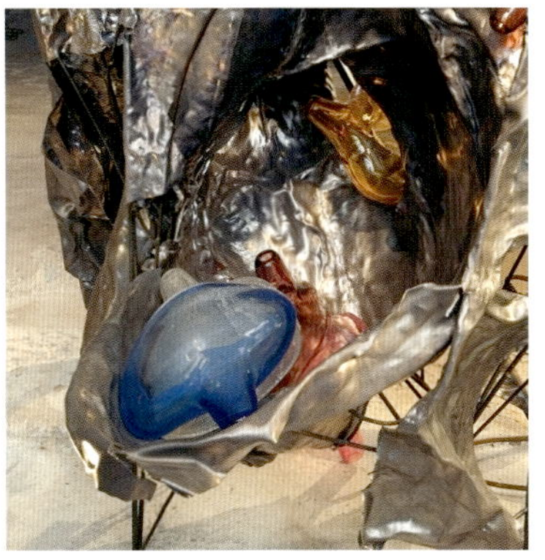

ANTJE RIECK
Soul Sister,
2011 / *detail*
170 x 310 x 310 cm

Courtesy Novalis Contemporary
Art, Turin
Exhibited at *Glasstress 2011*,
Venice (IT)

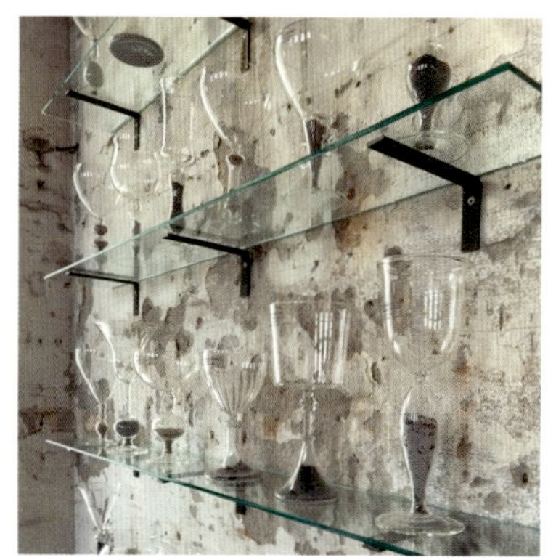

ANTONIO RIELLO
Ashes to Ashes,
2009/2010 / *detail*
35 x 20 cm diameter each /
variable dimensions

Courtesy Galleria Michela Rizzo,
Venice, and Berengo Private
Collection, Venice
Exhibited at *Glasstress 2011*,
Venice (IT)

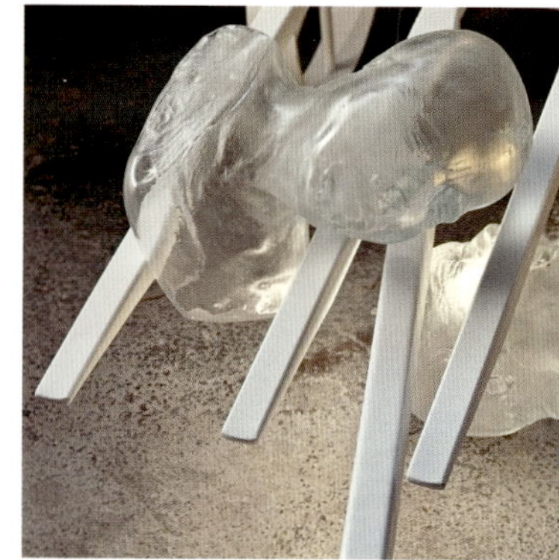

BERNARDÍ ROIG
**Il diavolo e le due teste
di San Giovanni,**
2011 / *detail*
variable dimensions

Courtesy Claire Oliver Gallery,
New York
Exhibited at *Glasstress 2011*,
Venice (IT)

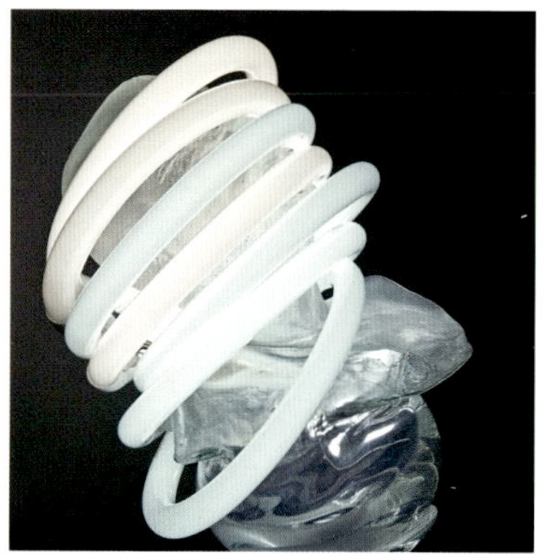

BERNARDÍ ROIG
St. John's Glass Head,
2011
50 x 40 x 35 cm

Courtesy Claire Oliver Gallery,
New York, and Berengo Private
Collection, Venice
Exhibited at *Glasstress 2011*,
Venice (IT)
Exhibited at *Glasstress Stockholm*
2011, Stockholm (SE)

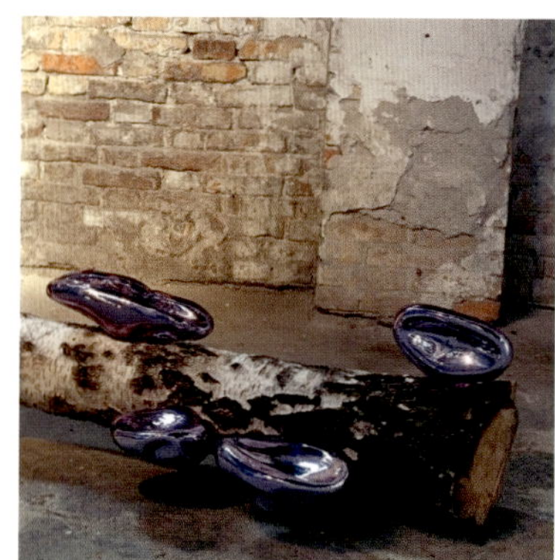

MARIA ROOSEN
Washed Tree Flour,
2009/2011
45 x 270 x 53 cm

Courtesy Collection Lise and
Thierry Prevot and Gallery Fons
Wetters, Amsterdam
Exhibited at *Glasstress 2011*,
Venice (IT)

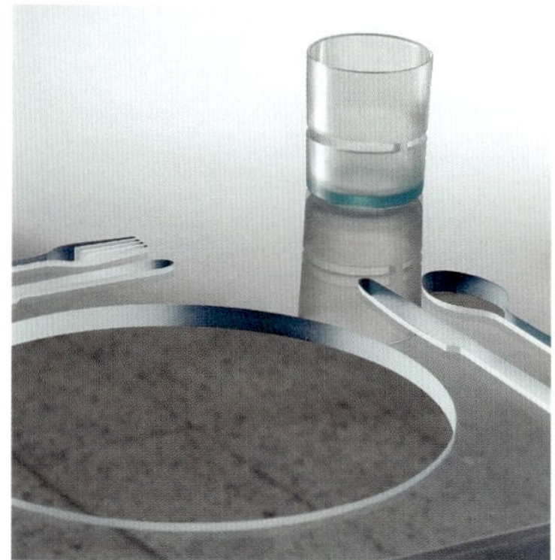

SILVANO RUBINO
Addizione sottrattiva,
2009 / *detail*
Ed. 1/3
80 x 400 x 100 cm

Courtesy the artist and Berengo
Private Collection, Venice
Exhibited at *Glasstress 2009*,
Venice (IT)
Exhibited at *Glasstress Stockholm*
2011, Stockholm (SE)
Exhibited at *Glasstress New York*,
New York (USA)

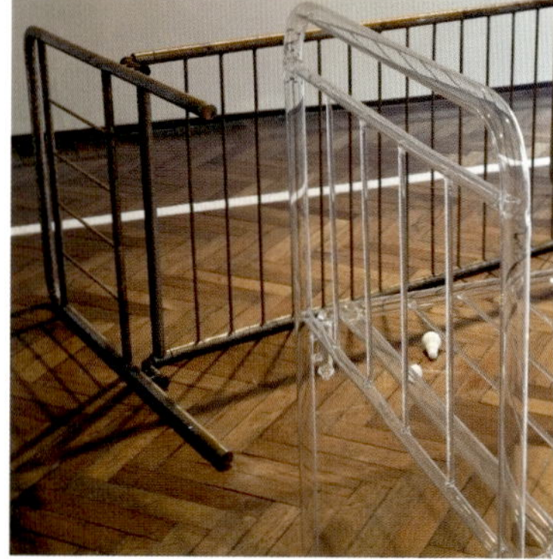

SILVANO RUBINO
**Death announced to
the ear of a deaf,**
2009/2010 / *detail*
variable dimensions

Courtesy the artist and Berengo
Private Collection, Venice
Exhibited at *Glasstress Riga* 2011,
Riga (LV)

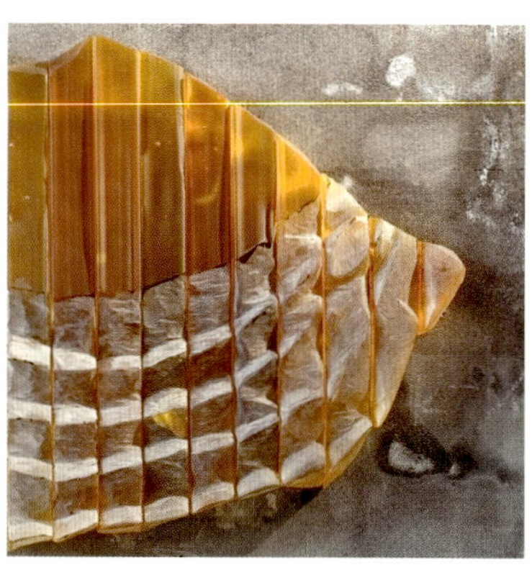

URSULA VON RYDINGSVARD
Glass Corrugated,
2010 / *detail*
130 x 76 x 5 cm

Courtesy the artist and Galerie
Lelong, New York
Exhibited at *Glasstress 2011*,
Venice (IT)
Exhibited at *Glasstress New York*,
New York (USA)

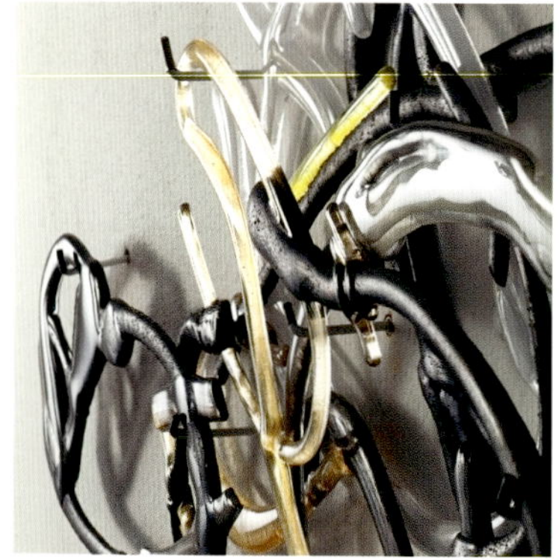

TANIA SÆTER
Transformers,
2011 / *detail*
350 x 300 x 15 cm /
variable dimensions

Courtesy the artist
Exhibited at *Glasstress 2011*,
Venice (IT)
Exhibited at *Glasstress Stockholm*
2011, Stockholm (SE)

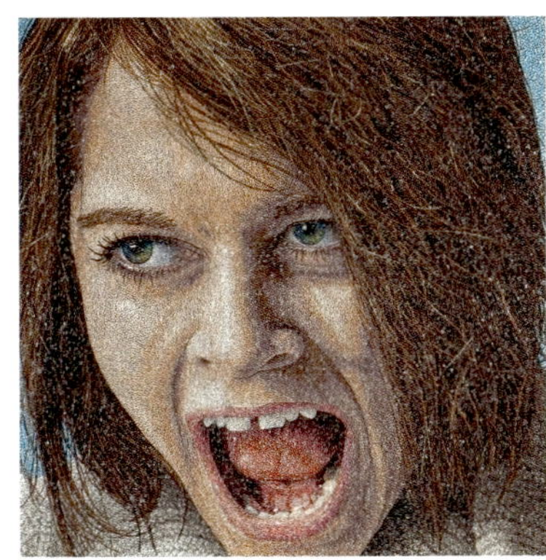

ANDREA SALVADOR
Giovanna d'Arco n.1, 2011
150 x 131.5 cm

Courtesy the artist and Berengo
Private Collection, Venice
Exhibited at *Glasstress 2011*,
Venice (IT)

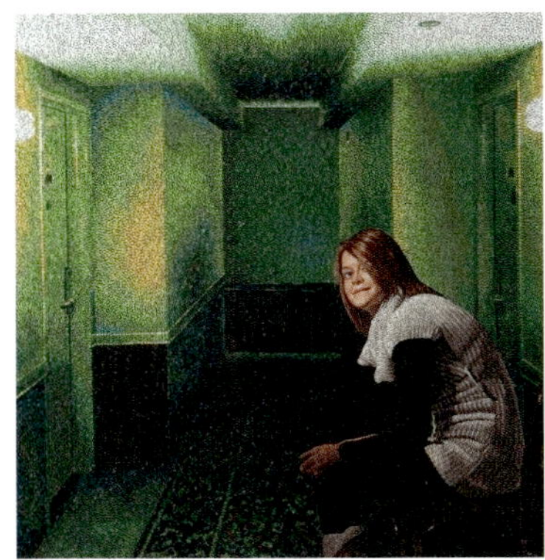

ANDREA SALVADOR
Giovanna d'Arco n.3, 2011
150 x 160 cm

Courtesy Berengo Private
Collection, Venice
Exhibited at *Glasstress Riga* 2011,
Riga (LV)

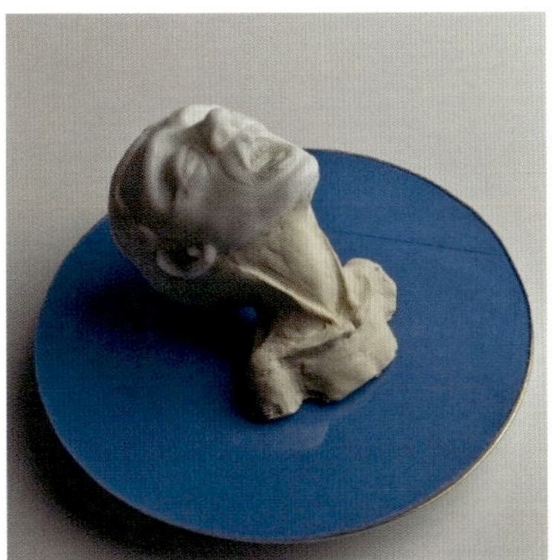

JUDITH SCHAECHTER
Drowning, 2012
30.5 x 18 x 18 cm

Courtesy Claire Oliver Gallery,
New York
Exhibited at *Glasstress New York*,
New York (USA)

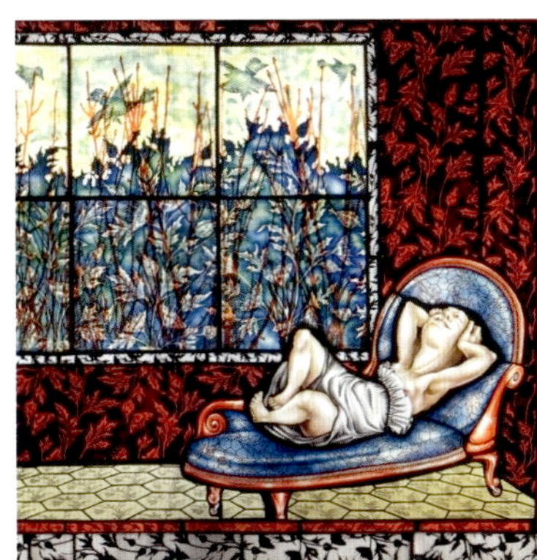

JUDITH SCHAECHTER
Nature, 2010 / *detail*
79 x 118 x 16 cm

Courtesy Claire Oliver Gallery,
New York
Exhibited at *Glasstress 2011*,
Venice (IT)

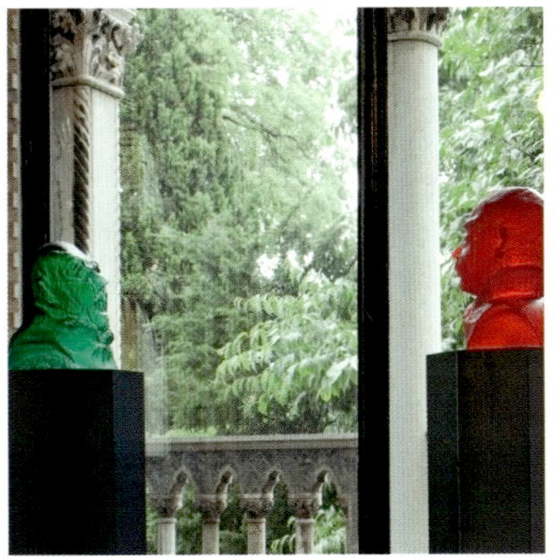

THOMAS SCHÜTTE
Berengo Head, 2011
45 x 30 x 27 cm
(green head) /
50 x 30 x 27 cm
(red head)

Courtesy the artist and Berengo
Private Collection, Venice
Exhibited at *Glasstress 2011*,
Venice (IT)
Exhibited at *Glasstress New York*,
New York (USA)

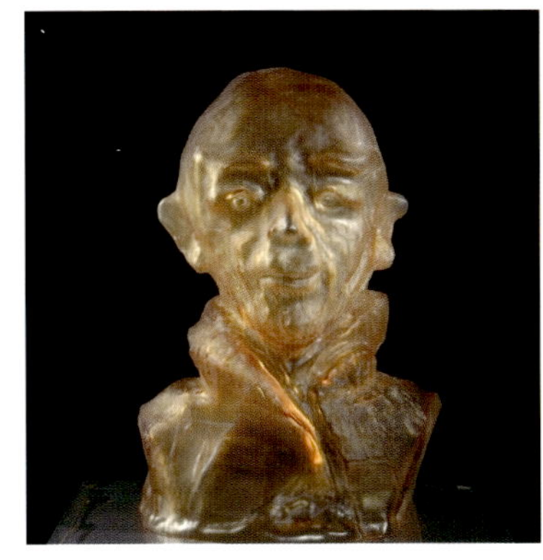

THOMAS SCHÜTTE
Berengo Head, 2011
49 x 25 x 30 cm
(yellow head)

Courtesy the artist and Berengo
Private Collection, Venice
Exhibited at *Glasstress Stockholm*
2011, Stockholm (SE)

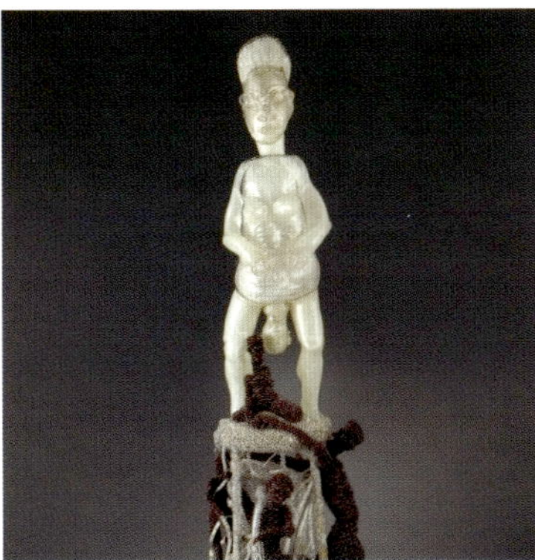

JOYCE JANE SCOTT
Milk Mammy 1,
2012 / *detail*
113 x 30.5 x 27 cm

Courtesy Goya Contemporary,
Baltimore, and Berengo Studio,
Venice
Exhibited at *Glasstress New York*,
New York (USA)

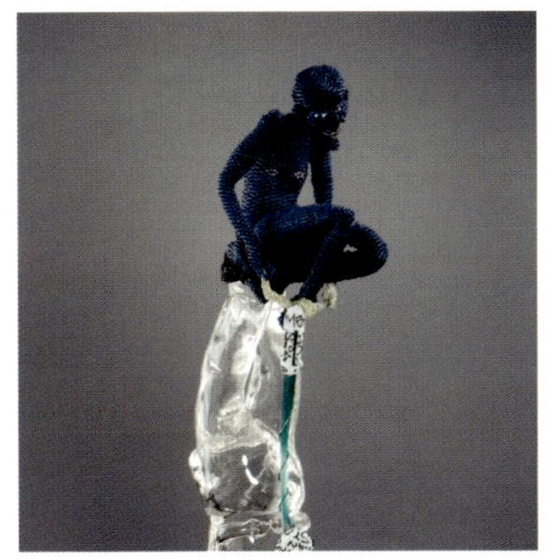

JOYCE JANE SCOTT
Water Mammy 1,
2012 / *detail*
89 x 16.5 x 25.5 cm

Courtesy Goya Contemporary,
Baltimore, and Berengo Studio,
Venice
Exhibited at *Glasstress New York*,
New York (USA)

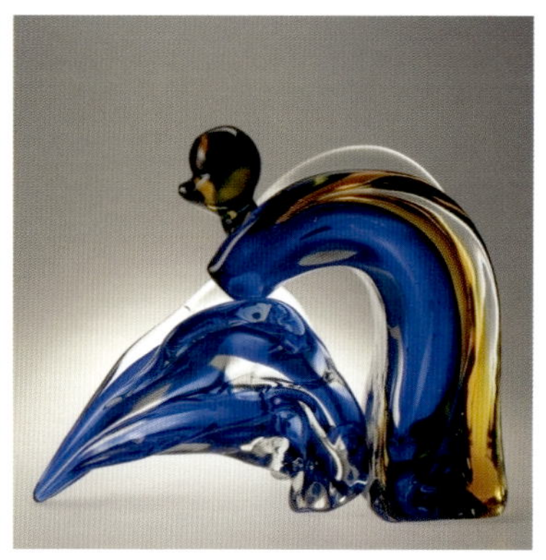

SANDRO SERGI
Uccello, 1970
35 x 46 x 18 cm

Courtesy Berengo Private
Collection, Venice
Exhibited at *Glasstress* 2009,
Venice (IT)

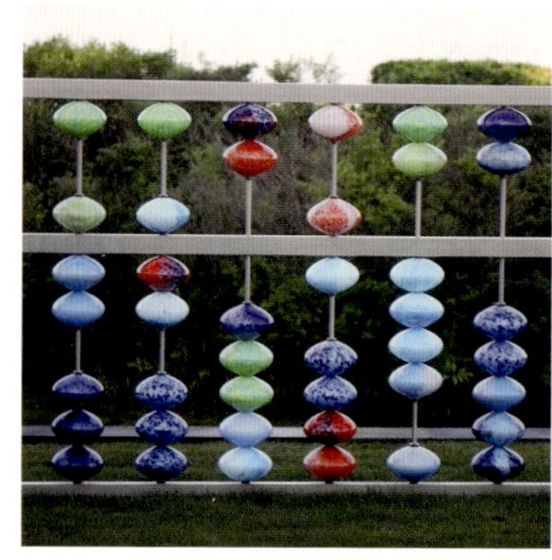

SHAN SHAN SHENG
Abacus-Western Zhou
Dynasty, BC 1046–BC 771,
2007 / *detail*
450 x 230 x 100 cm

Courtesy Joanne Katz Private
Collection, Florida
Exhibited at *Glasstress Stockholm*
2011, Stockholm (SE)

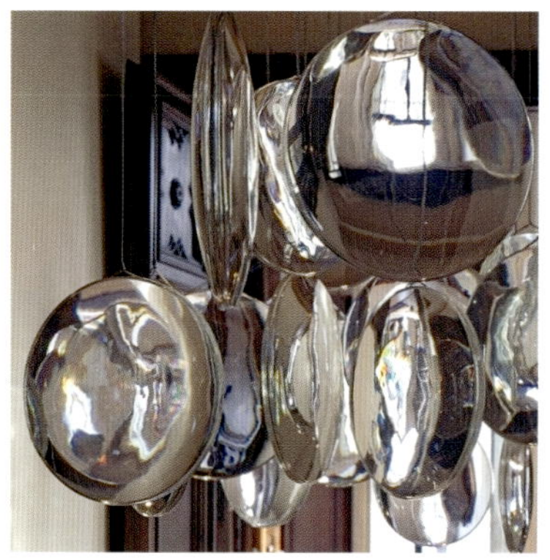

ANATOLY SHURAVLEV
Viewing Deception,
2011 / *detail*
25 cm diameter / 30 cm
diameter / 35 cm diameter
(lenses)

Courtesy Urs Meile Gallery,
Beijing, Lucerne, and Venice
Projects, Venice
Exhibited at *Glasstress 2011*,
Venice (IT)
Exhibited at *Glasstress Riga* 2011,
Riga (LV)

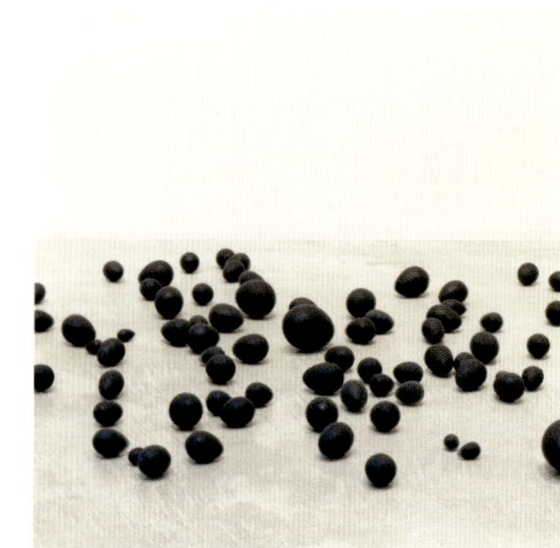

KIKI SMITH
Black Eggs,
1998 / *detail*
98 eggs, 4.4 x 7.6 x 5.7 cm
to 8.3 x 12.1 x 8.9 cm
each /
variable dimensions
(installation)

Collection of the artist,
courtesy The Pace Gallery
Exhibited at *Glasstress* 2009,
Venice (IT)

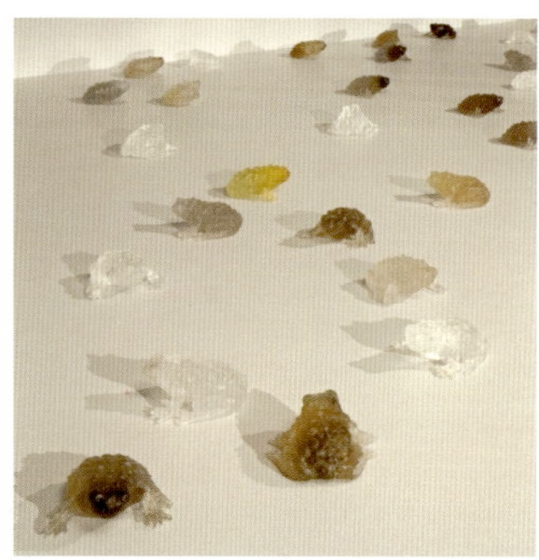

KIKI SMITH
Frogs, 1999 / *detail*
63 elements,
7.6 x 7.6 x 7.6 cm each /
variable dimensions
(installation)

Courtesy The Pace Gallery
Exhibited at *Glasstress New York*,
New York (USA)

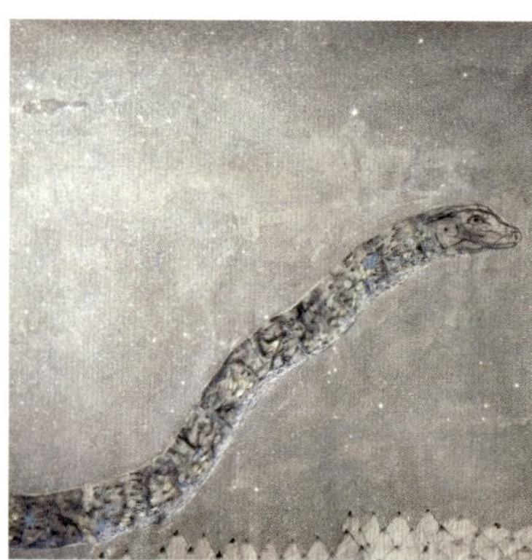

KIKI SMITH
Milky Way, 2011 / *detail*
182.9 x 193 cm

Courtesy The Pace Gallery
Exhibited at *Glasstress 2011*,
Venice (IT)

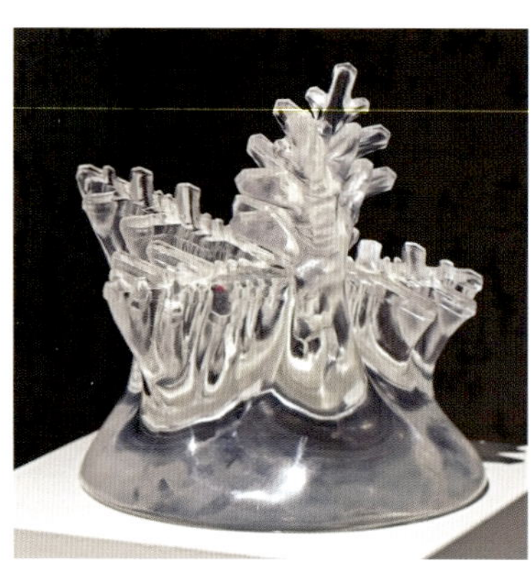

YUTAKA SONE
Every Snowflake Has
A Different Shape N.30 /
N.35, 2010 / *detail*
14.3 x 26.4 x 23.8 cm /
24.4 x 25.5 x 26.4 cm

Courtesy the artist
and David Zwirner, New York
Exhibited at *Glasstress 2011*,
Venice (IT)
Exhibited at *Glasstress New York*,
New York (USA)

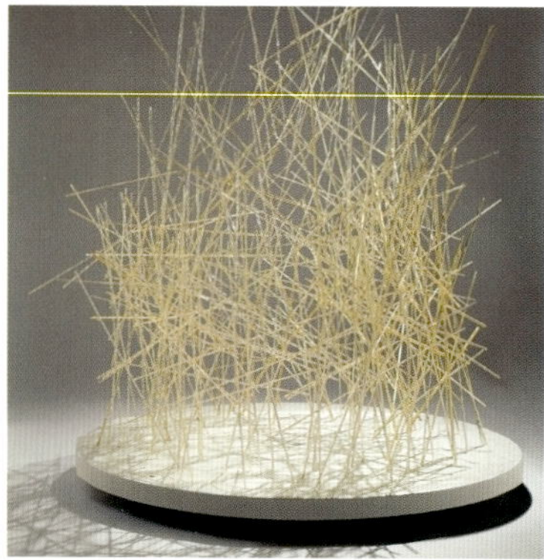

MIKE + DOUG STARN
Untitled, 2011
55 x 40 cm diameter

Courtesy Berengo Private
Collection, Venice
Exhibited at *Glasstress New York*,
New York (USA)

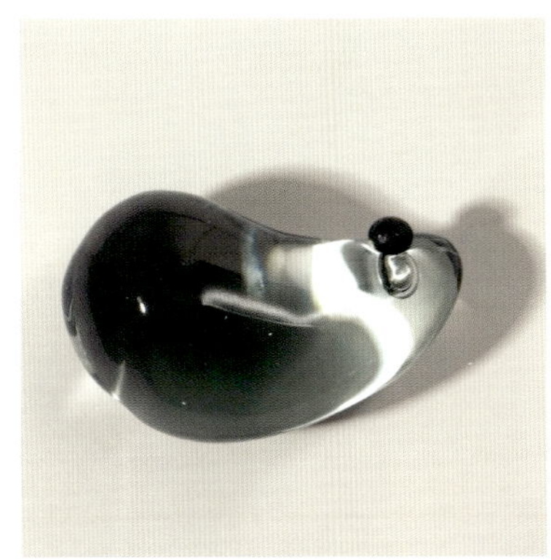

JANA STERBAK
Transpiration: Portrait Olfactif, 1995
16 x 28 x 14 cm diameter

Courtesy Galleria Raffaella Cortese, Milan, and Galeria Toni Tàpies, Barcelona
Exhibited at *Glasstress* 2009, Venice (IT)

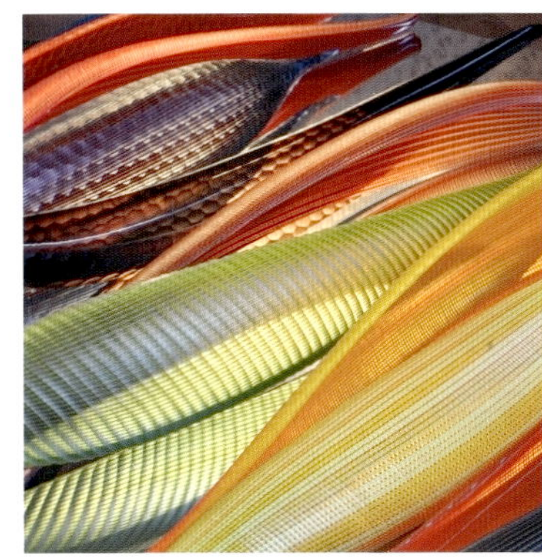

LINO TAGLIAPIETRA
Attesa, 2009 / *detail*
45 x 200 x 200 cm

Courtesy the artist
Exhibited at *Glasstress* 2009, Venice (IT)

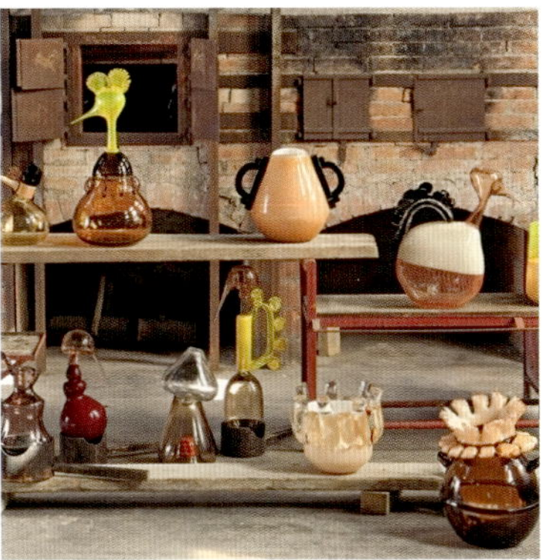

PATRICIA URQUIOLA
All Ambiq, 2011 /
detail
150 x 430 x 180 cm /
variable dimensions

Courtesy Studio Urquiola, Milan, and Berengo Private Collection, Venice
Exhibited at *Glasstress 2011*, Venice (IT)
Exhibited at *Glasstress New York*, New York (USA)

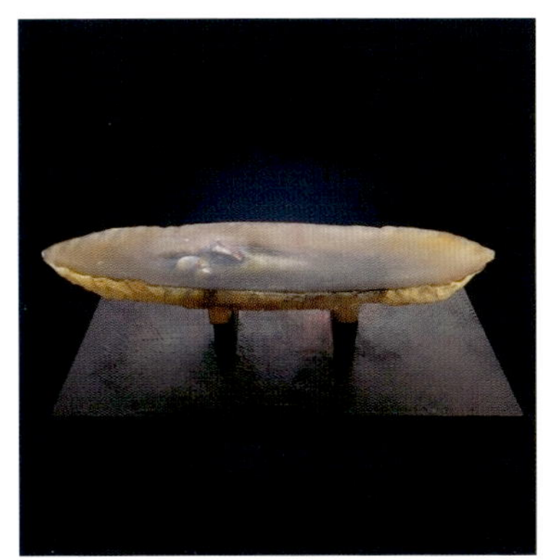

BERTIL VALLIEN
Hidden, 1987
10.5 x 15.5 x 65 cm

Courtesy Orrefors Kosta Boda AB, Orrefors
Exhibited at *Glasstress Stockholm* 2011, Stockholm (SE)

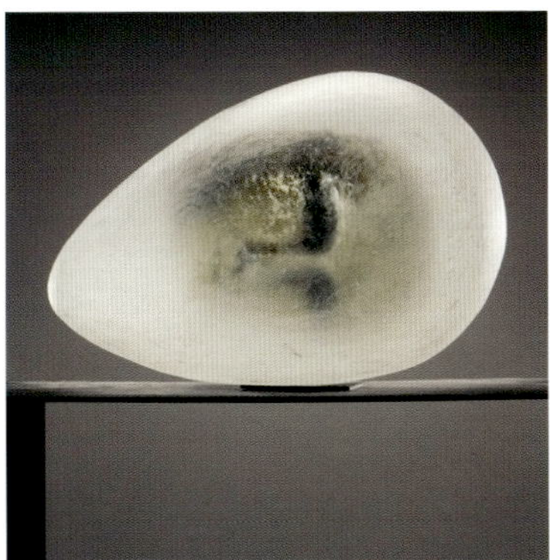

BERTIL VALLIEN
Resting Head, 2009
23 x 28 x 38 cm

Courtesy Orrefors Kosta Boda AB, Orrefors
Exhibited at *Glasstress Stockholm* 2011, Stockholm (SE)

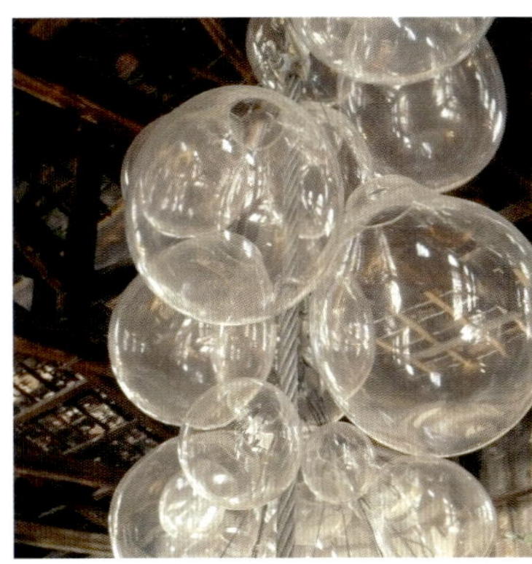

KOEN VANMECHELEN
Egg Cord,
2009 / *detail*
variable dimensions

Courtesy the artist and Berengo Private Collection, Venice
Exhibited at *Glasstress 2011*, Venice (IT)

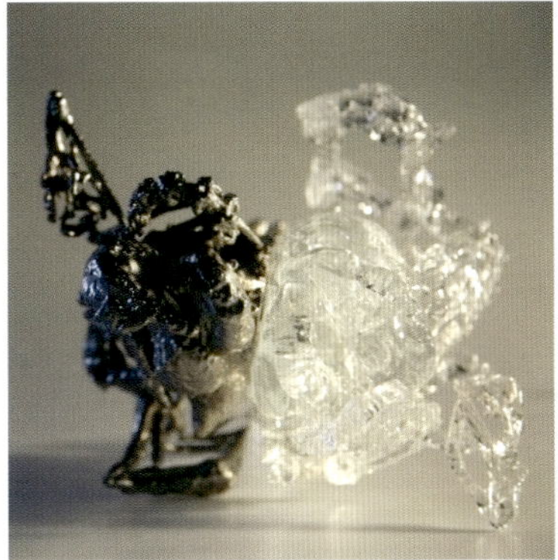

KOEN VANMECHELEN
Entwined, 2011
20 x 30 x 25 cm

Courtesy the artist
Exhibited at *Glasstress New York*, New York (USA)

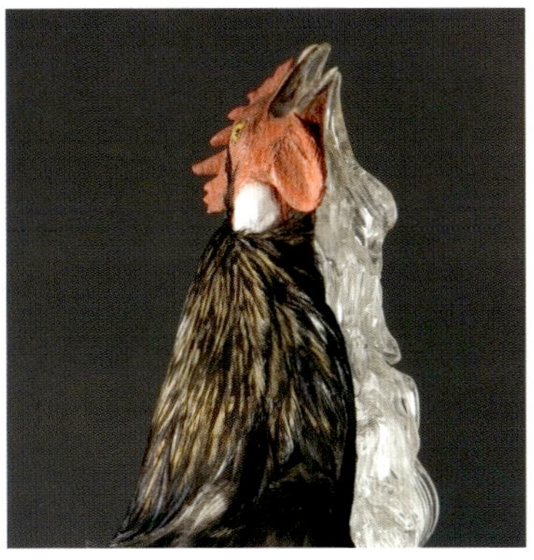

KOEN VANMECHELEN
The Accident,
2005 / *detail*
60 x 35 x 45 cm

Courtesy Moss Private Collection, Miami
Exhibited at *Glasstress* 2009, Venice (IT)

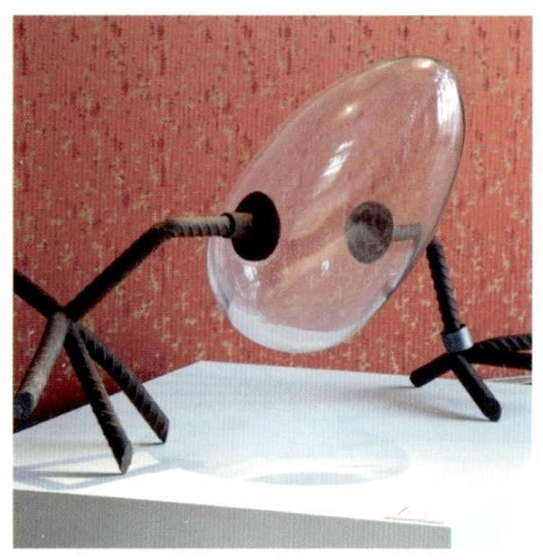

KOEN VANMECHELEN
The Walking Egg,
1989 / *detail*
70 x 156 x 58 cm

Courtesy Venice Projects, Venice
Exhibited at *Glasstress 2011*,
Venice (IT)
Exhibited at *Glasstress Stockholm*
2011, Stockholm (SE)

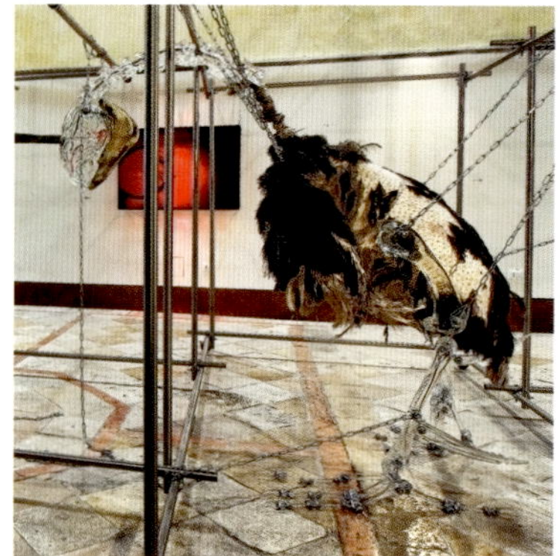

KOEN VANMECHELEN
Unicorn,
2009 / *detail*
200 x 400 x 800 cm

Courtesy the artist and Berengo
Private Collection, Venice
Exhibited at *Glasstress 2009*,
Venice (IT)

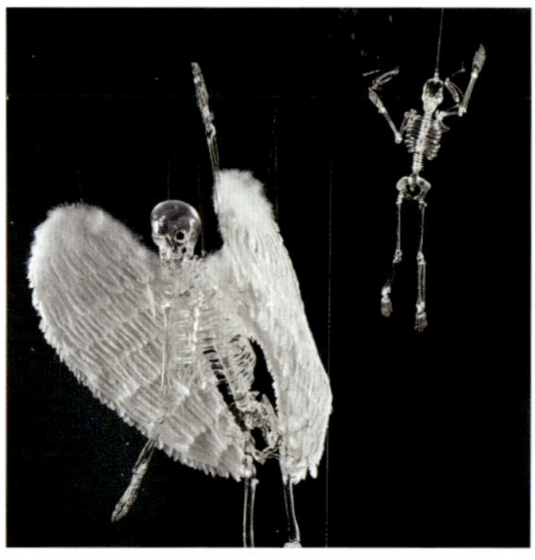

PHARRELL WILLIAMS
Inside Out, 2011
180 x 110 cm
(big skeleton) / 90 x 90 cm
(small skeleton)

Courtesy Venice Projects, Venice
Exhibited at *Glasstress 2011*,
Venice (IT)

FRED WILSON
Iago's Mirror, 2009
200 x 130 x 20 cm

Courtesy The Pace Gallery
and Berengo Private
Collection, Venice
Exhibited at *Glasstress 2009*,
Venice (IT)
Exhibited at *Glasstress Riga* 2011,
Riga (LV)
Exhibited at *Glasstress Stockholm*
2011, Stockholm (SE)

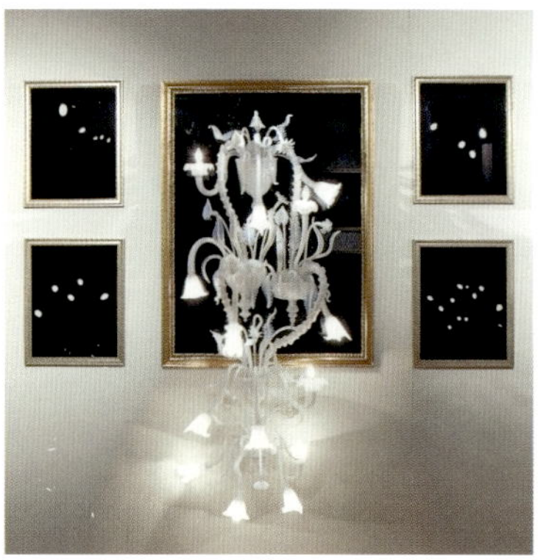

FRED WILSON
Sala Longhi, 2011
70 x 55 x 3 cm
(small frame) /
230 x 118 x 38 cm
(big frame) / 200 x 110 cm
(applique)

Courtesy The Pace Gallery
and Berengo Private
Collection, Venice
Exhibited at *Glasstress 2011*,
Venice (IT)

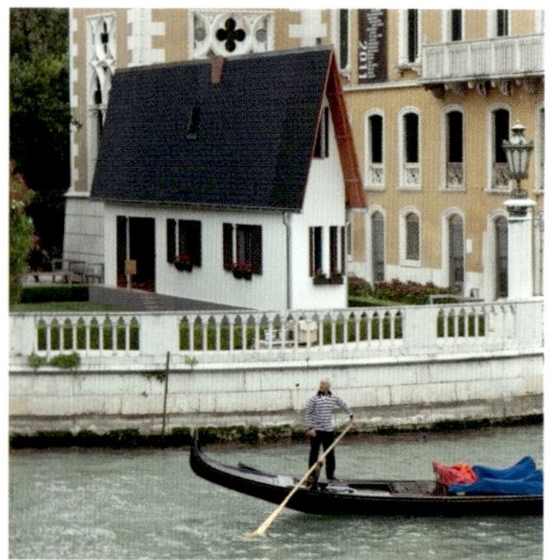

ERWIN WURM
Narrow House, 2010
Ed. 2/3
7 x 16 x 1.20 m

Courtesy Xavier Hufkens Gallery,
Brussels, Lehmann Maupin
Gallery, New York, and Thaddaeus
Ropac Gallery, Paris, Salzburg
Exhibited at *Glasstress 2011*,
Venice (IT)

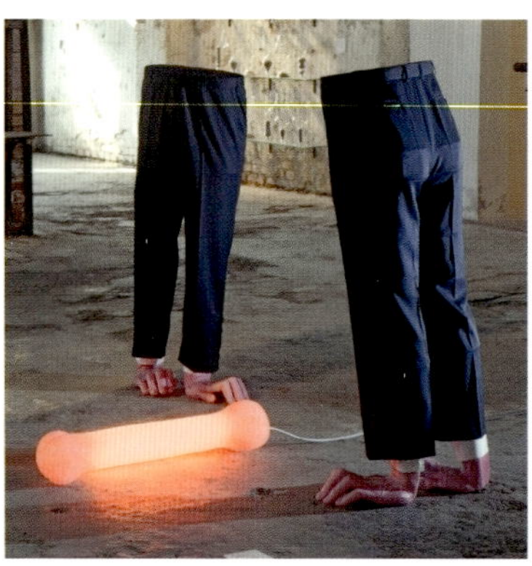

SHI YONG
The Moon's Hues Are
Teasing, 2011 / *detail*
14 x 80 x 18 cm (bone) /
126 x 70 x 40 cm
(pants with a pair
of hands)

Courtesy the artist, Venice
Projects, Venice, and Shanghart
Gallery, Shanghai
Exhibited at *Glasstress 2011*,
Venice (IT)

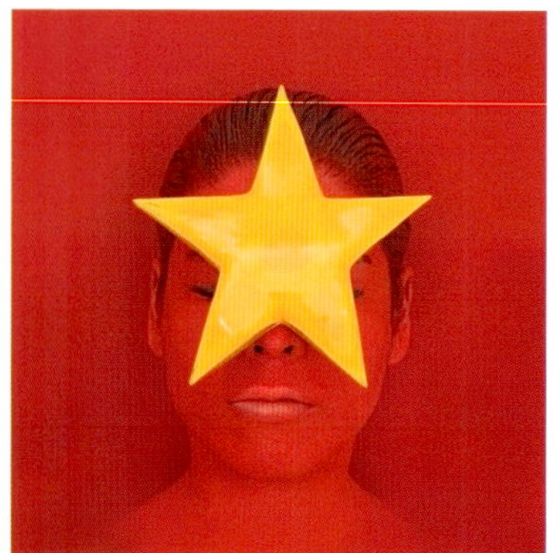

KIMIKO YOSHIDA
Blown Glass Symbols, 2009
28 x 28 cm each

Courtesy the artist and Berengo
Private Collection, Venice
Exhibited at *Glasstress Stockholm*
2011, Stockholm (SE)

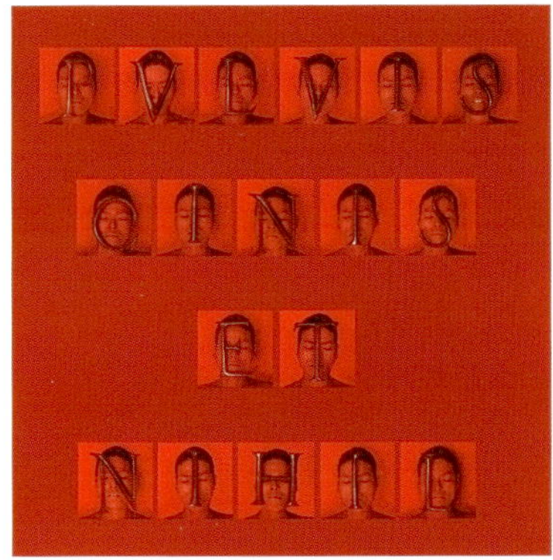

KIMIKO YOSHIDA
Tombeau. Self-Portrait
(after Cardinal Barberini's
Epitaph, Rome, 1646),
2005
28 x 28 cm each

Courtesy Guy Pieters Gallery,
Sint-Martens-Latem
Exhibited at *Glasstress* 2009,
Venice (IT)

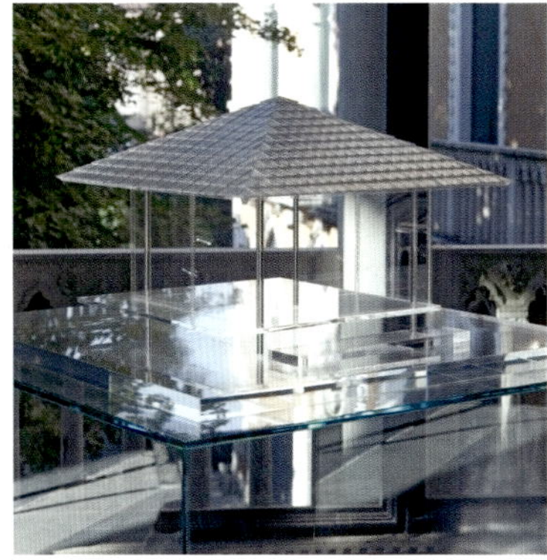

TOKUJIN YOSHIOKA
The Glass Tea House,
2011 / *detail*
40 x 80 x 80 cm

Courtesy Tokujin Yoshioka inc.,
Tokyo
Exhibited at *Glasstress 2011*,
Venice (IT)

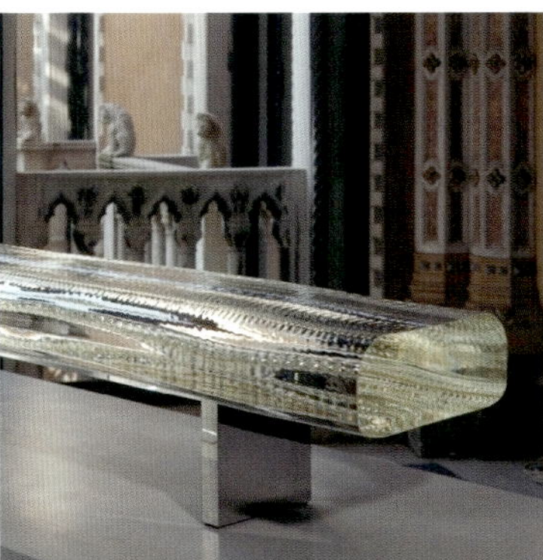

TOKUJIN YOSHIOKA
Water Block,
2002 / *detail*
75 x 450 x 70 cm

Courtesy Tokujin Yoshioka inc.,
Tokyo
Exhibited at *Glasstress 2011*,
Venice (IT)

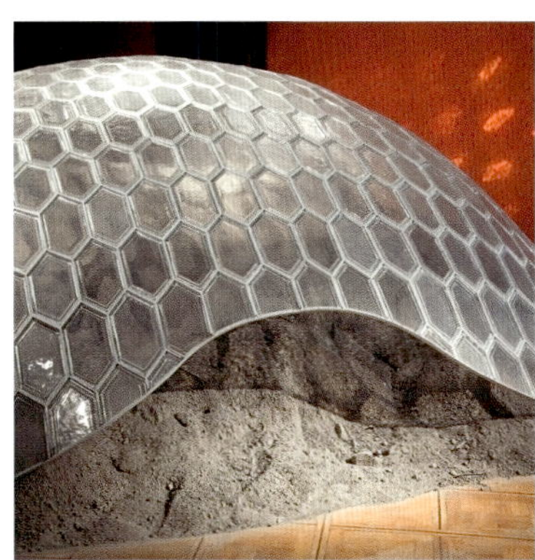

ZHANG HUAN
Ten Thousand Years Old
Turtle, 2011 / *detail*
160 x 500 x 600 cm

Courtesy Zhang Huan Studio,
Shanghai, and Venice Projects,
Venice
Exhibited at *Glasstress 2011*,
Venice (IT)

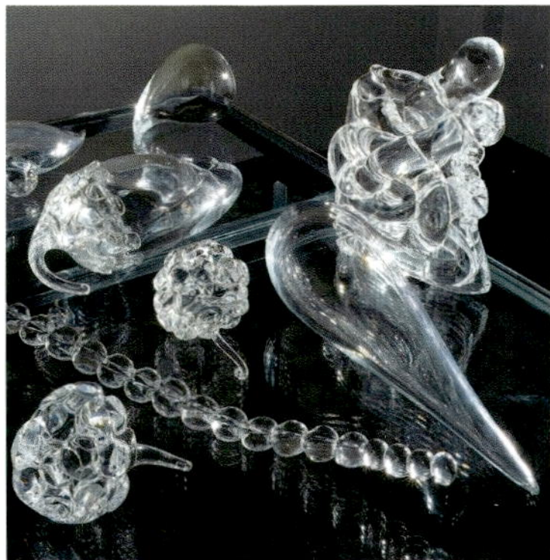

CHEN ZHEN
Crystal Landscape
of Inner Body,
2000 / *detail*
95 x 70 x 190 cm

Courtesy Galleria Continua, San
Gimignano, Beijing, Le Moulin
Exhibited at *Glasstress* 2009,
Venice (IT)

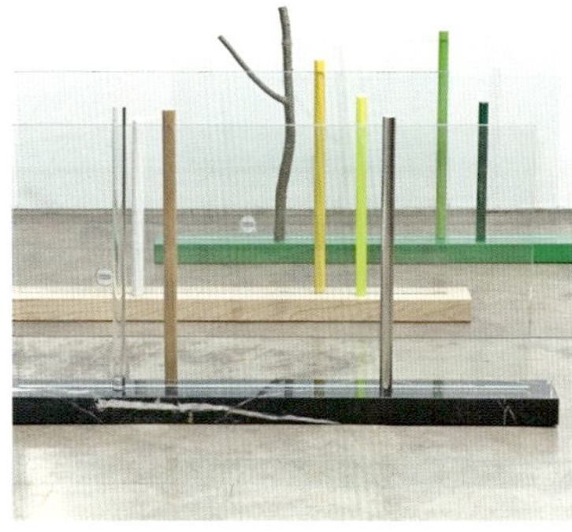

5.5 DESIGNERS
Matières à chaud,
2011 / *detail*
77 x 14 x 132 cm each

Courtesy the artists for Saazs, Paris
Exhibited at *Glasstress 2011*,
Venice (IT)

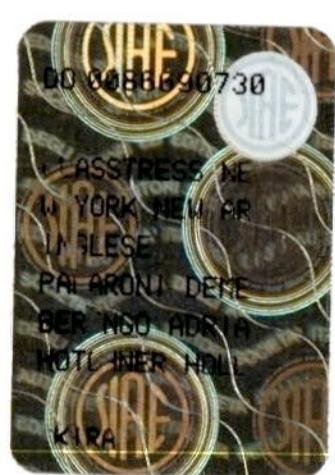